AMERICAN POLITICAL, ECONOMIC, AND SECURITY ISSUES

SUPREME COURT APPOINTMENTS AND NOMINATIONS

American Political, Economic, and Security Issues

Additional books in this series can be found on Nova's website under the Series tab.

Additional E-books in this series can be found on Nova's website under the E-books tab.

Law, Crime and Law Enforcement

Additional books in this series can be found on Nova's website under the Series tab.

Additional E-books in this series can be found on Nova's website under the E-books tab.

AMERICAN POLITICAL, ECONOMIC, AND SECURITY ISSUES

SUPREME COURT APPOINTMENTS AND NOMINATIONS

EDWARD P. BENNETT
EDITOR

Nova Science Publishers, Inc.
New York

For permission to use material from this book please contact us:
Telephone 631-231-7269; Fax 631-231-8175
Web Site: http://www.novapublishers.com

LIBRARY OF CONGRESS CATALOGING-IN-PUBLICATION DATA

Supreme Court appointments and nominations / editor, Edward P. Bennett.
p. cm.
Includes index.
ISBN 978-1-61209-249-2 (hardcover)
1. United States. Supreme Court--Officials and employees--Selection and appointment--History. 2. Judges--Selection and appointment--United States--History. I. Bennett, Edward P.
KF8742.S91185 2011
347.73'2634--dc22
2010048361

Published by Nova Science Publishers, Inc. † New York

CONTENTS

PREFACE

The appointment of a Supreme Court Justice is an event of major significance in American politics. Each appointment is of consequence because of the enormous judicial power the Supreme Court exercises as the highest appellate court in the federal judiciary. Appointments are usually infrequent, as a vacancy on the nine-member Court may occur only once or twice, or never at all, during a particular President's years in office. This new book examines the Supreme Court appointment and nominations process.

Chapter 1- The appointment of a Supreme Court Justice is an event of major significance in American politics. Each appointment is of consequence because of the enormous judicial power the Supreme Court exercises as the highest appellate court in the federal judiciary. Appointments are usually infrequent, as a vacancy on the nine-member Court may occur only once or twice, or never at all, during a particular President's years in office. Under the Constitution, Justices on the Supreme Court receive lifetime appointments. Such job security in the government has been conferred solely on judges and, by constitutional design, helps insure the Court's independence from the President and Congress.

Chapter 2- The speed with which appointments to the Supreme Court move through various stages in the nomination-and-confirmation process is often of great interest not only to all parties directly involved, but, as well, to the nation as a whole. This chapter provides information on the amount of time taken to act on all Supreme Court nominations occurring between 1900 and the present. It focuses on the *actual* amounts of time that Presidents and the Senate have taken to act (as opposed to the elapsed time between *official* points in the process). For example, rather than starting the nomination clock with the official notification of the President of a forthcoming vacancy, this chapter focuses on when the President first *learned* of a Justice's intention to leave the Court (e.g., via a private conversation with the outgoing Justice), or received word that a sitting Justice had died. Likewise, rather than starting the confirmation clock with the transmission of the official nomination to the Senate, this chapter focuses on when the Senate *became aware* of the President's selection (e.g., via a public announcement by the President).

Chapter 3- From 1789 through 2009, the President submitted to the Senate 159 nominations for positions on the Supreme Court. Of these nominations, 147 received action on the floor of the Senate, and 123 were confirmed. On May 10, 2010, the Senate received the nomination of Solicitor General Elana Kagan to be an Associate Justice of the Supreme Court. The data presented in this chapter do not include this nomination.

Chapter 4- The process of appointing Supreme Court Justices has undergone changes over two centuries, but its most basic feature, the sharing of power between the President and Senate, has remained unchanged. To receive a lifetime appointment to the Court, a candidate must first be nominated by the President and then confirmed by the Senate. A key role also has come to be played midway in the process by the Senate Judiciary Committee.

Chapter 5- From 1789 through August 2010, Presidents submitted 160 nominations to Supreme Court positions. Of these, 36 were not confirmed by the Senate. The 36 nominations represent 31 individuals whose names were sent forward to the Senate by Presidents (some individuals were nominated more than once). Of the 31 individuals who were not confirmed the first time they were nominated, however, six were later nominated again and confirmed. The Supreme Court nominations discussed here were not confirmed for a variety of reasons, including Senate opposition to the nominating President, nominee's views, or incumbent Court; senatorial courtesy; perceived political unreliability of the nominee; perceived lack of ability; interest group opposition; and fear of altering the balance of the Court. The Senate Committee on the Judiciary has played an important role in the confirmation process, particularly since 1868.

In: Supreme Court Appointments and Nominations
Editor: Edward P. Bennett
ISBN: 978-1-61209-249-2

Chapter 1

SUPREME COURT APPOINTMENT PROCESS: ROLES OF THE PRESIDENT, JUDICIARY COMMITTEE, AND SENATE

Denis Steven Rutkus

SUMMARY

The appointment of a Supreme Court Justice is an event of major significance in American politics. Each appointment is of consequence because of the enormous judicial power the Supreme Court exercises as the highest appellate court in the federal judiciary. Appointments are usually infrequent, as a vacancy on the nine-member Court may occur only once or twice, or never at all, during a particular President's years in office. Under the Constitution, Justices on the Supreme Court receive lifetime appointments. Such job security in the government has been conferred solely on judges and, by constitutional design, helps insure the Court's independence from the President and Congress.

The procedure for appointing a Justice is provided for by the Constitution in only a few words. The "Appointments Clause" (Article II, Section 2, clause 2) states that the President "shall nominate, and by and with the Advice and Consent of the Senate, shall appoint ... Judges of the supreme Court." The process of appointing Justices has undergone changes over two centuries, but its most basic feature—the sharing of power between the President and Senate—has remained unchanged: To receive lifetime appointment to the Court, a candidate must first be nominated by the President and then confirmed by the Senate. Although not mentioned in the Constitution, an important role is played midway in the process (after the President selects, but before the Senate considers) by the Senate Judiciary Committee.

On rare occasions, Presidents also have made Court appointments without the Senate's consent, when the Senate was in recess. Such "recess appointments," however, were temporary, with their terms expiring at the end of the Senate's next session. The last recess appointments to the Court, made in the 1950s, were controversial because they bypassed the Senate and its "advice and consent" role.

The appointment of a Justice might or might not proceed smoothly. From the first appointments in 1789 through its consideration of nominee Elena Kagan in 2010, the Senate confirmed 124 out of 160 Court nominations. Of the 36 unsuccessful nominations, 11 were rejected in Senate roll-call votes, while nearly all of the rest, in the face of committee or Senate opposition to the nominee or the President, were withdrawn by the President or were postponed, tabled, or never voted on by the Senate. (Six individuals, however, whose initial Supreme Court nominations were not confirmed, were later re-nominated and confirmed.)

Over more than two centuries, a recurring theme in the Supreme Court appointment process has been the assumed need for excellence in a nominee. However, politics also has played an important role in Supreme Court appointments. The political nature of the appointment process becomes especially apparent when a President submits a nominee with controversial views, there are sharp partisan or ideological differences between the President and the Senate, or the outcome of important constitutional issues before the Court is seen to be at stake.

BACKGROUND

The appointment of a Supreme Court Justice is an event of major significance in American politics. Each appointment to the nine-member Court is of consequence because of the enormous judicial power that the Court exercises, separate from, and independent of, the executive and legislative branches. While "on average, a new Justice joins the Court almost every two years,"[1] the time at which any given appointment will be made to the Court is unpredictable. Appointments may be infrequent (with a vacancy on the Court occurring only once or twice, or even never at all, during a particular President's years in office)[2] or occur in close proximity to each other (with a particular President afforded several opportunities to name persons to the Court).[3]

Thus far in his presidency, Barack Obama has been afforded two opportunities to make appointments to the Court. The first opportunity occurred on May 1, 2009, when Associate Justice David H. Souter notified President Obama of his intention to retire and subsequently, on June 29, 2009, stepped down from the Court. In response, President Obama on June 1 nominated Sonia Sotomayor, a U.S. court of appeals judge, to replace Justice Souter. It was the 159th time a President of the United States has nominated someone to be a Supreme Court Justice. On July 28, 2009, following four days of confirmation hearings, the Senate Judiciary Committee, by a vote of 13-6, favorably reported the Sotomayor nomination to the Senate. Following three days of floor debate, the Senate, on August 6, confirmed Judge Sotomayor to the Court by a vote of 68-31.

A second opportunity for President Obama to make a Court appointment came less than a year later. On April 9, 2010, Associate Justice John Paul Stevens wrote to the President that he would retire from the Court when it recessed for the summer. In response, President Obama on May 10, 2010, announced that he had selected Solicitor General Elana Kagan as his nominee to replace Justice Stevens. Subsequently, on June 28, 2010, the Court recessed for the summer, after issuing its final rulings for the 2009-2010 term and bidding farewell to departing Justice Stevens. Coincidentally, also on June 28, the Senate Judiciary Committee began four days of confirmation hearings on the Kagan nomination—with opening statements by committee members and the nominee occurring on the first day, questioning of the nominee by committee members on the second and third days, and statements by public witnesses on the fourth day (July 1). On July 20, 2010, the Judiciary Committee approved the Kagan nomination by a vote of 13-6. Following three days of floor debate, the Senate, on August 5, 2010, confirmed Ms. Kagan to the Court by a vote of 63-37.

Under the Constitution, Justices on the Supreme Court hold office "during good Behaviour,"[4] in effect receiving lifetime appointments. Once confirmed, Justices may hold office for as long as they live or until they voluntarily step down. Such job security in the federal government is conferred solely on judges and, by constitutional design, is intended to insure the independence of the federal judiciary, including the Supreme Court, from the President and Congress.[5] A President has no power to remove a Justice or judge from office. A Supreme Court Justice may be removed by Congress, but only through the process of impeachment by the House and conviction by the Senate. Only one Justice has ever been impeached (in an episode which occurred in 1804), and he remained in office after being acquitted by the Senate.[6] Many Justices serve for 20 to 30 years and sometimes are still on the Court decades after the President who nominated them has left office.[7]

The procedure for appointing a Justice to the Supreme Court is provided for in the Constitution of the United States in only a few words. The "Appointments Clause" in the Constitution (Article II, Section 2, Clause 2) states that the President "shall nominate, and by and with the Advice and Consent of the Senate, shall appoint ... Judges of the supreme Court."[8] While the process of appointing Justices has undergone some changes over two centuries, its most essential feature—the sharing of power between the President and the Senate—has remained unchanged: To receive lifetime appointment to the Court, one must first be formally selected ("nominated") by the President and then approved ("confirmed") by the Senate. Although not mentioned in the Constitution, an important role is also played midway in the process—after the President selects, but before the Senate as a whole considers the nominee—by the Senate Judiciary Committee. Since the end of the Civil War, almost every Supreme Court nomination received by the Senate has first been referred to and considered by the Judiciary Committee before being acted on by the Senate as a whole.

For the President, the appointment of a Supreme Court Justice can be a notable measure by which history will judge his Presidency.[9] For the Senate, a decision to confirm is a solemn matter as well, for it is the Senate alone, through its "Advice and Consent" function, without any formal involvement of the House of Representatives, which acts as a safeguard on the President's judgment. Traditionally, the Senate has tended to be less deferential to the President in his choice of Supreme Court Justices than in his appointment of persons to high executive branch positions.[10] The more exacting standard usually applied to Supreme Court nominations reflects the special importance of the Court, coequal to and independent of the presidency and Congress. Senators are also mindful that, as noted earlier, Justices—unlike persons elected to legislative office or confirmed to executive branch positions—receive lifetime appointments.[11]

Table 1. Current Members of the Supreme Court of the United States

Name	State[a]	Date of Birth	Appointing President	Date Senate Confirmed	Vote to Confirm
John G. Roberts Jr. (Chief Justice)	MD	Jan. 27, 1955	Bush, George W.	Sep. 29, 2005	78-22
Antonin Scalia	VA	Mar. 11, 1936	Reagan	Sep. 17, 1986	98-0
Anthony M. Kennedy	CA	July 23, 1936	Reagan	Feb. 3, 1988	97-0
Clarence Thomas	VA	June 23, 1948	Bush, George H.W.	Oct. 15, 1991	52-48
Ruth Bader Ginsburg	DC	Mar. 15, 1933	Clinton	Aug. 3, 1993	96-3
Stephen G. Breyer	MA	Aug. 15, 1938	Clinton	July 29, 1994	87-9
Samuel A. Alito Jr.	NJ	Apr. 1, 1950	Bush, George W.	Jan. 31, 2006	58-42
Sonia Sotomayor	NY	June 25, 1954	Obama	Aug. 6, 2009	68-31
Elena Kagan	MA	April 28, 1960	Obama	Aug. 5, 2010	63-37

a. State of Justice's residence at time of appointment.

The appointment of a Supreme Court Justice might or might not proceed smoothly. From the appointment of the first Justices in 1789 through its consideration of nominee Elena Kagan in 2010, the Senate has confirmed 124 Supreme Court nominations out of 160 received.[12] Of the 36 nominations which were not confirmed, 11 were rejected outright in roll-call votes by the Senate, while nearly all of the rest, in the face of substantial committee or Senate opposition to the nominee or the President, were withdrawn by the President, or were postponed, tabled, or never voted on by the Senate.[13] Six of the unconfirmed nominations, however, involved individuals who subsequently were re-nominated and confirmed.[14]

From the presidency of George Washington until early in the 20th century, the Senate took final action on the vast majority of Supreme Court nominations within one week of receiving them. In recent decades, by contrast, the Senate has tended to proceed much more slowly. From 1967 through August 5, 2010 (the date of the most recent Supreme Court confirmation), 15 of the 23 Court nominations that advanced to the committee hearing stage were pending in the Senate for more than nine weeks before receiving final action.[15] The contemporary Senate's inclination to proceed more slowly with Supreme Court nominations has been due at least in part to several developments:

- Starting with the "Warren Court" in the 1950s (under then-Chief Justice Earl Warren), the Supreme Court became an ongoing focal point of controversy, as it handed down a succession of rulings ushering in profound changes in American society and politics. By the late 1960s, the perceived potency of the Court as a catalyst for change underscored to many Senators, especially those on the Judiciary Committee, the importance of closely evaluating the attitudes and values of persons nominated to serve on the Court.[16]

- A general trend among Senate committees, beginning in the 1970s and 1980s, was to intensify their scrutiny of presidential nominations and to augment their investigative staffs for this purpose. Thorough and unhurried examination was regarded as especially justified in the case of Supreme Court nominations. Accordingly, close scrutiny by the Senate Judiciary Committee became the norm, even if a nominee were highly distinguished and untouched by controversy.
- Many, if not most, of the nominees in recent decades proved to be controversial because of questions raised concerning their backgrounds, qualifications, or ideological orientation.
- It has become increasingly common for Presidents to state the philosophical or ideological values that they look for in a Supreme Court nominee—a practice which may immediately raise concerns about the nominee on the part of Senators who do not share the President's philosophical preferences or vision for the Court.
- Many Court appointments in recent decades were made during times of "divided government," when one political party controlled the White House and the other was in the majority in the Senate.
- The frequency of 5-4 decisions by the Court has underscored to Senators how important even just one new appointment might be for future Court rulings.

President's Selection of a Nominee

The need for a Supreme Court nominee arises when a vacancy occurs on the Court, due to the death, retirement, or resignation of a Justice (or when a Justice announces the intention to retire or resign).[17] It then becomes the President's constitutional responsibility to select a successor to the vacating Justice.[18]

The Role of Senate Advice

Constitutional scholars have differed as to how much importance the Framers of the Constitution attached to the word "advice" in the phrase "advice and consent." The Framers, some have maintained, contemplated the Senate performing an advisory, or recommending, role to the President prior to his selection of a nominee, in addition to a confirming role afterwards.[19] Others, by contrast, have insisted that the Senate's "advice and consent" role was meant to be strictly that of determining, after the President's selection had been made, whether to approve the President's choice.[20] Bridging these opposing schools of thought, another scholar recently asserted that the "more sensible reading of the term 'advice' is that it means that the Senate is constitutionally entitled to give advice to a president on whom as well as what kinds of persons he should nominate to certain posts, but this advice is not binding."[21] Historically, the degree to which Senate advice has been sought or used has varied, depending on the President.

It is a common, though not universal, practice for Presidents, as a matter of courtesy, to consult with Senate party leaders as well as with members of the Senate Judiciary Committee before choosing a nominee.[22] Senators who candidly inform a President of their objections to a prospective nominee may help in identifying shortcomings in that candidate or the possibility of a confirmation battle in the Senate, which the President might want to avoid. Conversely, input from the Senate might draw new Supreme Court candidates to the President's attention, or provide additional reasons to nominate a person who already is on the President's list of prospective nominees.[23]

As a rule, Presidents are also careful to consult with a candidate's home-state Senators, especially if they are of the same political party as the President. The need for such care is due to the longstanding custom of "senatorial courtesy," whereby Senators, in the interests of collegiality, are inclined, though not bound, to support a Senate colleague who opposes a presidential nominee from that Member's state. While usually invoked by home-state Senators to block lower federal court nominees whom they find unacceptable, the custom of "senatorial courtesy" has sometimes also played a part in the defeat of Supreme Court nominations.[24]

Besides giving private advice to the President, Senators may also counsel a President publicly. A Senator, for example, may use a Senate floor statement or issue a statement to the news media indicating support for, or opposition to, a potential Court nominee, or type or quality of nominee, for the purpose of attracting the President's attention and influencing the President's choice.[25]

Advice from other Sources

Advice, it should be noted, may come to Presidents not only from the Senate but from many other sources. One key source of influence may be high-level advisers within the President's Administration.[26] Others who may provide advice include House Members, party leaders, interest groups, news media commentators, and, periodically, Justices already on the Court.[27] Presidents are free to consult with, and receive advice from, whomever they choose.

Criteria for Selecting a Nominee

While the precise criteria used in selecting a Supreme Court nominee vary from President to President, two general motivations appear to underlie the choices of almost every President. One is the desire to have the nomination serve the President's political interests (in the partisan and electoral senses of the word "political," as well as in the public policy sense); the second is to demonstrate that a search was successfully made for a nominee having the highest professional qualifications.

Virtually every President is presumed to take into account a wide range of political considerations when faced with the responsibility of filling a Supreme Court vacancy. For instance, most Presidents, it is assumed, will be inclined to select a nominee whose political or ideological views appear compatible with their own. "Presidents are, for the most part, results-oriented. This means that they want Justices on the Court who will vote to decide cases consistent with the president's policy preferences."[28] The President also may consider whether a prospective nomination will be pleasing to the constituencies upon whom he especially relies for political support or whose support he would like to attract. For political or other reasons, such nominee attributes as party affiliation, geographic origin, ethnicity, religion, and gender may also be of particular importance to the President.[29] A President also might take into account whether the existing "balance" among the Court's members (in a political party, ideological, demographic, or other sense) should be altered. The prospects for a potential nominee receiving Senate confirmation are another consideration. Even if a controversial nominee is believed to be confirmable, an assessment must be made as to whether the benefits of confirmation will be worth the costs of the political battle to be waged.[30]

Most Presidents also want their Supreme Court nominees to have unquestionably outstanding legal qualifications. Presidents look for a high degree of merit in their nominees not only in recognition of the demanding nature of the work that awaits someone appointed to the Court,[31] but also because of the public's expectations that a Supreme Court nominee be highly qualified.[32] With such expectations of excellence, Presidents often present their nominees as the best person, or among the best persons, available.[33] Many nominees, as a result, have distinguished themselves in the law (as lower court judges, legal scholars, or private practitioners) or have served as Members of Congress, as federal administrators, or as governors.[34] Although neither the Constitution nor federal law requires that a Supreme Court Justice be a lawyer, every person nominated to the Court thus far has been.[35] A President's search for excellence in a nominee, however, rarely proceeds without also taking political factors into account. Rather, "more typically," a President "seeks the best person from among a list of those who fulfill certain of these other [political] criteria and, of course, who share a president's vision of the nation and the Court."[36]

Closely related to the expectation that a Supreme Court nominee have excellent professional qualifications are the ideals of integrity and impartiality in a nominee. Most Presidents presumably will be aware of the historical expectation, dating back to Alexander Hamilton's pronouncements in the *Federalist Papers*, that a Justice be a person of integrity who is able to approach cases and controversies impartially, without personal prejudice.[37] In that same spirit, a bipartisan study commission on judicial selection in 1996 declared that it was "most important" to appoint judges who were not only learned in the law and conscientious in their work ethic but who also possessed "what lawyers describe as 'judicial temperament.'" This term, the commission explained, "essentially has to do with a personality that is evenhanded, unbiased, impartial, courteous yet firm, and dedicated to a process, not a result."[38] Accordingly, Presidents sometimes will cite the integrity or fairness of Supreme Court nominees to buttress the case for their appointment.[39]

Any given President also might single out other qualities as particularly important for a Supreme Court nominee to have, as President Barack Obama did in 2009, when announcing his nomination of Judge Sonia Sotomayor to the Court. In prefatory remarks to that announcement, President Obama cited selection criteria similar to those mentioned by other recent Presidents, such as "mastery of the law," the "ability to hone in on the key issues and provide clear answers to complex legal questions," and "a commitment to impartial justice." He added, however, that such qualities, while "essential" for anyone sitting on the Supreme Court, "alone are insufficient,"and that "[w]e need something more."[40] An additional requisite quality, President Obama said, was "experience," which he explained was …

> Experience being tested by obstacles and barriers, by hardship and misfortune, experience insisting, persisting, and ultimately, overcoming those barriers. It is experience

> that can give a person a common touch and a sense of compassion, an undertanding of how the world works and how ordinary people live. And that is why it is a necessary ingredient in the kind of Justice we need on the Supreme Court.[41]

A President, as well, may have additional concerns when the Supreme Court vacancy to be filled is that of the Chief Justice. Besides requiring that a candidate be politically acceptable, have excellent legal qualifications, and enjoy a reputation for integrity, a President might be concerned that his nominee have proven leadership qualities necessary to effectively perform the tasks specific to the position of Chief Justice. Such qualities, in the President's view, could include administrative and human relations skills, with the latter especially important in fostering collegiality among the Court's members. The President also might look for distinction or eminence in a Chief Justice nominee sufficient to command the respect of the Court's other Justices, as well as to further public respect for the Court. A President, too, might be concerned with the age of the Chief Justice nominee, requiring, for instance, that the nominee be at least of a certain age (to insure an adequate degree of maturity and experience relative to the other Justices) but not above a certain age (to allow for the likely ability to serve as a leader on the Court for a substantial number of years).[42]

Background Investigations

An important part of the selection process involves investigating the background of prospective nominees. In recent years the investigative effort generally has followed two primary tracks—one concerned with the public record and professional credentials of a person under consideration, the other with the candidate's private background. The private background investigation, which includes examination of a candidate's personal financial affairs, is conducted by the Federal Bureau of Investigation (FBI). The investigation into a candidate's public record and professional abilities ordinarily is headed by high Justice Department officials, White House aides, or both, working together.

The investigatory process may be preliminary in nature when the object is to identify potential candidates and consider their relative merits based on information already known or readily available. The investigations become more intensive as the list is narrowed. The object then becomes to learn as much as possible about the prospective nominees—to accurately gauge their qualifications and their compatibility with the President's specific requirements for a nominee, and, simultaneously, to flag anything in their backgrounds that might be disqualifying or jeopardize their chances for Senate confirmation. For help in evaluating the backgrounds of Court candidates, Presidents sometimes also have enlisted the assistance of private lawyers,[43] legal scholars,[44] or, on rare occasions, the American Bar Association (ABA).[45] Near the culmination of this investigative effort, the President might want to personally meet with one or more of the candidates before finally deciding whom to nominate.[46]

During the pre-nomination phase, Presidents vary in the degree to which they publicly reveal the names of individuals under consideration for the Court. Sometimes, Presidents seek to keep confidential the identity of their Court candidates. Such secrecy may allow a President to reflect on the qualifications of prospective nominees, and the background investigations to proceed, away from the glare of publicity, news media coverage, and outside political pressures. Other times, the White House may, at least in the early pre-nomination stage, reveal the names of Supreme Court candidates being considered. Such openness may be intended to serve various purposes—among them, to test public or congressional reaction to potential nominees, please political constituencies who would identify with identified candidates, or demonstrate the President's determination to conduct a comprehensive search for the most qualified person available.

An Administration, of course, need not wait until a vacancy occurs on the Court to begin investigating the backgrounds of potential nominees. Immediately after President George W. Bush was sworn into office in 2001, according to a recent book on Supreme Court nominations, "his staff began putting together a list of potential nominees and conducting extensive background research on them." The book continued:

> Officials believed [Chief Justice William H.] Rehnquist was likely to retire in the summer of 2001, and they were determined to be ready. Each young lawyer in the White House counsel's office, most of whom had clerked on the Supreme Court, was assigned a candidate and made responsible for writing a lengthy report about him or her. In the late spring, then-White House counsel Alberto Gonzalez and his deputy Tim Flanigan began secretly interviewing some of those possible replacements.
>
> The advance work was designed to ensure that George W. Bush would be prepared when a justice stepped down.... The early in-depth research and interviews with prospective nominees were important in ensuring Bush would have coolheaded advice, removed from any external political pressure to select a particular nominee in the hours after a retirement.[47]

Speed with Which President Selects Nominees

When a Supreme Court vacancy occurs, Presidents sometimes move quickly, selecting their nominee within a week of the vacancy being announced.[48] A President may be well positioned to make a quick announcement when a retiring Justice alerts the President beforehand (thus giving the President lead time, before the vacancy occurs, to consider whom to nominate as a successor). Even when receiving no advance warning from an outgoing Justice, the President may already have in hand a "short list," prepared precisely for the event of a Court vacancy, of persons already evaluated and acceptable to the President for the appointment. If the President has a strong personal preference for a particular individual, nominating the person quickly preempts the issue of whether someone else should be nominated. Rather than focus on a range of individuals who should be considered for the Supreme Court, the appointment process moves to the next stage, to the question of whether that individual should be confirmed.

Presidents also might be moved to nominate quickly in order to minimize the time during which there is a vacancy on the Court. If an actual vacancy is suddenly created—for example, due to an unexpected retirement, resignation, or death of a Justice—a President, as well as Members of the Senate, might be eager to bring the Court back to full strength as soon as possible. A similar sense of urgency might be felt if a Justice has announced the intention to step down from the Court by a date certain in the near future.

Selecting a Supreme Court nominee quickly, however, may sometimes have drawbacks. A President may be accused of charging ahead with a nominee without having first adequately consulted with the Senate, or without having taken the time necessary to determine who really would make the best nominee. Also, quick announcements might not allow time for the FBI to conduct a comprehensive background investigation prior to nomination, leaving open the possibility of unfavorable information about the nominee coming to light later.[49]

The speed with which a President chooses a nominee also, as noted above, can be affected by when a seat on the Court is vacated. Sometimes, Justices might announce their retirement when the Court recesses for the summer, in late June or early July, giving the President little or no advance notice. In such situations, a President might decide to nominate quickly, to allow the Senate confirmation process to begin as quickly as possible. A swiftly made nomination, in such a circumstance, affords the Senate Judiciary Committee and the Senate as long as three months (July through September) in which to consider the nomination before the start of the Court's term in early October, thereby increasing the chances of the Court being at full nine-member strength when it reconvenes.

Sometimes, when Justices give advance notice of their intention to retire, Presidents might be under relatively little pressure to nominate quickly. In the spring of 1993, for example, Justice Byron R. White announced he would step down when the Court adjourned for the summer. His advance notice gave President Clinton and the Senate together more than six months in which, respectively, to nominate and confirm a successor before the beginning of the Court's next term in October. A year later, in the spring of 1994, Justice Harry A. Blackmun announced his intention to retire at the end of the Court term then in progress, again affording the President and the Senate ample time to appoint a successor to a retiring Justice before the start of the next Court term.[50] Despite the long lead time afforded by Justice Blackmun's announcement, however,White House advisers reportedly believed it was "important to act quickly" to name a successor to Blackmun. To move quickly, it was reported, would serve to "avoid a repeat of the [previous] year's drawn out process" in which President Clinton engaged in a "very public, three-month search" before nominating Ruth Bader Ginsburg to the Court. [51] After Justice Blackmun's announcement, President Clinton deliberated five weeks before announcing, on May 13, 1994, his selection of U.S. appellate court judge Stephen G. Breyer to be his Supreme Court nominee.

President Barack Obama also was provided considerable advance notice of an upcoming Court vacancy when Justice David H. Souter, in a May 1, 2009 letter, informed the President of his intention to step down when the Court recessed for the summer. (The Court went into summer recess on June 29.) Three and a half weeks later, on May 26, President Obama announced his intention to nominate a U.S. appellate judge, Sonia Sotomayor, to succeed Justice Souter. The selection by President Obama was, on the one hand, not as quickly made as some of the nominee selections of Presidents Reagan, George H.W. Bush, and George W. Bush. On the other hand, President Obama took less time than President Clinton did in making his two Court selections.

During the 25 days between Justice Souter's retirement notice and the selection of Judge Sotomayor, President Obama had enough time, in his words, to seek "the advice of Members of Congress on both sides of the aisle, including every member of the Senate Judiciary Committee."[52] That he did not take additional time to decide whom to select might have been influenced by a concern for allowing the Senate to begin considering a Court nomination as soon as possible. The President and some Senate Democrats expressed the hope that the Senate would vote to confirm Judge Sotomayor not merely before the start of the Court's term in October, but before the Senate's August 2009 recess, in order to afford time for her to prepare for that term.[53] (The Senate ultimately confirmed the Sotomayor nomination on August 6, 2009.)[54]

Presidents also may have considerable latitude in deciding when to nominate if an outgoing Justice schedules his or her retirement to take effect only when a successor is confirmed or assumes office. The most recent instance of that occurred when Justice Sandra Day O'Connor, in a July 1, 2005, letter to President George W. Bush, announced her decision to retire from the Court "effective upon the nomination and confirmation" of her successor.[55] At the announcement of Justice O'Connor's retirement, President Bush declared he would "choose a nominee in a timely manner" so that the nominee would receive a Senate hearing and confirmation vote "before the new Supreme Court term begins."[56] Within three weeks he announced his selection of John G. Roberts Jr. to succeed Justice O'Connor.[57] The conditional nature of Justice O'Connor's planned retirement, however, meant that her seat on the Court would be occupied when the Court convened for its October 2005 term, whether or not her successor were confirmed by then.

Ultimately, Justice O'Connor remained on the Court for four months of the new Court term, retiring only on January 31, 2006, when the third person nominated by President Bush to succeed her, Samuel A. Alito Jr., was confirmed by the Senate. During the months that Justice O'Connor remained on the Court, awaiting the confirmation of her successor, the Associate Justice nomination of John G. Roberts Jr. was withdrawn so that President Bush could nominate Roberts to be Chief Justice (following the death of Chief Justice Rehnquist on September 3, 2005); a second nomination to succeed Justice O'Connor, that of White House Counsel Harriet E. Miers, was made, only to be withdrawn three weeks later; and, on November 10, 2005, a third person, Samuel A. Alito Jr., was nominated to succeed Justice O'Connor. For a President, the need to select an Associate Justice nominee might be seen as less urgent than the appointment of a Chief Justice, particularly if, as was the case in 2005, the Chief Justice position is actually vacant and the Associate Justice vacancy is not actual, but prospective.

Recess Appointments to the Court

On 12 occasions in our nation's history (most of them in the 19th century), Presidents have made temporary appointments to the Supreme Court without submitting nominations to the Senate. These occurred when Presidents exercised their power under the Constitution to make "recess appointments" when the Senate was not in session.[58] Historically, when recesses between sessions of the Senate were much longer than they are today, recess appointments served the purpose of averting long vacancies on the Court when the Senate was unavailable to confirm a President's appointees. The terms of these recess appointments, however, were limited, expiring at the end of the next session of Congress (unlike the lifetime appointments Court appointees receive when nominated and then confirmed by the Senate). Despite the temporary nature of these appointments, every person appointed during a recess of the Senate, except one, ultimately received a lifetime appointment to the Court after being nominated by the President and confirmed by the Senate.[59]

The last President to make recess appointments to the Court was Dwight D. Eisenhower. Of the five persons whom he nominated to the Court, three first received recess appointments and served as Justices before being confirmed—Earl Warren (as Chief Justice) in 1953, William Brennan in 1956, and Potter Stewart in 1958. President Eisenhower's recess appointments, however, generated controversy, prompting the Senate in 1960, voting closely along party lines, to pass a resolution expressing opposition to Supreme Court recess appointments in the future.[60]

While President Eisenhower's were the most recent recess appointments to the Supreme Court, recess appointments to the lower federal courts, since the late 1960s, also have become relatively rare. A President's constitutional power to make judicial recess appointments was upheld by a federal court in 1985[61] and again in 2004.[62] Such appointments, when they do occur, may cause controversy, in large part because they bypass the Senate and its "advice and consent" role. Because of the criticisms of judicial recess appointments in recent decades, the long passage of time since the last Supreme Court recess appointment, and the relatively short duration of contemporary Senate recesses (which arguably undercuts the need for recess appointments to the Court), a President in the 21st century might hesitate to make a recess appointment to the Court and do so only under the most unusual of circumstances.[63]

CONSIDERATION BY THE SENATE JUDICIARY COMMITTEE

Historical Background

While the Constitution of the United States assigns explicit roles in the Supreme Court appointment process only to the President and the Senate,[64] the Senate Judiciary Committee, throughout much of our nation's history, has also played an important, intermediary role. From 1816, when the Judiciary Committee was created, until 1868, more than two-thirds of nominations to the Supreme Court were referred to the committee, in each case by motion. In 1868, the Senate determined, as a general rule, that all nominations should automatically be referred to appropriate standing committees.[65] Since then, almost all Supreme Court nominations (90 of 96) have been referred to the committee.[66]

Senators Nominated to the Court

An important exception to the practice of referring Supreme Court nominees to the Judiciary Committee, however, usually has been made for nominees who, at the time of their nomination, were current or former Members of the U.S. Senate. These nominees benefitted from "the unwritten rule of the all but automatic approval of senatorial colleagues,"[67] with the Senate moving quickly to confirm without first referring the nominations to committee.[68] The most recent demonstration of this "unwritten rule" occurred on June 12, 1941. On that day, President Franklin D. Roosevelt submitted three Supreme Court nominations to the Senate, those of Associate Justice Harlan F. Stone to be Chief Justice, Senator James F. Byrnes (D-SC) to be Associate Justice, and Robert H. Jackson to be Associate Justice. The Stone and Jackson nominations were both referred to the Senate Judiciary Committee, which held one day of hearings on the former and four days of hearings on the latter, before reporting each favorably to the Senate. The overall time that elapsed between nomination and confirmation was 15 days for Stone and 25 days for Jackson.[69]

The Byrnes nomination, by contrast, was given expedited treatment by the Senate since the nominee was a Member of that body. The Senate considered and confirmed Senator Byrnes to the Court on the very day his nomination was received without referral of the nomination to the Judiciary Committee. When the Byrnes nomination was laid before the Senate, Senator Carter Glass (D-VA) moved that "the nomination of our colleague ... be now considered without reference to committee." In immediate response, Senator Charles L. McNary (R-OR) stated that "it has been the unbroken custom to adopt such a proposal as that made by the eminent Senator from Virginia, and I join him in his motion." The motion to consider the nomination without reference to committee was then seconded by the chair of the Judiciary Committee, Senator Frederick Van Nuys (D-IN). Moments later, the Senate confirmed the nomination by unanimous consent.[70]

The only instance since the Byrnes nomination in 1941 of a sitting Senator being named to the Court occurred in 1945. In this episode, the nomination of Senator Harold H. Burton (R-OH), unlike that of Byrnes, was referred to the Judiciary Committee. Referral to the committee, however, did not signal any problems ahead for Senator Burton, as the committee's handling of his nomination was swift and pro forma: A day after the nomination's receipt in the Senate, the committee, without holding a hearing, unanimously reported it to the Senate, where hours later it was confirmed by unanimous consent.[71]

The decades since 1945 have yet to test whether there remains an enduring Senate tradition of bypassing the Judiciary Committee when the Supreme Court nominee is a sitting U.S. Senator—as no President since then has nominated a sitting Senator. The last *former* Senator to be nominated to the Court, in 1949, was Judge Sherman Minton of Indiana. (After defeat for reelection to the Senate in 1940, Minton had been appointed by President Franklin D. Roosevelt to a federal appellate court judgeship.) In this instance, Senate tradition was not adhered to: The Supreme Court nomination of the former Senator was referred to the Judiciary Committee, which held a hearing on the nomination before reporting it favorably, by a vote of 9-2. On the Senate floor, confirmation came not by unanimous consent or voice vote but by a roll-call vote that was not unanimous (48-16).[72]

Movement Toward Open Hearings

During the 19th century, the Judiciary Committee routinely considered Supreme Court nominations behind closed doors, with its deliberations during the 20th century gradually becoming more public in nature. According to one expert source,[73] the earliest Supreme Court confirmation hearings held in open session were those in 1916 for the nomination of Louis D. Brandeis to be an Associate Justice. In 1925, Harlan F. Stone became the first Supreme Court nominee to appear in person and testify at his confirmation hearings.[74]

Neither the Brandeis nor the Stone hearings, however, served as binding precedents. Public confirmation hearings for Supreme Court nominations did not become a regular practice of the Judiciary Committee until the late 1930s. Of the five Supreme Court nominees after Stone in 1925, three (Charles Evans Hughes for Chief Justice in 1930, Owen J. Roberts for Associate Justice in 1930, and Senator Hugo C. Black for Associate Justice in 1937) did not receive confirmation hearings. Then, starting with the nomination of Stanley F. Reed in 1938, every Supreme Court nominee, except for two in the 1940s[75] and two in 2005,[76] would receive a hearing. Initially, however, the hearings in the 1930s and 1940s were usually brief and perfunctory, held only long enough to accommodate the small number of witnesses who wanted to testify against a nominee.[77]

Nominee Appearances at Confirmation Hearings

Also, notwithstanding Stone's appearance at his hearings in 1925, the Judiciary Committee, over the next 30 years, usually declined to invite Supreme Court nominees to testify if a confirmation hearing were held;[78] hence, as recently as 1954, Earl Warren did not appear at his confirmation hearings to be Chief Justice. However, hearings in 1955 on the Supreme Court nomination of John M. Harlan marked the beginning of a practice, continuing to the present, of each Court nominee testifying before the Judiciary Committee.[79] In 1981, Supreme Court confirmation hearings were opened to gavel-to-gavel television coverage for the first time, when the committee instituted the practice at the confirmation hearings for nominee Sandra Day O'Connor.[80]

Whereas, historically, nominees were routinely uninvolved in the appointment process, they have now become active participants. Indeed, at hearings, a nominee's demeanor, responsiveness and knowledge of the law may be crucial in influencing the committee members' and other Senators' votes on confirmation.

Lengthening of Committee Involvement in Appointment Proecess

Another important historical trend has involved the pace and thoroughness of the Judiciary Committee in acting on Supreme Court nominations. Throughout the second half of the 19th century and the first half of the 20th century, it was the standard practice, unless Senators at the outset found a nominee to be objectionable for some reason, for the committee to act on and dispose of a nomination within days of receiving it. In recent decades, by contrast, the committee has tended to proceed much more deliberately, with its official involvement in the appointment process now usually measured in weeks or months.[81]

Since the late 1960s, the Judiciary Committee's consideration of a Supreme Court nominee almost always has consisted of three distinct stages—a pre-hearing investigative stage, followed by public hearings, and concluding with a committee decision on what recommendation to make to the full Senate.

Pre-Hearing Stage

Immediately upon the President's announcement of a nominee, the Judiciary Committee initiates its own intensive investigation into the nominee's background. One primary source of information is a committee questionnaire to which the nominee responds in writing.[82] The questionnaire asks the nominee for detailed biographical and financial disclosure information,[83] with responses to some questions requiring the retrieval, listing and summarizing of voluminious information about the nominee's past experiences or activities.[84] Because of the labor intensive nature of the task, an administration typically will aid the nominee in preparing and transmitting the questionnaire to the Judiciary Committee.

A chief purpose of the questionnaire is to provide members of the the Judiciary Committee and their staffs with detailed pre-hearing information about the nominee. After delivery of the filled-in questionnaire to the committee, however, some Senators on the committee may formally request in writing that the nominee provide additional information to clarify or expand on what he or she has already submitted. The nominee may then provide the committee with written responses to specific questions from the Senators, which in turn are made available, as supplements to the questionnaire to all committee members prior to the start of the nominee's confirmation hearings.[85] The committee treats the questionnaire's biographical and financial disclosure sections as public information. The committee, however, treats as confidential (and not available to the news media or the public) the nominee's responses to more sensitive questions, such as whether he or she ever had been under investigation for possible violation of a civil or criminal statute.

Confidential FBI reports on the nominee are another important information source. These are available only to committee members and a small number of designated staff under strict security procedures designed to prevent unauthorized disclosure. Also, independently of the FBI, committee staff conduct their own confidential investigations into the nominee's background.

The Judiciary Committee's background investigation of a Supreme Court nominee closely reviews, among other things, the nominee's past professional activities. In this review, committee members and staff examine the mission of entitities that employed or otherwise retained the services of the nominee and the nature and quality of the work product of the nominee while in that service. To this end, the committee might seek and attain access to the nominee's confidential written work product or to other documents that the past employer might consider of an internal nature and ordinarily not suitable for public release.[86]

If the nominee's background includes prior service in the federal executive branch, the Judiciary Committee as a whole, or some of its members, can be expected to seek access to records of the nominee's written work product from that service. Sometimes, however, a President might resist such requests, citing the need to protect the confidentiality of advice provided, or decisions made, by the nominee while having served within an Administration—and typically invoking an "executive privilege" or attorney-client privilege to support his refusal to make such information available to the Judiciary Committee.[87] In such an event, committee members or their staff might then devote a significant amount of time, prior to confirmation hearings, to identifying and justifying disclosure of specific kinds of documents that would aid the committee in making a more informed evaluation of the nominee—as well as to examining whatever documents are eventually released. In some cases, the committee may be in a position to exert leverage over an Administration, particularly when a majority of the committee's members are insistent that at least some executive branch documents be released before the committee will act on the nomination. This, a CRS report notes, was the case in 1986, when the Judiciary Committee prepared to consider the nomination of William H. Rehnquist to be Chief Justice.

> During the confirmation proceeding for the elevation of Justice Rehnquist to be Chief Justice, the Judiciary Committee sought documents that he had authored on controversial subjects when he headed DOJ's Office of Legal Counsel. President Reagan asserted executive privilege, claiming the need to protect the candor and confidentiality of the legal advice submitted to Presidents and their assistants. But with opponents of Rehnquist [in the Judiciary Committee] gearing up to issue a subpoena, the nomination of not only Rehnquist but that of Antonin Scalia to be an Associate Justice, whose nominations were to be voted on in tandem,

were in jeopardy. President Reagan agreed to allow the Committee access to a smaller number of documents, and Rehnquist and Scalia were ultimately confirmed.[88]

Meanwhile, the nominee, in accordance with longstanding tradition, visits Capitol Hill to pay "courtesy calls" on individual Senators in their offices. For Senators not on the Judiciary Committee, that may be the only opportunity to converse in person with the nominee before voting on his or her confirmation to the Court. Senators may use these meetings to gain firsthand impressions of the nominee and to discuss with the nominee issues that are important to them in the context of the nomination.[89]

Also during the pre-hearing stage, the nominee is evaluated by the American Bar Association's Standing Committee on the Federal Judiciary,[90] which is publicly committed to providing the Senate Judiciary Committee with an impartial evaluation of the qualifications of each Supreme Court nominee. A publication of the ABA committee stresses that each evaluation focuses strictly on the candidate's "professional qualifications: integrity, professional competence and judicial temperament" and does "not take into account [his or her] philosophy, political affiliation or ideology."[91] Performance of this evaluation role, the committee states, is intended to help "ensure that the most qualified persons serve on the federal judiciary."[92] At the culmination of its evaluation, the ABA committee votes on whether to rate a nominee "well-qualified," "qualified," or "not qualified." The rating of the ABA committee is then reported to each member of the Senate Judiciary Committee, as well as to the White House, the Department of Justice, and the nominee. Also, the rating is posted for the public record, on the ABA committee's website, at http://www.abanet.org/scfedjud/.[93]

For the most part, from its inception in the late 1940s, and continuing through the next three decades, the ABA committee evaluated Supreme Court nominees, as well as nominees to lower court judgeships, with bipartisan support in the Senate. In the 1980s and 1990s, however, the committee came under criticism from some Senators, who questioned its impartiality and the usefulness of its nominee evaluations to the Judiciary Committee.[94] Notwithstanding those criticisms, and variations in the recognition afforded it by chairs of the Judiciary Committee,[95] the ABA committee has continued, in recent Congresses, to appear on a regular basis before the Judiciary Committee, under both Republican and Democratic chairs. In keeping with longstanding practice, the ABA committee chair was the first public witness to testify at the Supreme Court confirmation hearings in 2005, 2006, and 2009—to explain the ABA committee's rating of nominees John G. Roberts Jr., Samuel A. Alito Jr., and Sonia Sotomayor respectively.[96]

At the Alito hearings, the then-chair of the Judiciary Committee, Senator Arlen Specter (R-PA), observed that, in receiving the testimony of outside witnesses at Supreme Court confirmation hearings, "our tradition is to hear first from the American Bar Association and their evaluation of the judicial nominee."[97] Most recently, in 2010, in a minor break from this tradition, the ABA committee chair was not the first public witness to testify at the confirmation hearings for Supreme Court nominee Elena Kagan, but testified in a third panel of public witnesses (testifying first among those panelists).[98]

Meanwhile, it is common, well before the start of confirmation hearings, for public debate to begin on a nominee's qualifications and on the meaning of the nomination for the future of the Court. Much of this debate is waged by commentators in the news media and increasingly, in recent years, on Internet sites, and by advocacy groups that actively support or oppose a nominee.[99] Senators, too, sometimes contribute to this debate in Senate floor statements or other public remarks. Moreover, if a nominee is not quickly selected, groups who see their interests to be at stake by a new Court appointment can be expected to begin mobilizing members, or seeking to affect public or Senate opinion, before the President selects a nominee. Their purpose in doing might be to influence the President's choice or to galvanize the groups' members and political allies in anticipation of whomever the President chooses.[100]

If, ultimately, the President's choice of a nominee proves to be divisive, the pre-hearing phase will be of strategic concern both to those groups which support and those which oppose the nominee. During this phase, a political analyst has noted, "both sides will move quickly to try to define the nominee."[101] The analysis, published in July 2005, only days after Justice Sandra Day O'Connor announced her intention to retire, considered what might happen if President George W. Bush's choice to succeed Justice O'Connor created an immediate polarization in the Senate along party lines. In that event, it predicted the following scenario prior to the nominee's confirmation hearings:

> First impressions are lasting impressions. If Republicans can create a positive image of a Bush Supreme Court nominee in the public's mind right out of the gate, that could help the nominee withstand later efforts by critics to portray him or her as an extremist. Conversely, if Democrats can quickly paint the president's choice as ideologically driven and far out of the mainstream, that could be a deathblow.[102]

However, even if a nominee is not a "consensus" choice attracting immediate support across the political spectrum, the pre-hearing stage will not necessarily be marked by sharp polarization in the Senate or by the immediate emergence of Senate opposition. Such deep division, for instance, was absent when President Bush, on July 19, 2005, announced his selection of U.S. appellate court judge John G. Roberts Jr. to succeed the retiring Justice O'Connor. While "[l]iberal advocacy groups immediately assailed Roberts for his positions on abortion and other issues," and "Republican senators quickly rallied behind Roberts," Senate Democrats withheld immediate criticism of the nominee—reportedly out of concern about falling into what the Senate Democratic leader, according to aides, "considered a Republican trap of condemning a nominee before hearings...."[103]

As confirmation hearings approach, Judiciary Committee members and staff closely study the public record and investigative information compiled on the nominee,[104] and with the benefit of such research, they prepare questions to pose at the hearings. Sometimes committee members indicate in advance, either publicly or by communicating directly with the nominee, the kind of questions they intend to ask at the hearings.[105]

For his or her part, the nominee also intensively prepares for the hearings, focusing particularly on questions of law and policy likely to be raised by committee members. The Administration assists the nominee in this effort by providing legal background materials and by conducting mock hearing practice sessions for the nominee. At these sessions—also called "murder boards," because of "their grueling demands on a judicial nominee"[106]—the nominee is questioned on the full range of legal and constitutional issues that Senators on the Judiciary Committee can be expected to raise at the nominee's confirmation hearings.[107]

Hearings

A confirmation hearing typically begins with a statement by the chair of the Judiciary Committee welcoming the nominee and outlining how the hearing will proceed.[108] Other members of the committee follow with opening statements, and a panel of "presenters" introduces the nominee to the committee.[109] It is then the nominee's turn to make an opening statement, after which begins the principal business of the hearing—the questioning of the nominee by Senators serving on the Judiciary Committee. Typically, the chair begins the questioning, followed by the ranking minority member and then the rest of the committee in descending order of seniority, alternating between majority and minority members, with a uniform time limit for each Senator during each round. When the first round of questioning has been completed, the committee begins a second round, which may be followed by more rounds, at the discretion of the committee chair.[110]

In recent decades, most nominees have undergone rigorous questioning in varying subject areas. They have been queried, as a matter of course, about their legal qualifications, private backgrounds, and earlier actions as public figures. Other questions have focused on social and political issues, the Constitution, particular Court rulings, current constitutional controversies, constitutional values, judicial philosophy, and the analytical approach a nominee might use in deciding issues and cases.[111] Still other questions may concern past public statements made by the nominee, or (if the nominee is a judge) particular rulings handed down by the nominee.[112] To many Senators, eliciting testimony from the nominee may be seen as an important way to gain insight into the nominee's professional qualifications, temperament, and character. Some Senators, as well, may hope to glean from the nominee's responses signs of how the nominee, if confirmed to the Court, might be expected to rule on issues of particular concern to the Senators.[113]

For his or her part, however, a nominee might sometimes be reluctant to answer certain questions that are posed at confirmation hearings.[114] A nominee might decline to answer for fear of appearing to make commitments on issues that later could come before the Court.[115] A nominee also might be concerned that the substance of candid responses to certain questions could displease some Senators and thus put the nominee's chances for confirmation in jeopardy.[116]

For their part, committee members may differ in their assessments of a nominee's stated reasons for refusing to answer certain questions.[117] Some may be sympathetic and consider a nominee's refusal to discuss certain matters as of no relevance to his or her fitness for appointment, or as illustrative of a commendable inclination not to be "pinned down" on current legal controversies. Others, however, may consider a nominee's views on certain subjects as important to assessing the nominee's fitness and hence regard unresponsiveness to questions on these subjects as sufficient reason to vote against confirmation.[118] Protracted questioning, occurring over several days of hearings, is likely, especially if a nominee is relatively controversial or is perceived by committee members to be evasive or insincere in responding to certain questions, or if Senators perceive certain issues to merit extended discussion.

For members of the Judiciary Committee, questioning of the nominee may serve various purposes. As already noted, for Senators who are undecided about the nominee, the hearings may shed light on the nominee's fitness, and hence on how they should vote. Other Senators, as the hearings begin, may already be "reasonably certain about voting to confirm the nominee," yet "also remain reasonably open to counter-evidence," and thus use the hearings "to pursue a line of questioning designed to probe the validity of this initial favorable predisposition."[119] Still others, however, may come to the hearings "having already decided how they will vote on the nomination" and, accordingly, use their questioning of the nominee to try "to secure or defeat the nomination."[120] For some Senators, the hearings may be a vehicle through which to impress certain values or concerns upon a nominee, in the hope of influencing how he or she might approach issues later as a Justice.[121] The hearings also may represent to some Senators an opportunity to draw the public's attention to certain issues, to advocate their policy preferences, or to associate themselves with concern about certain problems. Senators, it has also been noted, "may play multiple roles in any given hearings."[122]

After questioning the nominee has been completed, the committee, in subsequent days of hearings, also hears testimony from public witnesses. As stated earlier, among the first to testify in recent decades has been the chair of the ABA's Standing Committee on the Federal Judiciary, who explains the committee's rating of a nominee. Other witnesses ordinarily include spokespersons for advocacy groups which support or oppose a nominee.

In a practice instituted in 1992, the Judiciary Committee also has conducted a closed-door session with each Court nominee. This session is held to address any questions about the nominee's background that confidential investigations might have brought to the committee's attention. In announcing this procedure in 1992, the then-chair of the committee, Senator Joseph R. Biden Jr. (D-DE), explained that such a hearing would be conducted "in all cases, even when there are no major investigative issues to be resolved so that the holding of such a hearing cannot be taken to demonstrate that the committee has received adverse confidential information about the nomination."[123]

The first such closed-door session was held for Supreme Court nominee Ruth Bader Ginsburg in 1993, separate from public hearings that the committee held on her nomination. Most recently, such sessions were held in 2005, 2006, 2009, and 2010 for nominees John G. Roberts Jr., Samuel A. Alito Jr., Sonia Sotomayor, and Elena Kagan respectively. At the Roberts, Alito, and Kagan confirmation hearings, a very brief executive session was held after the Judiciary Committee had concluded all of its rounds of questions for the nominees but before it received outside witness testimony.[124] At the Sotomayor confirmation hearings, an executive session was held between the Judiciary Committee's first and second rounds of questions for the nominee.[125]

Reporting the Nomination

Usually within a week of the end of hearings, the Judiciary Committee meets in open session to determine what recommendation to "report" to the full Senate. The committee may report favorably, negatively, or make no recommendation at all. A report with a negative recommendation or no recommendation permits a nomination to go forward, while alerting the Senate that a substantial number of committee members have reservations about the nominee.

If a majority of its members oppose confirmation, the committee technically may decide not to report a nomination, to prevent the full Senate from considering the nominee. However, since its creation in 1816, the Judiciary Committee's almost invariable practice has been to report even those Supreme Court nominations that were opposed by a committee majority,[126] thus allowing the full Senate to make the final decision on whether the nominee should be confirmed.[127] This committee tradition was reaffirmed in June 2001 by the committee's then-chair, Senator Patrick J. Leahy (D-VT), and its then-ranking member, Senator Orrin G. Hatch (R-UT), in a June 29, 2001, letter to Senate colleagues. The committee's "traditional practice," their letter stated,

> ... has been to report Supreme Court nominees to the Senate once the Committee has completed its considerations. This has been true even in cases where Supreme Court nominees were opposed by a majority of the Judiciary Committee.
>
> We both recognize and have every intention of following the practices and precedents of the committee and the Senate when considering Supreme Court nominees.[128]

In recent decades, reporting to the Senate frequently has included a printed committee report, although the four most recently reported Supreme Court nominations were done so without printed reports.[129] Prepared behind closed doors, after the committee has voted on the nominee, the printed report presents in a single volume the views of committee members supporting a nominee's confirmation as well as "all supplemental, minority, or additional views ... submitted by the time of the filing of the report...."[130] No Senate committee, however, is normally obliged to transmit a printed report to the Senate. Instead, the chair of the Judiciary Committee may simply file a one-page document reporting a nomination to the Senate and recommending whether the nomination should be confirmed.

A printed report, it can be argued, is valuable in providing for Senators not on the Judiciary Committee a review, in one volume, of all of the reasons that the committee's members cite for voting in favor or against a nominee.[131] A written report, however, might not always be considered a necessary reference for the Senate as a whole. For instance, in some cases, Senators not on the Judiciary Committee might believe they have received adequate information about a nominee from other sources, such as from news media reports or gavel-to-gavel video coverage of the nominee's confirmation hearings.[132] Further, preparation of a written report will mean additional days for a nomination to stay with the committee before it can be reported to the Senate.[133] In some situations, this might be viewed as creating unnecessary delay in the confirmation process, particularly if there is a desire to fill a Court vacancy as quickly as possible.[134]

The Senate usually, but not always, has agreed with Judiciary Committee recommendations that a Supreme Court nominee be confirmed.[135] Historically, negative committee reports, or reports without recommendation, have been precursors to nominations encountering substantial opposition in the full Senate, although a few of these nominations have eventually been confirmed by narrow margins.[136]

Senate Debate and Confirmation Vote

Bringing the Nomination to the Floor[137]

After the Judiciary Committee has reported a nomination, it is placed on the Executive Calendar and assigned a Calendar number by the executive clerk of the Senate.[138] As with other nominations listed in the Executive Calendar, information about a Supreme Court nomination includes the name and office of the nominee; the name of the previous holder of the office; whether the committee reported the nomination favorably, unfavorably, or without recommendation; and, if there is a printed report, the report number.[139] Business on the Executive Calendar, which consists of treaties and nominations, is considered in executive session.[140] Unless voted otherwise by the Senate, executive sessions are open to the public.[141] Floor debate on a Supreme Court nomination, in contemporary practice, invariably has been conducted in public session, open to the public and press and, since 1986, to live nationwide television coverage.[142]

Consideration of a nomination is scheduled by the majority leader, in consultation with the minority leader and with all interested Senators. At the time agreed on, or at the majority leader's initiative, the Senate proceeds to executive session, either by a motion or by unanimous consent. In recent decades, the almost invariable practice in calling up a Supreme Court nomination has been for the majority leader to ask for unanimous consent that the Senate consider the nomination. The leader may ask for unanimous consent to proceed to executive session to consider the nomination immediately,[143] or at some specified time in the future.[144]

Unanimous consent requests also may include a limit on the time that will be allowed for debate and specify the date and time on which the Senate will vote on a nomination.[145] Typically, the amount of time agreed upon for debate is divided evenly between the majority and minority parties, who usually have as their respective floor managers the chair and ranking minority member of the Judiciary Committee. If agreed to, a time limit on debate, with a date and time set for Senate vote, forecloses the use of unlimited debate by opponents of the nomination—a tactic known, in Senate procedural parlance, as the filibuster. Conversely, if the Senate agrees by unanimous consent to consider a nomination, but does not provide for a time limit on debate or specify when, or under what circumstances, a Senate vote will take place, unlimited debate is possible, although not necessarily inevitable.[146]

When unanimous consent to call up a nomination cannot be secured, a procedural alternative is to make a *motion* that the Senate proceed to consider the nomination. Such a motion may be made while the Senate is in executive or legislative session. If the majority leader moves to consider the nomination during executive session, the motion is debatable under Senate rules.[147] Closing debate on the motion, in turn, may require the Senate to invoke cloture by an affirmative vote of three-fifths of the entire Senate membership (60 Senators if there are no vacancies).[148] A majority leader today is unlikely to make such a motion while in executive session since the motion is debatable.

The debatable nature of a motion to consider, when made in executive session, was demonstrated in 1968, when the nomination of Associate Justice Abe Fortas to be Chief Justice was brought to the Senate floor. The episode marked the most recent Senate proceedings in which a *motion* was made to proceed to consider a Supreme Court nomination while the Senate was in *executive* session. Significant opposition within the Senate to the Fortas nomination raised the theoretical possibility of two filibusters being mounted—the first against the motion to consider, and then (if Fortas supporters were successful in ending debate on the first filibuster) a second, against the nomination itself.[149] The second filibuster, however, failed to materialize when the Senate declined, by the super-majority vote required, to close debate on the motion to consider.[150]

A motion to consider a nomination, however, may also be made while the Senate is in *legislative* session, and such a motion is not debatable. Since 1980, the Senate precedent has been explicitly established that when the Senate is in legislative session, a non-debatable motion may be made to go into executive session to take up a specified nomination.[151] If adhered to, the precedent, according to one congressional scholar, would limit a potential filibuster to the nomination itself.[152]

As discussed below,[153] the most recent instance in which Senate opponents of a Supreme Court nomination sought to block, or indefinitely delay, a vote on confirmation involved Associate Justice nominee Samuel A. Alito Jr., in January 2006. However, the possibility of two filibusters against the Alito nomination—namely, one against proceeding to consideration and a second against a vote on confirmation—was precluded the day after the nomination was reported to the Senate. On that day, January 25, 2006, the Senate, while in legislative session, agreed by unanimous consent to immediately proceed to executive session to consider the Alito nomination. From that point forward, debate in the Senate concerning the nomination had moved beyond the question of whether to consider and on to the question of whether to confirm. Under these circumstances, Senate approval of only one cloture motion, not two, was required to end debate and bring the nomination to a confirmation vote.[154]

Criteria Used to Evaluate Nominees

Once the Senate begins debate on a Supreme Court nomination, many Senators typically will take part in the debate. Some, in their remarks, underscore the importance of the Senate's "advice and consent" role, and the consequent responsibility to carefully determine the qualifications of a nominee before voting to confirm.[155] Invariably, each Senator who takes the floor states his or her reasons for voting in favor of or against a nominee's confirmation.

The criteria used to evaluate a Supreme Court nominee are a personal, very individual matter for each Senator.[156] In their floor remarks, some Senators may cite a nominee's professional qualifications or character as the key criterion,[157] others may stress the importance of the nominee's judicial philosophy or views on constitutional issues,[158] while still others may indicate that they are influenced in varying degrees by all of these criteria.[15]

In recent decades, Senate debate on virtually every Supreme Court nomination has focused to some extent on the nominee's judicial philosophy, ideology, constitutional values, or known positions on specific legal controversies. Many highly controversial decisions of the Court in recent decades have been closely decided, by 5-4 votes, appearing to underscore a longstanding philosophical or ideological divide in the Court between its more so-called liberal and so-called conservative members. A new appointee to the Court, Senators recognize, could have a potentially decisive impact on the Court's currently perceived ideological "balance" and on whether past rulings of the Court will be upheld, modified, or overturned in the future.[160] Announcements by the Court of 5-4 decisions, a journalist covering the Court in 2001 wrote, had "become routine, a familiar reminder of how much the next appointment to the court will matter."[161]

Senators sometimes will indicate in their floor statements whether they believe the views of a particular nominee, although not in complete accord with their own views, nonetheless, fall within a broad range of acceptable legal thinking.[162] Senators' concerns with a nominee's judicial philosophy or ideology may become heightened, and their positions more polarized relative to other Senators', if a nominee's philosophical orientation is seen as controversial, or if the President is perceived to have made the nomination with the specific intention of changing the Court's ideological balance.[163]

Other factors also may figure importantly into a Senator's confirmation decisions. One, it has been suggested, is peer influence in the Senate.[164] Particularly influential, for instance, might be Senate colleagues who are championing a nominee or spearheading the opposition,[165] or who played prominent roles in the Judiciary Committee hearings stage. Another consideration for Senators will be the views of their constituents, especially if many voters back home are thought to feel strongly about a nomination.[166] A third source of influence may be the views of a Senator's advisers, family, and friends, as well as the position taken on the nomination by advocacy groups that the Senator ordinarily trusts or looks to for perspective.[167]

Just as Presidents are assumed to do when considering prospective nominees for the Supreme Court, Senators may evaluate the suitability of a Supreme Court nominee according to whether certain groups, constituencies, or individuals with certain characteristics are adequately represented on the Court.[168] Among the representational criteria commonly considered have been the nominee's party affiliation, geographic origin, ethnicity, religion, and gender.[169]

When considering Supreme Court nominations, Senators may also take Senate institutional factors into account. For instance, the role, if any, that Senators from the home state of a nominee played in the nominee's selection, as well as their support for or opposition to the nominee, may be of interest to other Senators. At the same time, Senators may be interested in the extent to which the President, prior to selecting the nominee, sought advice from other quarters in the Senate—for instance, from Senate party leaders and from the chair, ranking minority member, and other Senators on the Judiciary Committee. A President's prior consultation with a wide range of Senators concerning a nominee may be a positive factor for other Members of the Senate, by virtue of conveying presidential respect for the role of Senate advice, as well as Senate consent, in the judicial appointments process.[170]

Sometimes, Senators may find themselves debating whether the Senate, in its "advice and consent" role, should defer to the President and give a nominee the "benefit of the doubt." This issue received particular attention during Senate consideration of the Supreme Court nomination of Clarence Thomas in 1991. In that debate, some Thomas supporters argued that the Senate, as a rule, should defer to the President's judgment concerning a nominee except when unfavorable information is presented overcoming the presumption in the nominee's favor.[171] Opponents, by contrast, rejected the notion that there was a presumption in favor of a Supreme Court nominee at the start of the confirmation process or that the President, in his selection of a nominee, is owed any special deference.[172]

That Senators continue to have differing views regarding appropriate evaluation criteria for Supreme Court nominees was apparent at Senate hearings on the judicial selection process held on June 26, 2001. At the hearings, a Senate Judiciary subcommittee examined the question of what role ideology should play in the selection and confirmation of federal judges.[173] In his opening remarks, the chair of the subcommittee, Senator Charles E. Schumer (D-NY), stated that it was clear that "the ideology of particular nominees often plays a significant role in the confirmation process." The current era, he said, "certainly justifies

Senate opposition to judicial nominees whose views fall outside the mainstream and who have been selected in an attempt to further tilt the courts in an ideological direction."[174]

By contrast, Senator Orrin G. Hatch (R-UT), in testimony before the subcommittee, declared that there "are myriad reasons why political ideology has not been—and is not—an appropriate measure of judicial qualifications. Fundamentally," he continued, "the Senate's responsibility to provide advice and consent does not include an ideological litmus test because a nominee's personal opinions are largely irrelevant so long as the nominee can set those opinions aside and follow the law fairly and impartially as a judge."[175]

Filibusters and Motions to End Debate[176]

Senate rules place no limits on how long floor consideration of a nomination may last.[177] With time limits lacking, Senators opposing a Supreme Court nominee may seek, if they are so inclined, to use extended debate or delaying actions to postpone or prevent a vote from occurring. The use of dilatory actions for such a purpose is known as the filibuster.[178]

By the same token, however, supporters of a Court nomination have available to them a procedure for placing time limits on consideration of a matter—the motion to invoke cloture. When the Senate agrees to a cloture motion, further consideration of the matter being debated is limited to 30 hours. The majority required for cloture on most matters, including nominations, is three-fifths of the full membership of the Senate—60, if there are no vacancies.[179] By invoking cloture, the Senate ensures that a nomination may ultimately come to a vote and be decided by a voting majority.

Motions to bring debate on Supreme Court nominations to a close have been made on only four occasions.[180] The first use occurred in 1968, when Senate supporters of Justice Abe Fortas tried unsuccessfully to end debate on the motion to proceed to his nomination to be Chief Justice. After the motion was debated at length, the Senate failed to invoke cloture by a 45-43 vote,[181] prompting President Johnson to withdraw the nomination. (The 45 votes in favor of cloture fell far short of the super-majority required—then two-thirds of Senators present and voting, a quorum being present.) A cloture motion to end debate on a Court nomination occurred again in 1971, when the Senate considered the nomination of William H. Rehnquist to be an Associate Justice. Although the cloture motion failed by a 52-42 vote,[182] Rehnquist was confirmed later the same day.[183] In 1986, a cloture motion was filed on a third Supreme Court nomination, this time of sitting Associate Justice Rehnquist to be Chief Justice. Supporters of the nomination mustered more than the three-fifths majority needed to end debate (with the Senate voting for cloture 68-31),[184] and Justice Rehnquist subsequently was confirmed as Chief Justice.

A cloture motion was presented to end consideration of a Supreme Court nomination a fourth time, during Senate consideration of the nomination of Samuel A. Alito Jr. in January 2006. The motion was presented on January 26, after two days of Senate floor debate on the nomination.[185] On January 30, the Senate voted to invoke cloture by a 72-25 vote,[186] and the next day it confirmed the Alito nomination by a vote of 58-42.

As one news analysis observed, Senators "are traditionally hesitant to filibuster judicial nominations."[187] Indicative of this, the article noted, was the fact that some of the "most divisive Supreme Court nominees in recent decades, including Associate Justice Clarence

Thomas, have moved through the Senate without opponents resorting to that procedural weapon."[188] In 1991, five days of debate on the Thomas nomination concluded with a 52-48 confirmation vote. The 48 opposition votes would have been more than enough to defeat a cloture motion if one had been filed. In three earlier episodes, Senate opponents of Supreme Court nominations appear to have refrained from use of the filibuster, even though their numbers would have been sufficient to defeat a cloture motion. In 1969, 1970, and 1987 respectively, lengthy debate occurred on the unsuccessful nominations of Clement F. Haynsworth, G. Harrold Carswell, and Robert H. Bork. In none of these episodes, however, was a cloture motion filed, and in each case debate ended with a Senate vote rejecting the nomination.

Although use of the filibuster against Supreme Court nominations has been relatively rare in the past, the number of filibusters conducted or threatened against lower court nominations has increased in recent years. During the 108th Congress, 10 of President George W. Bush's 34 nominees to U.S. circuit court of appeals judgeships were blocked when motions to end debate on the nominations failed to gain passage in the Senate.[189] Several of these nominations, after resubmission by President Bush in the 109th Congress, again faced the prospect of being filibustered by Senate Democrats, to the displeasure of the Senate's Republican leadership.[190] In May 2005, leaders of the Senate's Republican majority announced their intention, if filibusters against nominations continued, to change the chamber's rules or precedents to require the vote of only a simple Senate majority to end Senate debate on judicial nominations.[191]

A Senate confrontation between the two parties over judicial filibusters was averted on May 23, 2005, when an agreement was reached by a coalition of seven Democratic and seven Republican Senators. As part of the agreement, the coalition's Democratic Senators pledged not to lend their support to filibusters against judicial nominations except under "extraordinary circumstances," while the Republican Senators in the coalition agreed not to support any change in the Senate rules to bar filibusters against judicial nominations, as long as the "spirit and continuing commitments made in this agreement" were kept by all of Senators in the coalition.[192]

In recent years, prior to the May 23, 2005 agreement, some Senators had raised the possibility of a filibuster being conducted against a future Supreme Court nomination, particularly if a vacancy on the Court occurred during the presidency of George W. Bush.[193] Subsequently, in November 2005, the selection by President Bush of Samuel A. Alito Jr. for the Court immediately raised the question of whether Senators likely to oppose Alito might also support a filibuster against his nomination.[194] Ultimately, during Senate floor consideration of the Alito nomination in January 2006, some Senators opposed to Alito did seek to prevent ending debate on his nomination.[195] The effort, however, proved unsuccessful. On January 30, 2006, the Senate voted 72-25 in favor of a motion to end debate on the Alito nomination, well in excess of the 60 needed for the motion to carry.[196] The next day the Senate voted to confirm Alito by a 58-42 vote. The 58-42 vote, a newspaper editorial observed, "allowed Judge Alito to become Justice Alito even though enough Democrats opposed the nomination to stop it with a filibuster."[197]

Voice Votes, Roll Calls, and Vote Margins

When floor debate on a nomination comes to a close, the presiding officer puts the question of confirmation to a vote. In doing so, the presiding officer typically states, "The question is, Will the Senate advise and consent to the nomination of [nominee's name] of [state of residence] to be an Associate Justice [or Chief Justice] on the Supreme Court?"[198] A roll-call vote to confirm requires a simple majority of Senators present and voting, a quorum being present.[199] Since 1967, every Senate vote on whether to confirm a Supreme Court nomination has been by roll call.[200] Prior to 1967, by contrast, fewer than half of all of Senate votes on whether to confirm nominees to the Court were by roll call, with the rest by voice vote.[201]

Historically, vote margins on Supreme Court nominations have varied considerably. Some recorded votes, either confirming or rejecting a nomination, have been close.[202] Most votes, however, have been overwhelmingly in favor of confirmation.[203] On other occasions, as occurred with the three most recent nominations to the Court, a solid majority of the Senate has voted in favor of confirmation, but with a minority of more than 30% of the Senate's Members voting against confirmation.[204]

For roll-call votes on Supreme Court nominations, the formal procedure by which Senators cast their votes on the floor has varied over the years. In recent decades prior to 1991, it was the usual practice for Senators, during the calling of the roll, to be free to come and go, and not have to be present in the Senate chamber for the entire calling of the roll. However, for the seven most recent Supreme Court nominations to receive final Senate votes on confirmation, starting with nominee Clarence Thomas in 1991, the majority leader or the presiding officer, immediately prior to the calling of the roll, has asked all of the Senate's Members to remain seated at their desks during the entire vote—with each Senator rising and responding when his or her name is called.[205] Voting from the desk during roll calls is in keeping with a standing order of the Senate,[206] which rarely, however, is actually enforced;[207] nevertheless, the rule has been applied by Senate leaders, in recent years, to roll-call votes on Supreme Court nominations, to mark the special significance for the Senate of deciding whether to confirm an appointment to the nation's highest court.[208]

Reconsideration of the Confirmation Vote

After a Senate vote to confirm a Supreme Court nomination, a Senator who voted on the prevailing side may, under Senate Rule XXXI, move to reconsider the vote.[209] Under the rule, only one such motion to reconsider is in order on each nomination, and the tabling of the motion prevents any subsequent attempt to reconsider. The Senate typically deals with a motion to reconsider a Supreme Court confirmation in one of two ways. Immediately following the vote to confirm, a Senator may move to reconsider the vote, and the motion is promptly laid upon the table by unanimous consent.[210] Alternatively, well before the vote to confirm, in a unanimous consent agreement, the Senate may provide that, in the event of confirmation, the motion to reconsider be tabled.[211] The Senate, it should be noted, has never adopted a motion to reconsider a Supreme Court confirmation vote.

Nominations That Failed to Be Confirmed

Of the 160 nominations that have been made to the Supreme Court over the course of more than two centuries, 36 were not confirmed by the Senate. Of the 36 not confirmed, 11 were rejected by the Senate (all in roll-call votes), 11 were withdrawn by the President, and 14 lapsed at the end of a session of Congress without a Senate vote cast on whether to confirm.[212] The 36 nominations not confirmed by the Senate, a Congressional Research Service (CRS) report has found, represented 31 individuals, 6 of whom were later re-nominated and confirmed for positions on the Court. Of the other 25 nominees, 4 were nominated and failed confirmation more than once.[213]

Table 2, in the following pages, provides information on the outcome of each of the 36 unconfirmed nominations.[214]

Various scholars, as well as the aforementioned CRS report,[215] have analyzed or provided a broad overview of factors associated with unsuccessful Supreme Court nominations.[216] In a history of Supreme Court appointments from Presidents Washington to Clinton, one scholar identified eight of the more "prominent reasons" why Supreme Court nominations were "rejected either outright or simply were not acted on by the Senate," listing these reasons as the following:

> (1) opposition to the nominating president, not necessarily the nominee; (2) the nominee's involvement with one or more contentious issues of public policy or, simply, opposition to the nominee's perceived jurisprudential or sociopolitical philosophy (i.e., politics); (3) opposition to the record of the incumbent Court, which, rightly or wrongly, the nominee presumably supported; (4) senatorial courtesy (closely linked to the consultative nominating process); (5) a nominee's perceived political unreliability on the part of the party in power; (6) the evident lack of qualification or limited ability of the nominee; (7) concerted, sustained opposition by interest or pressure groups; and (8) fear that the nominee would dramatically alter the Court's jurisprudential lineup. Usually several of these reasons—not one alone—figure in the rejection of a nominee, to which poor timing and poor presidential management of a nomination—e.g., Reagan in Bork's case—could readily be added.[217]

Another scholar, in analyzing the ill-fated nominations of Abe Fortas (1968), Clement F. Haynsworth Jr. (1969), G. Harrold Carswell (1970) and Robert H. Bork (1987), has focused on the "rich interplay among the three leading factors associated with unsuccessful Supreme Court nominations," specifically, "the Senate's perception of the nominee's ideology," the "timing of the nomination," and "a less appreciated" factor, "presidential management of the confirmation process."[218]

The timing of a nomination may create problems for confirmation of a Supreme Court nominee, especially against an election backdrop. Timing, for example, might be less favorable for a nomination if it is made during the last year of a President's term, if the President is not seeking re-election, if his re-election prospects are doubtful, or if an off-year election is approaching in which the President's party is expected to lose Senate seats. Such circumstances might influence some Senators to delay action on a nomination, in order to allow the next President to make the appointment or the next Senate to decide whether to confirm.[219]

Table 2. Supreme Court Nominations Not Confirmed by the Senate

Nominee	President	Date received in Senate[a]	Final action by Senate and/or President[b]	Date(s) of Final Action
William Paterson	Washington	Feb. 27, 1793	Withdrawn	Feb. 28, 1793
John Rutledge (for Chief Justice)	Washington	Dec. 10, 1795	Rejected (10-14)	Dec. 15, 1795
Alexander Wolcott	Madison	Feb. 4, 1811	Rejected (9-24)	Feb. 13, 1811
John J. Crittenden	J.Q. Adams	Dec. 18, 1828	Postponed (23-17)	Feb. 12, 1829
Roger B. Taney	Jackson	Jan. 15, 1835	Postponed (24-21)	Mar. 3, 1835
John C. Spencer	Tyler	Jan. 9, 1844	Rejected (21-26)	Jan. 31, 1844
Reuben H. Walworth	Tyler	Mar. 13, 1844	Tabled (27-20), Withdrawn	June 15, 1844, June 17, 1844
Edward King	Tyler	June 5, 1844	Postponed (29-18)	June 15, 1844
John C. Spencer	Tyler	June 17, 1844	Withdrawn	June 17, 1844
Reuben H. Walworth	Tyler	June 17, 1844	No action recorded	
Reuben H. Walworth	Tyler	Dec. 10, 1844	Tabled, Withdrawn	Jan. 21, 1845, Feb 6, 1845
Edward King	Tyler	Dec. 10, 1844	Tabled, Withdrawn	Jan. 21, 1845, Feb. 8, 1845
John M. Read	Tyler	Feb. 8, 1845	No action recorded	
George W. Woodward	Polk	Dec. 23, 1845	Rejected (20-29)	Jan. 22, 1846
Edward A. Bradford	Fillmore	Aug. 21, 1852	Tabled	Aug. 31,1852
George E. Badger	Fillmore	Jan. 10, 1853	Postponed (26-25)	Feb. 11, 1853
William C. Micou	Fillmore	Feb. 24, 1853	No action recorded	
Jeremiah S. Black	Buchanan	Feb. 6, 1861	Motion to consider rejected (25-26)	Feb. 21, 1861
Henry Stanbery	A. Johnson	Apr. 16, 1866	No action recorded	
Ebenezer R. Hoar	Grant	Dec. 15, 1869	Rejected (24-33)	Feb. 3, 1870
George H. Williams (for Chief Justice)	Grant	Dec. 2, 1873	Withdrawn	Jan. 8, 1874
Caleb Cushing (for Chief Justice)	Grant	Jan. 9, 1874	Withdrawn	Jan. 14, 1874
Stanley Matthews	Hayes	Jan. 26, 1881	No action recorded	
Wm. B. Hornblower	Cleveland	Sep.19, 1893	No action recorded	
Wm. B. Hornblower	Cleveland	Dec. 6, 1893	Rejected (24-30)	Jan. 15, 1894
Wheeler H. Peckham	Cleveland	Jan. 22, 1894	Rejected (32-41)	Feb. 16, 1894
Pierce Butler	Harding	Nov. 23, 1922	No action recorded	
John. J. Parker	Hoover	Mar. 21, 1930	Rejected (39-41)	May 7, 1930

Table 2. (Continued)

Nominee	President	Date received in Senate[a]	Final action by Senate and/or President[b]	Date(s) of Final Action
John M. Harlan	Eisenhower	Nov. 9, 1954	No action recorded	
Abe Fortas (for Chief Justice)	L. Johnson	June 26, 1968	Cloture motion defeated (45-43), Withdrawn	Oct. 1, 1968, Oct. 4, 1968
Homer Thornberry	L. Johnson	June 26, 1968	Withdrawn	Oct. 4, 1968
Clement F. Haynsworth Jr.	Nixon	Aug. 18, 1969	Rejected (45-55)	Nov. 21, 1969
G. Harrold Carswell	Nixon	Jan. 19, 1970	Rejected (45-51)	Apr. 8, 1970
Robert H. Bork	Reagan	July 7, 1987	Rejected (42-58)	Oct. 23, 1987
John G. Roberts Jr.	Bush, G. W.	July 29, 2005	Withdrawn	Sep.6, 2005
Harriet E. Miers	Bush, G. W.	Oct. 7, 2005	Withdrawn	Oct. 28, 2005

Sources: *Journal of the Executive Proceedings of the Senate of the United States of America* (various volumes); CRS Report RL31171, *Supreme Court Nominations Not Confirmed, 1789-August 2010*, by Henry B. Hogue.

Notes: *Italics*—Later re-nominated and confirmed; **Boldface**—Later nominated for Chief Justice and confirmed.

a. The date in this column is the date on which the President's nomination message was received in the Senate. This date may differ from the date of the message itself.

b. Indicates whether there was final action by the Senate (rejecting, postponing action on, tabling, or rejecting a motion to close debate on the nomination) or by the President (withdrawing the nomination).

A nominee's prospects also may be put in jeopardy if a President has not used careful presidential management to pave the way for a smooth confirmation process. Among other things, sound presidential management of the process, it has been suggested, entails good-faith consultation with the Senate before choosing a nominee, especially if the President's party is in the Senate minority. Another element of sound presidential management is selecting a nominee without obvious liabilities or attributes that are likely to generate serious Senate opposition.[220]

Calling Upon the Judiciary Committee to Further Examine the Nomination

Sometimes, after a Supreme Court nomination has been reported, the Senate may delay considering or voting on the nomination, in order to have the Senate Judiciary Committee address new issues concerning the nominee or more fully examine issues that it addressed earlier. Opponents of a nomination may also seek such delay, through recommittal of the nomination to the committee, to defeat the nomination indirectly, by burying it in committee.

Recommittals of Supreme Court Nominations

Although the Senate has never adopted a motion to reconsider a Supreme Court nomination after a confirmation vote, there have been at least eight pre-vote attempts to recommit Supreme Court nominations to the Judiciary Committee.[221] Only two of those were successful. In the first of these two instances, in 1873-1874, the nomination, after being recommitted, stalled in committee until it was withdrawn by the President. In the second instance, in 1925, the Judiciary Committee re-reported the nomination, which the Senate then confirmed.

On December 15, 1873, on the second day of its consideration of the nomination of Attorney General George H. Williams to be Chief Justice, the Senate ordered the nomination to be recommitted to the Judiciary Committee.[222] The nomination had been favorably reported by the committee only four days earlier. During that four-day interval, however, various allegations were made against Williams, including charges that while Attorney General he had used his office to influence decisions profiting private companies in which he held interests.[223] In ordering the nomination to be recommitted, the Senate authorized the Judiciary Committee "to send for persons and papers"[224]—in evident reference to the new allegations made against the nominee. Although the Judiciary Committee held hearings after the recommittal, it did not re-report the nomination back to the Senate. Amid press reports of significant opposition to the nomination both in the Judiciary Committee and the Senate as a whole,[225] the nomination, at Williams's request, was withdrawn by President Ulysses S. Grant on January 8, 1874.[226]

On January 26, 1925, the Senate recommitted the Supreme Court nomination of Attorney General Harlan F. Stone to the Judiciary Committee. Earlier, on January 21, the Judiciary Committee had favorably reported the nomination to the Senate. However, one historian wrote, "Stone's unanimous Judiciary Committee approval ran into trouble when it reached the Senate floor."[227] A principal point of concern to some Senators was the decision made by Stone as Atorney General in December 1924 to expand a federal criminal investigation of Senator Burton K. Wheeler (D-MT)—an investigation initiated by Stone's predecessor as Attorney General, Harry Daugherty. Stone's most prominent critic on this point, Montana's other Democratic Senator, Thomas J. Walsh, demanded that the nomination be returned to the Judiciary Committee.[228] By unanimous consent the Senate agreed, ordering the nomination to be "rereferred to the Committee on the Judiciary with a request that it be reported back to the Senate as soon as practicable."[229] Two days after the recommittal, on January 28, the Judiciary Committee held hearings, with the nominee, at the committee's invitation, taking the then-unprecedented step of appearing before the committee. Under lengthy cross examination by Senator Walsh and several other Senators, the nominee defended his role in the Wheeler investigation.[230] On February 2, 1925, the Judiciary Committee again reported the Stone nomination favorably to the Senate, "by voice vote, without dissent,"[231] and on February 5, 1925, the Senate confirmed Stone by a 71-6 vote.

Delay for Additional Committee Hearings without Recommitting the Nomination

In 1991, during debate on Supreme Court nominee Clarence Thomas, the Senate—without recommitting the nomination to the Judiciary Committee—delayed its scheduled vote on the nomination specifically to allow the committee time for additional hearings on the nominee. On October 8, 1991, after four days of debate, the Senate, by unanimous consent, rescheduled its vote on the Thomas nomination, from October 8 to October 15. The purpose of this delay was to allow the Judiciary Committee to hold hearings on sexual harassment allegations made against the nominee by law professor Anita Hill, which had come to public light only after the Judiciary Committee had ordered the Thomas nomination to be reported, without recommendation, on September 27.[232] Following three days of hearings, on October 11, 12, and 13, 1991, at which the Judiciary Committee heard testimony from Judge Thomas, Professor Hill, and other witnesses, the Senate, pursuant to its unanimous consent agreement, voted on the Thomas nomination as scheduled, on October 15, 1991, confirming the nominee by a 52-48 vote.

After Senate Confirmation

Under the Constitution, the Senate alone votes on whether to confirm presidential nominations, the House of Representatives having no formal involvement in the confirmation process. If the Senate votes to confirm the nomination, the secretary of the Senate then attests to a resolution of confirmation and transmits it to the White House.[233] In turn, the President signs a document, called a commission, officially appointing the individual to the Court. Next, the signed commission "is returned to the Justice Department for engraving the date of appointment (determined by the actual day the president signs the commission) and for the signature of the attorney general and the placing of the Justice Department seal."[234] The department then arranges for expedited delivery of the commission document to the new appointee.

Once the President has signed the commission, the incoming Justice may be sworn into office.[235] In fact, however, the new Justice actually takes two oaths of office—a judicial oath, as required by the Judiciary Act of 1789,[236] and a constitutional oath, which, as required by Article VI of the Constitution, is administered to Members of Congress and all executive and judicial officers. Until recently, the most common practice of new appointees had been to take their judicial oath in private, usually within the Court, and, as desired by the Presidents who nominated them, to take their constitutional oaths in nationally televised ceremonies at the White House.[237] In 2009, however, in a departure from that practice, Supreme Court nominee Sonia Sotomayor, after Senate confirmation, took both her constitutional and judicial oaths of office at the Supreme Court—with the constitutional oath administered in a private ceremony, and the judicial oath broadcast on television ("marking the first live coverage of such a ceremony in the institution's history").[238] This break from the practice of administering one of the oaths at the White House was attributed, in one report, to President Obama "heeding concerns expressed by some justices—most recently John Paul Stevens—that a White House ceremony sends the inappropriate message that justices are beholden to their appointing president."[239] Following Sonia Sotomayor's example, President Obama's second Supreme Court nominee, Elena Kagan, took both her constitutional and judicial oaths of office at the Supreme Court as well.[240]

Subsequently, the Court itself, in its courtroom, also affords public recognition to the new Justice's appointment, in a formal ceremony called an "investiture," at which the Justice is sworn in yet again. This invitation-only event, for which reserved press seating is made available, is attended by the Court's other Justices, by family, friends, and former associates of the new Justice, and by outside dignitaries who may include the President and the attorney general.[241] The investiture typically occurs before the new Justice publicly takes his or her courtroom seat alongside the other members of the Court.[242]

CONCLUSION

Over the course of more than two centuries, the Supreme Court appointment process has undergone important changes, while remaining constant in other key respects. The process is now much longer than it used to be. From the appointment of the first Justices in 1789, continuing well into the 20th century, most Senate confirmations of Supreme Court nominees occurred within a week of the nominations being made by the President. In recent decades, by contrast, it has become the norm for appointment to the Court, from nomination by the President to confirmation by the Senate, to take from two to three months, with the process even longer if a nomination is controversial.[243]

Prior to 1868, the Senate Judiciary Committee sometimes was excluded from, or played a perfunctory role in, the appointment process. Now, however, the Judiciary Committee, rather than the Senate as a whole, invariably assumes the principal responsibility for investigating the background and qualifications of each Supreme Court nominee, and typically the committee conducts a close, intensive investigation of each nominee.

The process is also much more open now than it once was. From the outset, starting with George Washington, and for more than a hundred years thereafter, Presidents transmitted their nominations to the Senate without public fanfare, and the confirmation process that followed in the Senate Judiciary Committee and the Senate as a whole likewise occurred away from public view, in closed executive sessions. By contrast, in the modern appointment process, Presidents typically announce their Supreme Court nominations to the nation before broadcast television cameras in carefully staged presidential news events. In turn, nearly all of the official confirmation process that follows—confirmation hearings by the Judiciary Committee, the committee's vote on the nominee, Senate debate, and finally Senate vote on the nomination—is conducted in public session, receives intensive news media coverage, and is watched by hundreds of thousands (and sometimes millions) of American television viewers.

In another major change from earlier practice, there are now many more participants in the Supreme Court appointment process. Historically, nominees did not participate in the appointment process, but now they regularly appear before the Judiciary Committee. Likewise, in the modern era, public witnesses testify during each confirmation hearing. Among the witnesses are representatives of powerful interest groups, which often take positions in support of or in opposition to a nominee's confirmation. If a nominee is controversial, interest groups may commit themselves to sustained involvement in the confirmation process, mounting support for, or opposition to, a nominee at the very beginning of the process, and seeking through publicity, lobbying and grass-roots efforts of their members, to influence how both the Judiciary Committee and the Senate as a whole vote on the nomination.

From the beginning, an almost unchanging theme underlying the Supreme Court appointment process has been the assumed need for excellence or merit in a nominee as a requisite for appointment to the Court. The continuing expectation of high qualification in nominees has been demonstrated by the Senate's periodic rejection of nominees for alleged lack of qualification.

Also from the beginning, politics, as well as the search for excellence, has played a continuing, important role in Supreme Court appointments. The political nature of the Supreme Court appointment process becomes especially apparent when a President submits a nominee with controversial views, there are sharp partisan or ideological differences between the President and the Senate, or the outcome of important constitutional issues before the Court is seen to be at stake. Under these and other circumstances, divisions may occur in the Senate, bringing to the fore the differing political views of Senators supporting and those opposing the nominee.

If the nomination of a person to the Supreme Court sometimes produces confirmation battles, the appointment process at other times is remarkable for its lack of conflict, particularly when the Senate votes overwhelmingly for confirmation. Various factors might be present when a Supreme Court appointment process is characterized more by harmony than by conflict. At the start of the process, for example, there might be close consultation between the President and Senate Members over suitable candidates for the Court; the President may choose a distinguished, uncontroversial nominee who immediately attracts widespread support from Senators of both parties; the President's party might be in firm numerical superiority in the Senate (thus discouraging detractors of the nominee from mounting vigorous opposition); or a particular Court vacancy might not be regarded as of great moment to the future of the Court (in contrast to vacancy situations where opposing political interests perceive very much to be at stake).

Over more than two centuries, the Supreme Court appointment process has remained constant in one other, constitutionally fundamental respect—in the sharing of the appointment power between the President and the Senate. No Justice has ever been appointed for life to the Court except through this shared process of appointment (although, as noted earlier, Presidents on rare occasions have made temporary "recess appointments" to the Court without the Senate's consent).

Whenever a new Supreme Court vacancy occurs, the President and the Senate face a situation that is both unique and familiar. Unique are the political circumstances of the moment, and the legal controversies that loom before the Court at that point in time. Familiar are the basic roles to be performed in the appointment process. Following a pattern adhered to for more than 200 years, the President and the Senate will again share the appointment power. One will nominate, the other will decide whether to confirm. Only when the two reach agreement may a new Justice join eight others on the Supreme Court of the United States.

Additional Sources

Abraham, Henry J. *Justices, Presidents, and Senators: A History of the U.S. Supreme Court Appointments from Washington to Bush II*, 5th ed. (2008). Lanham, MD: Rowman & Littlefield Publishers, Inc.

——. *Justices and Presidents: A Political History of Appointments to the Supreme Court*, 5th ed. (2008). New York: Oxford University Press.

Atkinson, David N. (1999). *Leaving the Bench: Supreme Court Justices at the End.* Lawrence, KS: University Press of Kansas.

Comiskey, Michael. *Seeking Justices: The Judging of Supreme Court Nominees*. (2004). Lawrence, KS: University Press of Kansas.

Davis, Richard. (2005). *Electing Justice: Fixing the Supreme Court Nominating Process*. New York: Oxford University Press.

Eisgruber, Christopher L. (2007). *The Next Justice: Repairing the Supreme Court Appointment Process*. Princeton, NJ: Princeton University Press.

Epstein, Lee, et al. (2007). *The Supreme Court Compendium: Data, Decisions & Developments*, 4th ed. Washington: Congressional Quarterly Inc.

Gerhardt, Michael J. (2003). *The Federal Appointments Process*. Rev. ed. Durham, NC: Duke University Press.

Geyh, Charles Cardner. (2006). *When Courts & Congress Collide: The Struggle for Control of America's Judicial System*. Ann Arbor, MI: University of Michigan Press.

Greenburg, Jan Crawford. (2007). *The Inside Story of the Struggle for Control of the United States Supreme Court*. New York, Penguin Press.

Harris, Joseph P. (1968). *The Advice and Consent of the Senate: A Study of the Confirmation of Appointments by the United States Senate*. Berkeley, CA: University of California Press, 1953; reprint, New York: Greenwood Press.

Jacobstein, Myron, J. & Roy M. Mersky. (1993). *The Rejected: Sketches of the 26 Men Nominated for the Supreme Court but Not Confirmed by the Senate*. Milpitas, CA: Toucan Valley Publications.

Maltese, John Anthony. (1995). *The Selling of Supreme Court Nominees*. Baltimore: Johns Hopkins University Press. 193 pp.

Massaro, John. (1990). *Supremely Political: The Role of Ideology and Presidential Management in Unsuccessful Supreme Court Nominations*. Albany, NY: State University of New York Press. 272 pp.

Mersky, Roy M. & Myron J. Jacobstein, comp. (1977-1996). *The Supreme Court of the United States: Hearings and Reports on Successful and Unsuccessful Nominations of Supreme Court Justices by the Senate Judiciary Committee*, 1916-1994, 19 vols. Buffalo, NY: William S. Hein & Co.

Nemacheck, Christine L. (2007). *Strategic Selection: Presidential Nomination of Supreme Court Justices from Herbert Hoover Through George W. Bush*. Charlottesville, VA: University of Virginia Press.

Savage, David G. (2004). *Congressional Quarterly's Guide to the U.S. Supreme Court*, 4th ed., 2 vols. Washington: Congressional Quarterly Inc.

Silverstein, Mark. (1997). *Judicious Choices: The New Politics of Supreme Court Confirmations*, updated college ed. New York: W.W. Norton & Company.

Ward, Artemus. (2003). *Deciding To Leave: The Politics of Retirement from the United States Supreme Court*. Albany, NY: State University of New York Press.

Watson, George L. & John A. Stookey. (1995). *Shaping America: the Politics of Supreme Court Appointments*. New York: HarperCollins College Publishers.

Wittes, Benjamin. (2009). *Confirmation Wars: Preserving Independent Courts in Angry Times*. Lanham, MD: Rowman & Littlefield Publishers.

Wright, Benjamin Fletcher, ed. (1966). *The Federalist by Alexander Hamilton, James Madison, and John Jay*. Cambridge, MA: Belknap Press of Harvard University Press, pp. 480-484 (Federalist Paper 76—Hamilton, "The President and the Appointing Power"), pp. 489-496 (Federalist Paper 78—Hamilton, "The Judges as Guardians of the

Constitution"), and pp. 497-499 (Federalist Paper 79—Hamilton, "The Position of the Judiciary").

Yalof, David Alistair (1999). *Pursuit of Justices: Presidential Politics and the Selection of Supreme Court Nominees*. Chicago, University of Chicago Press.

CRS Reports

CRS Report RL32821. *The Chief Justice of the United States: Responsibilities of the Office and Process for Appointment*, by Denis Steven Rutkus and Lorraine H. Tong.

CRS Report RL32878. *Cloture Attempts on Nominations*, by Richard S. Beth and Betsy Palmer.

CRS Report RL32102. *Constitutionality of a Senate Filibuster of a Judicial Nomination*, by Todd B. Tatelman.

CRS General Distribution Memorandum. *Criteria Used by Senators to Evaluate Judicial Nominations*, by Denis Steven Rutkus (available from author).

CRS Report RL32843. *"Entrenchment" of Senate Procedure and the "Nuclear Option" for Change: Possible Proceedings and Their Implications*, by Richard S. Beth.

CRS Report RL31948. *Evolution of the Senate's Role in the Nomination and Confirmation Process: A Brief History*, by Betsy Palmer.

CRS Report R41299. *From Solicitor General to Supreme Court Nominee: Responsibilities, History, and the Nomination of Elena Kagan*, by Susan Navarro Smelcer and Kenneth R. Thomas.

CRS Report RL32971. *Judicial Recess Appointments: A Legal Overview*, by T. J. Halstead.

CRS Report RS22208. *The "Memorandum of Understanding": A Senate Compromise on Judicial Filibusters*, by Walter J. Oleszek.

CRS Report RL33059. *Proper Scope of Questioning of Supreme Court Nominees: The Current Debate*, by Denis Steven Rutkus.

CRS Report R41300. *Questioning Supreme Court Nominees About Their Views on Legal or Constitutional Issues: A Recurring Issue*, by Denis Steven Rutkus.

CRS Report RL31112. *Recess Appointments of Federal Judges*, by Louis Fisher (out of print, available from author).

CRS Report RL31980. *Senate Consideration of Presidential Nominations: Committee and Floor Procedure*, by Elizabeth Rybicki.

CRS Report RL33118, *Speed of Presidential and Senate Actions on Supreme Court Nominations*, 1900-2010, by R. Sam Garrett and Denis Steven Rutkus.

CRS Report R40802, *Supreme Court Justices: Demographic Characteristics, Professional Experience, and Legal Education*, 1789-2010, by Susan Navarro Smelcer.

CRS Report RL33225. *Supreme Court Nominations, 1789-2010: Actions by the Senate, the Judiciary Committee, and the President*, by Denis Steven Rutkus and Maureen Bearden.

CRS Report RL31171, *Supreme Court Nominations Not Confirmed*, 1789-August 2010, by Henry B. Hogue.

CRS Report RL33247, *Supreme Court Nominations: Senate Floor Procedure and Practice*, 1789-2010, by Richard S. Beth and Betsy Palmer.

End Notes

[1] U.S. Supreme Court, *The Supreme Court of the United States* (Washington: Published by the Supreme Court with the cooperation of the Supreme Court Historical Society, revised September 2006), p. 10. (Hereafter cited as Supreme Court, *Supreme Court of the United States.*)

[2] Of the 43 individuals who have served as President of the United States, 6 made only one Supreme Court nomination each, while 3 others were unable to make a single nomination to the Court since no vacancies occurred on the Court during their presidencies. See CRS Report RL33225, *Supreme Court Nominations, 1789 - 2010: Actions by the Senate, the Judiciary Committee, and the President*, by Denis Steven Rutkus and Maureen Bearden (under heading "Presidents Who Made the Nominations").

[3] For instance, nine vacancies occurred on the Court during a five-and-a-half year period of Franklin D. Roosevelt's presidency, with all of FDR's nine nominations to fill those vacancies confirmed by the Senate. The President with the largest number of Supreme Court confirmations in one term (apart from the first eight of George Washington's nominations—all in his first term, and all confirmed) was William Howard Taft, who, during his four years in office, made six Court nominations, all of which were confirmed by the Senate. Ibid.

[4] U.S. Constitution, art. III, §1.

[5] Alexander Hamilton, in Federalist Paper 78 ("The Judges as Guardians of the Constitution"), maintained that, while the judiciary was "in continual jeopardy of being overpowered, awed, or influenced by its coordinate branches ... , nothing can contribute so much to its firmness and independence as *permanency in office*." He added that if the courts "are to be considered as the bulwarks of a limited Constitution against legislative encroachments, this consideration will afford a strong argument for the *permanent tenure* of judicial offices, since *nothing will contribute so much as this to that independent spiritin the judges....*" (Emphases added.) Benjamin Fletcher Wright, ed., *The Federalist by Alexander Hamilton, James Madison, and John Jay* (Cambridge, MA: Belknap Press of Harvard University Press, 1966), p. 491 (first quote) and p. 494 (second quote). (Hereafter cited as Wright, *The Federalist.*)

[6] In 1804, the House of Representatives voted to impeach Justice Samuel Chase. The vote to impeach Chase, a staunch Federalist and outspoken critic of Jeffersonian Republican policies, was strictly along party lines. In 1805, after a Senate trial, Chase was acquitted after votes in the Senate fell short of the necessary two-thirds majority on any of the impeachment articles approved by the House. "Chase's impeachment and trial set a precedent of strict construction of the impeachment clause and bolstered the judiciary's claim of independence from political tampering." David G. Savage, *Guide to the U.S. Supreme Court*, 4th ed. (Washington: Congressional Quarterly Inc., 2004), vol. 1, p. 258. (Hereafter cited as Savage, *Guide to the U.S. Supreme Court.*) In a few other instances, Justices have been the object of preliminary House Judiciary Committee inquiries into allegations of conduct possibly constituting grounds for impeachment, but in none of these instances was impeachment recommended by the committee. In another instance, Justice Abe Fortas, on May 14, 1969, resigned from the Court three days after a House Member stated he had prepared articles of impeachment against the Justice, and one day after another House Member proposed that the House Judiciary Committee begin a preliminary investigation into allegations that the Justice was guilty of various ethical violations. See Charles Gardner Geyh, *When Courts & Congress Collide* (Ann Arbor, MI: The University of Michigan Press, 2009), pp. 119-125; Lee Epstein et al., *The Supreme Court Compendium: Data, Decisions & Developments*, 4th ed. (Washington: Congressional Quarterly Inc., 2007), p. 428. (Hereafter cited as Epstein, *Supreme Court Compendium.*); and U.S. Congress, House, *Hinds' Precedents of the House of Representatives of the United States*, prepared by Asher C. Hinds, clerk at the Speaker's table (Washington, GPO, 1907), vol. 3, sec. 2508.

[7] A Supreme Court booklet published in 2006 noted that since the formation of the Court in 1790, there had been only 17 Chief Justices and 98 Associate Justices, "with Justices serving for an average of 15 years." Supreme Court, *Supreme Court of the United States,* p. 10. More recently, the Congressional Research Service, accounting for all Justices having completed their Court service (including the most recent vacating Justice, John Paul Stevens), calculated an average length of service on the Court of 16.8 years.

[8] The decision of the Framers at the Constitutional Convention of 1787 to have the President and the Senate share in the appointment of the Supreme Court Justices and other principal officers of the government, one scholar wrote, was a compromise reached between "one group of men [who] feared the abuse of the appointing power by the executive and favored appointments by the legislative body," and "another group of more resolute men, eager to establish a strong national government with a vigorous administration, [who] favored the granting of the power of appointment to the President." Joseph P. Harris, *The Advice and Consent of the Senate: A Study of the Confirmation of Appointments by the United States Senate* (Berkeley, CA: University of California Press, 1953; reprint, New York: Greenwood Press, 1968), p. 33. (Hereafter cited as Harris, *Advice and Consentof the Senate.*)

[9] Consider, for example, President John Adams's fateful nomination in 1801 of John Marshall. During his more than 34 years of service as Chief Justice, Marshall, "more than any other individual in the history of the Court, determined the developing character of America's Federal constitutional system" and "raised the Court from

its lowly, if not discredited, position to a level of equality with the executive and legislative branches." Henry J. Abraham, *Justices and Presidents: A Political History of Appointments to the Supreme Court*, 3rd ed. (New York: Oxford University Press, 1992), p. 83. (Hereafter cited as Abraham, *Justices and Presidents.*) Looking back on his appointment a quarter century before, Adams in 1826 was quoted as saying, "My gift of John Marshall to the people of the United States was the proudest act of my life." Charles Warren, *The Supreme Court in United States History*, rev. edition, 2 vols. (Boston: Little Brown, 1926), vol. 1, p. 178.

[10] "By well-established custom, the Senate accords the President wide latitude in the selection of the members of his Cabinet, who are regarded as his chief assistants and advisers. It is recognized that unless he is given a free hand in the choice of his Cabinet, he cannot be held responsible for the administration of the executive branch." Harris, *Advice and Consentof the Senate*, p. 259.

[11] The Senate "is perhaps most acutely attentive to its [advise and consent] duty when it considers a nominee to the Supreme Court. That this is so reflects not only the importance of our Nation's highest tribunal, but also our recognition that while Members of the Congress and Presidents come and go ..., the tenure of a Supreme Court Justice can span generations." Sen. Daniel P. Moynihan, debate in Senate on Supreme Court nomination of Ruth Bader Ginsburg, *Congressional Record*, vol. 139, August 2, 1993, p. 18142.

[12] See CRS Report RL33225, *Supreme Court Nominations, 1789 - 2010: Actions by the Senate, the Judiciary Committee, and the President*, by Denis Steven Rutkus and Maureen Bearden, the table at the end of the report, which lists all 160 Supreme Court nominations made through 2010, starting with George Washington's first six nominations to the Court in 1789 and carrying through Barack Obama's nomination of Elena Kagan in 2010. The table shows that a lesser number of individuals, 141, were actually nominated to the Court, with some of them nominated more than once. The table includes the names of eight nominees who, subsequent to Senate confirmation, did not assume the office to which they had been appointed (with seven having declined the office, and one having died before assuming it).

[13] The first rejection by the Senate of a Supreme Court nominee occurred on December 15, 1795, when the Senate voted 14 to 10 not to confirm President George Washington's nomination of John Rutledge of South Carolina to be Chief Justice. See **Table 2** in the following pages of this chapter, listing all 36 Supreme Court nominations not confirmed by the Senate. Besides listing the unconfirmed nominations of persons nominated only once to the Court, the table includes the unconfirmed nominations of persons who were (1) nominated more than once and never confirmed; (2) re-nominated to the same Court position and then confirmed; or (3) nominated unsuccessfully for Associate Justice, only to be re-nominated for Chief Justice and then confirmed. For more complete information about the 36 Supreme Court nominations not confirmed by the Senate, including, most recently, the withdrawn nomination of Harriet E. Miers in 2005, see CRS Report RL31171, *Supreme Court Nominations Not Confirmed, 1789-August 2010*, by Henry B. Hogue. For short narratives regarding the Rutledge confirmation defeat and 25 subsequent Supreme Court nominees who failed to gain Senate confirmation, see J. Myron Jacobstein and Roy M. Mersky, *The Rejected* (Milpitas, CA: Toucan Valley Publications, 1993). (Hereafter cited as Jacobstein and Mersky, *The Rejected.*) Since it was published in 1993, *The Rejected* lacks a narrative for the failed Miers nomination. For such an account on the Miers nomination, see Jan Crawford Greenburg, *Supreme Conflict: The Inside Story of the Struggle for Control of the United States Supreme Court* (New York: Penguin Press, 2007), pp. 245-284. (Hereafter cited as Greenburg, *Supreme Conflict.*)

[14] The first Supreme Court nominee to be re-nominated and confirmed after his first nomination failed to be confirmed was William Paterson of New Jersey in 1793. Paterson was first nominated on February 27, 1793, by President George Washington. The President, however, withdrew the nomination a day later, citing a constitutional technicality. In his withdrawal message (U.S. Congress, Senate, *Journal of the Executive Proceedings of the Senate of the United States of America*, vol. 1, p. 135), President Washington indicated that the nomination was in violation of Article I, Section 6 of the Constitution, which provides: "No Senator or Representative shall, during the Time for which he was elected, be appointed to any civil Office ..., which shall have been created ... during such time ...." Paterson had been a member of the Senate when the Judiciary Act of 1789 was passed, creating the Associate Justice position to which Washington nominated Paterson in February 1793. Though Paterson had resigned from the Senate in 1790, the Senate term to which he had been elected would not conclude until March 3, 1793. Washington re-nominated Paterson on March 4, 1793, and later that day a special session of the Senate of a new Congress confirmed the nominee by voice vote.

Another Court nominee to be re-nominated and then confirmed was Pierce Butler of Minnesota in 1922. Butler was first nominated by President Warren G. Harding on November 23, 1922, during the 3rd session of the 67th Congress. Although reported favorably by the Judiciary Committee, the nomination failed to be confirmed before the end of the 3rd session. President Harding re-nominated Butler on December 5, 1922, during thc 4th session of the 67th Congrcss, and shortly thereafter, on December 22, 1922, the Senate confirmed Butler by a 61-8 roll-call vote.

A third Court nominee to be re-nominated and then confirmed was John M. Harlan II of New York. Harlan was first nominated by President Dwight D. Eisenhower on November 9, 1954, but the nomination received no action in the Senate before the final adjournment of the 83rd Congress less than a month later. President

Eisenhower re-nominated Harlan on January 10, 1955, at the beginning of the 84th Congress, and shortly thereafter, on March 16, 1955, the Senate confirmed Harlan by a 71-11 roll-call vote.

Two other nominees who were not confirmed the first time only to be later re-nominated and confirmed received Senate confirmation in spite of significant Senate opposition. One was Roger B. Taney, nominated twice by President Andrew Jackson in 1835, and Stanley Matthews, nominated first by President Rutherford B. Hayes in 1881 and by President James A. Garfield, later in 1881. Taney's first nomination, to Associate Justice, was postponed indefinitely by the Senate. During the next Congress, he was re-nominated and confirmed as Chief Justice by a 29-15 roll-call vote in the Senate. Mathews' first nomination was never reported out of committee, but in the following Congress, under a new President, he was re-nominated and confirmed by a 24-23 roll-call vote.

The final nominee not confirmed but later re-nominated and confirmed was current Chief Justice John G. Roberts. As noted previously in this chapter, Judge Roberts was first nominated to replace Associate Justice Sandra Day O'Connor, but when Chief Justice Rehnquist died suddenly, President Bush withdrew his nomination and resubmitted it for the position of Chief Justice.

[15] During the 1967-2010 period, two other Court nominations—the Associate Justice nominations in 2005 of John G. Roberts Jr. and Harriet E. Miers—were withdrawn by the President before receiving hearings. On the day his nomination was withdrawn, however, Judge Roberts was re-nominated to be Chief Justice and, 39 days later, confirmed.

[16] According to one author, when Justice Sandra Day O'Connor in 2005 announced her plan to retire, the Court was regarded as playing an extremely important role in American life. "For the past fifty years, beginning under the leadership of Earl Warren, the Court had confronted America's most pressing social controversies. The Court showed little hesitation in interjecting itself into those disputes and attempting to solve the nation's most vexing problems from the bench, even if that meant wresting them away from the state legislatures and the Congress." In the process, the Court "became a moral compass," identifying "new constitutional rights" not specifically addressed in the Constitution. "Liberals believed that was an entirely proper role for the court, especially since the other branches of government had failed so miserably in the area of civil rights." By contrast, conservatives "saw a Supreme Court that had arrogantly grabbed power for itself." Greenburg, *Supreme Conflict*, pp. 23-24.

[17] As noted above, a Supreme Court vacancy also would occur if a Justice were removed by Congress through the impeachment process, but no Justice has ever been removed from the Court in this way. For a comprehensive review of how and why past Supreme Court Justices have left the Court, see Artemus Ward, *Deciding To Leave: The Politics of Retirement from the United States Supreme Court* (Albany, NY: State University of New York Press, 2003), pp. 25-223. Ward, in introduction at p. 7, explained that his book, among other things, examines the extent to which Justices, in their retirement decisions, have been "motivated by strategic, partisan, personal, and institutional concerns."

[18] For a book-length examination of how several recent Presidents have selected nominees to serve on the Supreme Court, see David Alistair Yalof, *Pursuit of Justices: Presidential Politics and the Selection of Supreme Court Nominees* (Chicago: University of Chicago Press, 1999). (Hereafter cited as Yalof, *Pursuit of Justices*.) See also Greenburg, *Supreme Conflict*, which examined in depth the processes followed by the Administrations of Presidents Ronald Reagan, George H. W. Bush, William J. Clinton, and George W. Bush in selecting Supreme Court nominees; and Christine L. Nemacheck, *Strategic Selection: Presidential Nomination of Supreme Court Justices from Herbert Hoover Through George W. Bush* (Charlottesville, VA: University of Virginia Press, 2007).

[19] See, for example, John Ferling, "The Senate and Federal Judges: The Intent of the Founding Fathers," *Capitol Studies*, vol. 2, Winter 1974, p. 66: "Since the convention acted at a time when nearly every state constitution, and the Articles of Confederation, permitted a legislative voice in the selection of judges, it is inconceivable that the delegates could have intended something less than full Senate participation in the appointment process."

[20] See, for example, Harris, *Advice and Consent of the Senate*, p. 34: "The debates in the Convention do not support the thesis since advanced that the framers of the Constitution intended that the President should secure the advice—that is, the recommendations—of the Senate or of individual members, before making a nomination."

[21] Michael J. Gerhardt, *The Federal Appointments Process* (Durham, NC: Duke University Press, 2003), p. 33. (Hereafter cited as Gerhardt, *The Federal Appointment Process*.) The Constitution, Gerhardt added, "does not mandate any formal prenomination role for the Senate to consult with the president; nor does it impose any obligation on the president to consult with the Senate prior to nominating people to confirmable posts. The Constitution does, however, make it clear that the president or his nominees may have to pay a price if he ignores the Senate's advice." Ibid.

[22] "To a certain extent, presidents have always looked to the Senate for recommendations and subsequently relied on a nominee's backers there to help move the nomination through the Senate." George L. Watson and John A. Stookey, *Shaping America: The Politics of Supreme Court Appointments* (New York, HarperCollins College Publishers, 1995), p. 78. (Hereafter cited as Watson and Stookey, *Shaping America*.)

[23] President Clinton's search for a successor to retiring Justice Harry A. Blackmun, during the spring of 1994, is illustrative of a President seeking and receiving Senate advice. According to one report, the President, as he came close to a decision after holding his options "close to the vest" for more than a month, "began for the first time to consult with leading senators about his top candidates for the Court seat and solicited advice about prospects for easy confirmation." The advice he received included "sharp Republican opposition to one of his leading choices, Interior Secretary Bruce Babbitt." Gwen Ifill, "Clinton Again Puts Off Decision on Nominee for Court," *The New York Times*, May 11, 1994, p. A16.

In 2005, the Administration of President George W. Bush took pains to engage in a level of consultation with Senators over prospective Supreme Court nominations that White House officials called unprecedented. Prior to the President's nominations to the Court of John G. Roberts Jr., Harriet E. Miers, and Samuel A. Alito Jr., the President and his aides reportedly consulted with, and sought input from, the vast majority of the Senate's Members. Prior to announcing the Miers nomination, for instance, it was reported that "the President and his staff talked with more than 80 Senators," although "some Democrats questioned whether the process was just for show." Deb Riechmann, "Bush Expected to Name High Court Nominee," Associated Press Online, September 30, 2005, at http://www.nexis.com. According to a White House spokesman, the more than 80 Senators included all 18 members of the Senate Judiciary Committee and over two-thirds of Senate Democrats. Steve Holland, "Bush Completes Consultations, Nears Court Decision," Reuters News, September 30, 2005, at http://global.factiva.com.

Likewise, in 2009, President Barack Obama consulted Senators prior to selecting Sonia Sotomayor to succeed outgoing Justice David Souter. Announcing the nomination of Judge Sotomayor to the Court, President Obama said the selection process had been "rigorous and extensive" and included seeking "the advice of Members of Congress on both sides of the aisle, including every member of the Senate Judiciary Committee." U.S. President (Obama, Barack H.), "Remarks on the Nomination of Sonia Sotomayor To Be a Supreme Court Associate Justice," *Daily Compilation of Presidential Documents*, May 26, 2009, DCPD-200900402, p. 1

[24] "Numerous instances of the application of senatorial courtesy are on record, with the practice at least partially accounting for rejection of several nominations to the Supreme Court." Henry J. Abraham, *Justices, Presidents and Senators: A History of the U.S. Supreme Court Appointments from Washington to Clinton*, new and rev. ed. (New York: Rowman & Littlefield Publishers, 1999), pp. 19-20. (Hereafter cited as Abraham, *Justices, Presidents and Senators*.) Senatorial courtesy, Abraham wrote, appeared to have been the sole factor in President Grover Cleveland's unsuccessful nominations of William B. Hornblower (1893) and Wheeler H. Peckham (1894), both of New York. Each was rejected by the Senate after Senator David B. Hill (D-NY) invoked senatorial courtesy.

[25] In 1987, for instance, some Senators publicly warned President Reagan that he could expect problems in the Senate if he nominated U.S. appellate court judge Robert H. Bork to replace vacating Justice Lewis F. Powell. Among them, Sen. Robert C. Byrd (D-WV) said the Reagan Administration would be "inviting problems" by nominating Bork. The chair of the Senate Judiciary Committee, Joseph R. Biden Jr. (D-DE), said that, while Bork was a "brilliant man," it did "not mean that there should be six or seven or eight or even five Borks" on the Court. Helen Dewar and Howard Kurtz, "Byrd Threatens Stall on Court Confirmation," *The Washington Post*, June 30, 1987, p. A7. In what was regarded as a thinly veiled reference to a possible Bork nomination, Senate Majority Whip Alan Cranston (D-CA) called on Senate Democrats to form a "solid phalanx" to block an "ideological court coup" by President Reagan. Al Kamen and Ruth Marcus, "Nomination to Test Senate Role in Shaping of Supreme Court," *The Washington Post*, July 1, 1987, p. A9. President Reagan, nonetheless, nominated Judge Bork, only to have the nomination meet widespread Senate opposition and ultimate Senate rejection.

[26] Modern Presidents, one scholar wrote, "are often forced to arbitrate among factions within their own administrations, each pursuing its own interests and agendas." In recent Administrations, he maintained, the final choice of a nominee "has usually reflected one advisor's hard-won victory over his rivals, without necessarily accounting for the president's other political interests." Yalof, *Pursuit of Justices*, p. 3.

[27] For numerous examples of Justices advising Presidents regarding Supreme Court appointments, both in the 19th and 20th centuries, see Abraham, *Justices, Presidents and Senators*, pp. 21-23; see also in Abraham's earlier work, *Justices and Presidents*, pp. 186-187 (Chief Justice William Howard Taft's influence over President Warren G. Harding); pp. 233-234 (Justice Felix Frankfurter's advice to President Franklin D. Roosevelt); p. 243 (former Chief Justice Charles Evans Hughes's and former Justice Owen J. Roberts's advice to President Harry S Truman); and pp. 305-306 (Chief Justice Warren Burger's advice to President Richard M. Nixon).

[28] Watson and Stookey, *Shaping America*, pp. 58-59.

[29] Considerations of geographic representation, for example, influenced President George Washington in 1789, to divide his first six appointments to the Court between three nominees from the North and three from the South. See Watson and Stookey, *Shaping America*, p. 60, and Abraham, *Justices, Presidents, and Senators*, pp. 59-60. President Reagan in 1981, for example, was sensitive to the absence of any female Justices on the Court. In announcing his choice of Sandra Day O'Connor to replace vacating Justice Potter Stewart, President Reagan noted that "during my campaign for the Presidency, I made a commitment that one of my first appointments to the Supreme Court vacancy would be the most qualified woman that I could possibly find." U.S. President

(Reagan), "Remarks Announcing the Intention To Nominate Sandra Day O'Connor To Be an Associate Justice of the Supreme Court of the United States, July 7, 1981," *Public Papers of the Presidents of the United States, Ronald Reagan, 1981* (Washington: GPO, 1982), p. 596

[30] While the "desire to appoint justices sympathetic to their own ideological and policy views may drive most presidents in selecting judges," the field of potentially acceptable nominees for most presidents, according to Watson and Stookey, is narrowed down by at least five "subsidiary motivations"—(1) rewarding personal or political support, (2) representing certain interests, (3) cultivating political support, (4) ensuring a safe nominee, and 5) picking the most qualified nominee. Watson and Stookey, *Shaping America*, p. 59.

[31] Commenting on the nature of the Court's work, and the degree of qualification required of those who serve on the Court, the American Bar Association, in a recently published booklet, said the following: "The significance, range and complexity of the issues considered by the justices, as well as the finality and nation-wide impact of the Supreme Court's decisions, are among the factors that require the appointment of a nominee of exceptional ability." American Bar Association, *ABA Standing Committee on the Federal Judiciary: What It Is and How it Works*, pp. 9-10, accessed April 26, 2007, at http://www.abanet.org/scfedjud/).

[32] One of the "unwritten codes," two scholars on the judiciary have written, "is that a judicial appointment is different from run-of-the-mill patronage. Thus, although the political rules may allow a president to reward an old ally with a seat on the bench, even here tradition has created an expectation that the would-be judge have some reputation for professional competence, the more so as the judgeship in question goes from the trial court to the appeals court to the Supreme Court level." Robert A. Carp and Ronald A. Stidham, *Judicial Process in America*, 3rd ed. (Washington: CQ Press, 1996), pp. 240-241.

[33] President Gerald R. Ford, for example, said he believed his nominee, U.S. appellate court judge John Paul Stevens, "to be best qualified to serve as an Associate Justice of the Supreme Court." U.S. President (Ford), "Remarks Announcing Intention To Nominate John Paul Stevens To Be an Associate Justice of the Supreme Court, November 28, 1975," *Public Papers of the Presidents of the United States, Gerald R. Ford, 1975*, Book II (Washington: GPO, 1977), p. 1917. Similarly, in 1991, President George H. W. Bush said of nominee Clarence Thomas, "I believe he'll be a great justice. He is the best person for this position." U.S. President (Bush, George H.W.), "The President's News Conference in Kennebunkport, Maine, July 1, 1991," *Public Papers of the President of the United States*, *George Bush,1991*, Book II (Washington: GPO, 1992), p. 801. More recently, in 2005, President George W. Bush, in announcing his nomination of John G. Roberts Jr. to be an Associate Justice, described his nominee as having "superb credentials"; as serving "on one of the most influential courts in the Nation"; and as known, prior to becoming a judge, "as one of the most distinguished and talented attorneys in America." U.S. President (Bush, George W.), "Address to the Nation Announcing the Nomination of John G. Roberts, Jr. To Be an Associate Justice of the United States Supreme Court," *Weekly Compilation of Presidential* Documents, vol. 41, July 25, 2005, p. 1192.

[34] For lists of the professional, educational, and political backgrounds of every Justice serving on the Court from 1790 to 2007, see Epstein, *Supreme Court Compendium*, pp. 291-341.

[35] A legal scholar notes that while the Constitution "does not preclude a president from nominating nonlawyers to key Justice Department posts or federal judgeships," the delegates to the constitutional convention and the ratifiers "did occasionally express their expectation that a president would nominate qualified people to federal judgeships and other important governmental offices; but those comments were expressions of hope and concern about the consequences of and the need to devise a check against a president's failure to nominate qualified people, particularly in the absence of any constitutionally required minimal criteria for certain positions." Gerhardt, *The Federal Appointments Process*, p. 35.

[36] Watson and Stookey, *Shaping America*, p. 64.

[37] In Federalist Paper 78 ("Judges as Guardians of the Constitution"), Hamilton extolled the "benefits of the integrity and moderation of the Judiciary," which, he said, commanded "the esteem and applause of all the virtuous and disinterested." Further, he maintained, there could "be but few men" in society who would "unite the requisite integrity with the requisite knowledge" to "qualify them for the stations of judges." Wright, *The Federalist*, p. 495 (first quote) and p. 496 (second quote).

[38] Miller Center of Public Affairs, *Improving the Process of Appointing Federal Judges: A Report of the Miller Center Commission on the Selection of Federal Judges* (Charlottesville, VA: University of Virginia, May 1996), p. 10.

[39] For example, President George H.W. Bush, in announcing the nomination of David H. Souter to be an Associate Justice in 1990, declared that he wanted "a Justice who will ably and fairly interpret the law," and then added, "I believe that we've set a good example of selecting a fair arbiter of the law." U.S. President (Bush, George H.W.), "Remarks Announcing the Nomination of David H. Souter To Be an Associate Justice of the Supreme Court of the United States and a Question-and-Answer Session with Reporters," *Public Papers of the President of the United States*, *George Bush, 1990*, Book II (Washington: GPO, 1991), p. 1047. More recently, in 2005, in announcing the nomination of Samuel A. Alito Jr. to be an Associate Justice, President George W. Bush said he was confident that the Senate would be impressed not only by Judge Alito's "distinguished record" but also by his "measured judicial temperament and his tremendous personal integrity." U.S. President (Bush, George W.), "Remarks Announcing the Nomination of Samuel A. Alito Jr., To Be an Associate Justice

of the United States Supreme Court," *Weekly Compilation of Presidential Documents,* vol. 41, November 7, 2005, p. 1626.

[40] U.S. President (Obama, Barack H.), "Remarks on the Nomination of Sonia Sotomayor To Be a Supreme Court Associate Justice," *Daily Compilation of PresidentialDocuments*, May 26, 2009, DCPD-200900402, p. 1.

[41] Ibid.

[42] See CRS Report RL32821, *The Chief Justice of the United States: Responsibilities of the Office and Process for Appointment*, by Denis Steven Rutkus and Lorraine H. Tong (under heading "Criteria for Selecting a Nominee"). (See also Greenburg, *Supreme Conflict*, pp. 238-243 (discussing the assessment of the Administration of President George W. Bush in 2005 that John G. Roberts's leadership abilities and interpersonal skills were important qualities needed in a person under consideration for appointment to be Chief Justice).

[43] Perhaps the most extensive use of private attorneys for this purpose was made by President Clinton in the spring of 1993 during his consideration of candidates to fill the Supreme Court seat of retiring Justice Byron White. President Clinton, it was reported, utilized a team of 75 lawyers in the Washington, DC, area, who "pore[d] over briefs," analyzed "mountains of opinions and speeches" and "comb[ed] through financial records," of the "final contenders" for the Court appointment—from whom the President ultimately selected U.S. appellate court judge Ruth Bader Ginsburg. The team funneled their analyses to the White House counsel, "who, along with other aides, advised the president during the search for a justice." Under the team's ground rules, its work was performed on a confidential basis, with contact between its lawyers and White House aides prohibited. Private attorneys were relied on in this way at least partly because, at that early point in the Clinton presidency, a judicial search team for the Administration was not yet in place in the Department of Justice. Daniel Klaidman, "Who Are Clinton's Vetters, and Why the Big Secret?" *Legal Times*, vol. 16, June 21, 1993, pp. 1, 22-23.

[44] "During President Gerald R. Ford's search to fill a high court vacancy, Attorney General Edward Levi discreetly asked a small group of distinguished constitutional scholars to review opinions and other legal writings of a number of candidates." Ibid. (Klaidman), p. 23.

[45] Three Presidents—Dwight D. Eisenhower in 1957, Richard M. Nixon in 1971, and Gerald R. Ford in 1975—requested the ABA's Standing Committee on Federal Judiciary to evaluate the names of prospective Supreme Court candidates. Typically, however, the ABA committee is not invited by an administration to evaluate candidates under consideration for nomination to the Court. Instead, the committee performs its evaluation role later, after the President has selected a nominee, providing its evaluation of the nominee to the Senate Judiciary Committee prior to the start of confirmation hearings. See generally CRS Report 96-446, *The American Bar Association's Standing Committee on Federal Judiciary: A Historical Overview*, by Denis Steven Rutkus (out of print, available from author; hereafter cited as CRS Report 96-446, *ABA Historical Overview*), for a narrative tracing the evolution of the ABA committee's role from the 1940s to 1995, and specifically pp. 8-9, 31-32, and 35 regarding its role in advising Eisenhower, Nixon, and Ford, respectively.

[46] The five most recent Presidents—Reagan, George H.W. Bush, Clinton, George W. Bush, and Obama—all personally interviewed their final candidates before selecting a nominee. "Both Reagan and the elder Bush relied more on their staffs to pare down the list of nominees. They interviewed one or, at most, two prospects before making their decision, compared to the five George W. Bush interviewed to replace Sandra Day O'Connor." Greenburg, *Supreme Conflict*, p. 314. Sonia Sotomayor, nominated to the Court in 2009 by President Obama, was reportedly one of four candidates whom the President interviewed. Ruth Marcus, "An Easy Choice for Obama," *The Washington Post*, May 27, 2009, p. A19. Likewise, Elena Kagan, nominated to the Court in 2010 by President Obama, was reportedly also one of four candidates whom the President interviewed (and "was one of Mr. Obama's runners-up" the year before when he nominated Sonia Sotomayor to the Court). Peter Baker and Jeff Zeleny, *The New York Times*, May 10, 2010, p. 1.

[47] Greenburg, *Supreme Conflict*, p. 241.

[48] Presidents Reagan and George H. W. Bush, for instance, selected most of their Supreme Court nominees quickly, within days of the vacating Justices announcing their retirements from the Court. President Clinton, however, took more time in selecting his two Supreme Court nominees, nominating Ruth Bader Ginsburg on June 22, 1993, three months after the retirement announcement of Justice Byron R. White, and nominating Stephen G. Breyer on May 17, 1994, five weeks after the retirement announcement of Justice Harry A. Blackmun. Likewise, President George W. Bush's first two Supreme Court selections were not made immediately upon the heels of a Justice's retirement announcement: President Bush announced his choice of John G. Roberts Jr. to succeed Sandra Day O'Connor 18 days after she submitted her retirement letter to the President, and he announced his choice of Harriet E. Miers to succeed Justice O'Connor 28 days after withdrawing the aforementioned Roberts nomination. By contrast, President Bush moved much more swiftly in selecting a nominee to succeed Chief Justice William H. Rehnquist, announcing his choice of John G. Roberts Jr. for that office two days after the death of Chief Justice Rehnquist on September 3, 2005. Likewise, he moved swiftly in selecting a third nominee to succeed Justice O'Connor, announcing his choice of Samuel A. Alito Jr. for that office on October 31, 2005, four days after the Miers nomination to that office was withdrawn. For more detailed information about how quickly 20th century Presidents and Presidents George W. Bush and Barack

Obama selected Supreme Court nominees, see Tables 1 and 2 in CRS Report RL33118, *Speed of Presidential and Senate Actions on Supreme Court Nominations, 1900-2010*, by R. Sam Garrett and Denis Steven Rutkus.

[49] It is "precisely when presidents fail to require thorough checks," two scholars have written, "that trouble is likely." As illustrative, they cite the FBI investigation of President Richard M. Nixon's Supreme Court nominee Clement F. Haynsworth Jr. in 1969. "Unfortunately for both Haynsworth and the president, the cursory FBI check left unrevealed questions of financial dealings and conflicts of interest that would eventually doom the nomination. Without learning from the first mistake, the Nixon Administration rushed headlong into another hurried selection, Harrold Carswell, without full knowledge of flaws that would prove fatal in his background. A similar failure occurred as the Reagan Administration rushed to bring forth a nominee in the wake of the Bork defeat. In this instance, the rushed investigation failed to uncover the marijuana episodes of Douglas Ginsburg, which led to another presidential setback in the appointment process." Watson and Stookey, *Shaping America*, p. 82.

[50] Justice Blackmun reportedly had given even more advance notice to the President, having privately informed him, on or about January 1, 1994, of his intention to retire before the start of the next Court term in October 1994. See Douglas Jehl, "Mitchell Viewed as Top Candidate for High Court," *The New York Times,* April 7, 1994, p. A1; Tony Mauro, "How Blackmun Hid Retirement Plans," *New Jersey Law Journal*, April 25, 1994, p. 18, at http://www.nexis.com. Later, on the eve of his public retirement announcement, on April 6, 1994, Justice Blackmun was reported to have told friends "he wanted to make sure there would be ample time for a successor to be confirmed by the Senate and prepare for the start of a new term in October." Ruth Marcus, "Blackmun Set To Leave High Court," *The Washington Post*, April 6, 1994, p. A1.

[51] Ibid. (Marcus), pp. A1, A7.

[52] U.S. President (Obama, Barack H.), "Remarks on the Nomination of Sonia Sotomayor To Be a Supreme Court Associate Justice," *Daily Compilation of PresidentialDocuments*, May 26, 2009, DCPD-200900402, p. 1.

[53] See CRS Report RL33118, *Speed of Presidential and Senate Actions on Supreme Court Nominations, 1900-2010*, by R. Sam Garrett and Denis Steven Rutkus (under heading "Activity During 2009").

[54] A year later, President Obama was provided even more advance notice of an upcoming Court vacancy when Justice John Paul Stevens, in an April 9, 2010, letter, informed the President of his intention to step down when the Court recessed for the summer. Pesident Obama announced his selection of a nominee to succeed Justice Stevens, Elena Kagan, on May 10, 2010, taking 31 days to make and announce his selection (compared with the 25 days taken the year before to make and announce his selection of Sonia Sotomayor to succeed outgoing Justice Souter).

[55] Sandra Day O'Connor, letter to President George W. Bush, July 1, 2005, available at http://www.supremecourtus.gov/publicinfo/press/pr_07-01-05.html.

[56] U.S. President (Bush, George W.), "Resignation of Justice Sandra Day O'Connor from the Supreme Court of the United States," Weekly Compilation of Presidential Documents, vol. 41, July 4, 2005, p. 1108.

[57] While President Bush announced his selection of Roberts to be an Associate Justice nominee on July 19, 2005, he formally transmitted his nomination of Roberts to the Senate 10 days later.

[58] Specifically, Article II, Section 2, Clause 3 of the U.S. Constitution empowers the President "to fill up all Vacancies that may happen during the Recess of the Senate, by granting Commissions which shall expire at the End of their next Session."

[59] For a list and discussion of the 12 recess appointments to the Court, see Henry B. Hogue, "The Law: Recess Appointments to Article III Courts," *Presidential Studies Quarterly*, vol. 34, September 2004, pp. 656-673. For more information on judicial recess appointments, see CRS Report RL33009, *Recess Appointments: A Legal Overview*, by T. J. Halstead, and CRS Report RS22039, *Federal Recess Judges*, by Louis Fisher (out of print, available from author).

[60] Adopted by the Senate on August 29, 1960, by a 48-37 vote, S.Res. 334 expressed the sense of the Senate that recess appointments to the Supreme Court "should not be made, except under unusual circumstances and for the purpose of preventing or ending a demonstrable breakdown in the administration of the Court's business." Proponents of the resolution contended, among other things, that judicial independence would be affected if Supreme Court recess appointees, during the probationary period of their appointment, took positions to please the President (in order not to have the President withdraw their nominations) or to please the Senate (in order to gain confirmation of their nominations). It also was argued that Senate investigation of nominations of these recess appointees was made difficult by the oath preventing sitting Justices from testifying about matters pending before the Court. Opponents, however, said, among other things, that the resolution was an attempt to restrict the President's constitutional recess appointment powers and that recess appointments were sometimes called for in order to keep the Court at full strength and to prevent evenly split rulings by its members. "Opposition to Recess Appointments to the Supreme Court," debate in Senate on S.Res. 334, *Congressional Record*, vol. 106, August 29, 1960, pp. 18130-18145. See also CRS Report RL31112, *Recess Appointments of Federal Judges*, by Louis Fisher, pp. 16-18 (out of print, available from author).

[61] U.S. v. Woodley, 751 F.2d 1008 (9th Cir. 1985), *cert. denied*, 475 U.S. 1049 (1986).

[62] Evans v. Stephens, 387 F.3d 1220 (11th Cir. 2004), *cert. denied*, 544 U.S. 942 (2005).

[63] A notable, relatively recent instance in which the possibility of a recess appointment to the Court was raised occurred on July 28, 1987, when Senate Minority Leader Robert Dole (R-KS) observed that President Reagan had the constitutional prerogative to recess appoint U.S. appellate court judge Robert H. Bork to the Court. Earlier that month Judge Bork had been nominated to the Court, and, at the time of Senator Dole's statement, the chair of Senate Judiciary Committee, Sen. Joseph R. Biden Jr. (D-DE), had scheduled confirmation hearings to begin on September 15. With various Republican Senators accusing Senate Democrats of delaying the Bork hearings, Senator Dole offered as "food for thought" the possibility of President Reagan making a recess appointment of Judge Bork during Congress's August recess. Michael Fumento, "Reagan Has Power To Seat Bork While Senate Stalls: Dole," *The Washington Times*, July 28, 1987, p. A3; also, Edward Walsh, "Reagan's Power To Make Recess Appointment Is Noted," *The Washington Post*, July 28, 1987, p. A8. Judge Bork, however, did not receive a recess appointment and, as a Supreme Court nominee, was rejected by the Senate in a 58-42 vote on October 23, 1987.

[64] As explained earlier, Article II, Section 2, Clause 2, in pertinent part, provides simply that the President "shall nominate, and by and with the Advice and Consent of the Senate, shall appoint ... Judges of the supreme Court."

[65] U.S. Congress, Senate, *History of the Committee on theJudiciary, United States Senate, 1816-1981*, S. Doc. 97-18, 97th Cong., 1st sess. (Washington: GPO, 1982), p. iv.; also, U.S. Congress, Senate, *History of the Committee onRules and Administration—United States Senate,* prepared by Floyd M. Riddick, Parliamentarian Emeritus of the Senate, S. Doc. 96-27, 96th Cong., 1st sess. (Washington: GPO, 1980). Riddick provided, on pp. 21-28, the full text of the general revision of the Senate rules, adopted in 1868, including, on p. 26, the following rule: "When nominations shall be made by the President of the United States to the Senate, they shall, unless otherwise ordered by the Senate, be referred to appropriate committees.... "

[66] For a more detailed numerical breakdown of Supreme Court nominations referred or not referred to the Senate Judiciary Committee (as well as a listing of the nominations from 1868 to 2010 that were not referred), see CRS Report RL33225, *Supreme Court Nominations, 1789 - 2010: Actions by the Senate, the Judiciary Committee, and the President,* under heading "Referral of Nominations to Senate Judiciary Committee."

[67] Abraham, *Justices, Presidents, and Senators*, p. 33. One notable exception to this "unwritten rule," Abraham observed, was Franklin D. Roosevelt's "controversial selection" of Sen. Hugo L. Black (D-AL) in 1937, whose nomination was referred to the Judiciary Committee. Ibid., p. 34 (with discussion explaining various points of controversy over the Black nomination). See also Franklyn Waltman, "'Dark-Horse' Nomination of Alabaman Facing Study," *The Washington Post*, August 13, 1937, p. 1, which, on the day the Black nomination was received by the Senate, reported the following: "Efforts to have the Senate confirm the nomination immediately—a courtesy almost invariably granted when a member of the Senate is nominated for another post—were blocked by Senators Hiram Johnson (Republican), of California, and Edward R. Burke, Democrat, of Nebraska." Subsequently the Judiciary Committee, by a 13-4 vote, reported the Black nomination favorably, followed by a 63-16 vote of the Senate to confirm.

[68] Haynes's classic history of the Senate, published in 1938, noted what was then the "almost unbroken tradition that the nomination of a Senator or a former member of the Senate will be confirmed at once, without even being referred to a committee." Haynes cited, as illustrative, the contrasting experiences of two Supreme Court nominations in 1922—one of an attorney in private practice, Pierce Butler, which, prior to being confirmed, "was in controversy for nearly a month," the other of former Sen. George Sutherland (R-UT), which "without being referred to a committee, was confirmed by the Senate in open session within ten minutes after the name was received." George H. Haynes, *The Senate of the United States: Its History and Practice*, vol. 2 (Boston: Houghton Mifflin Company, 1938), p. 740.

[69] For a listing of the dates of actions by the Senate Judiciary Committee and full Senate on the Stone and Jackson nominations, see Table 1 in CRS Report RL33225, *Supreme Court Nominations, 1789 - 2010: Actions by the Senate, the Judiciary Committee, and the President.*

[70] "Nomination of Senator Byrnes To Be Associate Justice of the Supreme Court," *Congressional Record*, vol. 87, June 12, 1941, p. 5062.

[71] See "Senate Confirms Choice of Burton," *The New York Times*, September 20, 1945, p. 44; "Senate Quickly Confirms Burton to Supreme Court," *Los Angeles Times*, September 20, 1945, p. 4.

[72] For a narrative of the Judiciary Committee's consideration of the Minton nomination, including the nominee's declining a committee invitation that he testify before it, see James A. Thorpe, "The Appearance of Supreme Court Nominees Before the Senate Judiciary Committee," *Journal of Public Law*, vol. 18, 1969, pp. 380-385. (Hereafter cited as Thorpe, *Appearance of Supreme Court Nominees*.) See also Richard Baker, "October 1, 1949: Nominee Refuses to Testify," *The Hill*, September 24, 1997, in which the author, the Senate historian, characterized as a Senate custom "in decline" the practice of the Senate, prior to the Minton nomination of 1949, proceeding directly to consideration of a Supreme Court nominee, without referral to committee, when the nominee was a Senator.

It should be noted that not every Supreme Court nominee who was a Senator or former Senator when nominated was confirmed. While a Member of the Senate in 1853, George E. Badger of North Carolina was nominated to the Court but failed to gain Senate confirmation. Without being referred to the Judiciary

Committee, the Badger nomination was considered by the Senate, which ultimately voted to postpone taking any action on the nomination. Of eight sitting U.S. Senators ever nominated to the Court, Badger was the only one who failed to receive Senate confirmation. See Epstein, *Supreme Court Compendium*, pp. 345-353, listing every Supreme Court nominee's occupational position at time of nomination. In addition to the Badger nomination, however, the nomination in 1828 of a *former* U.S. Senator, John J. Crittenden of Kentucky, failed to be confirmed, after first being referred to the Judiciary Committee. After the committee reported with the recommendation that the Senate not act on the Crittenden nomination during that session, the Senate voted to postpone taking action on the nomination. See Jacobstein and Mersky, *The Rejected*, pp. 23-23 and 57-59, for brief accounts of Crittenden and Badger nominations, respectively; also, see Table 4 in CRS Report RL31171, *Supreme Court Nominations Not Confirmed, 1789-August 2010,* for dates of committee and Senate actions, if any, on Supreme Court nominations not confirmed (including the Badger and Crittenden nominations).

73 Roy M. Mersky, Tarlton Law Library, University of Texas at Austin Law School, telephone conversation with the author, April 3, 2003. Professor Mersky and J. Myron Jacobstein have jointly compiled 19 volumes of Senate Judiciary Committee hearings transcripts and reports for Supreme Court nominations, starting with the Brandeis nomination in 1916 and carrying through the nomination of Stephen G. Breyer in 1994. See Roy M. Mersky and J. Byron Jacobstein, comp., *The Supreme Court of the United States: Hearings and Reports on Successful and Unsuccessful Nominations of Supreme Court Justices by the Senate Judiciary Committee, 1916-1994*, 19 vols. (Buffalo, N.Y.: William S. Hein & Co., 1977-1996).

74 See Thorpe, *Appearance of Supreme Court Nominees*, pp. 371-373.

75 The nominees in both cases were Senators. As discussed above, the Senate considered the Supreme Court nomination of Senator James F. Byrnes in 1941, without referral to the Judiciary Committee; also, as discussed above, while the Supreme Court nomination of Senator Harold H. Burton in 1945 was referred to the Judiciary Committee, the committee voted to report the nomination to the Senate without holding a confirmation hearing.

76 The nominees in both cases saw their nominations withdrawn before hearings were held. As discussed above, the Associate Justice nominations of John G. Roberts Jr. and Harriet E. Miers in 2005 were withdrawn before the start of scheduled hearings. Roberts, however, on the day his nomination was withdrawn, was re-nominated to be Chief Justice, and his second nomination received a hearing, before being reported by the Judiciary Committee and confirmed by the Senate.

77 See David Gregg Farrelly, "Operational Aspects of the Senate Judiciary Committee," (Ph.D. diss., Princeton University, 1949), pp. 184-199, in which author examined the procedures followed by the committee in its consideration of 15 Supreme Court nominations referred to it between 1923 and 1947. The author observed, on p. 192, that six of the 15 nominations were "confirmed without benefit of public hearings. Of the remaining nine nominations, full public hearings were used on two occasions, another appointee received a limited hearing, and six were given routine hearings. Only [John J.] Parker and [Felix] Frankfurter received full, open hearings." A "routine hearing," the author explained, on pp. 194-195, "differs from a full, open hearing in that a date is set for interested parties to appear and present evidence against confirmation. In other words, a meeting is scheduled without requests for one; an open invitation is extended by the committee for the filing of protests against an appointment."

78 In 1930, although Supreme Court nominee John J. Parker had communicated his willingness to testify, the Judiciary Committee voted against inviting him to do so. "Committee, 10 to 6, Rejects Parker," *The New York Times*, April 22, 1930, pp. 1, 23.

79 Thorpe, *Appearance of Supreme Court Nominees*, pp. 384-402.

80 Although the standard practice of the Judiciary Committee, prior to the O'Connor hearings in 1981, was to prohibit broadcast coverage of Supreme Court confirmation hearings, there was at least one notable exception to this practice during the early years of television broadcasting. Archival records of the Columbia Broadcasting System (CBS), obtained by the Congressional Research Service (CRS), show that, on February 26 and 27, 1957, the CBS television network filmed and broadcast a few minutes of the confirmation hearings of Supreme Court nominee William J. Brennan Jr. Much earlier, in 1939, in a deviation from its standard practice of not allowing film coverage of confirmation hearings, the Judiciary Committee permitted newsreel coverage of its hearing on Supreme Court nominee Felix Frankfurter. A newsreel excerpt from the Frankfurter hearing is included in a CRS video product; see CRS Report MM70010, Supreme Court Appointment Process. Online Video and Audio. Video and Audio Tapes, by Denis Steven Rutkus (available from author).

81 A study by the Congressional Research Service has found that, prior to 1967, a median number of nine days elapsed between Senate receipt of Supreme Court nominations and the Judiciary Committee's final vote on reporting them to the full Senate. By contrast, from the Supreme Court nomination of Thurgood Marshall in 1967 through the nomination of Elena Kagan in 2010, the median number of days elapsed between Senate receipt and final committee vote was 51. See CRS Report RL33225, *Supreme Court Nominations, 1789-2010: Actions by the Senate, the Judiciary Committee, and the President*, by Denis Steven Rutkus and Maureen Bearden (under subheading "Days from Senate Receipt to Final Committee Vote").

82 Treated to date as public information are sections of the questionnaire that request biographical and financial disclosure information, as well as the nominee's responses to questions about the Constitution and the law.

Treated to date by the committee as confidential (and not available to the media or the public) are the nominee's responses to more sensitive questions, such as whether he or she ever had been under a federal, state or local investigation for possible violation of a civil or criminal statute or had ever been sued by a client or other party.

[83] Specifically, the Judiciary Committee's questionnaire for Supreme Court nominee Sonia Sotomayor in 2009, among other things, asked for:

- a complete employment recorcd;
- a list of all organizations in which the nominee had been a member;
- a list and copies of all her published writings and public statements;
- any judicial offices held and, if ever a judge, "the 10 most significant cases over which you presided,"
- citations for all opinions she had written, and citations to all cases in which she had been a panel member but did not write an opinion;
- a list of any cases in which a litigant or party had requested that she recuse herself as a judge due to an asserted conflict of interest, along with the reason for recusing or declining to recuse;
- identification of any position held or role played in a political campaign;
- a description of the 10 "most significant litigated matters which you personally handled, whether or not you were the attorney of record";
- teaching experience, including titles of courses and subject matter of courses taught;
- the sources, amounts and dates of all anticipated deferred income and future benefits;
- the sources and amounts of all income receving during the calendar year preceding nomination and for the current calendar year;
- "potential conflicts of interest when you first assume the position to which you have been nominated"; and
- a description of instances and amount of time devoted in the past "to serving the disadvantaged."

See, concerning the Sotomayor nomination, "Committee Questionnaire and Related Materials" link on the Senate Judiciary Committee's website, at http://judiciary.senate.gov/nominations/SupremeCourt/SotomayorIndex.cfm#Questionnaire.

[84] In 2009, for example, in response to the Judiciary Committee's questionnaire concerning her Supreme Court nomination, appellate judge Sonia Sotomayor accounted for almost 200 speeches she had delivered from the early 1990s to May 2009 and more than 140 confenences and events she had attended during her years as a federal judge. Following the initial submission of her questionnaire, Judge Sotomayor provided the committee more than 200 items of questionnaire supplement materials (including news articles, letters, memoranda, reports, videos, meeting minutes, seminar and speech transcripts, and case citatons.) Ibid.

[85] For example, prior to the start, on July 13, 2009, of confirmation hearings on the Supreme Court nomination of Sonia Sotomayor, the nominee's completed questionnaire to the Judiciary Committee was supplemented by at least 10 letters to the nominee from members of the committee or from the nominee responding to the Senators' letters. See, concerning the Sotomayor nomination, "Letters to and from Members of the Committee" link on the Judiciary Committee's website, at http://judiciary.senate.gov/nominations/SupremeCourt/upload/Sotomayor-MemberLetters.pdf

[86] In such a context, some members of the Judiciary Committee, prior to confirmation hearings for Supreme Court nominee Sonia Sotomayor in 2009, sought for the committee internal documents of the Puerto Rican Legal Defense and Education Fund (PRLDEF). Prior to becoming a federal judge, Judge Sotomayr, at various points during the period 1980-1992, had worked for PRLDEF, including as a board member. Soon after being nominated to the Court, Judge Sotomayor provided the Judiciary Committee with documents that she had contributed to or helped write as a board memer. Subsequently, however, some Judiciary Committee members requested more information, from the fund itself, about cases it had handled and policy positions it took while Sonia Sotomayor was working on its behalf, and ultimately the fund provided some of these requested materials to the Judiciary Committee. See Tom LoBianco, "Nominee Advised Critics of Bork; Legal Funding Tied to Sotomayor," *The Washington Times*, July 2, 2009, p. A8; also, "Papers Irrelevant, White House Says," *The Washington Times*, July 3, 2009, p. A2.

[87] In this vein, when President George W. Bush was asked at a news conference whether he would release to the Judiciary Committee some or all of Supreme Court nominee Harriet E. Miers's legal work as White House counsel, he replied, "I just can't tell you how important it is for us to guard executive privilege in order for there to be crisp decision making in the White House." Richard W. Stevenson, "President, Citing Executive Privilege, Indicates He'll Reject Requests for Counsel's Documents," *The New York Times,* October 5, 2005, at http://www.nexis.com. For the views, against the backdrop of the Miers nomination, of a range of legal scholars on the extent to which a President may properly invoke executive privilege to deny the Senate the work product of a White House counsel nominated to the Supreme Court, see Marcia Coyle, "Battle Looming over Privilege," *The National Law Journal*, vol. 28, October 10, 2005, pp. 1, 21.

[88] CRS Report RL32935, *Congressional Oversight of Judges and Justices*, by Elizabeth B. Bazan (under heading "Judicial Nominations"), citing, as the basis for the above paragraph, a more detailed narrative of the 1986 conflict between the Judiciary Committee and the Reagan Administration over the Rehnquist documents provided in Louis Fisher, *The Politics of Executive Privilege* (Durham, NC: Carolina Academic Press, 2004), pp. 76-77.

Comparable requests from the Judiciary Committee have produced mixed results in the case of President George W. Bush's Supreme Court nominees—John G. Roberts Jr., Harriet E. Miers, and Samuel A. Alito.Jr., whose backgrounds all included service in either the Department of Justice, the White House, or both. The Bush Administration allowed the release of some documents from each of the three nominees' executive branch service, but refused the release of other documents. See, for example: David G. Savage and Henry Weinstein, "Files from Roberts' Reagan Years Are Released," *Los Angeles Times,* August 16, 2005, p. 12; William Branigin, "Bush Will Not Release All Miers Documents," *The Washington Post*, October 24, 2005, at http://www.washingtonpost.com; and Susan Milligan, "Top Democrats Question Alito's Credibility," *Boston Globe*, December 2, 2005, at http://www.nexis.com.

[89] Several weeks before the start of confirmation hearings on her nomination, the most recent appointee to the Court, Elena Kagan, had reportedly made courtesy calls to "more than 50" Senate offices. Sheryl Gay Stolberg, "A KnockDown, Drag-Out—Yawn," *The New York Times*, June 3, 2010, p. 19. President Obama's first Supreme Court nominee, Sonia Sotomayor, reportedly made courtesy calls to 89 Senators prior to the start of her confirmation hearings on July 13, 2009. Mark Sherman, "Sotomayor Arrives, Supreme Ccourt Hearing Under Way," Associated Press Financial Wire, July 13, 2009, at http://www.nex.com. The nominee immediately prior to Sotomayor, Samuel A. Alito Jr., was reported to have met privately with more than 80 Senators between his nomination on November 10, 2005, and his confirmation on January 24, 2006. Jesse J. Holland (Associated Press), "Senate Moves Toward Alito's Confirmation," *Las Vegas Sun,* January 25, 2006, at http://www.lasvegassun.com. Of the two Supreme Court nominees who immediately preceded Alito, John G. Roberts Jr. and Harriet E. Miers, one paid numerous courtesy calls to Senate offices, while the other made fewer. "By the time Justice Roberts took the oath before the Senate Judiciary Committee, he had met with more than half of the 100 members of the Senate." By contrast, a week prior to the withdrawal of her nomination, Miers was reported to have met "with only about 25 senators," reportedly because the meetings that had been held "had been fraught with misunderstandings and disagreements, giving ammunition to detractors .... " Charles Hurt, "Miers to End Her Meetings with Senators; Supreme Court Nominee Will Cram for Hearings," *The Washington Times*, October 21, 2005, p. A1.

[90] Traditionally, this evaluation role has been performed at the official invitation of the chair of the Senate Judiciary Committee. In 1947, the ABA committee was first invited by the committee's chair, Sen. Alexander Wiley (R-WI), to testify or file a recommendation on each judicial nomination receiving a hearing. Grossman, Joel B. *Lawyers and Judges: The ABA and the Politics of Judicial Selection* (New York: John Wiley and Sons Inc., 1966), p. 64. A central purpose of the Judiciary Committee, when it first invited the ABA committee to evaluate judicial nominees, was to "help insure that only the highest caliber [of] men and women ascended to the bench.... " Statement of Sen. Joseph R. Biden Jr., chair of the Senate Judiciary Committee, in U.S. Congress, Senate Committee on the Judiciary, *The ABA Role in the Judicial Nomination Process*, hearing,101st Cong., 1st sess., June 2, 1989 (Washington: GPO, 1991), p. 2.

[91] American Bar Association, *The ABA Standing Committee on the Federal Judiciary: What It Is and How It Works*, p. 1, at http://www.abanet.org/scfedjud/federal_judiciary09.pdf

[92] Ibid. All 15 members of the ABA committee take part in its evaluation of a Supreme Court nominee. Committee members conduct confidential interviews nationwide wth practicing lawyers, judges, law professors and others "who are in a position to evaluate the prospective nominee's integrity, professional competence and judicial temperament." Meanwhile, teams of law school professors, as well as a separate team of practicing lawyers, examine the legal writing of a nominee. The nominee as well is interviewed, specifically by the committee member or members from the judicial circuit where the nominee has practiced or served as a judge; the chair of the committee also may participate in the interview, if he or she so chooses. The results of all of these inquiries are forwarded to the full ABA committee.

[93] Ibid., p. 10. Invariably, a nominee's ABA rating receives prominent news coverage when it is sent to the Senate Judiciary Committee. In the past, a unanimously positive rating by the ABA committee almost always presaged a very favorable vote by the Judiciary Committee on the nominee as well. Conversely, a divided vote, or less than the highest rating, by the ABA committee usually served to flag issues about the nominee for the Senate Judiciary Committee to examine at its confirmation hearings, and these issues in turn have sometimes been cited by Senators on the Judiciary Committee who voted against reporting a nomination favorably to the Senate floor.

Since the inception of the ABA committee's evaluating role, most, but not all, Supreme Court nominees have received the highest ABA rating, while none has been found by a committee majority to be "not qualified." See generally CRS Report 96-446, *ABA Historical Overview* (out of print, available from author).

[94] The ABA committee was accused by some Senators, as well as by some conservative groups, of holding a liberal ideological bias. The committee's ratings of judicial nominees Robert H. Bork in 1987 and Clarence Thomas

in 1991 in particular were cited as demonstrating prejudice against nominees with conservative judicial philosophies. The ABA rating of Bork was unusual, with 10 of the committee's 15 members finding the nominee "well qualified," 4 members rating him "not qualified," and 1 member voting "not opposed"—with no members voting for the intermediate "qualified" rating. For the Thomas nomination, 12 of the committee's 15 members found the nominee "qualified," 2 found him "unqualified," and 1 abstained. The mid-level rating by the 12-member majority was in contrast to the "well qualified" ratings that the ABA panel had unanimously given the two previous Supreme Court nominees, David H. Souter and Anthony M. Kennedy. See CRS Report 93-290, *The Supreme Court Appointment Process: Should It Be Reformed?* by Denis Steven Rutkus (out of print, available from author; hereafter cited as CRS Report 93-290, *Should Appointment Process Be Reformed?*); also see CRS Report 96-446, *ABA Historical Overview* (out of print, available from author).

[95] In 1997, Senator Orrin G. Hatch (R-UT), as chair of the Judiciary Committee, announced that, during his chairmanship, the ABA committee would no longer be accorded an "officially sanctioned role" in the judicial confirmation process. "One cannot assume," Chairman Hatch wrote, "that a group as politically active as the ABA can at the same time remain altogether neutral, impartial and apolitical when it comes to evaluating judicial qualifications." Sen. Orrin G. Hatch, Letter to Colleagues on the Senate Judiciary Committee, February 24, 1997; also, Associated Press, "Hatch Hits ABA's Screening Role, *The Washington Post,* February 19, 1997, p. A4. However, in 2001, the Judiciary Committee's next chair, Senator Patrick J. Leahy (D-VT), restored to the ABA committee a quasi-offocial evaluating role, stating that the Judiciary Committee's Democratic members would oppose votes on any of President Geroge W. Bush's judicial nominees who were not first reviewed by the ABA committee. Audrey Hudson, "Democrats Want ABA to Vet Judges," *The Washington Times*, March 28, 2001, p. A4; "Democrats Say ABA's Vetting of Nominees Still Counts," *The Washington Post*, March 28, 2001, p. A5. See also, for discussion of the ABA committee's role in evaluating judicial candidates, Sen. Patrick J. Leahy, "Nomination of Morrison C. England, Jr. To Be United States District Judge for the Eastern District of California," *Congresional Record*, daily edition, vol. 148, August 1, 2002, p. S7814.

[96] U.S. Congress, Senate Committee on the Judiciary, *Confirmation Hearing on the Nomination of John G. Roberts Jr. To Be Chief Justice of the United States,* 109th Cong., 1st sess., September 12-15, 2005 (Washington: GPO, 2005), pp. 451-455; U.S. Congress, Senate Committee on the Judiciary, *Confirmation Hearing on the Nomination of Samuel A. Alito Jr. To Be an Associate Justice of the Supreme Court of the United States,* 109th Cong., 2nd sess., January 9-13, 2006 (Washington: GPO, 2006), pp. 641-654; (Hereafter cited as Senate Judiciary Committee, *Confirmation Hearing on John G. Roberts*, and Senate Judiciary Committee, *Confirmation Hearing on Samuel A. Alito.*); "Senate Judiciary Committee Holds Hearing on the Nomination of Judge Sonia Sotomayor to be an Associate Justice of the U.S. Supreme Court," *CQ Congressional Transcripts*, July 16, 2009, at http://www.CQ.com.

The ABA committee unanimously, in each instance, gave Roberts, Alito, Sotomayor, and Kagan its "well qualified" rating.

[97] Senate Judiciary Committee, *Confirmation Hearing on Samuel A. Alito*, p. 640.

[98] See "Continuation of the Nomination of Elena Kagan to be an Associate Justice of the Supreme Court of he United States—Official Hearing Notice/Witness List," Senate Judiciary Committee, July 1, 2010, at http://judiciary.senate.gov/hearings/hearing.cfm?id=4679.

[99] For reportage on interest group support of, or opposition to, recent Supreme Court nominations during the pre-hearing stage, see "Interest Groups React," *The Natonal Law Journal*, vol. 31, June 1, 2009, p. 23 (reporting, less than a week after the selection of Sonia Sotomayor as a Supreme Court nominee, that her nomination "drew fervent praise and equally imipassed criticism"); David D. Kirkpatrick, "For Conservative Christians, Game Plan on the Nominee," *The New York Times,* August 12, 2005, p. 15; Jo Becker, "Television Ad War on Alito Begins; Liberals Try to Paint Court Pick as Tool of the Right Wing," *The Washington Post*, November 18, 2005, p. A3. For overviews of the role that interest groups played during an entire appointment process (from the point of Justice Sandra Day O'Connor's retirement announcement until the point that her successor, Samuel A. Alito Jr. was confirmed), see Lois Romano and Julie Eilperin, "Republicans Were Masters in the Race to Paint Alito; Democrats' Portrayal Failed to Sway the Public," *The Washington Post*, February 2, 2006, p. A1; David D. Kirkpatrick, "Paving the Way for Alito Began in Reagan Era," *The New York Times*, January 30, 2006, pp. A1, A18.

[100] In this vein, a news account reported that *before* George W. Bush's announcement, on July 19, 2005, of his selection of John G. Roberts Jr. to succeed Associate Justice Sandra Day O'Connor, the "prospect of filling the first Supreme Court vacancy in 11 years" had "already mobilized political forces on both sides to raise vast financial resources in preparation for a struggle akin to a presidential campaign. From the moment O'Connor announced her retirement July 1, interest groups have been airing television and Internet advertising, blitzing supporters with e-mail, and pressuring elected officials to stand strong." Peter Baker and Jim VanderHei, "Bush Chooses Roberts for Court," *The Washington Post*, July 20, 2005, p. A1. (Hereafter cited as Baker, "Bush Chooses Roberts".)

[101] Kirk Victor, "The Senate Showdown," *National Journal*, vol. 37, July 9, 2005, p. 2185.

[102] Ibid., p. 2186.

[103] Baker, "Bush Chooses Roberts," p. A1.

[104] See, for example, "Hanna Rosin," "They're Fishing on the Hill, but It's No Vacation," *The Washington Post*, August 4, 2005, p. C1 (describing the work of the "Noms Unit," a "special unit of the 50-member Democratic staff of the Senate Judiciary Committee, which in early August 2005 was tasked with investigating the background and past writings or statements of Supreme Court nominee John G. Roberts prior to Roberts's confirmation hearings scheduled to begin early the next month); see also Sheryl Gay Stolberg, "Out of Practice, Senate Crams for Battle over Court Nominee," *The New York Times*, July 8, 2005, pp. A1, A20 (describing the investigative and research roles of Republican staff on the Senate Judiciary Committee in early July 2005, as it prepared for President George W. Bush to select a nominee to succeed retiring Associate Justice Sandra Day O'Connor).

[105] See, for example, Seth Stern, "Leahy Says He Will Ask Roberts About So-Called Torture Memo," *CQ Today*, August 29, 2005, at http://www.cq.com; Gary Delsohn, "Feinstein to Seek Roberts' Abortion Views"), *Sacramento Bee*, August 25, 2005, p. A1, at http://www.nexis.com; Sen. Arlen Specter, Letter to Hon. John G. Roberts Jr., August 23, 2005. In his August 23, 2005, letter, Sen. Specter, then chair of the Judiciary Committee, began by stating, "Supplementing my letter on the Commerce Clause, this letter deals with Supreme Court decisions on the Americans with Disabilities Act (ADA), which I intend to ask you about at your confirmation hearing."

[106] Elisabeth Bumiller, "Lengthy Practices Prepare Court Nominee for his Senate Hearings," *The New York Times*, September 1, 2005, p. A11.

[107] Prior to the start of her confirmation hearings in July 2009, Supreme Court nominee Sonia Sotomayor reportedly "endured weeks of insults, obnoxious questions and unwelcome drilling into her work as a judge and a lawyer—and it was all on purpose, essentially a dress rehearsal for her confirmation hearings." Jesse J. Holland (The Associated Press), "Mock Exercises Prepare Sotomayor for Hearings," *The Washington Post*, July 10, 2009, at http://www.washingtonpost.com. A day before the start of the confirmation hearings, another story reported, quoting an Administration official, that Judge Sotomayor "and her helpers have been 'going over questions she would expect to be asked,' based on her record and what she has discussed in visits with senators over the last few weeks." Neil A. Lewis, "Nominee Wraps Up Rehearsals" *The New York Times*, July 12, 2009, p. 16.

In preparation for his confirmation hearings in September 2005, Associate Justice nominee John G. Roberts Jr. reportedly "participated in some 10 mock hearings of two to three hours each at the Justice Department, where administration lawyers and a revolving cast of Judge Roberts's colleagues and friends baited him with queries, including those they anticipated from the three Democratic senators who are widely expected to be toughest on the nominee.... " Ibid. After Judge Roberts's hearings were postponed (following the withdrawal of his Associate Justice nomination and then his re-nomination, this time to be Chief Justice), he apparently participated in even more mock hearings, for it was later reported that he "underwent at least a dozen murder boards in preparing for his hearings." Marcia Coyle, "Alito's 'Murder Board' a Mix of the Legal Elite," *The National Law Journal*, vol. 28, January 30, 2006, p. 7. Coyle, in the same article, reported that subsequently the next Supreme Court nominee, Samuel A. Alito Jr., also participated in a rigorous series of mock hearing sessions, in preparation for his confirmation hearings before the Senate Judiciary Committee in early January 2006. Alito, she noted, "was shepherded through all of the murder boards by a team that included Steve Schmidt, special advisor to the president in charge of the White House confirmation team, and Harriet Miers, counsel to the president." Coyle observed that the "well-handled U.S. Supreme Court nominee is now a fixture in the political process, and much of the credit goes to those so-called murder boards, or preparation sessions for the Senate confirmation hearings."

[108] The chair's opening statement might also express views on the nomination and confirmation process or on the nominee.

[109] The presenters often will include the Senators and, less frequently, Representatives from the state in which the nominee is a resident or the state in which the nominee was born or has resided for much of his or her life. Other presenters at recent Supreme Court confirmation hearings have included a former President (Gerald R. Ford, at the 1987 hearings for Robert H. Bork), the attorney general (William French Smith, at the 1981 hearings for Sandra Day O'Connor, and Edward Levi, at the 1975 hearings for John Paul Stevens); and a former attorney general (Griffin B. Bell, at the 1986 hearings for William H. Rehnquist).

[110] Almost invariably, the questioning is conducted exclusively by members of the committee. However, on at least two occasions in the 20th century, a Senator who was not a committee member was allowed to join in the questioning of the nominee. This first instance, in 1941, involved Sen. Millard E. Tydings (D-MD) at the confirmation hearings for nominee Robert H. Jackson; the second instance, in 1957, involved Sen. Joseph R. McCarthy (R-WI) at the confirmation hearings for nominee William J. Brennan Jr. See Thorpe, *Appearance of Supreme Court Nominees*, p. 378 (Jackson hearings) and p. 385 (Brennan hearings).

[111] See CRS Report R41300, *Questioning Supreme Court Nominees About Their Views on Legal or Constitutional Issues: A Recurring Issue*, by Denis Steven Rutkus; CRS Report RL33059, *Proper Scope of Questioning of Supreme Court Nominees: The Current Debate*, by Denis Steven Rutkus; and CRS Report 90-429,

Questioning Supreme Court Nominees—A Recurring Issue, by Denis Steven Rutkus (out of print, available from author).

[112] For instance, at her confirmation hearings in July 2009, Supreme Court nominee Sonia Sotomayor was asked questions about public statements she had made prior to her nomination (and which opponents of her nomination had criticized) of appellate judges making policy and of the experiences of a "wise Latina woman" versus those of a white male judge. Senators on the Judiciary Committee also asked her about about her participation in a controversial three-judge appellate panel ruling in a case involving reverse discimrinatinon allegations by a group of white firefighters against city officials in New Haven, Connectitcut (a ruling reversed by the Supreme Court in June 2009, after Judge Sotomayor's nomination to the Court but prior to the start of her confirmation hearings). See Tony Mauro, "During Senate Questioning, Sotomayor Explains Controversial Statements, Defends Rulings," *The National Law Journal,* July 15, 2009, at http://www.law.com;, Peter Baker and Neil A. Lewis, "Republicans Press Judge About Bias and Activism," *The New York Times*, July 15, 2009, pp. A1, A15; and Tom LoBianco, "Nominee Hit with Hot-Button Issues; Sotomayor Explains 'Wise Latina' Again," *The Washington Times*, July 16, 2009, p. A9.

[113] See, for example, Charles Babington, "On Question of Nominee Questions, No Clear Answer," *The Washington Post*, July 28, 2005, p. A6, which examined the issue facing Senators on the Judiciary Committee, prior to confirmation hearings for Supreme Court nominee John G. Roberts Jr, "of what should be asked and answered—or not answered—in confirmation hearings later this summer."

[114] See CRS Report 93-290, *The Supreme Court Appointment Process: Should It Be Reformed?* pp. 32-37 (out of print, available from author). See also William G. Ross, "The Questioning of Supreme Court Nominees at Senate Confirmation Hearings: Proposals For Accommodating the Needs of the Senate and Ameliorating the Fears of the Nominees," *Tulane Law Review*, vol. 62, November 1987, pp. 109-174.

[115] Illustrative of such a concern was the following statement by nominee David H. Souter, at a September 14, 1990, hearing, explaining his refusal to answer a question concerning the issue of a woman's right, under the Constitution, to have an abortion: "Anything which substantially could inhibit the court's capacity to listen truly and to listen with as open a mind as it is humanly possible to have should be off-limits to a judge. Why this kind of discussion would take me down a road which I think it would be unethical for me to follow is something that perhaps I can suggest, and I will close with this question.

"Is there anyone who has not, at some point, made up his mind on some subject and then later found reason to change or modify it? No one has failed to have that experience. ... With that in mind can you imagine the pressure that would be on a judge who had stated an opinion, or seemed to have given a commitment in these circumstances to the Senate of the United States, and for all practical purposes, to the American people?" U.S. Congress, Senate Committee on the Judiciary, *Nomination of David Souter To Be Associate Justice of the Supreme Court of the United* States, hearings, 101st Cong., 2nd sess., September 13, 14, 17, 18 and 19, 1990 (Washington: GPO, 1991), p. 194.

[116] In this vein, one journalist has written, the perspective of Supreme Court nominee John G. Roberts Jr., as he prepared for his 2005 confirmation hearings, was that he "knew he could afford no mistakes. He worried that one answer, one ten-second response to one question over the course of fifteen hours of questioning, could doom his chances." Greenburg, *Supreme Conflict*, p. 234.

[117] As early as 1959, at the confirmation hearings for Supreme Court nominee Potter Stewart, there is a record of Judiciary Committee members differing among themselves as to appropriateness of certain areas of questioning for the nominee. During the hearings, Sen. Thomas C. Hennings Jr. (D-MO) raised a point of order about interrogating a nominee on his "opinion as to any of the questions or the reasoning upon decisions which have heretofore ... [been] handed down" by the Supreme Court. The point of order, however, was overruled by the committee's chair, Sen. James O. Eastland (D-MS), who stated the rule he would follow: "[I]f the nominee thinks that the question is improper, that he can decline to answer. And that when he declines, his position will be respected." L.A. Powe Jr., "The Senate and the Court: Questioning a Nominee," *Texas Law Review*, vol. 54, May 1976, p. 892, citing an unpublished transcript of the April 9 and 14, 1959, hearings of the Senate Judiciary Committee on the Supreme Court nomination of Potter Stewart, pp. 43-44.

[118] That noncommittal replies by a Supreme Court nominee may be regarded differently by Senators on the Judiciary Committee appeared to be borne out at the confirmation hearings in September 2005 for Chief Justice nominee John G. Roberts Jr. In his first day of testimony, Roberts "was Delphic," according to one news analysis, "and his supporters and critics each ended the day saying his performance had hardened their enthusiasm or their doubts." Todd S. Purdum, "With His Goal Clear, the Nominee Provides a Profile in Caution During Questioning," *The New York Times,* September 14, 2005, p. 25.

[119] Watson and Stookey, *Shaping America*, p. 150.

[120] Ibid., p. 152.

[121] See Stephen J. Wermiel, "Confirming the Constitution: The Role of the Senate Judiciary Committee," *Law and Contemporary Problems*, vol. 56, Autumn 1993, p. 141, in which the author maintained that, since the 1987 hearings on Supreme Court nominee Robert H. Bork, a purpose of Senators on the Judiciary Committee has been "to identify points of constitutional concern and pursue those concerns with nominees, with the hope that,

once confirmed, the new Justices will remember the importance of the core values urged on them by the senators or at least feel bound by the assurance they gave during their hearings."

122 Watson and Stookey, *Shaping America*, p. 155.

123 Sen. Joseph R. Biden Jr., "Reform of the Confirmation Process," remarks in the Senate, *Congressional Record*, vol. 138, June 25, 1992, p. 16320.

124 On February 15, 2005 (following a morning of public testimony by nominee John G. Roberts Jr.), the chair of the Judiciary Committee, Sen. Arlen Specter (R-PA), announced that the committee would immediately be going into executive session, "to ask the nominee on the record under oath about all investigative charges against the person if there were any." Such hearings, Chairman Specter said, "are routinely conducted for every Supreme Court nominee, even where there are no investigative issues to be resolved. In so doing, those outside the Committee cannot infer that the committee has received adverse confidential information about a nominee." Thirty-one minutes after proceeding to closed session, the committee reconvened in open session. Chairman Specter noted that the committee had reviewed "the background investigations on Judge Roberts, which were routine," and that he and the committee's ranking member, Sen. Patrick J. Leahy (D-VT), had been "delegated to report that there are no disqualifying factors." (The committee then proceeded to hear outside witnesses in open session.) Senate Judiciary Committee, *Confirmation Hearing on John G. Roberts*, p. 450. See also Senate Judiciary Committee, *Confirmation Hearing on Samuel A. Alito,* p. 640, where, after a brief executive session, Chairman Specter, in public session, announced that the committee had "reviewed confidential data on the background of Judge Alito, and it was all found to be in order." Shortly before the conclusion of the Judiciary Comnmittee's questioning of Court nominee Elena Kagan on June 30, 2010, the chair of the committee, Senator Patrick J. Leahy (D-VT), informed committee members, "We'll finish the questions … and then … we will … go to the traditional closed session. And the presss won't be able to be there." [124] "Senate Judiciary Committee Holds Hearing on the Nomination of Solicitor General Elena Kagan to the U.S. Supreme Court, Day 3," *CQ Congressional Transcripts*, June 30, 2010, at http://www.CQ.com (no page numbering supplied).

125 On July 15, 2009, after all the Judiciary Committee's members had participated in a first round of questions for Judge Sotomayor, the chair of the committee, Senator Leahy requested, without objection, "for the committee now proceeding to a closed session, which is a routine practice we've followed for every [Supreme Court] nominee since back when Senator Biden was chairman of the committee." Upon conclusion of the brief closed-door session, the committee resumed public hearings that afternoon, starting with its second round of questions for Judge Sotormayor. "Senate Judiciary Committee Holds Hearing on the Nomination of Judge Sonia Sotomayor to be an Associate Justice of the U.S. Supreme Court," *CQ Congressional Transcripts*, July 15, 2009, at http://www.CQ.com.

126 Since its creation in 1816, the Judiciary Committee has reported to the Senate 106 Supreme Court nominations. Of the 106, seven were reported unfavorably—those of John Crittenden (1829), Ebenezer R. Hoard (1869), Stanley Matthews (1881), Lucius Q.C. Lamar (1888), William B. Hornblower (1894), John J. Parker (1930), and Robert H. Bork (1987). Two were reported without recommendation—those of Wheeler H. Peckham (1894) and Clarence Thomas (1991). See CRS Report RL33225, *Supreme Court Nominations, 1789 - 2010: Actions by the Senate, the Judiciary Committee, and the President* (under heading "Nominations Reported Out of Committee to Full Senate").

127 Of the 116 Supreme Court nominations referred to the Judiciary Committee, only eight were not reported by the committee to the Senate. The final outcome for all eight nominees, however, was determined not by the failure of their nominations to be reported out of committee, but by action, or lack of action, taken outside the committee—by the Senate, Congress as a whole, or the President. For instance, the most recent nominee not reported out of committee was Harriet E. Miers, whose nomination, in 2005, was withdrawn by President George W. Bush before the start of scheduled confirmation hearings. For details regarding the failure of each of the eight nominations not reported, see CRS Report RL33225, *Supreme Court Nominations, 1789 - 2010: Actions by the Senate, the Judiciary Committee, and the President* (under heading "Nominations Not Reported Out of Committee").

128 Sen. Patrick J. Leahy and Sen. Orrin G. Hatch, "Dear Colleague" Letter, June 29, 2001, *Congressional Record*, daily edition, vol. 147, June 29, 2001, p. S7282.

129 From the 1960s through 2010, the Judiciary Committee reported 25 Supreme Court nominations to the Senate, 16 of which included transmittals of printed reports. During this time span, the nine Supreme Court nominations reported to the Senate without printed report were those of Byron W. White and Arthur J. Goldberg in 1962, Abe Fortas in 1965, Warren E. Burger in 1969, John Paul Stevens in 1975, and the four most recent Court nominations—those of John G. Roberts Jr. (for Chief Justice) in 2005, Samuel A. Alito Jr. in 2006, Sonia Sotomayor in 2009, and Elena Kagan in 2010.

130 Rule 26, paragraph 10(c), *Standing Rules of the Senate.*

131 This argument, for instance, was raised in 1969, after the nomination of Warren E. Burger to be Chief Justice was reported by the Judiciary Committee to the Senate floor without a printed report. During floor consideration of the nomination, three Senators expressed concern about the absence of a printed committee report. The Senators maintained that it was important for the Senate, when considering an appointment of this

magnitude, to be able to consult a printed report from the Judiciary Committee that provided a breakdown of any recorded votes by the committee and an explanation of the committee's recommendation regarding the nominee. "The Supreme Court of the United States," debate in the Senate, *Congressional Record*, vol. 115, June 9, 1969, pp. 15174-15175 and 15192-15194. Shortly after this discussion, however, the Senate concluded debate on the Burger nomination and voted to confirm the nominee, 74-3.

[132] In one instance, involving the Supreme Court nomination of Ruth Bader Ginsburg in 1993, the Senate received the Judiciary Committee's printed report on the nomination on August 5, two days after voting to confirm the nominee. In that instance, it might be argued, the greater value of the the committee's report, in being transmitted after the Senate's confirmation vote, was not as an advisory resource for the Senate but as an official record for posterity that reviewed the nature of the committee's investigation of the nominee and the reasons for committee members unanimously favoring the nominee's confirmation.

[133] A written report ordinarily is produced within a week of the committee vote. On infrequent occasions, however, the report may entail weeks of preparation if the nomination is controversial or if the report is regarded as possibly crucial in influencing how the full Senate will vote on the nomination. In 1970, for instance, the committee submitted its written report on nominee Clement F. Haynsworth Jr. more than a month after voting 10-7 to recommend that Judge Haynsworth be confirmed. (Subsequently the full Senate rejected the Haynsworth nomination by a 55-45 vote.)

[134] Concern that vacancies on the Court be filled as expeditiously as possible appeared to figure in the decisions to report two recent Supreme Court nominees, John G. Roberts Jr. and Samuel A. Alito Jr., to the Senate without printed report. Dispensing with a written report for Roberts was briefly discussed on the Senate floor in July 29, 2005, the day his first nomination (for Associate Justice) was received by the Senate. (This nomination would later, on September 6, 2005, be withdrawn, with Roberts that same day re-nominated to be Chief Justice.) In a floor statement, the chair of the Judiciary Committee, Sen. Arlen Specter (R-Pa), described a joint agreement that he and the committee's ranking member, Sen. Patrick J. Leahy (D-VT), had reached with the Senate's party leaders concerning the scheduling procedures for the confirmation hearings on the Roberts nomination. The particulars of the agreement, Senator Specter said, were shaped by what he said was the Senate's "duty to have the nominee in place" on the Court by the start of its next term on October 3, 2005. In the list of particulars agreed to (including the start of hearings by a set date and the waiving by members of the Judiciary Committee of their right under committee rules to hold over the nomination for one week when first placed on the committee's executive agenda), Judiciary Committee members from both parties, Senator Specter said, "would waive their right to submit dissenting or additional or minority views to the committee report." "Hearings on Supreme Court Nominee John Roberts," *Congressional Record*, daily edition, vol. 151, July 29, 2005, p. S9420. Senator Leahy as well, in a floor statement immediately after Senator Specter, indicated that the joint agreement allowed for dispensing with a written committee report on the Roberts nomination: "And we recognize," Senator Leahy stated, "that nothing in the Senate or Judiciary Committee rules precludes the Senate from considering the nomination on the floor without a committee report." Ibid.
The scheduling of a Judiciary Committee vote on the Alito nomination, without a printed report by the committee to follow, also appeared to be grounded on concerns of acting as quickly on the nomination as possible. In Chairman Specter's initial announcement, on November 3, 2005, of a schedule for the Judiciary Committee and Senate floor action on the Alito nomination, he specified that floor action was to begin the day after the committee's vote (hence not allowing time for preparation of a printed report). Senator Specter observed that the Court was then in the midst of its October 2005 term, with the possibility of various cases already heard by the Court having to be reargued, if the departure of outgoing Justice Sandra Day O'Connor during the term were to result in 4-4 decisions. Thus, Senator Specter said, it was important to the Court for the Senate to act on the Alito nomination "as promptly as possible." "Senator Specter and Leahy Hold News Conference on Hearings for Supreme Court Justice Nominee Alito," CQ.Com Newsmaker Transcripts, November 3, 2005, at http://www.cq.com.

[135] The Senate disagreed with the Judiciary Committee's favorable assessment of a Supreme Court nominee three times in the 20th century, declining to confirm Supreme Court nominees Abe Fortas in 1968, Clement F. Haynsworth Jr. in 1969, and G. Harrold Carswell in 1970, even though their confirmation had been recommended by the committee. At least once in the 19th century, the Senate, in 1873, questioned a favorable committee report on a nominee to the Court, recommitting the nomination of George H. Williams to be Chief Justice; the nomination later was withdrawn by the President, without having been reported out a second time by the committee. A year later, in 1874, the nomination of Caleb Cushing to be Chief Justice failed to receive Senate confirmation after being reported favorably by the Judiciary Committee. Soon after the committee's action and in the face of growing Senate opposition, the nomination was withdrawn by President Ulysses S. Grant without, however, having received formal Senate consideration. See Jacobstein and Mersky, *The Rejected*, pp. 82-87 (Williams), pp. 87-89 (Cushing), pp. 125-137 (Fortas), pp. 141-147 (Haynsworth), and pp. 147-155 (Carswell).

[136] Specifically, the following three Supreme Court nominations, though reported out of committee without a favorable recommendation, nonetheless were confirmed by the Senate: Stanley Matthews (1881), by a 24-23 vote; Lucius Q.C. Lamar (1888), by a 32-28 vote; and Clarence Thomas (1991), by a 52-48 vote.

[137] For an examination of floor procedures used by the Senate in considering Supreme Court nominations, see CRS Report RL33247, *Supreme Court Nominations: Senate Floor Procedure and Practice, 1789-2010*, by Richard S. Beth and Betsy Palmer. The report examines the 146 Supreme Court nominations on which some form of formal proceedings took place on the Senate floor. It sketches the changing patterns of consideration that have been normal in successive historical periods since 1789, and, in considering all of the 146 nominations, discusses the kinds of dispositions that they received, the length of their floor consideration, and the kinds of procedural action taken during their consideration.

[138] "It is not in order for a Senator to move to consider a nomination that is not on the calendar, and except by unanimous consent a nomination on the calendar cannot be taken up until it has been on the calendar at least one day." Elizabeth Rybicki, CRS Report RL31980, *Senate Consideration of Presidential Nominations: Committee and Floor Procedure* (under heading Taking Up a Nomination"). The Senate may also discharge a matter from a committee, by motion or by unanimous consent.

[139] The latest issue of the Senate's Executive Calendar can be accessed electronically in the Legislative Information System of the U.S. Congress at http://www.senate.gov/legislative/LIS/executive_calendar/xcalv.pdf.

[140] See CRS Report RL31980, *Senate Consideration of Presidential Nominations: Committee and Floor Procedure.*

[141] In 1925, the full Senate for the first time considered a Supreme Court nomination—that of Harlan F. Stone to be an Associate Justice—in open session, waiving a rule requiring the chamber to consider nominations in closed session. In 1929, the Senate amended its rules to provide for debate on nominations in open session unless there were a vote to go into closed session. Thenceforth, it became the regular Senate practice to conduct debate on nominations, including those to the Supreme Court, in open session.

[142] The Senate has allowed gavel-to-gavel broadcast coverage of Senate floor debate since June 1986. The Senate's first floor debates on Supreme Court nominations ever to be televised were its September 1986 debates on the nominations of William H. Rehnquist to be Chief Justice and Antonin Scalia to be an Associate Justice.

[143] For instance, under a unanimous consent agreement propounded by Majority Leader Robert C. Byrd (D-WV), on October 21, 1987, the Senate proceeded immediately to consider the Supreme Court nomination of Robert H. Bork. Sen Robert C. Byrd, "Executive Session," remarks in the Senate, *Congressional Record*, vol. 133, October 21, 1987, p. 28654. Similarly, under a unanimous consent agreement requested by Majority Leader Bill Frist (R-TN) on January 25, 2006, the Senate proceeded immediately to consider the nomination to the Court of Samuel A. Alito Jr. Sen. Bill Frist, "Nomination of Samuel A. Alito, Jr., To Be an Associate Justice of the Supreme Court of the United States," remarks in the Senate, *Congressional Record*, daily edition, vol. 152, January 25, 2006, p. S35.

[144] For instance, on September 27, 1990, a unanimous consent agreement was propounded by Majority Leader George J. Mitchell (D-ME) providing for the Senate to proceed to the Supreme Court nomination of David H. Souter at 2:30 p.m., October 2. Sen. George J. Mitchell, "Nomination of David L. Souter To Be an Associate Justice of the Supreme Court of the United States," remarks in the Senate, *Congressional Record*, vol. 136, September 27, 1990, p. 26387. Likewise, on September 22, 2005, a unanimous consent agreement was obtained by Majority Leader Bill Frist (R-TN) providing for the Senate to proceed to the nomination of John G. Roberts Jr. to be Chief Justice of the United States, on September 26, 2005, "following the prayer and pledge" at 1 p.m. Sen. Bill Frist, "Orders for Monday, September 26, 2005," remarks in the Senate, *Congressional Record*, daily edition, vol. 151, September 22, 2005, p. S10392; on August 4, 2009, Majority Leader Harry Reid (D-NV) obtained a unanimous consent agreement providing that the Senate proceed to consider the Supreme Court nomination of Sonia Sotomayor later that day ("upon disposition of H.R. 2997"), Sen. Harry Reid, remarks in the Senate on proceeding to executive session, *Congressional Record*, daily edition, vol. 155, August 4, 2009, p. S8724; and, on August 2, 2010, Sen. Christopher J. Dodd (D-CT) asked and received unanimous consent that at 9:30 a.m., August 3, the Senate, immediately after its opening, proceed to consider the Supreme Court nomination of Elena Kagan. Sen. Christopher J. Dodd, "Unanimous Consent Agreement—Executive Calendar," *Congressional Record,* daily edition, vol. 156, August 2, 2010, p. S6593.

[145] In this vein, Majority Leader George J. Mitchell (D-ME), on July 28, 1994, while the Senate was in legislative session, asked unanimous consent that at 9 a.m. on July 29, the Senate proceed to executive session to consider the Supreme Court nomination of Stephen G. Breyer. The unanimous consent request also specified that there be six hours of debate, after which the Senate, "without any intervening action on the nomination," would vote on whether to confirm. Sen. George J. Mitchell, "Unanimous-Consent Agreement," remarks in the Senate, *Congressional Record*, vol. 140, July 28, 1994, p. 18544. Likewise, unanimous consent requests limited the time for debate and set the date and time for Senate votes on the Supreme Court nominations of Ruth Bader Ginsburg (1993), Clarence Thomas (1991), Anthony M. Kennedy (1988), and Sandra Day O'Connor (1981).

[146] For example, a September 27, 1990, unanimous consent agreement, which provided for the Senate to proceed to the Supreme Court nomination of David H. Souter at 2:30 p.m., October 2, did not, however, also provide for a time limit on the debate, or for a vote at the end of that debate. Despite the absence of these provisions in the unanimous consent agreement, the Senate concluded its debate and voted to confirm, on the same day that it began debate on the Souter nomination, October 2. Likewise, the Senate on August 29, 1967, by unanimous consent, proceeded to consider the Supreme Court nomination of Thurgood Marshall, without also providing for a time limit on the debate, or for a scheduled time for a vote on confirmation. "Supreme Court of the

United States," *Congressional Record*, vol. 113, August 29, 1967, p. 24437. In the absence of such provisions, the Senate concluded debate on, and voted to confirm, the Marshall nomination the next day, August 30. Also, the Senate, without providing for a vote on confirmation, may enter into one or more unanimous consent agreements, each with a time limit, to complete debate time and ultimately arrive at a time for a vote on confirmation. That was the scenario followed when the Senate in 2005 considered the nomination of John G. Roberts Jr. to be Chief Justice. Initial consideration of the Roberts nomination, on September 26, 2005, occurred pursuant to a unanimous consent agreement entered into on September 22, 2005. The agreement specified the precise amounts of time on September 26 to be allotted to the majority and minority party leaders or their designees for debate on the nomination, without, however, setting a date and time for a vote on confirmation. "Orders for Monday, September 26, 2005," *Congressional Record*, daily edition, vol. 151, September 22, 2005, p. S10392. Pursuant to three more UC agreements, further Senate consideration of the nomination followed, on September 27, 28, and 29, 2005, culminating in a 78-22 vote to confirm on September 29. (A complete chronology of Senate actions on the Roberts nomination, including all unanimous consent agreements reached on the nomination, can be accessed on the Legislative Information System's Nominations database at http://www.congress.gov/nomis/.)

[147] Charles Tiefer, *Congressional Practice and Procedure* (New York: Greenwood Press, 1989), p. 607. (Hereafter cited as Tiefer, *Congressional Practice and Procedure*.)

[148] For full details on the cloture process, see CRS Report RL30360, *Filibusters and Cloture in the Senate*, by Richard S. Beth, Valerie Heitshusen, and Betsy Palmer.

[149] For just as the motion to consider was a debatable question, permitting a filibuster by opponents, so, too, would be the question of whether to advise and consent to the nomination.

[150] The vote on the motion to close debate on the motion to consider the Fortas nomination was 45-43, well short of the super-majority then required by Senate rules for passage of a "cloture motion" (prior to 1975, two-thirds of Senators present and voting). Shortly after the unsuccessful attempt at cloture, the Fortas nomination was withdrawn by President Lyndon B. Johnson.

[151] Floyd M. Riddick and Alan S. Frumin, *Riddick's Senate Procedure*, S. Doc. 101-28, 101st Cong., 2nd sess. (Washington, GPO, 1992), pp. 941-942.

[152] Tiefer, *Congressional Practice and Procedure*, p. 608.

[153] See in following pages of this chapter, under the subheading "Filibusters and Motions To End Debate," discussion of the opposition, in January 2006, of some Senators to ending debate on the nomination of Samuel A. Alito Jr. to be an Associate Justice.

[154] The single cloture vote needed to limit debate on the Alito nomination occurred five days after the Senate, on January 25, 2006, agreed by unanimous consent to consider it. Specifically, after continuing its consideration of the Alito nomination on January 26 and 27, the Senate on January 30 invoked cloture by a 72-25 vote, and confirmed Judge Alito to the Court the next day, by a vote of 58-42. See Charles Babington, "Senate To Vote on Alito Today; Confirmation Near as Filibuster Fails," *The Washington Post*, January 31, 2006, p. A1; Charles Babington, "Alito Is Sworn In on High Court," *The Washington Post*, February 1, 2006, p. A1.

[155] "The advice-and-consent role of the Senate," one of its Members noted in 1994, "is something that we do not take lightly because this is the only opportunity for the people of this Nation to express whether or not they deem a nominee qualified to sit on the highest court in the land." Sen. Mark O. Hatfield, "Nomination of Stephen G. Breyer, of Massachusetts, To Be an Associate Justice of the Supreme Court of the United States," remarks in the Senate, *Congressional Record*, vol. 140, July 29, 1994, pp. 18692-18693.

[156] See CRS General Distribution Memorandum, *Criteria Used by Senators To Evaluate Judicial Nominations*, by Denis Steven Rutkus, June 14, 2002 (available from author).

[157] For example, during 1991 Senate debate on the Supreme Court nomination of Judge Clarence Thomas, the criterion of professional qualification was cited by both supporters and opponents of the nominee to explain their votes. A Senator supporting the Thomas nomination maintained that instead of the nominee's "philosophy on particular issues" which might come before the Supreme Court, the "more appropriate standard" was that the nominee "have outstanding legal ability and wide experience and meet the highest standards of integrity, judicial temperament, and professional competence." Judge Thomas, the Senator added, "clearly meets that standard." Sen. Frank H. Murkowski, "Nomination of Clarence Thomas to the Supreme Court," remarks in the Senate, *Congressional Record*, vol. 137, October 1, 1991, p. 24748. Other Senators, however, used the criterion of professional competence to find Judge Thomas unqualified. One, for example, found the nominee's "legal background and experience" inadequate and added that, if a President did not nominate to the court "well-qualified, experienced individuals, the American people have the right to expect that the members of the Senate will reject the nomination." Sen. Jeff Bingaman, "Justice Clarence Thomas," remarks in the Senate, *Congressional Record*, vol. 137, October 2, 1991, p. 24973.

[158] During debate over the nomination of Clarence Thomas in 1991, these criteria were used both by Senators favoring the nomination and by others opposing it. One Senator in support of the nomination, for example, declared his desire to have "Supreme Court Justices who will interpret the Constitution and not attempt to legislate or carry out personal agendas from the bench." Sen. Richard C. Shelby, "Nomination of Judge Clarence Thomas To Be an Associate Justice of the U.S. Supreme Court," remarks in the Senate,

Congressional Record, vol. 137, October 1, 1991, p. 24703. By contrast, another Senator, explaining his opposition to confirming Judge Thomas, said that if Senators were "not confident that nominees possess a clear commitment to the fundamental constitutional rights and freedoms at the heart of our democracy, they should not be confirmed." Sen. Edward M. Kennedy, "Nomination of Clarence Thomas, of Georgia, To Be an Associate Justice of the Supreme Court of the United States," remarks in the Senate, *Congressional Record*, vol. 137, October 3, 1991, p. 25271.

[159] "In addition to the obvious criteria any nominee for the Supreme Court ought to have—I suppose any nominee for any position on the judiciary ought to have—those of intellect, of integrity, and of judicial temperament, it is very appropriate of the Senate to inquire into a nominee's judicial philosophy. Of course, that includes the nominee's fidelity to the Constitution. It involves that nominee's understanding of the limited role of the courts, and it involves what I hope is a commitment to judicial restraint." Charles E. Grassley, "Supreme Court of the United States," remarks in the Senate, *Congressional Record*, vol. 139, August 2, 1993, p. 18133. Similarly evincing concern with both a nominee's professional qualification and his constitutional values was this 1991 Senate floor statement during debate on the nomination of Clarence Thomas: "When I face a Supreme Court nominee I have three questions: Is he or she competent? Does she or he possess the highest personal and professional integrity? And, third, will he or she protect and defend the core constitutional values and guarantees around free of speech, religion, equal protection of the law, and the right of privacy?" Sen. Barbara A. Mikulski, "Nomination of Clarence Thomas, of Georgia, To Be An Associate Justice of the Supreme Court of the United States," remarks in the Senate, *Congressional Record,* vol. 137, October 15, 1991, p. 26299.

[160] Three political scientists wrote in 2002 that although "speculation about possible Supreme Court vacancies is usually met with much interest by court watchers, it is particularly intense at present due to the ideological balance of the current Court and the recent politics of the judicial confirmation process. Given the delicate ideological balance on the current Court, a single vacancy could produce a dramatic shift in the ideological direction of future rulings." Kenneth L. Manning, Bruce A. Carroll, and Robert A. Carp, "George W. Bush's Potential Supreme Court Nominees: What Impact Might They Have?," *Judicature*, vol. 85, May-June 2002, p. 278.

[161] Linda Greenhouse, "Divided They Stand: The High Court and the Triumph of Discord," *The New York Times*, July 15, 2001, sec. 4, p. 1. Following the next two appointments to the Court—of Chief Justice John G. Roberts Jr. in 2005 and Associate Justice Samuel A. Alito Jr. in 2006—the proportion of 5-4 rulings by the Court increased. At the end of the Court's October 2006 term (the first full term with both Justices Roberts and Alito on the Court), Greenhouse reported that "[f]ully a third of the court's decisions, more than in any recent term, were decided by 5-to-4 margins. Most of those, 19 of 24, were decided along ideological lines, demonstrating the court's polarization whether on constitutional fundamentals or obscure questions of appellate procedure." Greenhouse added, "Of the ideological cases decided this term, the conservative majority, led by Chief Justice John G. Roberts Jr. and joined by Justices Antonin Scalia, Clarence Thomas and Samuel A. Alito Jr., prevailed in 13. The court's increasingly marginalized liberals—Justices John Paul Stevens, David H. Souter, Ruth Bader Ginsburg and Stephen G. Breyer—prevailed in only six...." Linda Greenhouse, "In Steps Big and Small, Supreme Court Moved Right," *The New York Times*, July 1, 2007, p. 1.

[162] For example, during 1994 floor debate on the Supreme Court nomination of Stephen G. Breyer, one Senator said of the nominee's views: "Certainly in terms of an expansive definition of the Constitution, I have no doubt that Judge Breyer is going to make rulings that represent a different interpretation of the great document than I have and that people who share my views have. But I also believe that Judge Breyer's views are mainstream liberal views. I believe that anyone who voted for Bill Clinton knew or should have known that the chances than anyone more conservative than Judge Breyer being nominated by Bill Clinton were almost zero." Sen. Phil Gramm, "Nomination of Stephen G. Breyer, of Massachusetts, To Be an Associate Justice of the Supreme Court of the United States," remarks in the Senate, *Congressional Record*, vol. 140, July 29, 1994, pp. 18671-18672.

[163] A key to Senate division over the nomination of Samuel A. Alito Jr. in 2005-2006, it can be argued, was a widespread perception that confirmation of Alito would change the ideological balance of the Court in that he might align in decisions with Justices whose views were regarded by some as conservative. See, for example, Seth Stern and Keith Perine, "Alito Confirmed After Filibuster Fails," *CQ Weekly,* vol. 64, February 6, 2006, p. 340 (characterizing Alito's confirmation, "by a mostly party-line vote of 58-42," as "the culmination of years of planning by conservatives to move the court to the right"); also, "A Supreme Nomination," *The Washington Times*, November 1, 2005, p. A18 (editorial describing the nomination as "the moment conservatives have been waiting for" and predicting a "confirmation battle" in the Senate).

Earlier, in 1987, Senate concern with a nominee's judicial philosophy was also especially heightened when President Reagan nominated appellate court judge Robert H. Bork to the Court. The nomination sparked immediate controversy, and polarized the Senate generally along party lines, in large part because of the nominee's judicial philosophy of "original intent" and the perception that he had been nominated by President Reagan to move the Court in the future in what was characterized as a more conservative direction. For analysis of how central an issue Judge Bork's judicial philosophy was in the Senate confirmation battle, see

John Massaro, *Supremely Political: The Role of Ideology and Presidential Management in Unsuccessful Supreme Court Nominations*. (Albany, NY: State University of New York Press, 1990), pp. 159-193. (Hereafter cited as Massaro, *Supremely Political*.)
In a Senate floor statement shortly after the Bork nomination was made, the then-chair of the Senate Judiciary Committee, Sen. Joseph R. Biden, Jr. (D-DE), faulted the President for his choice. Senator Biden declared that when a President selects nominees "with more attention to their judicial philosophy and less attention to their detachment and statesmanship," a Senator "has not only the right but the duty to respond by carefully weighing the nominee's judicial philosophy and the consequences for the country." The Senate, he continued, had both the right and the duty to raise political and judicial "questions of substance," for "we are once again confronted with a popular President's determined attempt to bend the Supreme Court to his political ends." Sen. Joseph R. Biden Jr., "Advice and Consent: The Right and Duty of the Senate To Protect the Integrity of the Supreme Court," remarks in the Senate," *Congressional Record*, vol. 133, July 23, 1987, p 20913 (first quote) and p. 20915 (second quote).
Various Senators who favored Judge Bork's confirmation, however, disagreed with Senator Biden regarding the importance of the nominee's judicial philosophy. Some expressed a preference for a narrower scope of Senate inquiry, focusing on Judge Bork's legal competence and character. Others considered Judge Bork's judicial philosophy and views of the Constitution appropriate areas of inquiry, but the crucial determination for the Senate to make in these areas, they argued, was whether his views fell within a broad range of acceptable thinking, not whether individual senators agreed with those views. Further, some Senators maintained, to evaluate a nominee according to political or judicial philosophy, or to vote to confirm only if Senators agreed with the nominee's views, would politicize the Supreme Court and undermine its independence of the legislative branch. See CRS Report 87-761, *Senate Consideration of the Nomination of Robert H. Bork To Be a Supreme Court Associate Justice—Background and an Overview of Issues*, by Denis Steven Rutkus (out of print, available from author), pp. 25-27.

[164] See Watson and Stookey, *Shaping America*, pp. 191-195, for discussion of how a relatively few number of Senators may serve as "cues" to other Senators during the consideration of controversial Supreme Court nominations.

[165] See, for example, Seth Stern, "'Bork's America' Resounds," *CQ Weekly*, vol. 67, September 7, 2009, p. 1987, where author suggests the profound influence that one floor speech by the late Sen. Edward M. Kennedy (D-MA) had in galvanizing Senate opposition to the Supreme Court nomination of Robert H. Bork in 1987.

[166] Illustrative of this, during 1991 Senate debate over the Clarence Thomas nomination, Sen. Frank H. Murkowski (R-AK) stated, "I have heard from a number of Alaskans and visited with them last week during our recess. Many have gone back and forth during the testimony, but now the hearings are concluded, and they are telling me by a substantial majority that they favor the confirmation of Judge Thomas by this body." Sen. Frank H. Murkowski, "Nomination of Clarence Thomas, of Georgia, To Be An Associate Justice of the Supreme Court of the United States," remarks in the Senate, *Congressional Record*, vol. 137, October 15, 1991, p. 26300.

[167] See Watson and Stookey, *Shaping America*, pp. 198-199.

[168] In recent decades, for instance, Presidents and Senators at various times have endorsed the goal of increasing the representation of women and persons of minority ethnicity in the lower courts, as well as on the Supreme Court, to make the judiciary more representative of the nation's population.

[169] Concern for adequate representation of women on the Court, for instance, was expressed by some Senators after President George W. Bush nominated Samuel A. Alito Jr. to succeed retiring Justice Sandra Day O'Connor. (President Bush had nominated Alito after withdrawing his earlier nomination of White House counsel Harriet E. Miers to succeed Justice O'Connor.) Confirmation of Alito, it was widely noted, would leave the Court with only one woman member, Justice Ruth Bader Ginsburg. In this context, Sen. Barbara A. Mikulski (D-MD), during January 25, 2006, floor debate on the Alito nomination, remarked, "After Harriet Miers was withdrawn, who did they give us? Certainly, I think in all of the United States of America there was a qualified woman who could have been nominated to serve on the Court." Sen. Barbara A. Mikulski, "Nomination of Samuel A. Alito Jr. To Be an Associate Justice on the Supreme Court of the United States," remarks in the Senate, *Congressional Record*, daily edition, vol. 152, January 25, 2006, p. S66.

[170] President George W. Bush, for instance, received bipartisan praise for personally, and through his aides, consulting widely with Members of the Senate, over a several week period, prior to nominating John G. Roberts Jr. to the Court in 2005. See, for example, the remarks of Majority Leader Bill Frist (R-TN), in "Supreme Court Confirmation Process," remarks in the Senate, *Congressional Record*, daily edition, vol. 151, July 12, 2005, pp. S8091-S8092, and of Senate Democratic Leader Harry Reid (D-NV) in "Pressing Issues," remarks in the Senate, *Congressional Record*, daily edition, vol. 151, July 11, 2005, pp. S7945-S7946. By contrast, President Bush's announcement of Samuel A. Alito Jr. on October 31, 2005, as a Court nominee, occurring four days after the withdrawal of a previous nominee to the same position (Harriet E. Miers), was faulted by some Senators as a selection made with little concern for consultation with Senators. Instead of an invitation to the White House, Senator Reid stated, "I received nothing more than a pro forma telephone call from the President's Chief of Staff, telling me he had selected Judge Alito about an hour before he announced

the nomination." Sen. Harry Reid, "The Nomination of Judge Alito," remarks in the Senate,"*Congressional Record,* daily edition, vol. 151, November 16, 2005, p. S12874.

[171] Among those Senators supporting the nomination, one declared that he strongly believed "that a nominee comes to the Senate with a presumption in his favor. Accordingly, opponents of the nominee must make the case against him, especially since Judge Thomas has been confirmed to positions of great trust and responsibility on four separate occasions." Sen. Strom Thurmond, "Supreme Court of the United States," remarks in the Senate, *Congressional Record*, vol. 137, October 3, 1991, p. 25257. Another Senator stated that while his vote in favor of Judge Thomas was not "cast without some doubt, ... I have tried to insist on every judicial nomination of every President that I would give both the President and the nominee the benefit of the doubt." Sen. Wyche Fowler Jr., "Supreme Court of the United States," remarks in the Senate, *Congressional Record*, vol. 137, October 3, 1991, p. 25270.

[172] During the Thomas nomination debate, for example, one Senator declared that "[i]n the selection of a person to serve on the Nation's highest court, in my view, the Senate is an equal partner with the President. The President is owed no special deference, and his nominee owed no special presumptions. We owe the public our careful and thorough consideration and our independent judgement." Sen. Frank R. Lautenberg, "Against the Confirmation of Clarence Thomas," remarks in the Senate, *Congressional Record*, vol., 137, September27, 1991, p. 24449. Likewise, another Senator maintained that, on "a question of such vast and lasting significance, where the course of our future for years to come is riding on our decision, the Senate should give the benefit of the doubt to the Supreme Court and to the Constitution, not to Judge Clarence Thomas." Sen. Edward M. Kennedy, "Nomination of Clarence Thomas, of Georgia, To Be an Associate Justice of the Supreme Court of the United States," remarks in the Senate, *Congressional Record*, vol. 137, October 15, 1991, p. 26290.

[173] For the complete record of the June 26, 2001 hearing, entitled "Judicial Nominations 2001: Should Ideology Matter?" see pp. 1-109 in U.S. Congress, Senate Committee on the Judiciary, Subcommittee on Administrative Oversight and the Courts, *The Judicial Nomination and Confirmation Process*, hearings, 107th Cong., 1st sess., June 26 & September 4, 2001 (Washington: GPO, 2002).

[174] Ibid., pp. 2-3.

[175] Ibid., p. 30. Soon thereafter, on September 4, 2001, the same Senate Judiciary subcommittee held a hearing on a related issue involving judicial nominations—namely, does the "burden of proof" lie with the nominee, to demonstrate that he or she merits appointment to the federal bench, or with Senate opponents, to demonstrate that the nominee is unfit for confirmation? The hearing, entitled "The Senate's Role in the Nomination and Confirmation Process: Whose Burden?," featured two panels of witnesses, some arguing for, and others against, placing the burden of proof on the nominee. See Ibid., pp. 111-218, for the complete record of the September 4 hearing.

[176] Much of the discussion under this subheading is based on, and borrows extensively from, CRS Report RL32878, *Cloture Attempts on Nominations*, by Richard S. Beth and Betsy Palmer.

[177] As discussed earlier, however, the Senate may set time limits on such debates by unanimous consent.

[178] See discussion earlier in this chapter, regarding debatable motions and filibusters, under subheading "Bringing the Nomination to the Floor."

[179] Prior to 1975, the majority required for cloture was two-thirds of Senators present and voting, a quorum being present. CRS Report RL32878, *Cloture Attempts on Nominations* (under heading "Historical Development of Cloture Attempts on Nominations").

[180] It has only been since 1949, under Senate rules, that cloture could be moved on nominations. Prior to 1949, dating back to the Senate's first adoption of a cloture rule in 1917, cloture motions could be filed only on legislature measures. Ibid.

[181] For the Senate's debate on the Fortas nomination immediately prior to the vote on the motion to close debate, see "Supreme Court of the United States," *Congressional Record*, vol. 114, October 1, 1968, pp. 28926-28933.

[182] For the Senate's debate on the Rehnquist nomination immediately prior to the vote on the motion to close debate, see "Cloture Motion," *Congressional Record*, vol. 117, December 10, 1971, pp. 46110-46117.

[183] The Senate, on December 10, 1971, confirmed the Rehnquist nomination by a vote of 68-26, after voting 22-70 to reject a motion that a vote on the nomination be deferred until January 18, 1972. *Congressional Record*, vol. 117, December 10, 1971, p. 46121 (vote on motion to defer) and p. 46197 (confirmation vote).

[184] "Nomination of William H. Rehnquist To Be Chief Justice of the United States," *Congressional Record*, vol. 132, September17, 1986, pp. 23729-23739.

[185] "Cloture Motion," *Congressional Record,* January 26, 2006, daily edition, vol. 152, p. S197.

[186] "Nomination of Samuel A. Alito, Jr., To Be an Associate Justice of the Supreme Court of the United States," *Congressional Record*, January 30, 2006, daily edition, vol. 152, pp. S260-S308.

[187] Matthew Tully, "Senators Won't Rule Out Filibuster of High Court Nominees," *CQ Daily Monitor*, March 21, 2002, p. 7.

[188] Ibid.

[189] See CRS Report RL31868, *U.S. Circuit and District Court Nominations by President George W. Bush During the 107th-109th Congresses*, by Denis Steven Rutkus, Maureen Bearden, and Kevin M. Scott (listing, in

Appendix 3, all of President Bush's circuit court nominations during the 108th Congress, including votes in the Senate on motions to end debate on 10 of the nominations).

[190] In March 2005, a Congressional Research Service report noted that in "recent years, final Senate action on several presidential nominations for federal judgeships has been impeded by filibusters or threatened filibusters." As a result, "some leading Senators have called for the Senate to change its procedures to prevent filibusters, or make them harder to sustain, at least on this class of business." CRS Report RL32843, *"Entrenchment" of Senate Procedure and the "Nuclear Option" for Change: Possible Proceedings and Their Implications*, by Richard S. Beth (under heading "Introduction").

[191] Senate Republican leaders announced that their move to change Senate precedents to bar filibusters against judicial nominations would occur in conjunction with their efforts to close floor debate on the nomination of Priscilla Owen to be a U.S. circuit court of appeals judge. (An earlier nomination of Owen to the same judgeship, during the 108th Congress, had been filibustered successfully by Senate Democrats four times.) Keith Perine and Daphne Retter, "Judicial Showdown Starts with Owen," *CQ Today*, vol. 41, May 18, 2005.

[192] Charles Babington and Shailagh Murray, "A Last-Minute Deal on Judicial Nominations," *The Washington Post*, May 24, 2005, pp. A1, A4. See also CRS Report RS22208, *The "Memorandum of Understanding": A Senate Compromise on Judicial Filibusters*, by Walter J. Oleszek; and CRS Report RL33094, *Congress and the Courts: Current Policy Issues*, by Walter J. Oleszek (under headings "The Bipartisan Agreement: A Memorandum of Understanding" and "Diverse Definitions of 'Extraordinary Circumstances'").

[193] Several Senate Democrats, it was reported in 2002, had said "they would consider staging a filibuster if President Bush nominates to the high court a conservative not to their liking." Matthew Tully, "Senators Won't Rule Out Filibuster of High Court Nominees," *CQ Daily Monitor*, March 21, 2002, p. 7. More recently, in June 2003, another Democratic Senator declared that he would filibuster any Supreme Court nominee that he found objectionable based on certain specified criteria. Adam Nagourney, "Senator Ready To Filibuster over Views of Court Pick," *The New York Times*, June 21, 2003, p. A13.

[194] See, for example, Jonathan Allen, "Dems Hint at Filibuster," *The Hill*, November 1, 2005, at http://www. hillnews. com/; also,, Charles Hurt, "Alito Nomination to Test 'Gang of 14"; GOP Sees No Reason to Allow Filibuster," *The Washington Times*, November 2, 2005, pp. A1, A12.

[195] See Seth Stern and Keith Perine, "Alito Confirmed after Filibuster Fails," *CQ Weekly*, vol. 64, February 6, 2006, pp. 340-341.

[196] See David D. Kirkpatrick, "Alito Clears Final Hurdle for Confirmation to Court," *The New York Times*, January 31, 2006, p. 1. The article reported that, on the afternoon before the cloture vote, the 14 Senators who were part of the May 23, 2005, agreement met and "agreed unanimously that the 'extraordinary circumstances' stipulation [to justify a filibuster] did not apply in Judge Alito's case" and that a week earlier "more than the requisite 60 senators had committed to opposing a filibuster."

[197] "The Filibuster That Wasn't," *The Washington Post*, February 5, 2006, p. B6.

[198] The wording of the question is dictated by Rule XXXI, paragraph 1, *Standing Rules of the Senate*, at http://rules.senate.gov/senaterules/rule31.php, which provides that "the final question on every nomination shall be, 'Will the Senate advise and consent to this nomination?"

[199] See CRS Report RL31980, *Senate Consideration of Presidential Nominations: Committee and Floor Procedure* (under heading "Consideration and Disposition"). This quorum requirement is derived from Article I, Section 5, Clause 1 of the Constitution, which states in part that "a Majority of each [House] shall constitute a Quorum to do Business...." Hence, the quorum for conducting business in a Senate of 100 Members is 51 Senators.

[200] See Table 2 in CRS Report RL33225, *Supreme Court Nominations, 1789 - 2010: Actions by the Senate, the Judiciary Committee, and the President*, by Denis Steven Rutkus and Maureen Bearden. The table breaks down numerically into four historical periods the 135 votes cast by the Senate, from 1789 to 2010, on whether to confirm particular Supreme Court nominees. The number of Senate votes within each historical period, in turn, is broken down according to whether they were voice votes or votes by unanimous consent on the one hand, or roll-call votes on the other.

[201] The most recent voice votes by the Senate on Supreme Court nominations were those confirming Abe Fortas in 1965 (to be an Associate Justice) and Arthur J. Goldberg and Byron R. White, both in 1962. Of the 135 Senate votes cast in all, from 1789 to 2010, on whether to confirm a Supreme Court nominee, 62 were done by roll-call votes, and the other 73 by voice votes or unanimous consent. See again Table 2 in CRS Report RL33225, *Supreme Court Nominations, 1789 - 2010: Actions by the Senate, the Judiciary Committee, and the President*, by Denis Steven Rutkus and Maureen Bearden.

[202] The closest roll calls ever cast on Supreme Court nominations were the 24-23 vote in 1881 confirming Stanley Matthews, the 25-26 vote in 1861 rejecting a motion to proceed to consider the nomination of Jeremiah S. Black, and the 26-25 Senate vote in 1853 to postpone consideration of the nomination of George E. Badger. Since the 1960s, the closest roll calls on Supreme Court nominations were the 52-48 vote in 1991 confirming Clarence Thomas, the 45-51 vote in 1970 rejecting G. Harrold Carswell, the 45-55 vote in 1969 rejecting Clement Haynsworth Jr., the 58-42 vote in 2006 confirming Samuel A. Alito Jr., the 42-58 vote in 1987 rejecting Robert H. Bork, the 63-37 vote in 2010 confirming Elena Kagan, and the 65-33 vote confirming William H. Rehnquist to be Chief Justice in 1986. Also noteworthy was the 45-43 vote in 1968 rejecting a

motion to end debate on the nomination of Abe Fortas to be Chief Justice; however, the roll call was not as close as the numbers by themselves suggested, since passage of the motion required a two-thirds vote of the Members present and voting. See Table 1 in CRS Report RL33225, *Supreme Court Nominations, 1789 - 2010: Actions by the Senate, the Judiciary Committee, and the President*, by Denis Steven Rutkus and Maureen Bearden.

[203] The most lopsided of these votes were the unanimous roll calls confirming Morrison R. Waite to be Chief Justice in 1874 (63-0), Harry A. Blackmun in 1970 (94-0), John Paul Stevens in 1975 (98-0), Sandra Day O'Connor in 1981 (99-0), Antonin Scalia in 1986 (98-0), and Anthony M. Kennedy in 1988 (97-0); and the near-unanimous votes confirming Noah H. Swayne in 1862 (38-1), Warren E. Burger in 1969 to be Chief Justice (74-3), Lewis F. Powell Jr. in 1971 (89-1), and Ruth Bader Ginsburg in 1993 (96-3). See again Table 1 in CRS Report RL33225, *Supreme Court Nominations, 1789 - 2009: Actions by the Senate, the Judiciary Committee, and the President*, by Denis Steven Rutkus and Maureen Bearden.

[204] The Senate confirmed the three most recent Supreme Court nominees—Samuel A. Alito Jr., Sonia Sotomayor, and Elena Kagan—by respective roll-call votes of 58-42, 68-31, and 63-37. In the much more distant past, the Senate confirmed two of President Andrew Jackson's nominees to the Court (Roger B. Taney to be Chief Justice in 1836 and John Catron in 1837) by comfortable vote margins; however, on both occasions more than one-third of the votes cast were against confirmation, with the Senate confirming Taney 29-15 and Catron 28-15.

[205] The seven most recent Senate confirmation votes on Supreme Court nominations were those for nominees Clarence Thomas in 1991, Ruth Bader Ginsburg in 1993, Stephen G. Breyer in 1994, John G. Roberts Jr. in 2005, Samuel A. Alito Jr. in 2006, Sonia Sotomayor in 2009, and Elena Kagan in 2010. In each instance, Senators remained at their desks during the calling of the roll.

[206] S.Res. 480, approved by the Senate on October 11, 1984, provided: "Resolved, That it is a standing order of the Senate that during yea and nay votes in the Senate, each Senator shall vote from the assigned desk of the Senator." See U.S. Congress, Senate, *Senate Manual Containing the Standing Rules, Orders, Laws , and Resolutions Affecting the Business of the United States Senate,* S. Doc. 107-1, 107th Cong., 1st sess. (Washington: GPO. 2002), p. 151.

[207] "Senators are required to vote from their desks, but this requirement rarely is enforced. On occasion, when a vote of special constitutional importance, such as a vote to convict in an impeachment trial, is about to begin, the majority leader will ask all Senators to come to the floor before the vote begins and then to vote from their desks...." CRS Report 96-452, *Voting and Quorum Procedures in the Senate*, by Betsy Palmer (under heading "Conducting Rollcall Votes").

[208] Immediately prior to the Senate's roll-call vote in 1994 on whether to confirm Stephen G. Breyer to be an Associate Justice, Majority Leader George J. Mitchell (D-ME) stated to his colleagues on the floor that "it has been the practice that votes on Supreme Court nominations are made from the Senator's desk. I ask that Senators cast their votes from their desks during this vote." *Congressional Record*, vol. 140, July 29, 1994, p. 18704. Again, in 2006, moments before the Senate's vote on nominee Samuel A. Alito Jr., the importance of a Supreme Court nomination was cited by the Senate's majority leader in applying the Senate rule that Members vote from their desks on a roll-call votes: "So, momentarily, we will vote from our desks, a time-honored tradition that demonstrates, once again, how important and consequential every Member takes his duty under the Constitution to provide advice and consent on a Supreme Court nomination and to give the nominee the fair up-or-down vote he deserves." Sen. Bill Frist, "Nomination of Judge Samuel Alito to the U.S. Supreme Court," remarks in the Senate, *Congressional Record,* daily edition, vol. 152, January 31, 2006, p. 348.

[209] "According to Senate Rule XXXI, any Senator who voted with the majority has the option of moving to reconsider a vote on the nomination. The motion to reconsider is in order on the day of the vote or the next two days the Senate meets in executive session. The motion is made in executive session or, by unanimous consent, 'as in executive session.'" CRS Report RL31980, *Senate Consideration of Presidential Nominations: Committee and Floor Procedure* (under subheading "Reconsideration").

[210] For example, immediately after the votes to confirm David Souter in 1990, Clarence Thomas in 1991, John G. Roberts Jr. in 2005, and Samuel A. Alito Jr. in 2006, a motion in each case was made to reconsider the vote, followed by a motion "to lay that motion on the table," which was agreed to without objection by the Senate. See *Congressional Record*, vol. 136, October 2, 1990, p. 26997; vol. 137, October 15, 1991, p. 26354; vol. 151 (daily edition), September 29, 2005, p. S10650; and vol. 152 (daily edition), January 31, 2006, p. S348. A slight variation of this procedure occurred in 2010, after the vote to confirm Elena Kagan, when the Senate's presiding officer, stated, "A motion to reconsider the vote is considered made and laid on the table." *Congressional Record*, daily edition, vol. 156, August 5, 2010. p. S6830.

[211] For example, by unanimous consent the Senate in 1993, 1994, and 2009 agreed that the motion to reconsider be tabled upon confirmation, respectively, of the Supreme Court nominations of Ruth Bader Ginsburg, Stephen G. Breyer, and Sonia Sotomayor. See "Unanimous-Consent Agreement," *Congressional Record*, vol. 139, July 30, 1993, p. 17996; "Unanimous-Consent Agreement," *Congressional Record*, vol. 140, July 28, 1994, p. 18544; and "Unanimous Consent Agreement—Executive Calendar," *Congressional Record*, daily edition, vol. 155, August 5, 2009, pp. S8887-S8888.

[212] CRS Report RL33225, *Supreme Court Nominations, 1789 - 2010: Actions by the Senate, the Judiciary Committee, and the President*, by Denis Steven Rutkus and Maureen Bearden (under heading "Final Action by the Senate or the President").

[213] CRS Report RL31171, *Supreme Court Nominations Not Confirmed, 1789-August 2010* (under heading "Summary of Unsuccessful Nominations"). The six individuals who were confirmed after being re-nominated, it will be recalled (from "Background" section, above), were William Paterson (1793). Roger B. Taney (1835), Stanley Matthews (1881), Pierce Butler (1922), John W. Harlan II (1954-1955), and John G. Roberts Jr. (2005).

[214] A more detailed table about each unsuccessful Supreme Court nomination is available in CRS Report RL31171, *Supreme Court Nominations Not Confirmed, 1789-August 2010*. Specifically, Table 4 in that report provides, for each unconfirmed Supreme Court nomination, the dates of relevant activity and votes in the Judiciary Committee as well as in the full Senate.

[215] See section in CRS Report RL31171, *Supreme Court Nominations Not Confirmed, 1789-August2010* (under heading "Factors Behind Unsuccessful Nominations").

[216] For a lengthy bibliographic listing of scholarly sources that deal directly with the factors associated with unsuccessful Supreme Court nominations, see Massaro, *Supremely Political*, p. 218, n. 4.

[217] Abraham, *Justices, Presidents and Senators*, p. 28. Abraham's book, it should be noted, predates the unsuccessful nomination of Harriet E. Miers to the Court in 2005. For a discussion of factors that appeared to contribute to the failure of the Miers nomination to be confirmed, see CRS Report RL31171, *Supreme Court Nominations Not Confirmed, 1789-August2010* (under heading "Application of the Factors to the Miers Nomination") and Greenburg, *Supreme Conflict*, pp. 277-282.

[218] Massaro, *Supremely Political*, p. xi.

[219] Massaro, in *Supremely Political*, p. 139, wrote that a nomination made "during the last full year of a president's term or in the interregnum period after a new chief executive has been elected presents an additional factor upon which to base opposition to confirmation." The vacancy's "unfavorable timing," he explained, can "generate opposition of its own as well as activate the otherwise dormant ideological resistance, significantly increasing the likelihood of the Senate's refusal to confirm. This is readily seen in the remarkably high refusal rate of seventy-one percent (ten of fourteen) for such nominations when they are also forwarded to a Senate in which the chief executive's party is in the minority."

[220] The Fortas, Haynsworth, Carswell, and Bork nominations, one scholar wrote, were all instances in which Presidents failed to give enough care to presidential management of the confirmation process. In the cases of the Fortas, Haynsworth and Carswell nominations, he wrote, opposition was "needlessly increased" when Presidents, without ensuring that "positive relationships with senators" were maintained, nominated individuals who were "vulnerable to non-ideological, non-partisan charges." Massaro, *Supremely Political*, pp. 140-142. In nominating Robert H. Bork, President Reagan, according to the author, fell short in exercising presidential management by failing to anticipate potential opposition in the Senate to a "controversial individual" at "a time demanding a careful and conciliatory course." Ibid., p. 190.
For a contrasting criticism of the Reagan Administration's strategy for the Bork nomination (one not faulting President Reagan for the fact that he chose, in Bork, a highly controversial nominee), see Greenburg, *Supreme Conflict*, who, at p. 50, wrote that the Reagan White House "never developed a strategy to sell Robert Bork to the senators and the American people" and "inexplicably chose not to defend Bork's constitutional approach to the law" or to launch the "ideological battle" that "many conservatives wanted to have." The result, according to Greenburg, was that Bork opponents "were able to define the nominee as a Stone Age extremist who would turn the clock back on civil rights for women and minorities."

[221] Besides the successful attempts in the Senate to recommit the nominations of George H. Williams as Chief Justice in 1873 and Harlan F. Stone as Associate Justice in 1925 (both discussed in this chapter), six other unsuccessful attempts to recommit Supreme Court nominations were recorded—specifically, the motions to recommit President Ulysses S. Grant's nomination of Joseph P. Bradley in 1870, President Warren G. Harding's nomination of Pierce Butler in 1922, President Herbert Hoover's nomination of Charles Evans Hughes as Chief Justice in 1930, President Franklin D. Roosevelt's nomination of Hugo L. Black in 1937, President Harry S. Truman's nomination of Sherman Minton in 1949, and President Richard M. Nixon's nomination of G. Harrold Carswell in 1970. *Congressional Quarterly Almanac, 1970*, vol. 26 (Washington: Congressional Quarterly, Inc., 1971), p. 161.

[222] U.S. Congress, Senate, *Journal of the Executive Proceedings of the Senate of the United States of America*, vol. 19 (Washington: GPO, 1901), p. 189. (Hereafter cited as *Senate Executive Journal.*)

[223] Jacobstein and Mersky, *The Rejected*, p. 86.

[224] *Senate Executive Journal*, vol. 19, p. 189.

[225] See, e.g., "The Chief Justiceship," *New York Tribune*, January 6, 1874, p. 1, which reported that the President "has at last discovered that the nomination of Mr. Williams to be Chief-Justice of the Supreme Court is not only a very unpopular one, but that his confirmation will be impossible...." See also Jacobstein and Mersky, *The Rejected*, pp. 84-86.

[226] *Senate Executive Journal*, vol. 19, p. 211.

[227] Abraham, *Justices, Presidents and Senators*, p. 147.

[228] Thorpe, *Appearance of Supreme Court Nominees*, p. 372.

[229] *Senate Executive Journal*, vol. 63, p. 293.

[230] Thorpe, *Appearance of Supreme Court Nominees*, pp. 372-373.

[231] Abraham, *Justices, Presidents and Senators*, p. 147.

[232] In October 8, 1991, floor remarks, Senate Majority Leader George J. Mitchell (D-ME) explained the need to delay the Thomas vote: "It is most unfortunate that we have been placed in this situation. But events which are unpredictable, unplanned, and unfortunate can and frequently do intervene and cause a change in the plans of human beings. That has now occurred in this matter, in my judgment.

"For that reason, I believe the action we have taken to change the time of the scheduled vote until next Tuesday [October 15], and to give time for further inquiry into this matter by the Judiciary Committee, is an appropriate action." Sen. George J. Mitchell, "Unanimous Consent Agreement," remarks in the Senate, *Congressional Record*, vol, 137, October 8, 1991, p. 25920.

[233] If, on the other hand, the Senate votes against confirmation, a resolution of disapproval is forwarded to the President.

[234] Sheldon Goldman, *Picking Federal Judges; Lower Court Selection form Roosevelt Through Reagan* (New Haven, CT: Yale University Press, 1997), p. 12.

[235] Sometimes, the swearing into office occurs before the new Justice actually receives the commission document. This, for instance, happened in 2005 with Chief Justice appointee John G. Roberts Jr. Immediately after President George W. Bush signed Roberts's commission, the new Chief Justice was sworn into office—receiving his commission document afterwards, when the Justice Department arranged for it to be hand-delivered to him at the Court.

[236] The Court itself regards the date a Justice takes the judicial oath as the beginning of his or her service, "for until that oath is taken he/she is not vested with the prerogatives of the office." Supreme Court, *Supreme Court of the United States*, p. 23.

[237] A news account noted the relatively recent advent of this pattern, when Justice Ruth Bader Ginsburg, on August 10, 1993, took her two oaths—the judicial oath, in private ceremony in the Court's conference room, and the constitutional oath, in a nationally televised ceremony in the White House's East Room. "Supreme Court appointees," the article observed, "always have taken both oaths, but only since 1986, when Ronald Reagan held a ceremony for the investiture of Associate Justice Antonin Scalia and Rehnquist, has the constitutional oath become part of a White House ceremony." Joan Biskupic, "Ginsburg Sworn In as 107th Justice and 2nd Woman on Supreme Court," *The Washington Post*, August 11, 1993, p. A6.

After Justice Ginsburg's appointment, the next three Court appointees took the judicial oath in private (though each in a different setting) and the constitutional oath in public (all at the White House). The judicial oath was administered to Stephen G. Breyer in private in 1994 by Chief Justice William H. Rehnquist at the latter's vacation home in Greensboro, VT; to John G. Roberts Jr. in a private ceremony at the White House by Justice John Paul Stevens; and to Samuel A. Alito Jr. in private at the Supreme Court's conference room in 2006 by Chief Justice Roberts. On the same occasions that they took their judicial oaths in private, Roberts and Alito took their constitutional oaths as well—while, however, also taking their constitutional oaths a second time, in televised White House ceremonies.

[238] Amy Goldstein, "Sotomayor Reaches Pinnacle of Law with Historic Oath," *The Washington Post*, August 9, 2009, p. A3. Chief Justice John G. Roberts Jr., a Court news release specified, would administer both the constitutional oath, "in a private ceremony in the Justices' Conference Room attended by members of the Sotomayor family," and the judicial oath, in the Court's East Conference Room " before a small gathering of Judge Sotomayor's family and friends," Untitled Press Release, August 6, 2009, Supreme Court of the United States, at http://www.supremecourtus.gov. The press release specified that the Court would allow televising of the latter ceremony by "pool coverage." See also Charlie Savage, "Sotomayor, After a Pair of Oaths, Officially Joins the Nation's Hghest Court, *The New York Times*, August 9, 2009, p. 10.

[239] Tony Mauro, "In Divided Vote, Senate Confirms Sotomayor for High Court," *The National Law Journal*, August 7, 2009, at http://www.law.com. Three days later, Mauro reported that "[a]t least one of the oaths taken by every current justice from Clarence Thomas on has been televised, but those events took place at the White House, not the Court. A White House source indicated Friday [August 7] that notwithstanding that practice, President Barack Obama made it clear from the start that, out of respect for the Court's independence, the entire ceremony should be at the Court, not the White House. As *The National Law Journal* reported last week, that's likely to be welcome news at the Court, where justices over the years have disapproved of White House oath-taking." Tony Mauro, "Cameras Come to the Supreme Court—in HD, No Less," August 10, 2009, *The National Law Journal*, at http://www.law.com.

[240] On August 7, 2010, Justice Kagan "was administered two oaths: the first, the Constitutional Oath in the Justice's Conference room, was attended by members of the Kagan family and several Jsutices; the second, the Judicial Oath, was in the West Conferenc Room before a small gathering of family and friends." "Swearing-In Ceremony for Kagan," *The Third Branch*, vol. 42, August 2010, p. 1.

[241] See, for example, Linda Greenhouse, "A Ceremonial Start to the Session as the Supreme Court Welcomes a New Chief Justice," *The New York Times*, October 4, 2005, p. 25.

[242] The investiture ceremony for newly appointed Justice Elena Kagan is scheduled to take place in the Supreme Court's courtroom on October 1, 2010, three days before the start of the Court's new term, on Monday, October 4.

The September 8, 2009 investiture for Justice Sonia Sotomayor, "marked the first time she joined her eight colleagues in the court's historic chambers.... " Robert Barnes, "Sotomayor Officially Takes Her Place on Supreme Court," *The Boston Globe*, September 9, 2009, p. 12. The event occurred a day before Justice Sotomayor and her eight colleagues were scheduled to hear oral arguments in an unusual summer session of the Court. See Adam Liptak, "The Newest Justice Takes Her Seat," *The New York Times*, September 9, 2009, p. 12.

Justice Samuel A. Alito Jr., who initially took his judicial and constitutional oaths of office on January 31, 2006, had "already been on the job two weeks and been sworn in twice" before his investiture on the Court on February 16, 2006, at which he "joined colleagues in the courtroom for the first time." Gina Holland, Associated Press, "New Justice Samuel Alito Welcomed at Supreme Court," *San Diego Union-Tribune*, February 16, 2006, at http://www.signonsandiego.com.

[243] See Table 1 in CRS Report RL33225, *Supreme Court Nominations, 1789 - 2010: Actions by the Senate, the Judiciary Committee, and the President*, by Denis Steven Rutkus and Maureen Bearden. The end of the table lists, for three time periods (1789-2009, 1789-1966, and 1967-2010), the median number of days from the date nominations were received in the Senate until the date that they received final action by the Senate or the President. The table also shows the length of this same time interval for individual Supreme Court nominations. For instance, it shows that for the three most recent nominees—Samuel A. Alito Jr., Sonia Sotomayor, and Elena Kagan—82, 66, and 87 days respectively elapsed between Senate receipt of their nominations and confirmation by the Senate.

In: Supreme Court Appointments and Nominations
Editor: Edward P. Bennett
ISBN: 978-1-61209-249-2

Chapter 2

SPEED OF PRESIDENTIAL AND SENATE ACTIONS ON SUPREME COURT NOMINATIONS, 1900-2010

R. Sam Garrett and Denis Steven Rutkus

SUMMARY

The speed with which appointments to the Supreme Court move through various stages in the nomination-and-confirmation process is often of great interest not only to all parties directly involved, but, as well, to the nation as a whole. This chapter provides information on the amount of time taken to act on all Supreme Court nominations occurring between 1900 and the present. It focuses on the *actual* amounts of time that Presidents and the Senate have taken to act (as opposed to the elapsed time between *official* points in the process). For example, rather than starting the nomination clock with the official notification of the President of a forthcoming vacancy, this chapter focuses on when the President first *learned* of a Justice's intention to leave the Court (e.g., via a private conversation with the outgoing Justice), or received word that a sitting Justice had died. Likewise, rather than starting the confirmation clock with the transmission of the official nomination to the Senate, this chapter focuses on when the Senate *became aware* of the President's selection (e.g., via a public announcement by the President).

The data indicate that the entire nomination-and-confirmation process (from when the President first learned of a vacancy to final Senate action) has generally taken almost twice as long for nominees after 1980 than for nominees in the previous 80 years. From 1900 to 1980, the entire process took a median of 59 days; from 1981 through 2010, the process took a median of 113 days. Although Presidents after 1980 have moved more quickly than their predecessors in announcing nominees after learning of vacancies (a median of 19.5 days compared with 34 days before 1980), the Senate portion of the process (i.e., from the nomination announcement to final Senate action) appears to take much longer than before (a median of 84 days from 1981 through 2009, compared with 17 days from 1900 through 1980). Notably, the amount of time between the nomination announcement and first Judiciary

Committee hearing has almost quadrupled—from a median of 12.5 days (1900-1980) to 49 days (1981-2010).

President Obama learned of another prospective vacancy on April 9, 2010. On May 10, 2010, President Obama announced he would nominate Solicitor General Elena Kagan to succeed Justice John Paul Stevens. From June 30 to July 1, 2010, the Senate Judiciary Committee held four days of hearings on the nomination, and on July 20, voted 13-6 to report the nomination to the Senate. On August 3, 2010, the Senate began its consideration of the nomination. The Senate confirmed Kagan as the nation's 112th Supreme Court Justice on August 5 by a 63-37 vote. The overall time for the Kagan appointment process was slightly longer than for other recent nominations. The entire period for presidential selection and Senate consideration and action on the 2009 Sonia Sotomayor nomination, for example, lasted 97 days, compared with 118 days for the Kagan nomination. Nonetheless, although the Kagan nomination took longer to move through the process than did the Sotomayor nomination, the total Kagan timetable was similar to those of other nominations since 1981. In fact, including the Kagan timetable data raised the median number of days for the entire process by only a day and a half—to 113 days, compared with 111.5 days for all Supreme Court nominations between 1981 and 2009.

Introduction

The nomination and confirmation of a Chief Justice or an Associate Justice to the U.S. Supreme Court is an infrequent event of major significance in American public life. To receive what may be lifetime appointment to the Court, a candidate must first be nominated by the President and then confirmed by the Senate. Midway in the appointment process, intensive hearings on a Supreme Court nomination, often taking at least three or four days, are routinely held by the Senate Judiciary Committee, which then can vote on whether to report the nomination to the Senate with a favorable recommendation.

Nominating and confirming Supreme Court Justices is an interdependent process. Neither the President nor the Senate acts alone. The decisions that each branch makes determine how quickly nominations are made and considered, and whether the nomination is successful. This chapter provides information on the pace of all Supreme Court nominations and confirmations since 1900, focusing on the *actual* amounts of time that Presidents and the Senate have taken to act (as opposed to the elapsed time between *official* points in the process).[1] As discussed below, the speed with which the President makes Supreme Court nominations and the Senate acts on those nominations has been of continuing concern to Congress in recent years.[2] Especially since 2005, a high priority has been assigned to making appointments according to timetables designed to assure that vacancies taking effect while the Court is in summer recess are filled in time for the nine-member Court to be at full strength when it convenes its next annual term.

RECENT NOMINATIONS ACTIVITY

Activity During 2010

On April 9, 2010, Associate Justice John Paul Stevens wrote to President Obama that he would retire from "regular active service" when the Court recesses for the summer.[3] Speculation about the retirement had been reported in the media for weeks, but even days before writing to President Obama Stevens' plans remained at least publicly unknown.[4] According to one media account, Stevens' letter arrived at the White House at 10:30 a.m. on April 9. White House counsel Robert Bauer then notified the President, who was traveling aboard Air Force One.[5]

Almost immediately, the President, Members of Congress, and members of the media began to comment on a potential schedule for considering Justice Stevens' replacement. In fact, the retirement letter itself referenced time concerns. Justice Stevens wrote he had concluded that "it would be in the best interests of the Court to have my successor appointed and confirmed well in advance of the commencement of the Court's next Term" in October 2010.[6] President Obama also expressed his desire for a new Justice to be seated by the start of the fall term, saying that he would "move quickly to name a new nominee." He also urged the Senate to "move quickly in the coming weeks to debate and then confirm my nominee so that a new Justice is seated in time for the fall term."[7] Senator Patrick Leahy, Chairman of the Judiciary Committee, has predicted that the new Supreme Court Justice would be confirmed by the Senate's August 2010 recess and said that there is "no question" that a nominee would be confirmed by the start of Court's fall term.[8]

On May 10, 2010, President Obama announced that he had selected Solicitor General Elena Kagan as his nominee to replace Justice Stevens. At that time, the President reiterated his call for quick action on the nomination, saying, "I hope that the Senate will act in a bipartisan fashion ... and that they will do so as swiftly as possible, so she can get busy and take her seat in time to fully participate in the work of the Court this fall."[9] Senator Leahy subsequently announced, on May 19, 2010, that Ms. Kagan's confirmation hearings would begin on June 28, 2010. Calling that timetable "a reasonable schedule that is in line with past practice," Senator Leahy noted that the Sotomayor confirmation hearings had begun 48 days after her nomination was announced (as noted in **Table 2** at the end of this chapter).[10] That schedule proceeded as expected. Forty-nine days elapsed between the May 10 announcement of the Kagan nomination and the start of hearings on June 28. Both time spans (49 and 48 days respectively for the Kagan and Sotomayor nominations) are close to or at the median 49 days that elapsed between the nomination announcement and the start of hearings for all Supreme Court nominees between 1981 and 2010. **Figure 1** and discussion in the rest of this chapter provide additional detail.

The entire Kagan appointment process, starting with when President Obama first learned that Justice Stevens would leave the Court, until Senate confirmation on August 5, lasted 118 days. This interval was relatively close to, but longer than, the median duration of 113 days of the entire appointment process for Court nominations which received final Senate action during the 1981-2010 period.

Some individual phases of the Kagan appointment process took longer than the corresponding intervals for previous Supreme Court nominations. One such phase, for example, is the time interval between final committee action and final Senate action. Sixteen days elapsed between final Judiciary Committee action on July 20, when the committee favorably reported the nomination, and August 5, when the Senate confirmed Kagan. That 16-day interval was almost twice the nine-day median elapsed time between final committee and final Senate actions on Supreme Court nominations between 1981 and 2010. In a few relatively recent instances, however, the full Senate has taken much longer to act on a reported Court nomination than it did with the Kagan nomination. Specifically, the Senate took 34 days to vote on the Rehnquist Chief Justice and the Scalia Associate Justice nominations in 1986. Overall, it took longer to announce and consider the Kagan nomination than any since Ruth Bader Ginsburg's in 1993. Although the Kagan appointment process lasted 118 days, then-Judge Ginsburg's lasted 137. The timetable for selecting and considering the Kagan nomination stretched 21 days beyond what was required for then-Judge Sotomayer's nomination in 2009. Timetables for action on Supreme Court nominations are affected by the selection process, the Senate schedule, and other factors. For any given nomination, the Senate may, of course, proceed at any pace it deems appropriate.

Activity During 2009

Before the Stevens announcement, the Senate most recently considered a Supreme Court nomination during the spring and summer of 2009. On May 1, 2009, President Barack Obama announced that Justice David H. Souter intended to retire when the Court recessed for the summer. During his brief appearance at a White House press briefing on May 1, the President expressed the "hope that we can swear in our new Supreme Court Justice in time for him or her to be seated by the first Monday in October when the Court's new term begins."[11]

On May 26, 2009, President Obama announced his intention to nominate Sonia Sotomayor, then a judge on the U.S. Court of Appeals for the Second Circuit, to the Souter seat. Shortly thereafter, discussion of various timetables began to emerge. The President and some Senate Democrats expressed the hope that the Senate would vote to confirm Judge Sotomayor before the Senate's August 2009 recess, in order to afford time for her to prepare for the start of the Court's term in October. Some Senate Republicans, however, were less supportive of a Senate vote before September, saying they wished to have as much time to examine the Sotomayor nomination as Senate Democrats were given in 2005-2006 for the Supreme Court nominations of Samuel A. Alito, Jr. and John G. Roberts, Jr.[12]

The Senate Judiciary Committee began hearings on the Sotomayor nomination on July 13, 2009, and favorably reported it (by a vote of 13-6) on July 28. The Senate confirmed Sotomayor (68-31) on August 8, 2009—the same day the new Justice took the constitutional and judicial oaths of office.[13]

Activity During 2005-2006

Late 2005 and early 2006 marked a period of transition among Supreme Court Justices. Associate Justice Sandra Day O'Connor's July 2005 retirement announcement marked the first pending Court vacancy since 1994. Within a few months, however, the Senate considered three nominations. As is discussed below, Judge John G. Roberts, Jr. was initially nominated to replace O'Connor, but that nomination was withdrawn when Chief Justice William H. Rehnquist died in early September. The Roberts nomination was withdrawn and re-submitted for the Chief Justice vacancy. The Senate confirmed Roberts in September 2005. Then-White House Counsel Harriet Miers was initially nominated to fill the again-pending O'Connor vacancy, but the Miers nomination was eventually withdrawn. Judge Samuel A. Alito, Jr. was confirmed to the O'Connor seat in January 2006.

As is noted throughout this chapter, media accounts and other research suggest that when these and other Court vacancies arise, the President, members of the Senate, and their staffs, can begin work on nominations immediately, even if official nominations are days or weeks away. Particularly when multiple vacancies occur in close succession or simultaneously, as they did in 2005, the President and the Senate might have different preferences about how quickly new nominees should be considered. Until 1980, the President often took longer to announce a nominee than the Senate did to take final action on nominees. By contrast, since 1981, Presidents have been quicker to announce nominations than the Senate has been to confirm or reject those nominations. The President and members of the Senate (especially the Judiciary Committee) each proposed their own timetables regarding the Roberts, Miers, and Alito nominations. The following discussion provides additional details.

The Roberts Nomination

On July 1, 2005, Associate Justice Sandra Day O'Connor surprised many in official Washington, and possibly President George W. Bush, with a one-paragraph letter announcing her retirement from the Supreme Court, effective upon the confirmation of her successor.[14] Her announcement created the first vacancy on the Court in 11 years. The Court had just concluded its 2004-2005 term, and the opening session of the Court's next term, on October 3, 2005, was three months away. Finding a new Associate Justice took on added urgency, given the failing health of then-Chief Justice William H. Rehnquist. Departure of the Chief Justice as well as Justice O'Connor could result in the need for two Court appointments, and create the possibility of at least one vacancy on the Court when it reconvened in October— unless the new appointments were made expeditiously.

Hours after Justice O'Connor announced her retirement, a senior aide to Senate Majority Leader Bill Frist told reporters that, "Our goal is to have the court back at full strength by the first Monday in October." Senate Judiciary Committee staff were reportedly "poised to begin reviewing background materials" on potential nominees.[15] Nevertheless, appointment of a new Justice in time for the Court's opening session seemed like a challenging goal. In recent years, the Senate Judiciary Committee, and the full Senate as well, had been embroiled in controversies over some of the President's nominations to the lower federal courts. Continued controversy seemed likely surrounding any future nominations to the Supreme Court.

On July 19, 2005, 18 days after receiving Justice O'Connor's retirement letter, President Bush announced his selection of John G. Roberts, Jr., a federal appellate judge, to be the next

Associate Justice. Ten days later, on July 29, the President formally nominated Judge Roberts to the Court, with the nomination document immediately transmitted to the Senate, where it was referred to the Senate Judiciary Committee. Hearings on this nomination were scheduled to begin September 6, but those hearings would never take place.

When Chief Justice William H. Rehnquist died on September 3, Judge Roberts became the first Supreme Court nominee to be withdrawn by the President for one seat on the Court and renominated for another. The Senate Judiciary Committee quickly cancelled its Associate Justice hearings, and began Roberts's Chief Justice hearings on September 12, 2005. After receiving a favorable 13-5 vote by the Judiciary Committee on September 22, the nomination of Judge Roberts to be Chief Justice was confirmed by the Senate on the morning of September 29, 2005, by a 78-22 vote. Later that day, the confirmed nominee took both his constitutional and judicial oaths of office at the White House.[16]

Due to the speed with which Judge Roberts was nominated to be Chief Justice and considered by the Senate Judiciary Committee and the full Senate, his appointment was completed in time for the Court to be at full strength at the start of its 2005-2006 term. With the start of that term, Justice O'Connor remained on the Court, in keeping with the intention stated in her retirement letter of stepping down only upon the confirmation of her successor. For his part, President Bush had declined to name a replacement for John Roberts to succeed Sandra Day O'Connor prior to the Senate vote on September 29 confirming Judge Roberts as Chief Justice.

The Miers Nomination

On October 3, 2005, President Bush announced his nomination of White House Counsel Harriet E. Miers to succeed Sandra Day O'Connor as Associate Justice on the Supreme Court. The President said that the Senate had shown during the confirmation of Chief Justice Roberts that it could act promptly, and called upon the Senate to "review [Miers's] qualifications thoroughly and fairly and to vote on her nomination promptly."[17] At a press conference the next day, the President said that he expected the Senate "to hold an up-or-down vote on Harriet's nomination by Thanksgiving" (i.e., by November 24, 2005).[18] Similarly, Senate Majority Leader Bill Frist called on his colleagues to move "expeditiously but carefully," and encouraged a floor vote "by Thanksgiving."[19] Several news reports suggested that confirmation hearings could begin as early as November 7, 2005. Senator Arlen Specter, Chairman of the Senate Judiciary Committee, reportedly told reporters that he hoped the committee would complete hearings by Thanksgiving,[20] but also reportedly emphasized that "thoroughness will be the objective," as opposed to meeting a particular timetable.[21] He also reportedly said that the timing of hearings on the nomination would in part be up to Miers, who would have to study "so that she would have the grasp of these very complex decisions."[22]

On October 27, 2005, Miers delivered a letter to the President withdrawing her nomination as Associate Justice, and the President "reluctantly accepted" her withdrawal.[23] Both Miers and the President indicated that the action was precipitated by the Senate's request for documents about her service in the White House. However, others suggested that other factors may have been involved.[24] In his statement accepting the withdrawal, the President said that he expected to fill the vacancy "in a timely manner."

The Alito Nomination

Four days after Harriet Miers's withdrawal, on October 31, 2005, President George W. Bush announced his nomination of Samuel A. Alito, Jr., a judge on the U.S. Court of Appeals for the Third Circuit, to replace Justice O'Connor. President Bush called on the Senate to "act promptly on this important nomination so that an up or down vote is held before the end of this year."[25] Senate Majority Leader Bill Frist also predicted a relatively quick timetable for Senate consideration,[26] but other Senators, including Minority Leader Harry Reid, suggested that Senate consideration of the nomination could last into the new year.[27]

On November 3, 2005, Senate Judiciary Committee Chairman Arlen Specter and Ranking Minority Member Patrick Leahy announced that confirmation hearings on Judge Alito's nomination would not begin until January 9, 2006, with a vote by the committee scheduled for January 17, 2006, after five days of hearings. They said that the full Senate would vote on the nomination on January 20, 2006.[28] Judiciary Committee hearings on the Alito nomination began and concluded as scheduled, although a targeted January 17 committee vote was postponed until January 24, 2006. A final floor vote was anticipated before President George W. Bush's January 31, 2006, State of the Union address.[29] After Senators Specter and Leahy reportedly reached agreement on the revised committee schedule over the January 14-16 weekend, Majority Leader Bill Frist announced that "as soon as the Judiciary Committee reports the nomination, the full Senate will begin debate on Judge Alito the next day and move swiftly to a fair up-or-down vote."[30] In a 10-8 party line vote, the Senate Judiciary Committee on January 24 reported Alito's nomination to the full Senate, which confirmed Alito, 58-42, on January 31, 2006.

MEASURING THE PACE OF SUPREME COURT APPOINTMENTS

For many Supreme Court appointments, the timing of individual events is determined by the decisions of various key players—by sitting Justices planning to leave the Court; by the President, who selects nominees to fill Court vacancies; and by Senate committee and party leaders, who respectively schedule committee and floor action on Supreme Court nominations. First, Justices who retire or resign from the Court must decide whether to provide the President with advance notice of that decision. For example, Justice Harry A. Blackmun told President William J. Clinton of his decision to retire in 1994, more than four months before the decision became public on April 6 of that year.[31] Justice O'Connor, on the other hand, did not appear to have given President George W. Bush any advance notice when she resigned on July 1, 2005. Also, the mode of presidential notification varies. While President Clinton learned of Justice Blackmun's plans to retire through an informal conversation, Justice O'Connor apparently notified President Bush of her decision through a formal letter.

Once the President chooses a nominee, he alerts the Senate—by public announcement as well as by formal transmission of a written nomination to the Senate. Frequently, the President will announce and formally nominate his Supreme Court choice on the same day, or take both actions within a few days of each other. Less commonly, Presidents announce their intention to nominate a candidate, then make the official nomination a week or more later. The most extreme case of the latter involved President Ronald Reagan in 1981. On July 7 of that year, President Reagan announced he would send the nomination of Sandra Day O'Connor, then an Arizona state appeals court judge, to the Senate "upon completion of all the necessary checks by the Federal Bureau of Investigation."[32] However, it was not until almost six weeks later, on August 19, that Judge O'Connor was officially nominated.[33] As noted above, after the Senate receives a Supreme Court nomination, the Judiciary Committee normally holds hearings, followed by final committee action, and consideration before the full chamber.

Official and Unofficial Timetables

The measurement of how long the President and the Senate take to execute their *official* duties surrounding Supreme Court nominations necessarily focuses on official dates of action taken. The most important of these action dates include those on which (1) an outgoing Justice officially informs the President of the intention to step down from the Court (or, alternatively, the date on which a Court seat is vacated due to the death of a Justice), (2) a President formally nominates someone to the Court, the Senate receives the President's nomination, and the nomination is referred to the Senate Judiciary Committee (almost always all on the same date),[34] (3) the Senate Judiciary Committee holds hearings on the nomination, (4) the committee votes on the nomination, and (5) the Senate votes on whether to confirm, or chooses to take no action.

In addition to these dates, however, the President and the Senate usually consider Supreme Court nominations outside official timetables. Just as the President can begin considering a new nominee as soon as he knows a vacancy will arise, the Senate can begin preparing to consider a nominee as soon as the President announces his choice, even if the receipt of the formal nomination is still days or weeks away. Fundamentally, nominations and confirmations to the Supreme Court involve both formal and informal decisions. While formal decisions are easily accessible in historical records, informal decisions—sparsely mentioned in the formal record, or not mentioned at all—might, in many cases, provide better insight into how long the process truly takes.

Objectives of This Chapter

This chapter explores the speed of presidential and Senate decision-making surrounding nominations to the Supreme Court from 1900 to the present. The analysis concentrates on the period 1900-2010: (1) relevant historical data for this period are much more readily available and reliable than for earlier Court appointments,[35] and (2) public confirmation hearings for Supreme Court nominations before the Senate Judiciary Committee—an important phase in the Supreme Court appointment process, and one of particular interest to this chapter—were unheard of before the 20th century.[36]

Although research on Supreme Court nominations often focuses on either presidential or Senate decision-making, this analysis considers the time *both* institutions take to make decisions about, and act on, nominees. The report also takes a unique approach in discussing—as well as can be determined—how long Presidents *actually* take to decide who their nominees will be, and how long the Senate *actually* takes to act on nominations. For example, rather than starting the nomination clock with the official notification of the President of a forthcoming vacancy (e.g., the receipt of a formal retirement letter), this analysis focuses on when the President first *learned* of the vacancy (e.g., a private conversation with the outgoing Justice). Likewise, rather than starting the confirmation clock with the transmission the official nomination to the Senate, this analysis focuses on when the Senate became aware of the President's selection (e.g., by a public announcement by the President).

In many cases, establishing precisely when a President knew that he would have the opportunity to make a Supreme Court nomination is impossible. Such information might never have been recorded or known by anyone except the President and his inner circle. However, historical research reveals several instances when a President had advance knowledge of an impending vacancy, well before the public announcement of a Justice's intention to leave the Court. Data sources used to determine when Presidents first knew of vacancies included historical newspapers, official documents such as public presidential papers (which contain Justices' retirement letters to various Presidents), and CRS consultations with presidential libraries.[37] Dates cited throughout this chapter and in **Table 1**, **Table 2**, and **Table 3**, at the end of the report, are based on that research.

The dates and intervals presented here may differ from those in other sources, such as media reports or even Congressional figures. In general, earlier starting dates and longer durations between dates presented here are likely due to this chapter's emphasis on when the President *first* learned of an opportunity to make a nomination and when the Senate *first* learned of an opportunity to act on a nomination—regardless of official timetables. In addition, events such as withdrawals, rejected nominations, and recess appointments can uniquely affect calculating intervals in the nomination and confirmation process. The tables and accompanying notes show which dates were selected to start and stop the nominations clock in these cases. Different methodologies could yield different results. This chapter takes no position on the appropriateness of other methodologies, and contrasting this chapter's methodology with alternatives is beyond the scope of the report.

How Supreme Court Vacancies Occur

The need for a new appointment to the Court arises when a Justice position becomes vacant, due to death, retirement, or resignation, or when a Justice announces his intention to retire or resign. If the vacated seat is that of the Chief Justice, the President, if he chooses, may nominate a sitting Associate Justice to be Chief, thus setting the stage for the creation of an Associate Justice vacancy as well. Vacancies on the Court also will occur if Justices resign to receive new government appointments or to seek new government positions. When a nomination fails in the Senate, the President must select a new nominee (unless the President chooses to re-nominate his first choice).

Death of a Sitting Justice

Supreme Court Justices receive what may be lifetime appointments, "good Behaviour" being the only constitutionally specified requirement for continued service.[38] Lifetime tenure, interesting work, and the prestige of the office result in Justices often choosing to serve as long as possible. Historically, a number of Justices have died in office. Most recently, Chief Justice William H. Rehnquist died on September 3, 2005, after battling thyroid cancer for almost a year. Death in office was common on the Court during the first half of the 20th century—14 of 34 vacancies between 1900-1950. In fact, all five Court vacancies occurring between 1946 and 1954 were due to death of a sitting Justice (see **Table 1**). Of the 23 vacancies since 1954, though, no Justice had died while still on the Court until Chief Justice Rehnquist in 2005.

Retirement or Resignation of a Sitting Justice

Since 1954, retirement has been by far the most common way in which Justices have left the bench (19 of 23 vacancies occurring after 1954 resulted from retirements). Resignation (i.e., leaving the bench before becoming eligible for retirement compensation) is rare.[39] In recent history, two Justices have resigned from the Court. Justice Arthur Goldberg resigned in 1965 to assume the post of U.S. Ambassador to the United Nations.[40] Justice Abe Fortas resigned in 1969 after protracted criticism over controversial consulting work while on the bench and a failed nomination to be elevated from Associate Justice to Chief Justice.[41] When Justices retire or resign, the President is usually notified by formal letter. As noted previously, there is evidence in a few cases that a President informally learned of a forthcoming retirement in advance.

Pursuant to a law enacted in 1939, a Justice (or any other federal judge receiving lifetime appointment) may also retire if "unable because of permanent disability to perform the duties of his office," by furnishing the President a certificate of disability.[42] Prior to 1939, specific legislation from Congress was required to provide retirement benefits to a Justice departing the Court because of disability who otherwise would be ineligible for such benefits, due to insufficient age and length of service. In such circumstances in 1910, for instance, Congress took legislative action granting a pension to Justice William H. Moody. As the *Washington Post* reported at the time, although illness had kept Justice Moody from the bench for "almost a year," he was not yet eligible for retirement.[43]

Nomination of a Sitting Justice to Another Position

When a Chief Justice vacancy arises, the President may choose to nominate a sitting Associate Justice for the Court's top post. If the Chief Justice nominee is confirmed, he or she must, to assume the new position, resign as Associate Justice, requiring a new nominee from the President to fill the newly vacated Associate Justice seat. However, this scenario is relatively rare. During the 1900-2009 period, Presidents attempted to elevate Associate Justices to Chief Justice four times, with the Senate confirming three nominees. Most recently, in 1986, President Ronald Reagan nominated then-Associate Justice William H. Rehnquist to be Chief Justice.[44]

Presidents may also nominate sitting Justices to other political posts, which (if accepted) require resignation from the Court. Between 1900 and 2009, three Justices resigned to pursue other formal public service. In 1916, Justice Charles Evans Hughes resigned to pursue the Republican nomination for President.[45] Justice James F. Byrnes resigned on October 3, 1942, becoming Director of Economic Stability for President Franklin D. Roosevelt.[46] As noted previously, Justice Arthur Goldberg resigned in 1965 to become the U.N. Ambassador.

Controversial, Withdrawn, and Rejected Nominations

When any Court nomination (whether for an Associate or Chief Justice seat) fails in the Senate, the President may either re-submit the nomination or choose another candidate to fill the bench. The entire process thus begins anew. Withdrawals and rejections can greatly increase the amount of time taken to confirm Justices to the Court. Controversial nominees who are eventually confirmed also usually take more time to consider. The late 1960s and early 1970s were one of the most tumultuous periods of nominations and rejections in the Court's history. On May 14, 1969, Justice Abe Fortas resigned from the bench. Fortas had been embroiled in a scandal surrounding his consulting income, and failed to win confirmation as Chief Justice when President Johnson nominated him to the seat in 1968.[47] Previously, on October 14, 1968, President Johnson had withdrawn the Fortas nomination as well as the nomination of Homer Thornberry to fill the vacancy that would have been created by Fortas's elevation. The Senate rejected President Richard M. Nixon's first two nominees to the Fortas seat—Clement F. Haynsworth, Jr. and G. Harrold Carswell.[48] President Nixon's third choice, Harry A. Blackmun, was not confirmed until May 12, 1970—almost a year after Fortas's resignation.

DATA PRESENTATION

Table 1 (at the end of this chapter) lists dates for the following events regarding each nomination to the Supreme Court since 1900: (1) when the actual or prospective vacancy apparently became known to the President, (2) when the President announced the nominee, (3) when the Senate Judiciary Committee held its first hearing on the nominee, (4) when final committee action took place, and (5) when final Senate action took place. **Table 2** presents the number of days elapsed for six related time intervals: (1) from when the President apparently learned of the actual or prospective vacancy to the his announcement of a new nominee, (2) from the nomination announcement to the first Judiciary Committee hearing, (3) from the first hearing to the committee's final action, (4) from the committee's final action to the Senate's final action, (5) from nomination announcement to final Senate action (duration of total Senate action), and (6) from the vacancy starting date (when the President apparently first became aware of the opportunity to make a nomination) to final Senate action. **Table 3** provides summary statistics for the number of days elapsed during each of these intervals, for all nominations from 1900 until 2010, and for two periods within those dates—1900-1980 and 1981-2010.[49] As discussed later in this chapter, those periods were chosen because the data indicate a sharp difference in the pace of most nominations before and after 1980.

Date of Actual or Prospective Vacancy

As noted previously, it is often difficult or impossible to determine the specific date that a President first knew he would have the opportunity to name a new Justice to the Supreme Court. The President always has the constitutional obligation to make nominations to the Court when vacancies arise, and is certainly aware of the possibility that vacancies could arise at any time. However, the "Actual or Prospective Vacancy Became Known to President" columns in **Table 1** and **Table 2** focus on documented, specific instances when the President knew he had, or soon would have, the opportunity to name a new Justice to the Court.[50] These dates are based on extensive research about when the Justice's impending departure (or death) was made public, and whether the President had advance knowledge of the vacancy before it became public. In cases in which research revealed no public evidence that the President had advance notice (or in which the data are inconclusive), the date of the first public account of the vacancy marks the beginning of the process (the "When" column in **Table 1** and **Table 2**).[51]

For example, Justice Sandra Day O'Connor announced her retirement, pending confirmation of a successor, on July 1, 2005. There is no evidence that President George W. Bush definitely knew that O'Connor would retire until her announcement. Therefore, July 1, 2005, is used as the starting point for what became the Associate Justice nomination of John G. Roberts, Jr.[52] On the other hand, although Chief Justice Warren Burger's retirement letter to Ronald Reagan was not released until June 17, 1986, President Reagan's public papers reveal that Burger informed the President of his decision to retire on May 27, 1986.[53] Therefore, May 27, 1986, is used as the starting point for what became the William H. Rehnquist elevation to Chief Justice. Notes throughout **Table 1** and **Table 2** provide information on historical context.

Announcement-of-Nominee Date

Unless otherwise noted, the "President's Announcement-of-Nominee" date in **Table 1** is the day when the President announced his nomination to the public or released the text of his nomination letter (whichever came first). This date is significant because it marks the Senate's first opportunity to begin considering the nomination, even if informally. There are a few cases, explained by table notes, in which Presidents announced their decisions less formally, but still publicly. For example, President Harry S. Truman casually told reporters during a July 28, 1949, press conference that he had offered an Associate Justice nomination to then-Attorney General Thomas C. Clark, even though Clark had not yet accepted the nomination.[54] As discussed previously, in some cases, the announcement date differs by days or even weeks from the date the nomination was formally submitted to the Senate.

Use of Medians to Summarize Intervals

Table 2 provides the duration of each major interval in the process of nominating and considering Supreme Court Justices.[55] **Table 3** provides the *median* number of days for each major interval in the process. The median is the middle number in a set of observations (in this case, the number of days involved in each stage of considering Supreme Court nominations). The median is generally the preferred measure of central tendency in social science research.[56] As statistician William H. Greene notes, "Loosely speaking, the median corresponds more closely than the mean to the middle of a distribution [group of numbers]. It is unaffected by extreme values."[57] In other words, the median represents the best example of the "average" case, regardless of extremely short or long individual confirmations.

However, in describing the speed of the Supreme Court nomination-and-confirmation process, even median values should be considered carefully. Each nomination is different, and political context and historical factors can have a major impact on when various events occur. Several factors affecting individual nominations to the Court are discussed later in this chapter.

The Duration of the Nomination-and-Confirmation Process

During the entire period covered by this chapter (1900-2010), the President and the Senate have each taken varying amounts of time to act on Supreme Court nominations and confirmations. As **Table 3** shows, from 1900-2010, Presidents took a median of 28 days after a vacancy occurred to announce their nominees, compared with a median of 23.5 days for final Senate action once the nomination was announced. The entire process, from actual or prospective vacancy to final Senate action, lasted a median of 79 days from 1900-2010.

However, the amount of time involved in each stage of the nomination-and-confirmation process varies widely when individual cases are examined. Some Supreme Court nominations are unusually fast, coming immediately on the heels a sitting Justice's departure from the bench. In these cases, the President almost certainly knew in advance of the outgoing Justice's intention to retire yet delayed announcement of the retirement to coincide with announcing a new nominee. For example, on May 27, 1986, President Reagan simultaneously announced the retirement of Chief Justice Warren Burger, the elevation of William H. Rehnquist to Chief Justice, and the nomination of Antonin Scalia to assume the Associate Justice seat being vacated by Justice Rehnquist.[58] On the other hand, some nomination decisions can take months—at least to become public. For example, although Justice Harold H. Burton submitted his retirement letter to President Dwight D. Eisenhower on October 6, 1958, Eisenhower did not publicly announce Potter Stewart's nomination until January 17, 1959—103 days after announcing Justice Burton's retirement. The entire interval between Burton's announced retirement and Stewart's confirmation lasted 211 days, the bulk of the interval due to a long congressional recess.[59]

Changes Since 1981

The data indicate that the median decision-making intervals surrounding Supreme Court nominations have changed substantially since 1981.[60] When comparing Supreme Court nominations from 1900-1980 with those from 1981-2010, five patterns stand out. First, after apparently learning of vacancies, Presidents have typically been quicker to announce nominees since 1981 than in the previous 80 years. As shown in **Figure 1** (and **Table 3**), from 1900-1980, Presidents took a median of 34 days to announce their nominees after apparently learning of vacancies, compared with only 19.5 days from 1981-2010.

Second, and perhaps most notably, the median interval between the President's announcement of his nominee and the first Judiciary Committee hearing was substantially longer from 1981-2009 than from 1900-1980. As shown in **Figure 1** (and **Table 3**), this period almost quadrupled—from 12.5 days during the 1900-1980 period to 49 days from 1981-2010. Again, however, context is important. Even before hearings begin, the Senate can be actively working on the nomination. For example, prior to the start of John G. Roberts's hearings (and even before his nomination was submitted to the Senate), Senators met privately with Judge Roberts, and some pressed the White House to release records from Roberts's Department of Justice service.[61] The Harriet Miers and Samuel Alito nominations followed similar patterns.

Third, committee and floor action from 1981-2010 also took slightly longer than prior to 1981. From 1981-2010, the Judiciary Committee took a median of 15 days to reach a decision after starting hearings, while the interval between final committee action and final Senate action took nine days (compared with six and three days respectively from 1900-1980).

Fourth, as shown in **Figure 1** (and **Table 3**), total Senate activity (the interval between the President's announcement of the nominee and final Senate action) increased from a median of 17 days (1900-1980) to 84 days (1981-2010).

Finally, the entire nomination-and-confirmation process took substantially longer after 1980 than during the previous 80 years. The median duration for the entire process (from when the President apparently became aware of a vacancy until the Senate's final action on the nomination) was almost twice as long from 1981-2010 than during 1900-1980 (113 days versus 59 days, respectively).

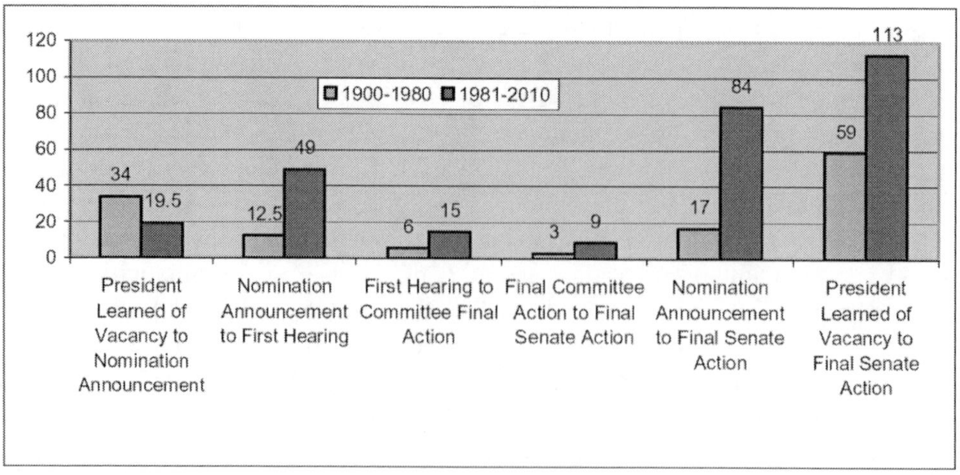

Source: Computations based on data compiled by the CRS authors. See **Table 3** for rounding information.

Note: Intervals in the figure refer to median number of days.

Figure 1. Speed in Days of Intervals Surrounding Supreme Court Nominations and Confirmations, 1900-2010

Factors Influencing the Speed of the Process

Some elements of the decision-making process surrounding the naming and the confirmation or rejection of Supreme Court nominees are known only to Presidents, nominees, and a few select advisors. Other elements are more obvious. Each nomination has its own political context, making each nomination somewhat different. However, several factors appear to be relatively constant in affecting the speed of Supreme Court nominations and Senate decisions.

How the Vacancy Occurs

How quickly the President announces his nominee and how quickly the Senate considers that nomination can depend on how the vacancy occurred. When Justices die unexpectedly, Presidents can be eager to bring the Court back to full strength as soon as possible. On July 19, 1949, for example, Justice Frank Murphy unexpectedly died of a heart attack after a brief illness.[62] President Harry S. Truman announced his nomination of Thomas C. Clark at a press conference nine days later, on July 28.[63] The Senate also considered the nomination quickly, beginning hearings on August 9. Clark's entire nomination-and-confirmation process lasted just 30 days. A few months later, Sherman Minton was confirmed even faster—in 24 days—after the death of Justice Wiley B. Rutledge. Nonetheless, sudden death does not guarantee that either the President or the Senate will make nomination-and-confirmation decisions quickly. For example, when Justice Rufus W. Peckham died unexpectedly on October 24, 1909, President William Howard Taft waited 50 days to announce a nominee. Once Taft announced his choice, the Senate confirmed Horace H. Lurton seven days later.

Retirements and resignations are often expected, allowing the President time to prepare for his choice even before an official announcement that a sitting Justice will step down. For example, at the time of his retirement, Justice William O. Douglas's health had been so poor and abilities allegedly in such decline that seven of his fellow Justices voted on October 17, 1975, to "effectively strip Douglas of his power" and excluded the aging Justice from deliberations.[64] By the time Justice Douglas officially wrote to President Gerald R. Ford on November 12, 1975, announcing his retirement, the President was prepared to act quickly. He announced the nomination of John Paul Stevens just 16 days later. Congress, too, acted quickly, confirming Stevens 19 days later, on December 17, 1975.

Sometimes, though, even when retirements or resignations come with advance notice, the process moves slowly. For example, Justice Harry A. Blackmun privately told President William J. Clinton around January 1, 1994, that he was planning to leave the Court. Soon afterward, the White House staff began quietly considering replacements.[65] However, President Clinton did not publicly announce Justice Blackmun's retirement until April 6, did not publicly announce Judge Stephen G. Breyer's nomination until May 13, and did not formally nominate Breyer until May 17.[66] The Judiciary Committee began hearings 60 days after the nomination was announced, and the entire process surrounding Breyer's nomination lasted 209 days. However, decisions affecting the nomination were apparently being made even before Blackmun's retirement became public knowledge.

The Senate's Schedule

Congress's schedule, especially whether the Senate is in session at all, plays an important role in how long Supreme Court nominations take to reach a conclusion. In the early 1900s, several vacancies arose during summer recess or election years when Congress was away from the Capitol. In 1910, for example, Congress adjourned on June 25 and did not return until December 5—a break of more than five months.[67] In the interim, Chief Justice Melville W. Fuller died of a heart attack on July 4.[68] As press coverage noted at the time, although potential nominees were immediately considered, President William Howard Taft waited to formally submit a nomination to the Senate until Congress reconvened.[69] On December 12, five days after the Senate reconvened, President Taft announced and formally submitted to the Senate his nomination of former Senator Edward D. White of Louisiana to be Chief Justice. That same day, without referring the nomination to the Judiciary Committee, the Senate quickly confirmed Senator White.

Three times during the 1950s, President Eisenhower resorted to recess appointments when Justices died or announced their retirement after Congress had already adjourned for the year.[70] In each case, President Eisenhower formally submitted the nomination after the Senate convened the following January. Of the five persons whom he nominated to the Court, three first received recess appointments and served as Justices before being confirmed—Earl Warren (as Chief Justice) in 1953, William Brennan in 1956, and Potter Stewart in 1958. President Eisenhower's recess appointments, however, generated controversy, prompting the Senate in 1960, voting closely along party lines, to pass a resolution expressing opposition to Supreme Court recess appointments in the future.[71]

President Eisenhower's actions were the most recent recess appointments to the Supreme Court, and recess appointments to the lower federal courts also have become relatively rare since the late 1960s. While a President's constitutional power to make judicial recess appointments was upheld by a federal court in 1985,[72] such appointments, when they do occur, may cause controversy, in large part because they bypass the Senate and its "advice and consent" role. Because of the criticisms of judicial recess appointments in recent decades, the long passage of time since the last Supreme Court recess appointment, and the relatively short duration of contemporary Senate recesses (which arguably undercuts the need for recess appointments to the Court), a President in the 21st century might be expected to make a recess appointment to the Supreme Court only under the most unusual of circumstances.[73]

Today, Congress's availability is less of an obstacle to speedy consideration of nominations than in the past. Given Congress's increasingly year-round schedule, extended decision-making is more often the result of waiting for presidential decisions, background investigations of nominees, or preparations for Judiciary Committee hearings.

Committee Involvement and Institutional Customs

Today, it would be highly unusual for the Judiciary Committee not to hold Supreme Court confirmation hearings lasting at least a few days. In the past, however, the Judiciary Committee often handled Supreme Court nominations without holding hearings at all. As **Table 1** shows, of the 22 nominees to the Court from 1900 to 1937, only three had Judiciary Committee hearings (Louis D. Brandeis in 1916, Harlan F. Stone in 1925, and John J. Parker in 1930 (whose nomination was eventually rejected)). In contrast, of the 41 nominees after

1937, only three *did not* have hearings.[74] Nominees did not begin regularly testifying at their own hearings until John M. Harlan did so in 1955.[75]

When the Judiciary Committee holds hearings, Senate floor consideration can be pushed back sometimes by weeks or even months. Controversial nominees often spur protracted hearings. For example, the Judiciary Committee spent 19 days considering Justice Louis D. Brandeis's nomination in 1916, and the interval between the start of hearings and final committee action lasted 105 days. The final Senate vote came eight days later. More recently, the Judiciary Committee, after learning of President Ronald Reagan's selection of Robert H. Bork, took 76 days to hold its first day of hearings on the nomination, and then 21 more days to conclude action on the nomination.

Senate custom plays an especially large role when sitting or former Senators are nominated to the Court. The Senate has almost always considered their colleagues' nominations to the Court within days of receiving the nomination, often without committee hearings or floor debate.[76] For example, although President Taft waited five months to nominate Edward D. White (a former Senator from Louisiana) for Chief Justice, the Senate confirmed the nomination with no debate in less than one hour.[77] Since 1900, three sitting Senators—Hugo L. Black of Alabama (1937), James F. Byrnes of South Carolina (1941), and Harold H. Burton of Ohio (1945)—have been nominated to the Court, and all were quickly confirmed.[78] Senators George Sutherland of Utah (1922) and Sherman Minton of Indiana (1949) were nominated to the Court after having concluded their Senate service. Sutherland was confirmed on the same day on which President Warren Harding announced the nomination, and Minton was confirmed in 19 days.

The decades since 1945 have yet to test again the Senate tradition of bypassing the Judiciary Committee when the Supreme Court nominee is a sitting U.S. Senator; no President since then has nominated a sitting Senator. The last *former* Senator to be nominated to the Court, in 1949, was Judge Sherman Minton of Indiana. (After defeat for re-election to the Senate in 1940, he had been appointed by President Franklin D. Roosevelt to a federal appellate court judgeship.) In a break with tradition, the Supreme Court nomination of former Senator Minton was referred to the Judiciary Committee, and Senate confirmation followed the day after the committee approved the nomination.

Controversial Nominations

As noted previously, withdrawn, rejected, or controversial nominations can substantially lengthen the process. In these cases, although Presidents often name nominees fairly quickly, consideration of the nominations can be drawn out in the Senate. During Judge Robert H. Bork's controversial nomination, for example, Senate consideration of Bork lasted more than a month, from the first Judiciary Committee hearing on September 15, 1987, until the Senate's floor vote to reject the nomination on October 23, 1987. The entire process—from President Reagan's announcement of his intention to nominate Bork to Senate rejection—took 119 days.

Controversy can also delay confirmation of nominees who are ultimately successful. Despite a relatively quick nomination-and-confirmation process of 42 days in late 1924 and early 1925 for then-Attorney General Harlan F. Stone, his nomination was temporarily set back when it was recommitted to the Senate Judiciary Committee, apparently because of Stone's investigation as Attorney General of Senator Burton K. Wheeler.[79] More recently, although Judge Clarence Thomas narrowly won confirmation in 1991, nominating and confirming him took 110 days, including a second round of Judiciary Committee hearings surrounding law professor Anita Hill's allegations against Thomas of sexual harassment.

Discussion and Conclusions

Understanding how long the previous Supreme Court nomination-and-confirmation process has taken, and what factors affected that schedule, can provide useful perspective on presidential decision-making and the Senate's preparations for future nominations. While Presidents and supporters of nominees want Justices confirmed quickly, some Senators will continue to emphasize their right to consider nominees carefully and their responsibility to hold sufficient hearings. Against that political backdrop, this chapter demonstrates that the length of time required to nominate and confirm or reject a nominee varies widely. Even median durations must be interpreted cautiously. The context surrounding each nomination is particularly important in understanding how long the process takes.

This chapter indicates that, from 1900-1980, the President's portion of the process took longer than the Senate's. Since 1981, though, there has been a substantial increase in the median duration between the President's announcement of a nominee and the start of Judiciary Committee hearings. As a result, the Senate's portion of the process has taken longer than the President's.

Prior to 1981, lengthy nomination-and-confirmation processes usually occurred because either the Senate was out of session when a vacancy on the Court arose, or the nomination was controversial. In recent decades, by contrast, slower decision-making has taken place during an era when Congress is in session longer than during the early 20th century.

Since 1981, the nomination-and-confirmation process has lasted a median of 113 days—almost twice as long as the 59-day median from 1900-1980. Although the data in **Table 1**, **Table 2**, and **Table 3** provide a median measure of the process, political context is an essential backdrop for understanding the numbers. The President and the Senate share decision-making responsibilities for placing new Justices on the Court. Ultimately, the choices each institution makes determine how long nominations and confirmations take.

One possible explanation for the paradox of slower decisions despite more time in session is that, as some critics on both sides of the aisle contend, Supreme Court nominations have become battlegrounds for larger political debates.[80] Another possibility is that the Senate is considering nominations more carefully than in the past, and therefore taking more time to make decisions about nominees. Similarly, the Senate might be using longer decision-making and scrutiny of nominees as a method of counterbalancing presidential power, especially when Senators believe that the President has chosen an unqualified nominee.

Some early 20th century appointments to the Supreme Court were confirmed within days of a vacancy occurring. More recent nominations and confirmations, by contrast, typically have taken several weeks or months. How and when a vacancy occurs, the Senate's schedule, Judiciary Committee involvement, institutional customs, and whether or not the nomination is controversial, all affect the speed with which the President nominates, and the Senate passes judgment, on prospective Justices.

Table 1. Major Events in the Supreme Court Nomination-and-Confirmation Process, 1900-2010

Nominating President	Outgoing Justice	Actual or Prospective Vacancy Apparently Became Known to President		President's Announcement of Nominee		Senate Action Dates on Nomination		
		When	How	Nominee	Date	First Hearing	Committee Final Action	Senate Final Action
Theodore Roosevelt	Horace Gray	09/15/1902	Death of outgoing Justice	Oliver Wendell Holmes	12/02/1902	No record of hearing	12/04/1902	12/04/1902
Theodore Roosevelt	George Shiras, Jr.	08/20/1902[a]	Public reports of imminent retirement	William R. Day	01/14/1903[b]	No record of hearing	02/23/1903	02/23/1903
Theodore Roosevelt	Henry B. Brown	03/08/1906[c]	Outgoing Justice notified President of intention to retire[d]	William H. Moody	11/07/1906	No record of hearing	12/10/1906	12/12/1906
William Howard Taft	Rufus W. Peckham	10/24/1909	Death of outgoing Justice	Horace H. Lurton	12/13/1909[e]	No record of hearing	12/16/1909	12/20/1909
William Howard Taft	David J. Brewer	3/28/1910	Death of outgoing Justice	Charles Evans Hughes	4/25/1910	No record of hearing	05/02/1910	05/02/1910
William Howard Taft	Melville W. Fuller, *Chief Justice*	07/04/1910	Death of outgoing Chief Justice	Edward D. White	12/12/1910	Nomination was not referred to Judiciary Committee		12/12/1910
William Howard Taft	Edward D. White	12/12/1910	Justice Edward D. White nomination to be Chief Justice	Willis Van Devanter	12/12/1910	No record of hearing	12/15/1910	12/15/1910
William Howard Taft	William H. Moody	06/15/1910[f]	Congressional action authorizing retirement	Joseph R. Lamar	12/12/1910	No record of hearing	12/15/1910	12/15/1910
William Howard Taft	John Marshall Harlan	10/14/1911	Death of outgoing Justice	Mahlon Pitney	02/19/1912	No record of hearing	03/04/1912	03/13/1912
Woodrow Wilson	Horace H. Lurton	07/12/1914	Death of outgoing Justice	James C. McReynolds	08/19/1914[g]	No record of hearing	08/24/1914	08/29/1914

Table 1. (Continued)

Nominating President	Outgoing Justice	Actual or Prospective Vacancy Apparently Became Known to President		President's Announcement of Nominee		Senate Action Dates on Nomination		
		When	How	Nominee	Date	First Hearing	Committee Final Action	Senate Final Action
Woodrow Wilson	Joseph R. Lamar	01/02/1916	Death of outgoing Justice	Louis D. Brandeis	01/28/1916	02/09/1916	05/24/1916	06/01/1916
Woodrow Wilson	Charles Evans Hughes	06/10/1916[h]	Resignation letter submitted to President	John H. Clarke	07/14/1916	No record of hearing	07/24/1916	07/24/1916
Warren Harding	Edward D. White	05/19/1921	Death of outgoing Justice	William Howard Taft	06/30/1921	Nomination was not referred to Judiciary Committee		06/30/1921
Warren Harding	John H. Clarke	09/05/1922	Resignation letter submitted to President	George Sutherland	09/05/1922	Nomination was not referred to Judiciary Committee		09/05/1922
Warren Harding	William R. Day	09/05/1922[i]	Public reports of imminent retirement	Pierce Butler	11/23/1922	No record of hearing	11/28/1922	Placed on Executive Calendar on 11/28/1922, with no record of further action[j]
		12/04/1922	Lack of action on first nomination of Butler	Pierce Butler	12/05/1922	No record of hearing	12/18/1922	12/21/1922
Warren Harding	Mahlon Pitney	12/16/1922	White House announced fort-hcoming retirement[k]	Edward T. Sanford	01/09/1923[l]	No record of hearing	01/29/1923	01/29/1923
Calvin Coolidge	Joseph McKenna	12/25/192[m]	Public reports of forthcoming retirement	Harlan F. Stone	01/05/1925	01/28/1925	01/21/1925	Recommitted 01/26/1925
							02/02/1925	02/05/1925

Table 1. (Continued)

Nominating President	Outgoing Justice	Actual or Prospective Vacancy Apparently Became Known to President		President's Announcement of Nominee		Senate Action Dates on Nomination		
		When	How	Nominee	Date	First Hearing	Committee Final Action	Senate Final Action
Herbert Hoover	William Howard Taft *Chief Justice*	02/03/1930	Retirement letter submitted to President	Charles Evans Hughes	02/03/1930	No record of hearing	02/10/1930	02/13/1930
Herbert Hoover	Edward T. Sanford	03/08/1930	Death of outgoing Justice	John J. Parker	03/21/1930	04/05/1930	04/21/1930	Rejected 05/07/1930
Herbert Hoover	Edward T. Sanford	05/07/1930	Parker nomination rejected by Senate	Owen J. Roberts	05/09/1930	No record of hearing	05/19/1930	05/20/1930
Herbert Hoover	Oliver Wendell Holmes, Jr.	01/12/1932	Retirement letter submitted to President	Benjamin N. Cardozo	02/15/1932	02/19/1932	02/23/1932	02/24/1932
Franklin D. Roosevelt	Willis Van Devanter	05/18/1937[n]	Retirement letter submitted to President	Hugo L. Black	08/12/1937	No record of hearing	08/16/1937	08/17/1937
Franklin D. Roosevelt	George Sutherland	01/05/1938	Retirement letter submitted to President	Stanley F. Reed	01/15/1938[o]	01/20/1938	01/24/1938	01/25/1938
Franklin D. Roosevelt	Benjamin N. Cardozo	07/09/1938[p]	Death of outgoing Justice	Felix Frankfurter	01/05/1939	01/10/1939	01/16/1939	01/17/1939
Franklin D. Roosevelt	Louis D. Brandeis	02/13/1939[q]	Retirement letter submitted to President	William O. Douglas	03/20/1939	03/24/1939	03/27/1939	04/04/1939
Franklin D. Roosevelt	Pierce Butler	11/16/1939	Death of outgoing Justice	Frank Murphy	01/04/1940	01/11/1940	01/15/1940	01/16/1940
Franklin D. Roosevelt	James Clark McReynolds	01/22/1941	Outgoing Justice notified President of intention to retire[r]	James F. Byrnes	06/12/1941	Nomination was not referred to Judiciary Committee		06/12/1941

Table 1. (Continued)

<table>
<tr><th rowspan="2">Nominating President</th><th rowspan="2">Outgoing Justice</th><th colspan="2">Actual or Prospective Vacancy Apparently Became Known to President</th><th colspan="2">President's Announcement of Nominee</th><th colspan="3">Senate Action Dates on Nomination</th></tr>
<tr><th>When</th><th>How</th><th>Nominee</th><th>Date</th><th>First Hearing</th><th>Committee Final Action</th><th>Senate Final Action</th></tr>
<tr><td>Franklin D. Roosevelt</td><td>Charles Evans Hughes Chief Justice</td><td>06/02/194[s]</td><td>Retirement letter submitted to President</td><td>Harlan F. Stone</td><td>06/12/1941</td><td>06/21/1941</td><td>06/23/1941</td><td>06/27/1941</td></tr>
<tr><td>Franklin D. Roosevelt</td><td>Harlan F. Stone</td><td>06/12/1941</td><td>Harlan F. Stone nomination to be Chief Justice</td><td>Robert H. Jackson</td><td>06/12/1941</td><td>06/21/1941</td><td>06/30/1941</td><td>07/07/1941</td></tr>
<tr><td>Franklin D. Roosevelt</td><td>James F. Byrnes</td><td>10/03/1942[t]</td><td>Byrnes appointment to other public office</td><td>Wiley B. Rutledge</td><td>01/11/1943</td><td>01/22/1943</td><td>02/01/1943</td><td>02/08/1943</td></tr>
<tr><td>Harry S. Truman</td><td>Owen J. Roberts</td><td>06/30/1945[u]</td><td>Retirement letter submitted to President</td><td>Harold H. Burton</td><td>09/18/1945</td><td>No record of hearing</td><td>09/19/1945</td><td>09/19/1945</td></tr>
<tr><td>Harry S. Truman</td><td>Harlan F. Stone Chief Justice</td><td>04/22/1946</td><td>Death of outgoing Chief Justice</td><td>Fred M. Vinson</td><td>06/06/1946</td><td>06/14/1946</td><td>06/19/1946</td><td>06/20/1946</td></tr>
<tr><td>Harry S. Truman</td><td>Frank Murphy</td><td>07/19/1949</td><td>Death of outgoing Justice</td><td>Thomas C. Clark</td><td>07/28/1949</td><td>08/09/1949</td><td>08/12/1949</td><td>08/18/1949</td></tr>
<tr><td>Harry S. Truman</td><td>Wiley B. Rutledge</td><td>09/10/1949</td><td>Death of outgoing Justice</td><td>Sherman Minton</td><td>09/15/1949</td><td>09/27/1949</td><td>10/03/1949</td><td>10/04/1949</td></tr>
<tr><td rowspan="2">Dwight D. Eisenhower</td><td rowspan="2">Fred M. Vinson Chief Justice</td><td rowspan="2">09/08/1953</td><td rowspan="2">Death of outgoing Chief Justice</td><td rowspan="2">Earl Warren</td><td colspan="4">Recess appointment, 10/02/1953</td></tr>
<tr><td>01/11/1954</td><td>02/02/1954</td><td>02/24/1954</td><td>03/01/1954</td></tr>
<tr><td rowspan="2">Dwight D. Eisenhower</td><td rowspan="2">Robert H. Jackson</td><td>10/09/1954</td><td>Death of outgoing Justice</td><td>John Marshall Harlan II</td><td>11/08/1954[v]</td><td colspan="3">No record of hearing, committee vote, or Senate vote</td></tr>
<tr><td>01/05/1955 (Congress reconvenes)</td><td>Lack of action on first nomination of Harlan nomination</td><td>John Marshall Harlan II</td><td>01/10/1955</td><td>02/24/1955</td><td>03/10/1955</td><td>03/16/1955</td></tr>
</table>

Table 1. (Continued)

Nominating President	Outgoing Justice	Actual or Prospective Vacancy Apparently Became Known to President		President's Announcement of Nominee		Senate Action Dates on Nomination		
		When	How	Nominee	Date	First Hearing	Committee Final Action	Senate Final Action
Dwight D. Eisenhower	Sherman Minton	09/07/1956	Retirement letter submitted to President	William J. Brennan	*Recess appointment, 10/15/1956*			
					01/14/1957	02/26/1957	03/04/1957	03/19/1957
Dwight D. Eisenhower	Stanley F. Reed	01/31/1957	Press conference held by Reed announcing retirement[w]	Charles E. Whittaker	03/02/1957	03/18/1957	03/18/1957	03/19/1957
Dwight D. Eisenhower	Harold H. Burton	10/06/1958	Retirement letter submitted to President	Potter Stewart	*Recess Appointment, 10/14/1958*			
					01/17/1959	04/09/1959	04/20/1959	05/05/1959
John F. Kennedy	Charles E. Whittaker	03/28/1962	Retirement letter received by President[x]	Byron R. White	03/30/1962[y]	04/11/1962	04/11/1962	04/11/1962
John F. Kennedy	Felix Frankfurter	08/28/1962[z]	Retirement letter submitted to President	Arthur J. Goldberg	08/29/1962	09/11/1962	09/25/1962	09/25/1962
Lyndon B. Johnson	Arthur J. Goldberg	07/20/1965	Goldberg appointment to other public office[aa]	Abe Fortas	07/28/1965[bb]	08/05/1965	08/10/1965	08/11/1965
Lyndon B. Johnson	Thomas C. Clark	02/28/1967	Outgoing Justice notified President of intention to retire[cc]	Thurgood Marshall	06/13/1967[dd]	07/13/1967	08/03/1967	08/30/1967
Lyndon B. Johnson	Earl Warren *Chief Justice*	06/13/1968[ee]	Retirement letter submitted to President	Abe Fortas	06/26/1968	07/11/1968	09/17/1968	10/01/1968 (Cloture motion rejected)
Lyndon B. Johnson	Abe Fortas	06/26/1968[ff]	Fortas nomination to be Chief Justice	Homer Thornberry	06/26/1968	07/11/1968	No record of committee vote	Nomination withdrawn by President, 10/04/1968

Table 1. (Continued)

Nominating President	Outgoing Justice	Actual or Prospective Vacancy Apparently Became Known to President		President's Announcement of Nominee		Senate Action Dates on Nomination		
		When	How	Nominee	Date	First Hearing	Committee Final Action	Senate Final Action
Richard M. Nixon	Earl Warren *Chief Justice*	01/20/1969[gg]	Fortas Chief Justice nomination with-drawn by President Johnson (10/04/1968)	Warren E. Burger	05/21/1969	06/03/1969	06/03/1969	06/09/1969
Richard M. Nixon	Abe Fortas	05/14/1969	Resignation letter submitted to President	Clement F. Haynsworth, Jr.	08/18/1969[hh]	09/16/1969	10/09/1969	11/21/1969 (Rejected)
		11/21/1969	Haynsworth nomination rejected by Senate	G. Harrold Carswell	01/19/1970	01/27/1970	02/16/1970	04/08/1970 (Rejected)
		04/08/1970	Carswell nomination rejected by Senate	Harry A. Blackmun	04/14/1970	04/29/1970	05/06/1970	05/12/1970
Richard M. Nixon	Hugo L. Black	09/17/1971	Retirement letter submitted to President	Lewis F. Powell, Jr.	10/21/1971	11/03/1971	11/23/1971	12/06/1971
Richard M. Nixon	John Marshall Harlan II	09/23/1971	Retirement letter submitted to President	William H. Rehnquist	10/21/1971	11/03/1971	11/23/1971	12/10/1971
Gerald R. Ford	William O. Douglas	11/12/1975[ii]	Retirement letter submitted to President	John Paul Stevens	11/28/1975[jj]	12/08/1975	12/11/1975	12/17/1975
Ronald Reagan	Potter Stewart	05/18/1981[kk]	Retirement letter submitted to President	Sandra Day O'Connor	07/07/1981[ll]	09/09/1981	09/15/1981	09/21/1981
Ronald Reagan	Warren E. Burger *Chief Justice*	05/27/1986[mm]	Chief Justice priva-tely alerted President of intention to retire	William H. Rehnquist	06/17/1986	07/29/1986	08/14/1986	09/17/1986
Ronald Reagan	William H. Rehnquist	05/27/1986[nn]	Rehnquist nomination by Reagan to be Chief Justice	Antonin Scalia	06/17/1986	08/05/1986	08/14/1986	09/17/1986

Table 1. (Continued)

Nominating President	Outgoing Justice	Actual or Prospective Vacancy Apparently Became Known to President		President's Announcement of Nominee		Senate Action Dates on Nomination		
		When	How	Nominee	Date	First Hearing	Committee Final Action	Senate Final Action
Ronald Reagan	Lewis F. Powell, Jr.	06/26/ 1987[oo]	Press conference held by Powell announcing retirement	Robert H. Bork	07/01/1987	09/15/1987	10/06/1987	10/23/1987 (Rejected)
		10/23/1987	Bork nomination rejected by Senate	Douglas H. Ginsburg	10/29/1987	Ginsburg withdrew (11/07/1987) before official nomination[pp]		
		11/07/1987	Ginsburg withdrawal	Anthony M. Kennedy	11/11/1987	12/14/1987	01/27/1988	02/03/1988
George H.W. Bush	William J. Brennan	07/20/1990	Retirement letter submitted to President	David H. Souter	07/23/ 1990[qq]	09/13/1990	09/27/1990	10/02/1990
George H.W. Bush	Thurgood Marshall	06/27/1991	Retirement letter submitted to President	Clarence Thomas	07/01/1991	09/10/1991	09/27/1991	10/15/1991
William J. Clinton	Byron R. White	03/19/1993[rr]	Retirement letter submitted to President	Ruth Bader Ginsburg	06/14/ 1993[ss]	07/20/1993	07/29/1993	08/03/1993
William J. Clinton	Harry A. Blackmun	01/01/1994[tt]	Justice privately alerted President of forthcoming retirement	Stephen G. Breyer	05/13/1994	07/12/1994	07/19/1994	07/29/1994

Table 1. (Continued)

Nominating President	Outgoing Justice	Actual or Prospective Vacancy Apparently Became Known to President		President's Announcement of Nominee		Senate Action Dates on Nomination		
		When	How	Nominee	Date	First Hearing	Committee Final Action	Senate Final Action
George W. Bush	Sandra Day O'Connor	07/01/2005	Retirement letter submitted to President	John G. Roberts, Jr.	07/19/2005	Nomination was with-drawn by President (09/05/2005) before the start of Judiciary Committee hearings; renominated as Chief Justice (09/05/2005)		
		09/05/2005	Announcement of Roberts nomination withdrawal and re-submission by President	Harriet E. Miers	10/03/2005	Miers withdrew as nominee (10/27/2005) before the start of Judiciary Committee hearings		
		10/27/2005	Announcement of Miers withdrawal	Samuel A. Alito, Jr.	10/31/2005	01/09/2006	01/24/2006	01/31/2006
George W. Bush	William H. Rehnquist	09/03/2005	Death of outgoing Justice	John G. Roberts, Jr.	09/05/2005	09/12/2005	09/22/2005	09/29/2005
Barack Obama	David H. Souter	05/01/2009	Retirement letter submitted to President	Sonia Sotomayor	05/26/2009	07/13/2009	07/28/2009	08/06/2009
Barack Obama	John Paul Stevens	04/09/2010	Retirement letter submitted to President	Elena Kagan	05/10/2010	06/28/2010	07/20/2010	08/05/2010

Sources: As described in the text, this research relied on historical newspapers, official presidential papers, and CRS correspondence with Presidential Libraries. Ward's *Deciding to Leave* was especially useful in compiling data on the reasons why Justices left the bench. Additional source information appears in the table notes below.

a. It is unclear when President Theodore Roosevelt learned of Justice Shiras's intention to retire. However, *Washington Post* coverage suggests that Shiras's forthcoming departure was well known in Washington, DC by at least August 20, 1902 ("Knox May Not Want It: Belief that He Would Decline Justice Shiras's Position," *Washington Post*, August 20, 1902, p. 1).

b. President Roosevelt did not formally announce Day's nomination until February 19, 1903. However, the *Washington Post* reported as early as January 14, 1903 that President Roosevelt had already offered Day the nomination, after William Howard Taft declined the offer in favor of continuing his position as Civil Governor of the Philippine Islands ("Declined by Taft," *Washington Post*, January 14, 1903, p. 1).

c. According to the *Washington Post*, Justice Brown notified the President, on March 8, 1906, that he wished to retire ("To Leave the Bench: Justice Brown Will Retire in the Fall," *Washington Post*, March 8, 1906, p. 3).

d. It is unclear from the historical record whether the President learned of Justice Brown's desire to retire by letter, personal conversation, etc.

e. Despite the delay between Justice Peckham's death and President William Howard Taft's nomination of Horace H. Lurton, President Taft, in nominating Lurton, was reportedly "adhering to his original purpose to promote Judge Lurton, whom he has known for years, and with whom he served on the bench," ("Taft Names Lurton," *Washington Post*, December 14, 1909, p. 3).

f. Justice Moody did not actually depart the Court until November 20, 1910 (Ward, *Deciding to Leave*, p. 5). However, "Illness of a serious nature has kept Justice Moody from his duties in the Supreme Court for almost a year. There have been occasional rumors of retirement, but Senator Lodge [on June 15, 1910] presented the real harbinger of that action, in the form of a bill extending the statute relating to retirement from the Supreme Court to cover the case of Mr. Moody" ("Moody Will Retire," *Washington Post*, June 15, 1910, p. 1).

g. Although Justice McReynolds's nomination was not announced until August 20, 1914, the *Washington Post* reported on August 19 that President Woodrow Wilson had "definitely decided" on McReynolds ("Picks M'Reynolds," *Washington Post*, August 19, 1914, p. 1), thereby informally alerting Congress to the President's choice.

h. On June 10, 1916, Justice Hughes resigned to pursue the 1916 Republican presidential nomination ("Hughes, With Words That Ring, Obeys Call to Lead Republicans," *Washington Post*, June 11, 1916, p. 1). Although historical media research does not indicate that President Wilson knew for certain that Justice Hughes would resign, media reports had hinted at a Hughes resignation throughout the spring of 1916.

i. Day did not leave the Court until November 13, 1922. However, the *Washington Post* reported that Day's consideration of retirement was mentioned at a White House briefing on September 5, 1922 ("Justice Day May Leave the Bench," *Washington Post*, September 6, 1922, p. 1).

j. After the Senate took no final action on Butler's nomination by the end of the third session of the 67th Congress on December 4, 1922, President Warren Harding renominated Butler on December 5, 1922. See "Fight Over Butler's Nomination Forecast," *Washington Post*, December 6, 1922, p. 12; and "Fight Against Butler Opened by Shipstead," *Washington Post*, December 9, 1922, p. 2.

k. Although Justice Pitney's resignation was effective as of December 31, 1922, the White House announced Pitney's forthcoming departure on December 16, 1922 ("Resigns," *Chicago Daily Tribune*, December 17, 1922, p. 17).

l. President Warren Harding did not officially nominate Sanford until January 24, 1923. However, the media reported as early as January 9, 1923, that President Harding intended to nominate Sanford ("E.T. Sanford Choice for Supreme Court," *Washington Post*, January 9, 1923, p. 1).

m. Justice McKenna did not officially retire until January 5, 1925. However, the media reported his imminent retirement on December 25, 1924 ("M'Kenna to Retire Soon as a Justice of the Supreme Court," *Washington Post*, December 25, 1924, p. 2).

n. For an account of Justice Van Devanter privately alerting a reporter of his decision to retire on the morning of the announcement, see "News 'Beat' Aided by Van Devanter," *New York Times*, May 23, 1937, p. 40.

o. Justice Reed had also been a frontrunner for the 1937 seat that eventually went to Justice Hugo Black. This perhaps explains President Franklin D. Roosevelt's relatively quick nomination of Reed, despite what many reporters considered to be a surprise retirement announcement from Sutherland. See Robert C. Albright, "Sutherland, 75, Quits U.S. Supreme Court," *New York Times*, January 6, 1938, p. X1; and Franklyn Waltman, "Stanley F. Reed Named to U.S. Supreme Court." *New York Times*, January 16, 1938, p. 1.

p. Although Justice Cardozo had been ill and away from the bench since December 1937 (United Press, "Supreme Court Liberal Succumbs to Heart Ailment in N.Y., *Washington Post*, July 10, 1938, p. M1), a definite need to nominate a new Justice did not occur until Cardozo's death on July 9, 1938.

q. Justice Brandeis had been away from the bench for a month, recovering from a heart attack, prior to announcing his retirement (United Press, "Justice Brandeis, Dean of Supreme Court, Quits," *Los Angeles Times*, February 14, 1939, p. 1). Nonetheless, his retirement was considered abrupt, suggesting that President Roosevelt had little advance notice to consider a successor.

r. It is unclear from the historical record whether the President learned of Justice McReynolds's desire to retire by letter, personal conversation, etc.

s. Although Chief Justice Hughes's retirement due to age and poor health had been "rumored some months" prior to submission of his formal retirement letter (Walter Trohan, "Hughes Retires From Court," *Chicago Daily Tribune*, June 3, 1941, p. 1), the definite need for a new nominee did not arise until Hughes announced his retirement.

t. Justice Byrnes resigned at President Roosevelt's request on October 3, 1942, becoming Director of Economic Stability. Roosevelt was, therefore, aware of an impending vacancy on the Court prior to the formal resignation, although the precise date is unclear. For a summary of Byrnes's transition from the Court to his new post, see Associated Press, "Byrnes Resigns From Bench in Letter to President," *New York Times*, October 4, 1942, p. 45.

u. Although President Truman did not announce Justice Roberts's intention to retire until July 5, 1945 (United Press, "Morganthau and Roberts Resign," *Los Angeles Times*, July 6, 1945, p. 1), Justice Roberts's retirement letter is dated July 30, 1945. Truman received the letter on that date "or soon thereafter" (e-mail communication between CRS Information Specialist Dana Ely and Truman Library Archivist Randy Sowell, September 2, 2005).

v. The Senate took no final action on the Harlan nomination before the 83rd Congress's final adjournment on December 2, 1954. President Eisenhower re-nominated Harlan to the Court on January 10, 1955, five days after the start of the first session of the 84th Congress. Evidence does not suggest that another announcement of the nomination was made.

w. Whether President Eisenhower first learned of Justice Reed's retirement through the press conference or a letter from Reed is unclear. Contemporary media coverage mentioned a press conference and a letter to Eisenhower (Edward T. Folliard, "Reed Is Retiring From High Court," *Washington Post*, February 1, 1957, p. A1). However, political scientist Artemus Ward's account asserts that Reed announced his retirement through a press conference (Ward, *Deciding to Leave*, pp. 162-163). Regardless, both events occurred on January 31, 1957. For the January 31 correspondence between Reed and Eisenhower, see "Letter to Stanley Reed Regarding His Retirement From Active Service as An Associate Justice of the Supreme Court," U.S. National Archives and Records Administration, Office of the Federal Register, *Public Papers of the Presidents of the United States: Dwight D. Eisenhower, 1957* (Washington: GPO, 1958), pp. 109-110.

x. This information is based on e-mail communication between CRS Information Specialist Dana Ely and Kennedy Library Reference Technician Sharon Kelly, September 14, 2005.

y. According to a press account, President Kennedy's decision to nominate White "was apparently made just a few hours before the selection was announced Friday night" (on March 30, 1962) (James E. Clayton, "White Was One of Three In Line for High Court," *Washington Post*, April 1, p. A1). Given the relatively quick action, however, Kennedy might have considered White as a Supreme Court candidate in advance of the March 28, 1962, announced vacancy.

z. August 28, 1962, is the only definitive date which can be established based on available data, as the earliest point at which President Kennedy learned of Justice Frankfurter's intention to retire. However, President Kennedy's quick nomination of Goldberg, and Justice Frankfurter's poor health in the weeks leading up to his retirement, suggest that President Kennedy was considering prospective nominees well before Frankfurter stepped down. Kennedy's letter to Justice Frankfurter accepting his retirement references a visit the President paid to Frankfurter to check on his health sometime during the summer of 1962 (U.S. National Archives and Records Administration, Office of the Federal Register, *Public Papers of the Presidents of the United States: John F. Kennedy, 1962*, (Washington: GPO, 1963), p. 656). According to Kennedy Library Reference Technician Sharon Kelly, Kennedy's office files suggest that correspondence between Frankfurter, Special Assistant for National Security Affairs McGeorge Bundy, and the President would have alerted Kennedy to Frankfurter's declining health around May 17, 1962 (e-mail communication between CRS Information Specialist Dana Ely and Kennedy Library Reference Technician Sharon Kelly, September 14, 2005).

aa. President Lyndon B. Johnson unexpectedly nominated Justice Goldberg to be U.S. Ambassador to the United Nations following the death on July 14, 1965, of the previous ambassador, Adlai E. Stevenson. See Carroll Kilpatrick, "Goldberg is Named to Stevenson Post," *Washington Post*, July 21, 1965, p. A1.

bb. Although Justice Fortas was not nominated until July 28, 1965, President Johnson apparently decided to nominate Fortas long before the Goldberg vacancy, making the gap of only one week between Goldberg's resignation and Fortas's nomination unsurprising. At the press conference announcing Fortas's nomination, President Johnson said that he and Fortas had discussed the nomination "on numerous occasions in the 20 months," (U.S. National Archives and Records Administration, Office of the Federal Register, *Public Papers of the Presidents of the United States: Lyndon B. Johnson, 1966*, vol. 2 (Washington: GPO), 1967, p. 798).

cc. Despite the fact that Justice Clark announced his forthcoming retirement on February 28, 1967, historical evidence suggests that Johnson might have prompted Clark's retirement as early as January 1967, when the President prepared to nominated Justice Clark's son, Ramsey, to be Attorney General. "On January 25, 1967, Johnson told Ramsey that he could only be named the permanent attorney general if his father stepped down from the Court" (Ward, *Deciding to Leave*, p. 170).

dd. Like the 1965 Fortas nomination, Marshall's nomination was no surprise, since Johnson was reportedly considering Marshall for appointment to the Court before the formal nomination. According to a 1967 *Washington Post* report, "Marshall's resignation two years ago, at the President's request, from a lifetime seat on the 2d U.S. Circuit Court of Appeals to become Solicitor General, had seemed clearly a move to groom him for the Nation's highest court" (John P. MacKenzie, "LBJ Names Marshall to Court," June 14], 1967, *Washington Post*, p. A1).

ee. Although President Johnson did not announce Chief Justice Warren's retirement until June 26, he received Warren's retirement letter on June 13, 1968 (U.S. National Archives and Records Administration, Office of the Federal Register, *Public Papers of the Presidents of the United States: Lyndon B. Johnson, 1968-69*, vol. 1 (Washington: GPO), 1970, p. 746).

ff. Although a specific opportunity to name a new Associate Justice did not arise until the Fortas Chief Justice nomination on June 26, 1968, it was reported that "[s]ome Texans at the Capitol are sure that Mr. Johnson has planned for the last four years to name Thornberry to the Supreme Court before he [Johnson] left office," (Richard L. Lyons, "Homer Thornberry: 'Constructive Liberal,' Close LBJ friend," *Washington Post,* June 27, 1969, p. 1).

gg. January 20, 1969 (the date of Richard M. Nixon's inauguration), is used as the starting date for the vacancy because it marks the beginning of President Nixon's official decision-making powers. After the Abe Fortas Chief Justice nomination failed, President Johnson announced on October 2, 1968, that he would not name another nominee (U.S. National Archives and Records Administration, Office of the Federal Register, *Public Papers of the Presidents of the United States: Lyndon B. Johnson, 1968-69*, vol. 2 (Washington: GPO), 1966, p. 509). Eight days later, Johnson elaborated on his decision. The President wrote that although he would have made another nomination in "ordinary times," the situation was extraordinary and that, "Under the circumstances, the foundations of government would be better served by the present Chief Justice [Earl Warren] remaining [in office] until emotionalism subsides, reason and fairness prevail (U.S. National Archives and Records Administration, Office of the Federal Register, *Public Papers of the Presidents of the United States: Lyndon B. Johnson, 1968-69*, vol. 2 (Washington: GPO, 1970), p. 1024). On December 3, 1968, Chief Justice Warren informed President-elect Richard M. Nixon that he was willing to continue serving until a successor was confirmed ("Statement by the Chief Justice," December 4, 1968, Earl Warren Papers, Manuscript Division, Library of Congress, Washington, DC). In a May 1969, conversation with reporters, President Nixon offered an unusually detailed discussion of his decision-making process surrounding the Burger nomination. Nixon reported that he thought "it would not be a proper mark of respect for the Court and for the Chief Justice to have a nomination go down, say, in February or March, and then have possibly the Senate hearings and the like at a time that the Court was sitting," and that his target date for a nomination decision was between May 1 and June 1, 1968 (U.S. National Archives and Records Administration, Office of the Federal Register, *Public Papers of the Presidents of the United States: Richard Nixon, 1970*, (Washington: GPO), 1971, p. 390).

hh. Although President Richard M. Nixon waited until August 18, 1969, to nominate Haynsworth, media accounts speculated that Haynsworth would be the nominee at least as early as August 6. See AP, "Possible High Court Choice Hit," *Washington Post*, August 7, 1969, p. B4.

ii. Chief Justice Warren Burger reportedly "hint[ed] at a possible vacancy" on the Court in a letter to President Gerald Ford on November 10, 1975, and offered "factors for [the President] to consider when appointing a new justice," (e-mail communication between CRS Information Specialist Dana Ely and Ford Library Archivist Technician Joshua Cochran, September 12, 2005). Justice Douglas's health had been in question since December 31, 1974, when he suffered a stroke (John P. MacKenzie, "Douglas Retires From Court," *Washington Post*, November 13, 1975, p. A1). However, President Ford would have had relatively little time to consider a replacement Justice since he did not assume the presidency until August 9, 1975, and a vacancy did not officially arise until Justice Douglas's November 12, 1975, retirement letter.

jj. During a November 29, 1975, press conference, White House Press Secretary Ron Nessen revealed that the President had decided to nominate, as well as announce his choice of, Stevens the same day (Spencer Rich, "Ford Picks Chicago Jurist," *Washington Post*, November 29, 1975, p. A1). The announcement occurred on November 28, 1975.

kk. Although Justice Stewart's decision to retire was not made public until June 18, 1981, Stewart delivered a letter, stating his desire to retire, to President Ronald Reagan on May 18, 1981 (U.S. National Archives and Records Administration, Office of the Federal Register, *Public Papers of the Presidents of the United States: Ronald Reagan, 1981* (Washington: GPO, 1982), p. 539.

ll. In this case, the distinction between the dates of announcement of the nominee and the formal nomination is particularly important. On July 7, 1981, President Reagan "announced his intention" to nominate Judge O'Connor upon completion of a required FBI background check (U.S. National Archives and Records Administration, Office of the Federal Register, *Public Papers of the Presidents of the United States: Ronald Reagan, 1981, (*Washington: GPO, 1982), p. 597). President Reagan did not formally nominate her until August 19, 1981, after she had passed the background check.

mm. Although Chief Justice Burger officially notified President Reagan, by letter on June 17, 1986, of his desire to retire, Burger privately informed Reagan of his plans on May 27, 1986 ("Remarks on the Resignation of Supreme Court Chief Justice Warren E. Burger and the Nominations of William H. Rehnquist To Be Chief Justice and Antonin Scalia To Be an Associate Justice," U.S. National Archives and Records Administration, Office of the Federal Register, *Public Papers of the Presidents of the United States: Ronald Reagan, 1986,* vol. 2 (Washington: GPO, 1989), p. 781).

nn. The May 27, 1986, date is used because Chief Justice Burger's intention to retire (known to President Reagan on May 27) alerted the President of the forthcoming opportunity to elevate Rehnquist from Associate Justice to Chief Justice, and in turn, of the opportunity to nominate someone to succeed Rehnquist as an Associate Justice.

oo. President Reagan reportedly "had no advance warning of the resignation" (Al Kamen, "Nixon-Appointed Democrat Cites Age, Health," *Washington Post*, June 27, 1987, p. A1).

pp. Judge Ginsburg withdrew his name from consideration before being officially nominated, but after President Reagan had announced his intention to nominate Ginsburg. Among other controversies surrounding the nomination, Ginsburg admitted shortly before withdrawing that he "had smoked marijuana while a Harvard law professor" (Lou Cannon and Ruth Markus, "Judge Kennedy Likely Choice," *Washington Post*, November 9, 1987, p. A6).

qq. President George H. W. Bush stated in a July 23, 1990, press conference nominating Souter that he had not decided on a final nominee until that day (U.S. National Archives and Records Administration, Office of the Federal Register, *Public Papers of the Presidents of the United States: George Bush, 1990,* vol. 2 (Washington: GPO, 1992), p. 1051).

rr. On the details of transferring Justice White's retirement letter to the President beginning on March 18, 1993, see Dennis J. Hutchinson, *The Man Who Was Once Whizzer White: A Portrait of Justice Byron R. White* (New York: Free Press , 1998, p. 437) and Ward, *Deciding to Leave,* p. 183, n. 183. One of Justice White's former law clerks, by then working in the White House, delivered the letter on the March 19, 1993.

ss. President William J. Clinton announced Ginsburg's nomination on June 14, 1993. However, President Clinton noted in his nomination speech that he asked Ginsburg to accept the nomination on the evening of June 13 (U.S. National Archives and Records Administration, Office of the Federal Register, *Public Papers of the Presidents of the United States: William J. Clinton, 1993,* vol. 1 (Washington: GPO, 1994), p. 843).

tt. January 1, 1994, is a slight estimation, since Justice Blackmun reportedly "told President Bill Clinton at Renaissance Weekend over the New Year's holiday in Hilton Head, S.C., that this would be his last term (Tony Mauro, "How Blackmun Hid Retirement Plans," *New Jersey Law Journal,* April 25, 1994, p. 18.). Clinton publicly announced Blackmun's retirement on April 6, 1994. (U.S. National Archives and Records Administration, Office of the Federal Register, *Public Papers of the Presidents of the United States: William J. Clinton, 1994,* vol. 1 (Washington: GPO, 1995), p. 597).

Table 2. Duration in Days Between Major Events in the Supreme Court Nomination-and-Confirmation Process, 1900-2010

Nominating President	Outgoing Justice	Actual or Prospective Vacancy Apparently Became Known to President		Nominee	Number of Days Elapsed from...					
		When	How		Vacancy to Nomination Announcement	Nomination Announcement to First Hearing	First Hearing to Committee Final Action	Committee Final Action to Senate Action	Nomination Announcement to Final Senate Action	Starting Date to Final Senate Action
Theodore Roosevelt	Horace Gray	09/15/1902	Death of outgoing Justice	Oliver Wendell Holmes	78	No record of hearing	No record of hearing	0	2	80
Theodore Roosevelt	George Shiras, Jr.	08/20/1902[a]	Public reports of imminent retirement	William R. Day	147	No record of hearing	No record of hearing	0	40	187
Theodore Roosevelt	Henry B. Brown	03/08/1906[b]	Outgoing Justice notified President of intention to retire[c]	William H. Moody	244	No record of hearing	No record of hearing	2	35	279
William Howard Taft	Rufus W. Peckham	10/24/1909	Death of outgoing Justice	Horace H. Lurton	50	No record of hearing	No record of hearing	4	7	59
William Howard Taft	David J. Brewer	03/28/1910	Death of outgoing Justice	Charles Evans Hughes	28	No record of hearing	No record of hearing	0	7	35
William Howard Taft	Melville W. Fuller *Chief Justice*	07/04/1910	Death of outgoing Chief Justice	Edward D. White	161	Nomination was not referred to Judiciary Committee	Nomination was not referred to Judiciary Committee	Nom. was not referred to Judiciary Committee	0	161
William Howard Taft	Edward D. White	12/12/1910	White nomination by President to be Chief Justice	Willis Van Devanter	0	No record of hearing	No record of hearing	0	3	3

Table 2. (Continued)

Nominating President	Outgoing Justice	Actual or Prospective Vacancy Apparently Became Known to President		Nominee	Number of Days Elapsed from...					
		When	How		Vacancy to Nomination Announce-ment	Nomination Announce-ment to First Hearing	First Hearing to Committee Final Action	Committee Final Action to Senate Action	Nomination Announce-ment to Final Senate Action	Starting Date to Final Senate Action
William Howard Taft	William H. Moody	06/15/1910[d]	Congressional action authorizing retirement	Joseph R. Lamar	180	No record of hearing	No record of hearing	0	3	183
William Howard Taft	John Marshall Harlan	10/14/1911	Death of outgoing Justice	Mahlon Pitney	128	No record of hearing	No record of hearing	9	23	151
Woodrow Wilson	Horace H. Lurton	07/12/1914	Death of outgoing Justice	James C. McReynolds	38	No record of hearing	No record of hearing	5	10	48
Woodrow Wilson	Joseph R. Lamar	01/02/1916	Death of outgoing Justice	Louis D. Brandeis	26	12	105	8	125	151
Woodrow Wilson	Charles Evans Hughes	06/10/1916[e]	Resignation to pursue political office	John H. Clarke	34	No record of hearing	No record of hearing	0	10	44
Warren Harding	Edward D. White	05/19/1921	Death of outgoing Justice	William Howard Taft	42	Nomination was not referred to Judiciary Committee	Nomination was not referred to Judiciary Committee	Nomination was not referred to Judiciary Committee	0	42
Warren Harding	John H. Clarke	09/05/1922	Resignation letter submitted to President	George Sutherland	0	Nomination was not referred to Judiciary Committee	Nomination was not referred to Judiciary Committee	Nomination was not referred to Judiciary Committee	0	0
Warren Harding	William R. Day	09/05/1922[f]	Public reports of imminent retirement	Pierce Butler	79	No record of hearing	No record of hearing	No record of hearing	No Senate action	No final action

Table 2. (Continued)

Nominating President	Outgoing Justice	Actual or Prospective Vacancy Apparently Became Known to President		Nominee	Number of Days Elapsed from...					
		When	How		Vacancy to Nomination Announcement	Nomination Announcement to First Hearing	First Hearing to Committee Final Action	Committee Final Action to Senate Action	Nomination Announcement to Final Senate Action	Starting Date to Final Senate Action
		12/04/1922	Lack of action on first nomination of Butler	Pierce Butler	1	No record of hearing	No record of hearing	3	16	4
Warren Harding	Mahlon Pitney	12/16/1922	White House announced forthcoming retirement[g]	Edward T. Sanford	24	No record of hearing	No record of hearing	0	20	44
Calvin Coolidge	Joseph McKenna	12/25/1924[h]	Public reports of imminent retirement	Harlan F. Stone	11	23	5[h]	3	31	42
Herbert Hoover	William Howard Taft	02/03/1930	Retirement letter submitted to President	Charles Evans Hughes	0	No record of hearing	No record of hearing	3	10	10
Herbert Hoover	Edward T. Sanford	03/08/1930	Death of outgoing Justice	John J. Parker	13	15	16	16	47	60
Herbert Hoover	Edward T. Sanford	05/07/1930	Parker nomination rejected by Senate	Owen J. Roberts	2	No record of hearing	No record of hearing	1	11	13
Herbert Hoover	Oliver Wendell Holmes, Jr.	01/12/1932	Outgoing Justice notified President of intention to retire	Benjamin N. Cardozo	34	4	4	1	9	43
Franklin D. Roosevelt	Willis Van Devanter	05/18/1937[i]	Retirement letter	Hugo L. Black	86	No record of hearing	No record of hearing	1	5	91

Table 2. (Continued)

Nominating President	Outgoing Justice	Actual or Prospective Vacancy Apparently Became Known to President		Nominee	Number of Days Elapsed from...					
		When	How		Vacancy to Nomination Announcement	Nomination Announcement to First Hearing	First Hearing to Committee Final Action	Committee Final Action to Senate Action	Nomination Announcement to Final Senate Action	Starting Date to Final Senate Action
			submitted to President							
Franklin D. Roosevelt	George Sutherland	01/05/1938	Retirement letter submitted to President	Stanley F. Reed	10	5	4	1	10	20
Franklin D. Roosevelt	Benjamin N. Cardozo	07/09/1938[j]	Death of outgoing Justice	Felix Frankfurter	180	5	6	1	12	192
Franklin D. Roosevelt	Louis D. Brandeis	02/13/1939[k]	Retirement letter submitted to President	William O. Douglas	35	4	3	8	15	50
Franklin D. Roosevelt	Pierce Butler	11/16/1939	Death of outgoing Justice	Frank Murphy	49	7	4	1	12	61
Franklin D. Roosevelt	James C. McReynolds	01/22/1941	Outgoing Justice notified President of intention to retire[l]	James F. Byrnes	141	Nomination was not referred to Judiciary Committee	Nomination was not referred to Judiciary Committee	Nomination was not referred to Judiciary Committee	0	141
Franklin D. Roosevelt	Charles Evans Hughes *Chief Justice*	06/02/1941[m]	Retirement letter submitted to President	Harlan F. Stone	10	9	2	4	15	25
Franklin D. Roosevelt	Harlan F. Stone	06/12/1941	Stone nomination by President to be Chief Justice	Robert H. Jackson	0	9	9	7	25	25

Table 2. (Continued)

Nominating President	Outgoing Justice	Actual or Prospective Vacancy Apparently Became Known to President		Nominee	Number of Days Elapsed from...					
		When	How		Vacancy to Nomination Announcement	Nomination Announcement to First Hearing	First Hearing to Committee Final Action	Committee Final Action to Senate Action	Nomination Announcement to Final Senate Action	Starting Date to Final Senate Action
Franklin D. Roosevelt	James F. Byrnes	10/03/1942[n]	Byrnes appointment to other public office	Wiley B. Rutledge	100	11	10	7	28	128
Franklin D. Roosevelt	Benjamin N. Cardozo	07/09/1938[j]	Death of outgoing Justice	Felix Frankfurter	180	5	6	1	12	192
Franklin D. Roosevelt	Louis D. Brandeis	02/13/1939[k]	Retirement letter submitted to President	William O. Douglas	35	4	3	8	15	50
Franklin D. Roosevelt	Pierce Butler	11/16/1939	Death of outgoing Justice	Frank Murphy	49	7	4	1	12	61
Franklin D. Roosevelt	James C. McReynolds	01/22/1941	Outgoing Justice notified President of intention to retire[l]	James F. Byrnes	141	Nomination was not referred to Judiciary Committee	Nomination was not referred to Judiciary Committee	Nomination was not referred to Judiciary Committee	0	141
Franklin D. Roosevelt	Charles Evans Hughes *Chief Justice*	06/02/1941[m]	Retirement letter submitted to President	Harlan F. Stone	10	9	2	4	15	25
Franklin D. Roosevelt	Harlan F. Stone	06/12/1941	Stone nomination by President to be Chief Justice	Robert H. Jackson	0	9	9	7	25	25
Franklin D. Roosevelt	James F. Byrnes	10/03/1942[n]	Byrnes appointment	Wiley B. Rutledge	100	11	10	7	28	128

Table 2. (Continued)

Nominating President	Outgoing Justice	Actual or Prospective Vacancy Apparently Became Known to President		Nominee	Number of Days Elapsed from...					
		When	How		Vacancy to Nomination Announce-ment	Nomination Announce-ment to First Hearing	First Hearing to Committee Final Action	Committee Final Action to Senate Action	Nomination Announce-ment to Final Senate Action	Starting Date to Final Senate Action
			to other public office							
Harry. S. Truman	Owen J. Roberts	06/30/1945[o]	Retirement letter submitted to President	Harold H. Burton	80	No record of hearing	No record of hearing	0	1	81
Harry S. Truman	Harlan F. Stone *Chief Justice*	04/22/1946	Death of outgoing Chief Justice	Fred M. Vinson	45	8	5	1	14	59
Harry S. Truman	Frank Murphy	07/19/1949	Death of outgoing Justice	Thomas C. Clark	9	12	3	6	21	30
Harry S. Truman	Wiley B. Rutledge	09/10/1949	Death of outgoing Justice	Sherman Minton	5	12	6	1	19	24
Dwight D. Eisenhower	Fred M. Vinson *Chief Justice*	09/08/1953	Death of outgoing Chief Justice	Earl Warren	24	*Recess appointment, 10/02/1953*				
					125[p]	22	22	5	49	174
Dwight D. Eisenhower	Robert H. Jackson	10/09/1954	Death of outgoing Justice	John Marshall Harlan II	30	No record of hearing	No record committee action	No record of committee action	No record of final action after committee referral	No record of final action after comm-ittee referral
					5	45	14	6	65	70

Table 2. (Continued)

Nominating President	Outgoing Justice	Actual or Prospective Vacancy Apparently Became Known to President		Nominee	Number of Days Elapsed from...					
		When	How		Vacancy to Nomination Announcement	Nomination Announcement to First Hearing	First Hearing to Committee Final Action	Committee Final Action to Senate Action	Nomination Announcement to Final Senate Action	Starting Date to Final Senate Action
Dwight D. Eisenhower	Sherman Minton	09/07/1956	Retirement Letter submitted to President	William J. Brennan	38	*Recess appointment, 10/15/1956*				
					129[q]	43	6	15	64	193
Dwight D. Eisenhower	Stanley F. Reed	01/31/1957	Press conference held by Reed announcing retirement[r]	Charles E. Whittaker	30	16	0	1	17	47
Dwight D. Eisenhower	Harold H. Burton	10/06/1958	Retirement letter submitted to President	Potter Stewart	8	*Recess appointment, 10/14/1958*				
					103[s]	82	11	15	108	211
John F. Kennedy	Charles E. Whittaker	03/28/1962	Retirement letter received by President[t]	Byron R. White	2	12	0	0	12	14
John F. Kennedy	Felix Frankfurter	08/28/1962[u]	Retirement letter submitted to President	Arthur J. Goldberg	1	13	14	0	27	28
Lyndon B. Johnson	Arthur J. Goldberg	07/20/1965	Goldberg appointment to other public office[v]	Abe Fortas	8	8	5	1	14	22
Lyndon B. Johnson	Thomas C. Clark	02/28/1967	Outgoing Justice notified President of intention to retire[w]	Thurgood Marshall	105	30	21	27	78	183

Table 2. (Continued)

Nominating President	Outgoing Justice	Actual or Prospective Vacancy Apparently Became Known to President			Number of Days Elapsed from...					
		When	How	Nominee	Vacancy to Nomination Announce-ment	Nomination Announce-ment to First Hearing	First Hearing to Committee Final Action	Committee Final Action to Senate Action	Nomination Announce-ment to Final Senate Action	Starting Date to Final Senate Action
Lyndon B. Johnson	Earl Warren *Chief Justice*	06/13/1968[x]	Retirement letter submitted to President	Abe Fortas	13	15	68	14	97	110
Lyndon B. Johnson	Abe Fortas	06/26/1968[y]	Fortas nomination by Johnson to be Chief Justice	Homer Thornberry	0	15	No record of committee vote	No record of final committee action	Nomination withdrawn by President (10/04/1968)	Nominati on With-drawn by President
Richard M. Nixon	Earl Warren *Chief Justice*	01/20/1969[z]	Fortas Chief Justice nomination withdrawn by President (10/4/1968)	Warren E. Burger	121	13	0	6	19	140
Richard M. Nixon	Abe Fortas	05/14/1969	Resignation letter submitted to President	Clement F. Haynsworth, Jr.	96	29	23	43	95	191
		11/21/1969	Haynsworth nomination rejected by Senate	G. Harrold Carswell	59	8	20	51	79	138
		04/08/1970	Carswell nomination rejected by Senate	Harry A. Blackmun	6	15	7	6	28	34
Richard M. Nixon	Hugo L. Black	09/17/1971	Retirement letter	Lewis F. Powell, Jr.	34	13	20	13	46	80

Table 2. (Continued)

Nominating President	Outgoing Justice	Actual or Prospective Vacancy Apparently Became Known to President		Nominee	Number of Days Elapsed from...					
		When	How		Vacancy to Nomination Announcement	Nomination Announcement to First Hearing	First Hearing to Committee Final Action	Committee Final Action to Senate Action	Nomination Announcement to Final Senate Action	Starting Date to Final Senate Action
			submitted to President							
Richard M. Nixon	John Marshall Harlan II	09/23/1971	Retirement letter submitted to President	William H. Rehnquist	28	13	20	17	50	78
Gerald R. Ford	William O. Douglas	11/12/1975[aa]	Retirement letter submitted to President	John Paul Stevens	16	10	3	6	19	35
Ronald Reagan	Potter Stewart	05/18/1981[bb]	Retirement letter submitted to President	Sandra Day O'Connor	50	64	6	6	76	126
Ronald Reagan	Warren E. Burger *Chief Justice*	05/27/1986[cc]	Justice privately alerted President of intention to retire	William H. Rehnquist	21	42	16	34	92	113
Ronald Reagan	William H. Rehnquist	05/27/1986[dd]	Rehnquist nomination by Reagan to be Chief Justice	Antonin Scalia	21	49	9	34	92	113
Ronald Reagan	Lewis F. Powell, Jr.	06/26/1987[ee]	Press conference held by Powell announcing retirement	Robert H. Bork	5	76	21	17	114	119

Table 2. (Continued)

Nominating President	Outgoing Justice	Actual or Prospective Vacancy Apparently Became Known to President		Nominee	Number of Days Elapsed from...					
		When	How		Vacancy to Nomination Announcement	Nomination Announcement to First Hearing	First Hearing to Committee Final Action	Committee Final Action to Senate Action	Nomination Announcement to Final Senate Action	Starting Date to Final Senate Action
		10/23/1987	Bork nomination rejected by Senate	Douglas H. Ginsburg	6	Ginsburg withdrew (11/07/1987) before official nomination[ff]				
		11/07/1987	Ginsburg withdrawal	Anthony M. Kennedy	4	33	44	7	84	88
George H. W. Bush	William J. Brennan	07/20/1990	Retirement letter submitted to President	David H. Souter	3	52	14	5	71	74
George H. W. Bush	Thurgood Marshall	06/27/1991	Retirement letter submitted to President	Clarence Thomas	4	71	17	18	106	110
William J. Clinton	Byron R. White	03/19/1993[gg]	Retirement letter submitted to President	Ruth Bader Ginsburg	87	36	9	5	50	137
William J. Clinton	Harry A. Blackmun	01/01/1994[hh]	Justice privately alerted President	Stephen G. Breyer	132	60	7	10	77	209
George W. Bush	Sandra Day O'Connor	07/01/2005	Retirement letter submitted to President	John G. Roberts	18	Nomination withdrawn by President (09/05/2005) before the first Judiciary Committee hearing; re-nominated as Chief Justice (09/05/2005)				

Table 2. (Continued)

Nominating President	Outgoing Justice	Actual or Prospective Vacancy Apparently Became Known to President			Number of Days Elapsed from...					
		When	How	Nominee	Vacancy to Nomination Announcement	Nomination Announcement to First Hearing	First Hearing to Committee Final Action	Committee Final Action to Senate Action	Nomination Announcement to Final Senate Action	Starting Date to Final Senate Action
		09/05/2005	Announcement of Roberts nomination withdrawal and re-submission by President	Harriet Miers	28	Miers withdrew as nominee (10/27/2005) before the start of Judiciary Committee hearings				
		10/27/2005	Announcement of Miers withdrawal	Samuel A. Alito, Jr.	4	70	15	7	92	96
George W. Bush	William H. Rehnquist	09/03/2005	Death of outgoing Justice	John G. Roberts	2	7	10	7	24	26
Barack Obama	David H. Souter	05/01/2009	Retirement letter submitted to President	Sonia Sotomayor	25	48	15	9	72	97
Barack Obama	John Paul Stevens	04/09/2010	Retirement letter submitted to President	Elena Kagan	31	49	22	16	87	118

Sources: Durations for major intervals in the nomination-and-confirmation process were computed by the CRS authors. As described in the text, this research relied on historical newspapers, official presidential papers, and CRS correspondence with Presidential Libraries. Ward's *Deciding to Leave* was especially useful in compiling data on the reasons why Justices left the bench. Additional source information appears in the table notes below.

a. It is unclear when President Theodore Roosevelt learned of Justice Shiras's intention to retire. However, *Washington Post* coverage suggests that Shiras's forthcoming departure was well known in Washington by at least August 20, 1902 ("Knox May Not Want It: Belief that He Would Decline Justice Shiras' Position," *Washington Post*, August 20, 1902, p. 1).

b. According to the *Washington Post*, Justice Brown notified the President, on March 8, 1906, that he wished to retire ("To Leave the Bench: Justice Brown Will Retire in the Fall," *Washington Post*, March 8, 1906, p. 3).

c. It is unclear from the historical record whether the President learned of Justice Brown's desire to retire by letter, personal conversation, etc.

d. Justice Moody did not actually depart the Court until November 20, 1910 (Ward, *Deciding to Leave*, p. 5). However, "Illness of a serious nature has kept Justice Moody from his duties in the Supreme Court for almost a year. There have been occasional rumors of retirement, but Senator Lodge [on June 15, 1910] presented the real harbinger of that action, in the form of a bill extending the statute relating to retirement from the Supreme Court to cover the case of Mr. Moody" ("Moody Will Retire," *Washington Post*, June 15, 1910, p. 1).

e. On June 10, 1916, Justice Hughes resigned to pursue the 1916 Republican presidential nomination ("Hughes, With Words That Ring, Obeys Call to Lead Republicans," *Washington Post*, June 11, 1916, p. 1). Although historical media research does not indicate that President Wilson knew for certain that Justice Hughes would resign, media reports had hinted at a Hughes resignation throughout the spring of 1916.

f. Day did not leave the Court until November 13, 1922. However, the *Washington Post* reported that Day's consideration of retirement was mentioned at a White House briefing on September 5, 1922 ("Justice Day May Leave the Bench," *Washington Post*, September 6, 1922, p. 1).

g. Although Justice Pitney's resignation was effective as of December 31, 1922, the White House announced Pitney's forthcoming departure on December 16, 1922 ("Resigns," *Chicago Daily Tribune*, December 17, 1922, p. 17).

h. Justice McKenna did not officially retire until January 5, 1925. However, the media reported his imminent retirement on December 25, 1924 ("M'Kenna to Retire Soon as a Justice of the Supreme Court," *Washington Post*, December 25, 1924, p. 2). Duration calculations for final Senate action on Stone are based on the February 5, 1925, confirmation date shown in Table 1, not the January 26, 1925, recommittal.

i. For an account of Justice Van Devanter privately alerting a reporter of his decision to retire on the morning of the announcement, see "News 'Beat' Aided by Van Devanter," *New York Times*, May 23, 1937, p. 40.

j. Although Justice Cardozo had been ill and away from the bench since December 1937 (United Press, "Supreme Court Liberal Succumbs to Heart Ailment in N.Y.," *Washington Post*, July 10, 1938, p. M1), a definite need to nominate a new Justice did not occur until Cardozo's death on July 9, 1938.

k. Justice Brandeis had been away from the bench for a month, recovering from a heart attack, prior to announcing his retirement (United Press, "Justice Brandeis, Dean of Supreme Court, Quits," *Los Angeles Times*, February 14, 1939, p. 1). Nonetheless, his retirement was considered abrupt, suggesting that President Roosevelt had little advance notice to consider a successor.

l. It is unclear from the historical record whether the President learned of Justice McReynolds's desire to retire by letter, personal conversation, etc.

m. Although Chief Justice Hughes's retirement due to age and poor health had been "rumored some months" prior to submission of his formal retirement letter (Walter Trohan, "Hughes Retires From Court," *Chicago Daily Tribune*, June 3, 1941, p. 1), the definite need for a new nominee did not arise until Hughes announced his retirement.

n. Justice Byrnes resigned at President Roosevelt's request on October 3, 1942, becoming Director of Economic Stability. Roosevelt was, therefore, aware of an impending vacancy on the Court prior to the formal resignation, although the precise date is unclear. For a summary of Byrnes's transition from the Court to his new post, see Associated Press, "Byrnes Resigns From Bench in Letter to President," *New York Times*, October 4, 1942, p. 45.

o. Although President Truman did not announce Justice Roberts's intention to retire until July 5, 1945 (United Press, "Morganthau and Roberts Resign," *Los Angeles Times*, July 6, 1945, p. 1), Justice Roberts's retirement letter is dated June 30, 1945. Truman received the letter on that date "or soon thereafter" (e-mail communication between CRS Information Specialist Dana Ely and Truman Library Archivist Randy Sowell, September 2, 2005).

p. Congress was not in session when Chief Justice Vinson died on September 8, 1953 (U.S. Congress, Joint Committee on Printing, *2003-2004 Official Congressional Directory: 108th Congress* (Washington: GPO), p. 519). President Eisenhower recess-appointed Earl Warren as Chief Justice on October 2, 1953 and nominated him to the Court, on January 11, 1954, after Congress reconvened for the second session of the 83rd Congress. Therefore, although the interval between the starting date (September 8, 1953, as shown in **Table 1**) and announcement date (January 11, 1954) is 125 days, and the entire interval from the starting date until final Senate action (March 1, 1954) is 174 days, the President's actual decision-making timetable could also be classified as 24 days, or the interval between Vinson's death (September 8, 1953) and Eisenhower's recess appointment of Chief Justice Warren (October 2, 1953). Both intervals are used to calculate the median elapsed time from vacancy to nomination announcement. Nonetheless, the long intervals have a minimal impact on computing the median durations between stages in the process because the median is less sensitive than the mean to extremely high or low values.

q. Congress was not in session when Justice Minton submitted his retirement letter to the President on September 7, 1956 (U.S. Congress, Joint Committee on Printing, *2003-2004 Official Congressional Directory: 108th Congress,* (Washington: GPO), p. 519). President Eisenhower recess-appointed William J. Brennan as Associate Justice on October 15, 1956, and nominated him to the Court, on January 14, 1957, after Congress convened for the first session of the 85th Congress. Therefore, although the interval between the starting date (September 7, 1956, as shown in Table 1) and announcement date (January 14, 1957) is 129 days, and the entire interval from the starting date until final Senate action (March 19, 1957) is 193 days, the President's actual decision-making timetable could also be classified as 38 days, or the interval between Brennan's retirement announcement (September 7, 1956) and Eisenhower's recess appointment of Justice Brennan (October 15, 1956). Both intervals are used to calculate the median elapsed time from vacancy to nomination announcement. Nonetheless, the long intervals have a minimal impact on computing the median durations between stages in the process because median is less sensitive than the mean to extremely high or low values.

r. Whether President Eisenhower first learned of Justice Reed's retirement through the press conference or a letter from Reed is unclear. Contemporary media coverage mentioned a press conference and a letter to Eisenhower (Edward T. Folliard, "Reed Is Retiring From High Court," *Washington Post*, February 1, 1957, p. A1). However, political scientist Artemus Ward's account asserts that Reed announced his retirement through a press conference (Ward, *Deciding to Leave*, pp. 162-163). Regardless, both events occurred on January 31, 1957. For the January 31 correspondence between Reed and Eisenhower, see "Letter to Stanley Reed Regarding His Retirement From Active Service as An Associate Justice of the Supreme Court," U.S. National Archives and Records Administration, Office of the Federal Register, *Public Papers of the Presidents of the United States: Dwight D. Eisenhower, 1957* (Washington: GPO, 1958), pp. 109-110.

s. Congress was not in session when Burton submitted his retirement letter to the President on October 6, 1958 (U.S. Congress, Joint Committee on Printing,*2003-2004 Official Congressional Directory: 108th Congress* (Washington: GPO), p. 519). President Eisenhower recess-appointed Potter Stewart as Associate Justice on October 14, 1958, and nominated him to the Court, on January 17, 1959, after Congress convened for the first session of the 86th Congress. Therefore, although the interval between the starting date (October 6, 1958, as shown in Table 1) and nomination date (January 17, 1959) is 103 days, and the entire interval from the starting date until final Senate action (May 5, 1959) is 211 days, the President's actual decision-making timetable could also be classified as eight days, or the interval between Burton's retirement announcement (October 6, 1958) and Eisenhower's recess appointment of Justice Stewart (October 14, 1958). Both intervals are used to calculate the median elapsed time from vacancy to nomination announcement. Nonetheless, the long intervals have a minimal impact on computing the median durations between stages in the process because the median is less sensitive than the mean to extremely high or low values.

t. This information is based on e-mail communication between CRS Information Specialist Dana Ely and Kennedy Library Reference Technician Sharon Kelly, September 14, 2005.

u. August 28, 1962, is the only definitive date which can be established, based on available data, as the earliest point at which President Kennedy learned of Justice Frankfurter's intention to retire. However, President Kennedy's quick nomination of Goldberg, and Justice Frankfurter's poor health in the weeks leading up to his retirement, suggest that President Kennedy was considering prospective nominees well before Frankfurter stepped down. Kennedy's letter to Justice Frankfurter accepting his retirement references a visit the President paid to Frankfurter to check on his health sometime during the summer of 1962 (U.S. National Archives and Records Administration, Office of the Federal Register, *Public Papers of the Presidents of the United States: John F. Kennedy, 1962*, (Washington: GPO, 1963), p. 656). According to Kennedy Library Reference Technician Sharon Kelly, Kennedy's office files suggest that correspondence between Frankfurter, Special Assistant for National Security Affairs McGeorge Bundy, and the President would have alerted Kennedy to Frankfurter's declining health around May 17, 1962 (e-mail communication between CRS Information Specialist Dana Ely and Kennedy Library Reference Technician Sharon Kelly, September 14, 2005).

v. President Lyndon B. Johnson unexpectedly nominated Justice Goldberg to be U.S. Ambassador to the United Nations following the death on July 14, 1965, of the previous ambassador, Adlai E. Stevenson. See Carroll Kilpatrick, "Goldberg is Named to Stevenson Post," *Washington Post*, July 21, 1965, p. A1.

w. Despite the fact that Justice Clark announced his forthcoming retirement on February 28, 1967, historical evidence suggests that Johnson might have prompted Clark's retirement as early as January 1967, when the President prepared to nominated Justice Clark's son, Ramsey, to be Attorney General. "On January 25, 1967, Johnson told Ramsey that he could only be named the permanent attorney general if his father stepped down from the Court" (Ward, *Deciding to Leave*, p. 170).

x. Although President Johnson did not announce Chief Justice Warren's retirement until June 26, he received Warren's retirement letter on June 13, 1968 (U.S. National Archives and Records Administration, Office of the Federal Register, *Public Papers of the Presidents of the United States: Lyndon B. Johnson, 1968-69*, vol. 1 (Washington: GPO, 1966), p. 746).

y. Although a specific opportunity to name a new Associate Justice did not arise until the Fortas Chief Justice nomination on June 26, 1968, it was reported that "[s]ome Texans at the Capitol are sure that Mr. Johnson has planned for the last four years to name Thornberry to the Supreme Court before he [Johnson] left office," (Richard L. Lyons, "Homer Thornberry: 'Constructive Liberal,' Close LBJ friend," *Washington Post,* June 27, 1969, p. 1).

z. January 20, 1969 (the date of Richard M. Nixon's inauguration), is used as the starting date for the vacancy because it marks the beginning of President Nixon's official decision-making powers. After the Abe Fortas Chief Justice nomination failed, President Johnson announced on October 2, 1968, that he would not name another nominee (U.S. National Archives and Records Administration, Office of the Federal Register, *Public Papers of the Presidents of the United States: Lyndon B. Johnson, 1968-69*, vol. 2 (Washington: GPO, 1966), p. 509). Eight days later, Johnson elaborated on his decision. The President wrote that although he would have made another nomination in "ordinary times," the situation was extraordinary and that, "Under the circumstances, the foundations of government would be better served by the present Chief Justice [Earl Warren] remaining [in office] until emotionalism subsides, reason and fairness prevail (U.S. National Archives and Records Administration, Office of the Federal Register, *Public Papers of the Presidents of the United States: Lyndon B. Johnson, 1968-69*, vol. 2 (Washington: GPO, 1970), p. 1024). On December 3, 1968, Chief Justice Warren informed President-elect Richard M. Nixon that he was willing to continue serving until a successor was confirmed ("Statement by the Chief Justice," December 4, 1968, Earl Warren Papers, Manuscript Division, Library of Congress, Washington, DC). In a May 1969, conversation with reporters, President Nixon offered an unusually detailed discussion of his decision-making process surrounding the Burger nomination. Nixon reported that he thought "it would not be a proper mark of respect for the Court and for the Chief Justice to have a nomination go down, say, in February or March, and then have possibly the Senate hearings and the like at a time that the Court was sitting," and that his target date for a nomination decision was between May 1 and June 1, 1968 (U.S. National Archives and Records Administration, Office of the Federal Register, *Public Papers of the Presidents of the United States: Richard Nixon, 1970*, (Washington: GPO, 1971), p. 390).

aa. Chief Justice Warren Burger reportedly "hint[ed] at a possible vacancy" on the Court in a letter to President Gerald Ford on November 10, 1975, and offered "factors for [the President] to consider when appointing a new justice" (e-mail communication between CRS Information Specialist Dana Ely and Ford Library Archivist Technician Joshua Cochran, September 12, 2005). Justice Douglas's health had been in question since December 31, 1974, when he suffered a stroke (John P. MacKenzie, "Douglas Retires From Court," *Washington Post*, November 13, 1975, p. A1). However, President Ford would have had relatively little time to consider a replacement Justice since he did not assume the presidency until August 9, 1975, and a vacancy did not officially arise until Justice Douglas's November 12, 1975 retirement letter.

bb. Although Justice Stewart's decision to retire was not made public until June 18, 1981, Stewart delivered a letter, stating his desire to retire, to President Ronald Reagan on May 18, 1981 (U.S. National Archives and Records Administration, Office of the Federal Register, *Public Papers of the Presidents of the United States: Ronald Reagan, 1981* (Washington: GPO, 1982), p. 539).

cc. Although Chief Justice Burger officially notified President Reagan of his desire to retire, by letter on June 17, 1986, Burger privately informed Reagan of his plans on May 27, 1986 ("Remarks on the Resignation of Supreme Court Chief Justice Warren E. Burger and the Nominations of William H. Rehnquist To Be Chief Justice and Antonin Scalia To Be an Associate Justice," U.S. National Archives and Records Administration, Office of the Federal Register, *Public Papers of the Presidents of the United States: Ronald Reagan, 1986,* vol. 2 (Washington: GPO, 1989), p. 781).

dd. The May 27, 1986, date is used because Chief Justice Burger's intention to retire (known to President Reagan on May 27) alerted the President of the forthcoming opportunity to elevate Rehnquist from Associate Justice to Chief Justice, and in turn, of the opportunity to nominate someone to succeed Rehnquist as an Associate Justice.

ee. President Reagan reportedly "had no advance warning of the resignation" (Al Kamen, "Nixon-Appointed Democrat Cites Age, Health," *Washington Post*, June 27, 1987, p. A1).

ff. Judge Ginsburg withdrew his name from consideration before being officially nominated, but after President Reagan had announced his intention to nominate Ginsburg. Among other controversies surrounding the nomination, Ginsburg admitted shortly before withdrawing that he "had smoked marijuana while a Harvard law professor" (Lou Cannon and Ruth Markus, "Judge Kennedy Likely Choice," *Washington Post*, November 9, 1987, p. A6).

gg. On the details of transferring Justice White's retirement letter to the President beginning on March 18, 1993, see Dennis J. Hutchinson, *The Man Who Was Once Whizzer White: A Portrait of Justice Byron R. White* (New York: Free Press , 1998, p. 437) and Ward, *Deciding to Leave,* p. 183, n. 183. One of Justice White's former law clerks, by then working in the White House, delivered the letter on the March 19, 1993.

hh. January 1, 1994, is an estimation, since Justice Blackmun reportedly "told President Bill Clinton at Renaissance Weekend over the New Year's holiday in Hilton Head, S.C., that this would be his last term (Tony Mauro, "How Blackmun Hid Retirement Plans," *New Jersey Law Journal,* April 25, 1994, p. 18.). Clinton publicly announced Blackmun's retirement on April 6, 1994. (U.S. National Archives and Records Administration, Office of the Federal Register, *Public Papers of the Presidents of the United States: William J. Clinton, 1994,* vol. 1 (Washington: GPO), 1995, p. 597).

Table 3. Median Duration in Days between Major Events in the Supreme Court Nomination-and-Confirmation Process, 1900-2010

	Median Number of Days Elapsed from ... [a]					
Time Period	**President Apparently Learned of Actual or Prospective Vacancy to Nomination Announcement**	**Nomination Announcement to First Hearing**	**First Hearing to Committee Final Action**	**Committee Final Action to Final Senate Action**	**Nomination Announcement to Final Senate Action**	**President Apparently Learned of Actual or Prospective Vacancy to Final Senate Action**
1900-1980	34	12.5	6	3	17	59
1981- 2009	19.5	49	15	9	84	113
1900- 2010	28	15	9.5	5.5	23.5	79

Sources: Durations for major intervals in the nomination-and-confirmation process were computed by the CRS authors. As described in the text, this research relied on historical newspapers, official presidential papers, and CRS correspondence with Presidential Libraries. Artemus Ward's, *Deciding to Leave: The Politics of Retirement from the United States Supreme Court* (Albany: State University of New York Press, 2003) was especially useful in compiling data on the reasons why Justices left the bench.

Note: For a listing of all Supreme Court nominations made during the 1900-2009 period and, for each nomination, the dates of the "major events" accounted for in the columns in **Table 3**, see the preceding **Table 1**. For a listing, for each nomination, of the duration in days between major events in the Supreme Court nomination-and-confirmation process, see **Table 2**.

a. In **Table 3**, the median amount of time from vacancy to final Senate action within each time period does not necessarily equal the sum of the medians for each stage in the nomination-and-confirmation process. Likewise, the median length of time for all Senate actions (i.e., from nomination announcement to final Senate action) within each time period does not equal the sum of the medians for each stage. The median identifies the mid-point for individual sets of observations. Because each stage of the process can have a different number of observations, and because the data are also not a "normal" (i.e., "bell-shaped") distribution, the sum of the medians for individual stages generally is not equal to the median for the entire period. For more information, see chapter 4 in Ya-lun Chou, *Statistical Analysis for Business and Economics* (New York: Elsevier, 1989).

End Notes

[1] The methodology for identifying relevant dates and calculating durations is explained throughout the report. Research that relies on different methodology may yield different results.

[2] For a discussion of *official* actions for all Supreme Court nominations since 1789, see CRS Report RL33225, *Supreme Court Nominations, 1789 - 2009: Actions by the Senate, the Judiciary Committee, and the President*, by Denis Steven Rutkus and Maureen Bearden.

[3] Letter from John Paul Stevens, Associate Justice, to Barack Obama, President of the United States, April 9, 2010, http://www.supremecourt.gov/publicinfo/press/JPSLetter.pdf. Assuming the Court follows its normal schedule, the current term will end in late June or early July 2010.

[4] See, for example, Robert Barnes, "For Justice Stevens, a Weighty Decision," *Washington Post*, April 4, 2010, p. A-1.

[5] Les Fleet and Cheryl Bolen, "Stevens Announces He Will Retire at End of Current Supreme Court Term," *Daily Report for Executives*, April 12, 2010, pp. A-6.

[6] Letter from John Paul Stevens to Barack Obama, April 9, 2010.

[7] The White House, Office of the Press Secretary, "Remarks by the President on the Retirement of Justice Stevens and on the West Virginia Mining Tragedy," April 9, 2010, http://www.whitehouse.gov/the-press-office/remarks-president-retirement-justice-stevens-and-west-virginia-mining-tragedy.

[8] See NBC News Transcripts, "Senator Patrick Leahy and Senator Jeff Sessions Discuss Supreme Court Vacancy and Possible Nominees," "Meet the Press," April 11, 2010, transcript obtained via Nexis (subscription required), p. 5; and Kathleen Hunter, "Leahy: New Justice to Be Confirmed by August," *Roll Call*, April 11, 2010, http://www.rollcall.com/news/45036-1.html. On timing concerning the current nomination, see also Seth Stern, "For High Court Nominations, Timing is Critical," *CQ Today*, vol. 46, no. 47 (April 16, 2010), p. 1; and Federal News Service, "Press Conference with Senator Patrick Leahy (D-VT); Senator Chuck Schumer (D-NY)," April 13, 2010, transcript obtained via Nexis (subscription required), p. 4. Both of the latter sources suggest that timing intervals can be measured differently, and produce different results, than some of the intervals noted in this chapter. See the "Objectives of This chapter" section for additional discussion.

[9] The White House, Office of the Press Secretary, "Remarks by the President and Solicitor General Elena Kagan at the Nomination of Solicitor General Elena Kagan to the Supreme Court," May 10, 2010, http://www.whitehouse.gov/the-press-office/remarks-president-and-solicitor-general-elena-kagan-nomination-solicitor-general-el.

[10] Sen. Patrick Leahy, "Statement Of Senator Patrick Leahy (D-Vt.), Chairman, Senate Judiciary Committee, Regarding The Nomination Of Solicitor General Elena Kagan To Be Associate Justice On The U.S. Supreme Court," May 19, 2010, http://leahy.senate.gov/press/press_releases/release/?id=041D951E-0B3D-45FE-A6EC-27C809E60327.

[11] U.S. President (Barack Obama), Remarks at Press Briefing By Press Secretary Robert Gibbs, May 1, 2009, The White House, http://www.whitehouse.gov/the_press_office/Press-Briefing-By-Press-Secretary-Robert-Gibbs-5-1-09/. Justice Souter's retirement letter is also dated May 1. See Letter from Justice David H. Souter to President Obama, May 1, 2009, http://www.supremecourtus.gov/publicinfo/press/DHSLetter.pdf.

[12] For differing views on the appropriate speed at which the Senate should consider and act on the Sotomayor nomination, see Senate floor debate over the scheduling decision of the Chair of the Senate Judiciary Committee to begin hearings on the nomination on July 13, 2009 (including remarks of the Chair of the Judiciary Committee, the committee's Ranking Member, the Senate Majority Leader, and the Senate Republican Leader), at "Sotomayor Nomination," *Congressional Record*, daily edition, vol. 155 , June 9, 2009, pp. S-6342-S6347. See also See Sen. Jeff Sessions, "Sessions: Supreme Court Hearings Will Focus On Proper Role of Judge and Court In American Legal System," press release, May 26, 2009, http://sessions.senate.gov/public/index.cfm?FuseAction=PressShop.NewsReleases&ContentRecord_id= 7da096fe-0676-632e-291a-91176c710fcb. White House press secretary Robert Gibbs also discussed timing issues at a May 26, 2009, press conference. See Press Briefing By Press Secretary Robert Gibbs, May 26, 2009, The White House, http://www.whitehouse. gov/the_press_office/Briefing-by-White- House-Press-Secretary-Robert-Gibbs-5-26-09/. See also National Public Radio, "Senate Will Debate Sotomayor's Nomination," Morning Edition, May 27, 2009, transcript accessed via LexisNexis (subscription required).

[13] Supreme Court of the United States, Office of the Curator, *Oaths of Office Taken by the Current Court*, information sheet, Washington, DC, p. 2, http://www.supremecourtus. gov/about/oathsof thecurrentcourt2009.pdf.

[14] Justice O'Connor's retirement letter is available at http://www.supremecourtus.gov/publicinfo/press/ oconnor 070105.pdf.

[15] "Senate GOP Leaders Seek Quick Action on Nominee to Replace Justice O'Connor," *Daily Report for Executives*, July 5, 2005, p. A-33.

[16] The judicial oath is required by the Judiciary Act of 1789, and the constitutional oath (which is administered to Members of Congress and all executive and judicial officers) is required by Article VI of the Constitution of the United States.

[17] See http://www.whitehouse.gov/news/releases/2005/10/20051003.html for the President's nomination statement and Miers's remarks.

[18] See http://www.whitehouse.gov/news/releases/2005/10/20051004-1.html for the text of this press conference.

[19] See http://frist.senate.gov/index.cfm?FuseAction=Speeches.Detail&Speech_id=293 for a copy of Senator Frist's statement.

[20] Kimberly Heffling, "Specter Decries Bush 'Pummeling' on Miers," *Washington Post*, October 11, 2005 http://www.washingtonpost.com/wp-dyn/content/article/2005/10/11/AR2005101101310.html.

[21] John Stanton, "Leaders Seeking To Place Miers On Court By Thanksgiving," *CongressDailyPM*, October 3, 2005.

[22] Sheryl Gay Stolberg, "Some Liberals and Conservatives Find Themselves in Awkward Spots," *New York Times*, October 4, 2005, p. A23.

[23] For a copy of the President's statement, see http://www.whitehouse.gov/news/releases/2005/10/20051027-2.html.

[24] For example, former Senator Daniel R. Coats, who shepherded Miers in the Senate, said "It was not all about the documents. It was a cumulation of things." See Keith Perine and Seth Stern, "Bush Faces Dilemma With New Pick," *CQ Today*, October 27, 2005. See http://www.cq.com/display.do?dockey=/cqonline/prod/ data/docs/ html/news/109/ news109-000001936032.html@allnews&metapub=CQ-NEWS&searchIndex=0 &seq Num=1.

[25] For President George W. Bush's nomination remarks and Judge Alito's response, see http://www.white house.gov/ news/releases/2005/10/print/20051031.html.

[26] For a copy of Senator Frist's press release, see http://frist.senate.gov/index. cfm?Fuse Action =Press Releases. Detail& PressRelease_id=2144&Month=10&Year=2005.

[27] See The Associated Press, "Reaction to the Alito Nomination," *Washington Post*, October 31, 2005, available at http://www.nexis.com/research/home?key=1130786095&_session=9eef720a-4a42-11da-9394-00008a0c593e.1.3308238895.296188.%20.0.0&_state=&wchp=dGLbVtb-zSkBl&_md5=93f06c0fe1c37fbd5b4c52fe4519bbbb.

[28] See "Senate Judiciary Will Begin Alito Hearings Jan. 9, Vote Jan. 17; Floor Vote Set Jan. 20, "*Daily Report for Executives*, November 4, 2005, available at http://ippubs.bna.com/ip/BNA/DER.NSF/9311bd429c19a79485256b57005ace13/819c3d1e4ca734da852570af0010aeaf?OpenDocument. For a transcript of Senators Specter and Leahy's remarks, see http://www.cq.com/display.do?docid=1948157.

[29] Amy Goldstein, "Senate Panel's Vote on Alito Delayed Until Next Week," *Washington Post*, January 17, 2006, p. A3.

[30] For a copy of Senator Frist's January 16, 2006, press release, see http://frist.senate.gov/index.cfm?FuseAction=PressReleases.Detail&PressRelease_id=2221&Month=1&Year=2006.

[31] U.S. National Archives and Records Administration, Office of the Federal Register, *Public Papers of the Presidents of the United States: William J. Clinton, 1993,* vol. 1 (Washington: GPO, 1994), p. 597.

[32] U.S. National Archives and Records Administration, Office of the Federal Register, *Public Papers of the Presidents of the United States: Ronald Reagan, 1981* (Washington: GPO, 1982), p. 596.

[33] U. S. Congress, Senate, *Journal of the Executive Proceedings of the Senate of the United States of America*, 97th Cong., 1st sess., August 19, 1981 (Washington: GPO, 1982), p. 644.

[34] Although these three events usually occur on the same day, a nomination sometimes, on rare occasions, is received by the Senate on a day after it was signed by the President, or is referred to the Judiciary Committee on a day after its receipt by the Senate.

[35] This particularly is the case for coverage of Supreme Court appointments in on-line full-text historical newspapers, where coverage, as might be expected, typically is found to be less comprehensive regarding the procedures of Supreme Court appointments farther back into the 19th century.

[36] The earliest Supreme Court confirmation hearings held in open session were those in 1916 for the nomination of Louis D. Brandeis to be an Associate Justice. See CRS Report RL31989, *Supreme Court Appointment Process: Roles of the President, Judiciary Committee, and Senate*, by Denis Steven Rutkus.

[37] CRS Knowledge Services Group Information Research Specialist Dana Ely, Karen Anson (Franklin D. Roosevelt Library), Valoise Armstrong (Eisenhower Library), Joshua Cochran (Ford Library), Jennifer Evans (Nixon Presidential Materials), Sharon Kelly (Kennedy Library), Matthew Schaefer (Hoover Library), Randy Sowell (Truman Library), Jennifer Sternaman (Reagan Library), Deborah Wheeler (George Bush Library), and Adam C. Bergfeld (Clinton Library) provided consultations on this portion of the project.

[38] U.S. Constitution, Article III, Section 1.

[39] Under 28 U.S.C. §371, Supreme Court Justices, like other Article III (tenure "during good Behaviour") federal judges, may *retire*, and be entitled to receive retirement compensation, in one of two ways—either by taking "senior status" or by "retiring from office." Beginning at age 65, they are entitled to receive retirement compensation, if having served a minimum 10 years as an Article III judge, their age and overall Article III judicial experience totals 80 years. (Hence, under this "Rule of 80," a Justice of age 65 must have served 15 years to become eligible for retirement compensation; a Justice of age 66, 14 years; a Justice of age 67, 13

years; etc.) Judges who take senior status retire from regular active service but retain their judicial office and the salary of the office, subject to annual certification of their having performed certain judicial or administrative duties in the preceding year. Judges who retire from office completely relinquish their judicial office with the right to a frozen lifetime annuity equal to the salary of the office at the time of retirement. In contrast, a Justice's *resignation* entails voluntarily relinquishing his or her judicial office without meeting the age and service requirements of the Rule of 80 (and thus being ineligible to receive retirement compensation). See U.S. Administrative Office of the United States Courts, *Senior Status and Retirement for Article III Judges*, April 1999 (Judges Information Series, No. 4), pp. vii-viii.

[40] Carroll Kilpatrick, "Goldberg is Named to Stevenson Post," *Washington Post*, July 21, 1965, p. A1.

[41] On the controversies surrounding Justice Fortas's nomination and resignation, see Artemus Ward, *Deciding to Leave: The Politics of Retirement from the United States Supreme Court* (Albany: State University of New York Press, 2003), pp. 171-175; and Philip Warden and Aldo Beckman, "Fortas Agrees to Quit, Nixon Aide Says," *Chicago Tribune*, May 15, 1969, p. 7.

[42] The law provides that a Justice retiring under these provisions shall receive for the remainder of his lifetime "the salary he is receiving at the date of retirement" or, if his service was less than ten years, one-half of that salary. Act of August 5, 1939, ch. 433, 53 Stat. 1204-1205; 28 U.S.C. §372(a).

[43] "Moody Will Retire," *Washington Post*, June 15, 1910, p. 1.

[44] The other Associate Justices nominated for Chief Justice during the period were: Edward D. White (1910), Harlan F. Stone (1941), and Abe Fortas (1968). As noted previously, Justice Fortas's nomination failed to receive Senate confirmation.

[45] "Hughes, With Words That Ring, Obeys Call to Lead Republicans," *Washington Post*, June 11, 1916, p. 1.

[46] Associated Press, "Byrnes Resigns From Bench in Letter to President," *New York Times*, October 4, 1942, p. 45.

[47] On the controversies surrounding Justice Fortas's nomination and resignation, see Ward, *Deciding to Leave*, pp. 171-175; and Philip Warden and Aldo Beckman, "Fortas Agrees to Quit, Nixon Aide Says," *Chicago Tribune*, May 15, 1969, p. 7.

[48] Haynsworth and Carswell were both rejected due to Senate doubts about their personal views and professional qualifications. For a summary of these and other cases of rejected Supreme Court nominees, see CRS Report RL31171, *Supreme Court Nominations Not Confirmed, 1789-2009*, by Henry B. Hogue, Supreme Court Nominations Not Confirmed, 1789-2008, by Henry B. Hogue.

[49] In **Table 3**, the median amount of time from vacancy to final Senate action within each time period does not necessarily equal the sum of the medians for each stage in the nomination-and-confirmation process. Likewise, the median lengths of time for all Senate actions (i.e., from nomination announcement to final Senate action) within each time period do not equal the sum of the medians for each stage. The median identifies the mid-point for individual sets of observations. Because each stage of the process can have a different number of observations, and because the data are also not a "normal" (i.e., "bell-shaped") distribution, the sum of the medians for individual stages generally is not equal to the median for the entire period. For more information, see chapter 4 in Ya-lun Chou, *Statistical Analysis for Business and Economics* (New York: Elsevier, 1989).

[50] In **Table 1** and **Table 2**, actual vacancies are those that already have been announced or occurred (i.e., a sitting Justice announces a retirement date or dies). Prospective vacancies, for the purposes of this chapter, are not merely speculative. They require firm notice, either through notification from a sitting Justice or major media accounts, that a Justice will leave the Court imminently, even if an exact date is not specified.

[51] This chapter, it should be re-emphasized, bases the starting point at when Presidents apparently learned of actual or prospective Court vacancies. These dates are based on published information or information obtained from presidential archives. Readers should be alerted, as a caveat, that there might well have been instances, unreported at the time as well as still unknown to present-day scholars, in which various Presidents privately were alerted of upcoming Court vacancies or had reasons to believe that vacancies were imminent in advance of the starting dates listed in this chapter. To the extent that such instances are unaccounted for, the full extent of time during which such Presidents were aware of prospective Court vacancies and were able to consider future Court candidates before publicly announcing their choices, is under-measured in this chapter.

[52] As noted elsewhere in this chapter, President George W. Bush withdrew Roberts's nomination as Associate Justice on September 5, 2005.

[53] President Reagan had a private conversation with Chief Justice Burger on May 27, 1986, when Burger alerted the President to his impending retirement ("Remarks on the Resignation of Supreme Court Chief Justice Warren E. Burger and the Nominations of William H. Rehnquist To Be Chief Justice and Antonin Scalia To Be an Associate Justice," U.S. National Archives and Records Administration, Office of the Federal Register, *Public Papers of the Presidents of the United States: Ronald Reagan, 1986*, vol. 2 (Washington: GPO, 1989) p. 781).

[54] President Truman did not announce that Clark had accepted the nomination until August 1, 1949 (Edward T. Folliard, "Clark Accepts High Court Proffer," *Washington Post*, August 2, 1949), p. 1.

[55] When calculating durations, the date on which the final event occurs is not counted as a full day. For example, if committee hearings began on July 12 and the committee took its final action on July 13, the duration is one day, not two. For cases in which durations are less than one day (i.e., the committee final action and final Senate vote took place on the same day), the duration is listed as 0 days.

[56] Although the arithmetic mean (the sum of all observations divided by the number of observations) is the true "average" number, it has the disadvantage of being skewed by extremely high or low values. For an introduction to median versus mean and arguments surrounding when each should be used, see chapter 3 in Alan Agresti and Barbara Finlay, *Statistical Methods for the Social Sciences*, 3rd ed. (Upper Saddle River, NJ: Prentice Hall, 1997).

[57] William H. Greene, *Econometric Analysis*, 5th ed. (Upper Saddle River, NJ: Prentice Hall, 2003, p. 847).

[58] As previously noted, although Chief Justice Burger, by letter on June 17, 1986, officially notified President Reagan of his desire to retire, Burger privately informed Reagan of his plans on May 27, 1986 ("Remarks on the Resignation of Supreme Court Chief Justice Warren E. Burger and the Nominations of William H. Rehnquist To Be Chief Justice and Antonin Scalia To Be an Associate Justice," U.S. National Archives and Records Administration, Office of the Federal Register, *Public Papers of the Presidents of the United States: Ronald Reagan, 1986*, vol. 2, p. 781).

[59] Context provides important caveats, as is always the case when exploring median decision-making surrounding Supreme Court nominations. President Eisenhower recess-appointed Justice Stewart because Congress was not in session on October 6, 1958, when Justice Burton announced his retirement. The 85th Congress had adjourned *sine die* on August 24, 1958. The President nominated Potter Stewart to the Court on January 17, 1959, after Congress had reconvened for the first session of the 86th Congress. Therefore, although the interval between the starting date (October 6, 1958, as shown in **Table 1**) and nomination date (January 17, 1959) is 103 days, and the entire interval from the starting date until final Senate action (May 5, 1959) is 211 days, the President's actual decision-making timetable could also be classified as eight days, or the interval between Burton's retirement announcement (October 6, 1958) and Eisenhower's recess appointment of Justice Stewart (October 14, 1958). Both intervals are used to calculate the median elapsed time from vacancy to nomination announcement. Nonetheless, the long intervals have a minimal impact on computing the median durations between stages in the process because the median is less sensitive than the mean to extremely high or low values.

[60] For an analysis of the decision-making speed surrounding Supreme Court nominations between 1962-1987, see CRS Report 87-576, *The Speed With Which Action Has Been Taken on Supreme Court Nominations in the Last 25 Years*, by Denis Steven Rutkus (out of print but available from author).

[61] See, for example, Charles Babington, "Access to Records May Be a Sticking Point; Democrats Push for Prompt Review," *Washington Post*, July 28, 2005, p. A6; and Mike Allen and Jo Becker, "A Clash Over Roberts Documents; Justice Department Balks at Senate Democrats' Demands," *Washington Post*, August 7, 2005, p. A4.

[62] For a profile of Murphy and his death, see *Chicago Daily Tribune*, "Justice Murphy Dies of Heart Attack at 59," *Chicago Daily Tribune*, July 20, 1949, p. 2.

[63] President Truman did not announce that Clark had accepted the nomination until August 1, 1949 (Edward T. Folliard, "Clark Accepts High Court Proffer, *Washington Post*, August 2, 1949, p. 1).

[64] Justice Byron R. White disagreed with the decision. See Ward, *Deciding to Leave*, p. 187.

[65] Tony Mauro, "How Blackmun Hid Retirement Plans," *New Jersey Law Journal*, April 25, 1994, p. 18.

[66] U.S. National Archives and Records Administration, Office of the Federal Register, *Public Papers of the Presidents of the United States: William J. Clinton, 1994*, vol. 1 (Washington: GPO, 1995), p. 597.

[67] U.S. Congress, Joint Committee on Printing, *2003-2004 Official Congressional Directory: 108th Congress* (Washington: GPO), p. 517.

[68] "Justice Fuller Dies Suddenly," *Washington Post*, July 5, 1910, p. 1.

[69] In addition to waiting for the Senate to return, President Taft reportedly considered more than 200 nominees, a far more thorough process than the media predicted after Fuller's death (ibid. and "White Heads Bench," *Washington Post*, December 13, 1910, p. 1).

[70] The discussion of recess appointments in the following two paragraphs is adapted from CRS Report RL31989, *Supreme Court Appointment Process: Roles of the President, Judiciary Committee, and Senate*, by Denis Steven Rutkus.

[71] Adopted by the Senate on August 29, 1960, by a 48-37 vote, S.Res. 334 expressed the sense of the Senate that recess appointments to the Supreme Court "should not be made, except under unusual circumstances and for the purpose of preventing or ending a demonstrable breakdown in the administration of the Court's business." Proponents of the resolution contended, among other things, that judicial independence would be affected if Supreme Court recess appointees, during the probationary period of their appointment, took positions to please the President (in order not to have the President withdraw their nominations) or to please the Senate (in order to gain confirmation of their nominations). It also was argued that Senate investigation of nominations of these recess appointees was made difficult by the oath preventing sitting Justices from testifying about matters pending before the Court. Opponents, however, said, among other things, that the resolution was an attempt to restrict the President's constitutional recess appointment powers and that recess appointments were sometimes called for in order to keep the Court at full strength and to prevent evenly split rulings by its members. See "Opposition to Recess Appointments to the Supreme Court," debate in the Senate on S.Res. 334, *Congressional Record*, vol. 106, August 29, 1960, pp. 18130-18145. See also CRS Report RL32971, *Judicial*

Recess Appointments: A Legal Overview, by T. J. Halstead. For an overview of judicial recess appointments during the George W. Bush presidency (none of which were to the Supreme Court), see CRS Report RL33310, *Recess Appointments Made by President George W. Bush*, by Henry B. Hogue and Maureen Bearden, Recess Appointments Made by President George W. Bush, by Henry B. Hogue and Maureen Bearden.

[72] *U.S. v. Woodley*, 751 F.2d 1008 (9th Cir. 1985).

[73] A notable, relatively recent instance in which the possibility of a recess appointment to the Supreme Court was raised occurred on July 28, 1987, when Senate Minority Leader Robert Dole observed that President Reagan had the constitutional prerogative to recess appoint U.S. appellate court judge Robert H. Bork to the Court. Earlier that month Judge Bork had been nominated to the Court, and at the time of Senator Dole's statement, the chair of Senate Judiciary Committee, Sen. Joseph R. Biden, Jr. had scheduled confirmation hearings to begin on September 15. With various Republican Senators accusing Senate Democrats of delaying the Bork hearings, Senator Dole offered as "food for thought" the possibility of President Reagan recess appointing Judge Bork during Congress's August recess. See Michael Fumento, "Reagan Has Power To Seat Bork While Senate Stalls: Dole," *Washington Times*, July 28, 1987, p. A3; also, Edward Walsh, "Reagan's Power To Make Recess Appointment Is Noted," *Washington Post*, July 28, 1987, p. A8. Judge Bork, however, did not receive a recess appointment and, as a Supreme Court nominee, was rejected by the Senate in a 58-42 vote on October 23, 1987.

[74] This number does not include instances such as the John G. Roberts *Associate Justice* nomination, in which the Judiciary Committee did not have the opportunity to hold hearings. Hearings before the Judiciary Committee were dispensed with for three nominees: Frank Murphy in 1939, James F. Byrnes in 1941, and Harold H. Burton in 1945, all of whom had prior service in high public office. Murphy had previously served as Governor of Michigan and U.S. Attorney General. Byrnes was a sitting Senator from South Carolina when nominated to the Court. Harold H. Burton was a Senator from Ohio. (Biographical information obtained from the Federal Judicial Center's Federal Judges Biographical Database, available at http://www.fjc .gov/public/home.nsf/hisj).

[75] See CRS Report RL31989, *Supreme Court Appointment Process: Roles of the President, Judiciary Committee, and Senate*, by Denis Steven Rutkus.

[76] For additional background information on Senators giving current or former colleagues deference when nominated to the Court, see Rutkus, *Supreme Court Appointments Process*, pp. 17-18.

[77] "White Heads Bench," *Washington Post*, December 13, 1910, p. 1.

[78] Senators Burton and Byrnes's nominations were not referred to the Judiciary Committee. Sen. Black's nomination was referred to the committee, which recommended his confirmation, although by a divided 13-4 vote.

[79] On Stone's testimony before the Judiciary Committee regarding the investigation, see Albert W. Fox, "Stone Tells Senate Committee He Assumes Full Responsibility For Pressing New Wheeler Case," *Washington Post*, January 29, 1925, p. 1.

[80] On increasingly controversial judicial nominations, see chapter 4 in Walter F. Murphy, C. Herman Pritchett, and Lee Epstein, *Courts, Judges, & Politics: An Introduction to the Judicial Process*, 5th ed. (Boston: McGraw Hill, 2002); [Thomas O. Sargentich, Paul D. Carrington, Barbara E. Reed, Charles Gardner Geyh, and Erwin Chemerinsky], *Uncertain Justice: Politics and America's Courts: The Reports of the Task Forces of Citizens for Independent Courts* (New York: The Century Foundation, 2000); and Mark Silverstein, *Judicious Choices: The New Politics of Supreme Court Confirmations* (New York: W.W. Norton & Company, 1994).

In: Supreme Court Appointments and Nominations
Editor: Edward P. Bennett
ISBN: 978-1-61209-249-2

Chapter 3

SUPREME COURT NOMINATIONS: SENATE FLOOR PROCEDURE AND PRACTICE, 1789-2010

Richard S. Beth and Betsy Palmer

SUMMARY

From 1789 through 2009, the President submitted to the Senate 159 nominations for positions on the Supreme Court. Of these nominations, 147 received action on the floor of the Senate, and 123 were confirmed. On May 10, 2010, the Senate received the nomination of Solicitor General Elana Kagan to be an Associate Justice of the Supreme Court. The data presented in this chapter do not include this nomination.

The forms of proceeding by which the Senate considered the 147 nominees to reach the floor break down relatively naturally into five patterns over time. First, from 1789 through about 1834, the Senate considered the nominations on the floor a day after they were received from the President. The second period (1835-1867) was distinguished by the beginning of referral of nominations to the Committee on the Judiciary. The third period (1868-1921) was marked by rule changes that brought about more formalization of the process. During the fourth period (1922-1967), the Senate began using the Calendar Call to manage the consideration of Supreme Court nominations, and the final time period, 1968 to the present, is marked by routine roll call votes on confirmation and the use of unanimous consent agreements to structure debate.

Of the 123 votes by which the Senate confirmed nominees, 73 took place by voice vote and 50 by roll call, but on only 25 of the roll calls did 10 or more Senators vote against. Of the 36 nominations not confirmed, the Senate rejected 11 outright, and 12 others never received floor consideration (some because of opposition; others were withdrawn). The remaining 13 nominations reached the floor but never received a final vote, usually because some procedural action terminated consideration before a vote could occur (and the President later withdrew some of these). Including those that received incomplete consideration, were rejected, or drew more than 10 negative votes, just 49 of the 159 total nominations experienced opposition that might be called "significant."

Of the 147 nominations that reached the floor, 100 received one day of consideration, while 25 received more than two days, including four on which floor action took seven days or more. Of these 147 nominations, optional procedural actions that could have been used to delay or block a confirmation vote occurred on 58, of which 26 involved procedural roll calls. Among a wide variety of procedural actions used, the more common ones have included motions to postpone, recommit, and table; motions to proceed to consider or other complications in calling up; live quorum calls, and unanimous consent agreements.

Neither extended consideration, the presence of extra procedural actions, nor the appearance of "significant" opposition affords definitive evidence, by itself, that proceedings were contentious. For example, some nominations considered for one day still faced procedural roll calls, some considered for three days or more faced no optional procedures, and some opposed by more than 10 Senators were still considered only briefly and without optional procedures. Of the 147 nominations to reach the floor, however, 76 were confirmed in a single day of action with neither optional procedural actions nor more than scattered opposition.

INTRODUCTION

The nomination of a Justice to the Supreme Court of the United States is one of the rare moments when all three branches of the federal government come together: the executive branch nominates, and the legislative branch considers the nomination, deciding whether the nominee will become a member of the high court. Presidents and Senators have said that, short of declaring war, deciding who should be on the Supreme Court is the most important decision they will make while in office.

The Constitution, in Article II, Section 2, divides the responsibility for selecting and confirming members of the Supreme Court between the President and the Senate. It says that the President "shall nominate, and by and with the Advice and Consent of the Senate, shall appoint Ambassadors, other public Ministers and Consuls, Judges of the Supreme Court, and all other Officers of the United States, whose Appointments are not herein otherwise provided for...."

The Senate has traditionally deferred to the President on nominations to the Cabinet, but they have shown less deference to a President's choice for the Supreme Court.[1] Of the 159 nominations Presidents made to the Supreme Court since 1789, 36 were not confirmed. Of the hundreds of cabinet officials nominated over the same time period, just 15 failed of confirmation.[2]

Some nominations to the Supreme Court have won confirmation with little debate and no procedural complications, while others have been debated extensively, with significant resort to parliamentary procedures during consideration. It appears that the Senate has never felt strictly bound by past practice in considering these nominations, but that it has used procedures and forms of consideration that the body has at the time deemed appropriate to each individual case. Nothing in Senate rules, procedures, or practice requires that the Senate proceed to a final vote on a nomination, for example, although in most instances it has done so. Of the 159 nominations for the Supreme Court, 12 never reached the floor and 13 others never received a final vote, although they were debated on the floor. The remaining 11 nominations that failed of confirmation reached a final vote, but were rejected by the Senate.

This chapter examines the ways in which the Senate has handled the 159 Supreme Court nominations the President has sent to the Senate in the past.[3] As the purpose of this chapter is to examine the forms taken by Senate proceedings on these 159 nominations, it treats each nomination as a separate case.[4] It is not couched in terms of the smaller number of different individuals nominated or the ultimate outcome the confirmation process may have had for each individual.[5]

Supreme Court confirmation debates, of course, do not occur in a vacuum. They are a product of the President making the choice, the state of the Senate at the time, the nominee and his or her views, and the prevailing mood of the country. These elements, while critical to understanding specific cases, are not considered in this chapter, and discussions of them can be found in other reports on the Supreme Court.[6] This chapter focuses on the kinds of actions the Senate has taken during consideration of Supreme Court nominees, how they have changed over time, and how they have affected the process of confirmation.

The emphasis of this chapter is on the 147 nominations on which some form of formal proceedings took place on the Senate floor, not on the ways in which the nominations might have been handled in committee or other pre-floor stages.[7] The information presented was drawn from a comprehensive search of the *Executive Journals* of the Senate, which are its official record of procedural actions taken in relation to executive business (i.e., nominations and treaties, which are the forms of business submitted to the Senate by the President). For recent Congresses for which the *Journal* was not yet available, information was taken from the *Congressional Record* and the Nominations data base of the congressional Legislative Information System.

The following discussion first sketches the changing patterns of consideration that have been normal in successive historical periods since 1789, noting their relation to changes in the procedural rules and practice of the Senate. For each period, it not only describes normal and exceptional practice, but also provides examples of proceedings that were either typical or notable. The report then successively addresses three key characteristics of floor action on these nominations: the dispositions the Senate made of them, the length of floor consideration, and the kinds of procedural action taken during consideration.

Historical Trends in Floor Consideration

Although the Constitution mandates a role for the Senate in the consideration of nominees to the Supreme Court, it does not include any specific method for doing so. The process by which the Senate has considered these nominations has typically included several stages, from receipt and committee referral through committee consideration and reporting, to scheduling for floor action, followed by floor debate and a final vote. Within this broad outline, the Senate has answered the basic question—what should the procedure be for consideration of nominations?—in different ways at different times.

A review of all Supreme Court nominations since 1789 yields two general conclusions about the procedures used. First, the Senate has not felt bound to consider each nomination in exactly the same way that the others before it were considered. Although some Supreme

Court nominations, for example, never reached the Senate floor (and hence, did not receive a vote), the Senate spent numerous days debating other nominations. Neither of those practices has been routine, but their use shows how the Senate has reserved to itself the right to take the course of action that it believes best suits consideration of a particular nomination. This stance becomes even more evident when the Senate considers a well-known person for a Supreme Court seat. The Senate received, debated and confirmed the nomination of former President William Howard Taft to be Chief Justice on the same day, for example.

Second, although the form of confirmation proceedings has varied, the Senate's process has tended to become longer and more formal over time. Although members of the first Supreme Court were confirmed just two days after their nominations were received, the norm in modern times has tended toward weeks, if not months, between the receipt of the nomination and disposition by the Senate.[8] Early in the Senate's history, it was not typical for Supreme Court nominations to be referred to committee at all; by modern times, it was the norm for the Senate Committee on the Judiciary to spend significant time reviewing nominees.

A study of the 159 nominations sent to the Senate finds that the Senate's floor consideration of Supreme Court nominations breaks down relatively naturally into five patterns over time.

Beginning Patterns, 1789-1834

In the earliest years, the Senate normally considered a Supreme Court nomination, as a matter of course, on the second day after it had been received from the President. There was no routine referral to committee, although at least one nominee, Alexander Wolcott, was referred to a select committee in 1811 (his nomination was defeated). From the beginning, the Senate has considered nominations in executive session, that portion of the Senate's business that was established to consider business that comes directly from the President (nominations and treaties). At this time, executive session also meant that the doors were closed, only Senators and select staff were permitted to be in the chamber and the proceedings were to remain secret.[9]

The first set of Senate rules, developed and adopted in 1789, did not include any specific provisions for handling nominations. In 1806, the Senate adopted a general revision of its rules, which included a new provision on nominations. This rule required that "when nominations shall be made in writing by the President of the United States to the Senate, a future day shall be assigned, unless the Senate unanimously direct otherwise, for taking them into consideration."[10]

Despite adoption of this rule, however, there is no indication that the Senate either fixed a date for consideration of nominations when they were received, or that the Senate waived this rule.

The journal which records the Senate's action on nominations, the *Executive Journal*, records no motion to consider these early nominations, instead stating simply that "the Senate proceeded to consider" the message from the President. The message from the President became the de facto method of organizing the nominations, apparently representing a precursor of the Calendar Call the Senate was to employ later. Of the 31 Supreme Court nominations sent to the Senate during this period, all 28 confirmations occurred by voice vote; the two rejections were by roll call (one nomination was considered by the Senate but left unfinished).

Also, the normal period of floor consideration during this period was one day for each nomination. Five nominations were considered for more than one day: the three nominations not confirmed, Wolcott, John Rutledge (1795) and John J. Crittenden (1828), and two others, that of Alfred Moore (1799) and Robert Trimble (1826).

This pattern of consideration is shown in the confirmation of the very first Supreme Court, in the following case study.

The Original Court, 1789

The court's first six members, a Chief Justice and five Associate Justices, were nominated by President George Washington on September 24, 1789. The nominations were not referred to committee. These men were personally known to many, if not all, members of the Senate, and there was no extensive investigation into their background. On September 26, the Senate proceeded to consider each of the six men, and on each, "on the question to advise and consent thereto, it passed in the affirmative."[11] There is no indication of lengthy debate; all six nominations were confirmed on the same day, in the same way. John Jay was confirmed as Chief Justice, and John Rutledge, of South Carolina, James Wilson, of Pennsylvania, William Cushing, of Massachusetts, Robert H. Harrison, of Maryland, and John Blair, of Virginia, were confirmed as Associate Justices.

Although the vast majority of nominations during this time was handled in the same way as the above, there were instances of extraordinary procedure, particularly when the nomination appeared to be controversial, as shown in the following case study.

John Crittenden, 1828

On December 17, 1828, President John Quincy Adams nominated John Crittenden, a Kentucky lawyer, to be an Associate Justice of the Supreme Court, to replace Justice Robert Trimble, who had died. The nomination took place after Adams' successor, Andrew Jackson, had been elected in November. Opposition to Crittenden by supporters of Jackson prevented the Senate from confirming him.[12]

Crittenden's supporters did not give in without a fight, and the Senate debated the nomination for nine days. In an unusual proceeding, rather than consider the nomination itself, the Senate debated a resolution, offered by opponents of the nomination. It read:

> Resolved, That it is not expedient to act upon the nomination of John I. Crittenden, as a Justice of the Supreme Court of the United States, until the Senate shall have acted finally on the report of the Judiciary Committee, relative to the amendment of the Judicial System of the United States.[13]

One purpose of the above report was to address the question of whether to change the size of the Supreme Court, which might have had the effect of abolishing the seat to which Adams had nominated Crittenden. Supporters of the nomination offered a lengthy amendment to the resolution, which, in essence, said that it was the duty of the President to fill vacant slots no matter at what point in a Presidency they occurred. An amendment to this amendment was then offered, declaring:

> That the duty of the Senate to confirm or reject the nominations of the President, is as imperative as his duty to nominate; that such has heretofore been the settled practice of the government; and that it is not now expedient or proper to alter it.[14]

The Senate rejected this amendment to the amendment by voice vote, voted 17-24 to reject the original amendment, and then voted 23-17 on February 12, 1829, to adopt the original resolution declaring it "not expedient" to act on the Crittenden nomination. By this action, the early Senate declined to endorse the principle that proper practice required it to consider and proceed to a final vote on every nomination.

Committee Referral, 1835-1867

A new pattern of bringing up and considering Supreme Court nomination emerged in 1835, when the Senate began to refer nominations routinely to the Senate Committee on the Judiciary, which had been created in 1816. Once the committee reported the nomination to the Senate, the chamber tended to act upon it immediately. In most cases, the nomination was reported and then confirmed, almost as one action. As with the previous practice, most of these confirmations were accomplished by voice vote. The Senate followed this form of proceeding through 1867.

In some cases, a Senator, apparently opposed to a particular nomination, would move to table the nomination immediately after it was reported from committee. The effect of a motion to table, however, was not the same as it is in current Senate parliamentary practice, where the motion, if successful, has the same effect as rejection. At this point in the development of the Senate, it appears that the motion to table had an effect more like a motion to postpone, and was used as a way to avoid taking action on the nomination on that day. When the Senate considered the nomination of Roger B. Taney to be Chief Justice in 1835, for example, the nomination was immediately tabled after the committee reported it. Later, however, the Senate voted 25-19 to proceed to consider the nomination, and he was confirmed.

The nomination of Robert C. Grier shows the typical features of this time period.

Robert C. Grier, 1846

President Polk nominated Grier on August 3, 1846, to replace Henry Baldwin, who had died. Grier had served as president judge of the District of Allegheny Court in Pennsylvania. The nomination was referred to the Judiciary Committee, which reported it out the next day. The Senate considered the nomination immediately after it was reported and confirmed Grier by voice vote.[15]

Tyler Presidency, 1844-1845

The major departure from the normal pattern of consideration for Supreme Court nominations during this time period took place during the presidency of John Tyler. He had been elected Vice President on the Whig ticket with William Henry Harrison in 1840. Harrison died 31 days after taking the oath of office, and Tyler became President. His relations with the Whig party were strained, and after he vetoed a banking bill, Tyler's entire cabinet but for one resigned, and Tyler was later expelled from the Whig party. Not surprisingly, Tyler had difficulties winning confirmation of his Supreme Court nominations from a Whig-dominated Senate.[16]

Tyler tried nine times to win Senate confirmation of a Supreme Court nomination, but he was successful only once, with the nomination of Samuel Nelson in 1845. Tyler nominated four other men over the course of more than a year to fill vacancies on the court. He sent the name of Edward King to the Senate twice, that of John C. Spencer twice, and that of Reuben H. Walworth three times. The Senate responded with disdain. Four times the Senate voted to table Tyler nominations (and took no further action on them); one, the 1844 nomination of Spencer, the Senate rejected outright by a vote of 21-26.

The standoff between the President and the Senate took on such intensity that in one day, June 17, 1844, Tyler changed his mind about whom to nominate twice. At the time, the Senate had tabled the nomination of Walworth to be an Associate Justice. According to the Senate *Executive Journal*, Tyler sent the following message to the Senate:

> I have learned that the Senate has laid on the table the nomination, heretofore made, of Reuben H. Walworth, to be associate justice of the Supreme Court, in place of Smith Thompson, deceased. I am informed that a large amount of business has accumulated in the second district, and that the immediate appointment of a judge for that circuit is essential to the administration of justice. Under those circumstances, I feel it is my duty to withdraw the name of Mr. Walworth, whose appointment the Senate by their action seems not now prepared to confirm, in the hopes that another name might be more acceptable. The circumstances under which the Senate heretofore declined to advise and consent to the nomination of John C. Spencer have so far changed as to justify me in my again submitting his name to their consideration. I, therefore, nominate John C. Spencer, of New York, to be appointed as an associate justice of the Supreme Court, in the place of Smith Thompson, deceased.[17]
>
> JOHN TYLER

Tyler then sent several other appointment messages to the Senate, which were read. The Senate confirmed several of the other appointments. The journal then records a dispute over whether the Senate should receive a further message from the President, as the time previously set to end the Congress had arrived. Senators agreed to hear the message, which read "I withdraw the nomination of John C. Spencer to be associate justice of the Supreme Court of the United States, and I renominate Reuben H. Walworth to be associate justice of the Supreme Court of the United States."

A motion was made to consider Walworth, but objection was heard, and the Senate then adjourned sine die.[18]

Increased Formalization, 1868-1922

In 1868, the Senate passed another general revision of its rules. It contained a lengthier and far more specific method for dealing with nominations.

> When nominations shall be made by the President of the United States to the Senate, they shall, unless otherwise ordered by the Senate, be referred to appropriate committees; and the final question on every nomination shall be "Will the Senate advise and consent to this

> nomination?" which question shall not be put on the same day on which the nomination is received nor on the day on which it may be reported by committee, unless by unanimous consent of the Senate. Nominations neither approved nor rejected by the Senate during the session at which they are made shall not be acted upon at any succeeding session without being again made by the President; and if the Senate shall adjourn or take a recess for more than thirty days, all nominations pending and not finally acted upon at the time of such adjournment or recess shall be returned to the President and shall not be afterwards acted upon, unless again submitted to the Senate by the President; and all motions pending to reconsider a vote upon a nomination shall fall on such adjournment or recess; and the Secretary of the Senate shall thereupon make out and furnish to the heads of departments and other officers the list of nominations rejected or not confirmed, as required by law.[19]

This rule codified what had since 1835 become the practice of the Senate, at least in regard to Supreme Court nominations, of referring the nomination to committee. It also called for a layover of at least a one day from the time a committee reported on a nomination to Senate action on that nomination, unless the Senate decided by unanimous consent to do otherwise.

Despite the rule, however, the Senate did tend to decide otherwise. Of the 41 nominations in this period, nearly half, 18, were considered by the Senate by unanimous consent on the same day they were reported out of committee. Nine other nominations were considered within two days of the committee's report. The remaining 10 nominations which saw floor action came up on the floor more than two days after the committee reported, sometimes significantly more than two days later. In the case of Melville W. Fuller to be Chief Justice (1888), for example, the Senate took up the nomination 17 days after the committee reported it.

In a change from past practice, the Senate Committee on the Judiciary began issuing reports that characterized the committee's support for the nomination: the committee would usually report favorably, but sometimes adversely. Prior to 1869, the committee had simply reported the nomination, without such characterizations.

Roll call votes on the confirmation of the pending nomination became more common during this period, occurring on 16 of the 41 nominations. The Senate rejected three nominations decided by roll call votes and confirmed the 13 others.

The nomination of William B. Woods illustrates the key patterns of consideration at this time.

William B. Woods, 1880

When Associate Justice William Strong resigned, President Rutherford B. Hayes looked for a southerner to replace him. Woods was born and educated in the north, and had been a leader in the Ohio legislature and subsequently a Union general. After the war, however, he had settled in Alabama, and had become a circuit court judge on the Fifth Circuit. Hayes nominated Woods on December 15, 1880. The nomination was referred to the Judiciary Committee, which reported it favorably on December 20. The next day the Senate considered the nomination and, by a vote of 39-8, confirmed it.[20]

Also during this period, however, confirmation ceased to be virtually automatic for Supreme Court nominations, even when the nominee was a sitting Senator, as illustrated by the case of George E. Badger.

George E. Badger, 1853

On January 10, 1853, President Millard Fillmore nominated George E. Badger to be an Associate Justice, to replace Justice John McKinley, who had died. Although Fillmore, a Whig, was a "lame duck" President following the fall election of Democrat Franklin Pierce, he nevertheless desired to place a nominee on the Supreme Court. Badger, who was an incumbent Senator from North Carolina and who had served as Secretary of the Navy under Presidents Harrison and Tyler, would seem to have been a good choice. "It was thought that the Senate would exercise Senatorial courtesy and not reject a fellow a Senator," according to historians.[21]

The Senate, however, was controlled by Democrats, by a margin of 38 Democrats to 22 Whigs and 2 Free Soilers. The Senate debated the Badger nomination for portions of four days. The Senate postponed consideration several times, and in the course of one day's debate on the nomination, it voted 26-25 to adjourn. Finally, on February 11, the Senate agreed by a vote of 26-25 to postpone consideration of the nomination until March 4, the date when the term of the Congress would expire and the new President would take office.

Debates on Supreme Court nominations during these years still took place behind closed doors, and Senators were supposed to maintain the secrecy of these proceedings. The nomination of Ebenezer Rockwood Hoar is one of the few instances in which some information is available about what went on during the Senate debate.

Ebenezer Rockwood Hoar, 1869

Hoar, who was serving as Attorney General, was nominated for the Supreme Court by President Grant in 1869. Republicans then controlled the Senate by a large margin, 62-12, and it was thought, at first, that Hoar would have no trouble winning confirmation. But, as it turned out, Hoar had badly alienated the Senate as Attorney General during implementation of the law which created the circuit court system in early 1869. The law created a series of new federal judgeships, and Hoar was responsible for choosing names to recommend to the President for filling these positions. Hoar undertook the job without consulting Senators on those positions. According to Hoar's biography, "Nearly every Senator had a candidate of his own for the Circuit Court, but in almost every instance the President took the Attorney General's advice." The same biography also notes that "Unhappily, the judge's manner in discharging his duty was not engaging. He had the plain speech and trying sincerity of latitude 42 degrees N., in an extreme degree, and it proved hard to bear at Washington."[22]

The Senate received Hoar's nomination on December 15, 1869. It was referred to the Judiciary Committee, and on December 22 the committee reported it out with an adverse recommendation. The Senate began debate on the nomination on the same day it was reported. A motion was offered to adjourn, which failed by a vote of 23-31, as was a motion to table the nomination, which also failed 24-30. But supporters of the nomination evidently saw the writing on the wall and eventually agreed later that same day, by voice vote, to table the nomination, which, at that time, still meant only to delay its further consideration, and not necessarily to kill it.

In a letter to Hoar, Massachusetts Senator Henry Wilson said it had been a difficult fight. "I write simply to say that your friends for more than four hours battled for you, that all was said and done that could be. When it was clearly seen that a majority had determined on a vote of rejection, we struggled for more than two hours against coming to a vote, before we secured an adjournment. Never have I seen such action in the Senate." Another letter, from J.D. Cox, a former House Member who was then Secretary of the Interior, said he had met with several senators about the nomination fight. He said of those opposed to Hoar: "They were determined to be content with nothing but a prompt rejection, and did not even consent to a motion to table the business, after four hours exciting struggle, until [Alexander G.] Cattell [a Senator from New Jersey] told them he would make dilatory motions all night before he would permit such an outrage. The result was the tabling of the question, with (as the opposition claim) an understanding that it shall not be again taken up."[23]

The Senate reconvened in 1870 and, on February 3, rejected Hoar's nomination by a vote of 24-33.

The Calendar Call Becomes Formalized, 1922-1967

Beginning in 1922, the Senate began to call up Supreme Court nominations under a system known as the Call of the Calendar or a Calendar Call. Under this procedure, the Senate would consider the nominations that had been reported by committee and placed on the *Executive Calendar* in the order in which they appeared on that calendar. Under this system, there was no need to make a motion or ask unanimous consent to take up a Supreme Court nomination. The Senate would instead begin with the first available nomination and work its way through the calendar until reaching the Supreme Court nomination. If a nomination was experiencing difficulty, the Senate could pass it over when it was reached on the Calendar Call. It would come up again the next time the Senate took up the Calendar. Particularly in cases for which there was no controversy, on the other hand, the Senate could call up a nomination out of order by unanimous consent. These practices appear to represent a formalization of the process used from 1868 to 1922.

Twenty of the 30 Supreme Court nominations during this time period came up when their place on the Calendar had been reached. Several others were considered out of order by unanimous consent, including Edward T. Sanford in 1923 and Byron White and Arthur J. Goldberg in 1962.

Another major development, as well, took place early in this period: debate on nominations became public. After years of debating the issue, in 1929 the Senate decided to conduct its executive business (consideration of treaties and nominations) in open session. Increasingly in the preceding years, although the doors had been closed and debate on nominations was supposed to remain secret, very often detail of the sessions would leak out to the press. In addition, the rule of secrecy had been set aside several times, so that certain debates, such as that on Louis D. Brandeis to be an Associate Justice in 1916, could be opened to the public.

The immediate trigger for the rules change was the disclosure, by the United Press, of the roll call vote on the nomination of Roy O. West to be Secretary of the Interior. Soon after, UP also published the vote on the nomination of former Senator Irvine Lenroot to be a judge of the Customs Court of Appeals. The Senate Rules Committee began an investigation into who leaked the Lenroot vote, and, for a variety of reasons, it was forced to hold this inquiry in open session. The reporter, Paul Mallon, refused to disclose who his source had been, and the committee came to no conclusion on the matter. The Senate then considered a rules change that would have allowed a majority to vote to open any executive session. An alternative was proposed to make all debates open unless a majority voted to close them. The Senate approved this amendment, 69-5.[24]

The nomination of William O. Douglas shows how the Calendar Call operated when there was controversy.

William O. Douglas, 1939

President Roosevelt nominated Douglas to be an Associate Justice on March 20, 1939, to replace retiring Justice Louis D. Brandeis. Douglas was the head of the Securities and Exchange Commission, and he seemed well-known to the Senate. The Senate Committee on the Judiciary referred the nomination to a subcommittee, which held a hearing at which no one testified. The subcommittee unanimously reported the nomination to the full committee, which then unanimously reported the nomination favorably to the full Senate on March 27. A news report stated that Douglas attended the full committee's meeting so that he could "meet the members."[25]

Between the committee session and floor debate, however, opposition developed. Senator Lynn Frazier of North Dakota argued Douglas had an improper relationship with the leaders of the New York Stock Exchange. The nomination was passed over twice on the Call of the Calendar, in order to facilitate fuller debate. In particular, the first time the nomination was passed over it was because Senator Frazier could not be in the chamber, and he wanted the Senate to wait until he was able to be a part of the debate. Three live quorum calls were taken during consideration of the nomination. The first of these was demanded at the start of the debate, and the second during the middle of Senator Frazier's speech. The third live quorum call was demanded just prior to the final speech of the debate, made by Senator Maloney in favor of the nomination. The vote to confirm Douglas was 62-4, with 30 Senators not voting.[26]

Unanimous Consent Agreements, 1968 to present

In the modern era, Senate practices of floor consideration generally have come to be dominated by the use of unanimous consent agreements, under which Senators agree to limit their rights to debate and to take procedural actions. The pervasiveness of these agreements has extended to the consideration of Supreme Court nominations. From about 1968 to the present, unanimous consent agreements have been reached that typically provide for when the Senate will take up nominations, limit and structure the debate, and, in many instances, provide for a final confirmation vote.

These agreements allow the Senate leadership to move to consider a nomination at a time, and in a way, they desire, instead of waiting until the nomination is reached on the Calendar. In fact, majority leaders began to ask unanimous consent to go into executive session to consider a specific Supreme Court nomination. This proceeding had been used as early as 1959 for the consideration of the nomination of Potter Stewart, and it was the method used, for example, when Majority Leader Mike Mansfield called up Harry A. Blackmun for Senate floor consideration in 1970. Under a later precedent of the Senate, a motion to go into executive session to consider a specific nomination is not debatable, though the nomination itself is.[27]

Another change also took place roughly around the same time. The Senate routinely began to decide the question of confirmation by roll call votes. Since 1967, indeed, the Senate has evidently come to consider it appropriate always to take roll call votes on Supreme Court nominations. In addition, nominations during this period have typically received longer floor consideration than in any previous period.

A further characteristic of the modern era is the use of the cloture motion. The Senate cloture rule, which permits a super-majority to limit the time for consideration of a matter by a roll call vote, did not exist until 1917, and it could not be applied to nominations until 1949. Since then, supporters have attempted to use the motion to impose limits on the consideration of only four Supreme Court nominations. The first attempt was on the motion to proceed to the 1968 nomination of Abe Fortas, already a member of the Court, to be Chief Justice. Cloture failed, as did the 1971 cloture attempt on the nomination of William H. Rehnquist to be an Associate Justice (though Rehquist was confirmed, while Fortas was not). The Senate did invoke cloture on the consideration of the 1986 elevation of Rehnquist to the position of Chief Justice and the 2005 nomination of Samuel Alito to be an Associate Justice.

The 1971 nomination of William H. Rehnquist illustrates the use of cloture on a Supreme Court nomination.

William H. Rehnquist, 1971

President Nixon named Rehnquist to be an Associate Justice of the Supreme Court on October 26, 1971, to replace retiring Justice John Marshall Harlan. Rehnquist had been Assistant Attorney General for two years and was well known on Capitol Hill, but opponents contended that he had shown insufficient commitment to civil rights and civil liberties.[28]

The Judiciary Committee held five days of hearings on the Rehnquist nomination, and opponents delayed the Committee vote on recommending the nomination to the full Senate for a week. The Committee voted 12-4 to report the nomination favorably. The nomination was debated on the Senate floor for five days. A motion to invoke cloture, and limit debate on the nomination, failed on the fifth day by a vote of 52-42 (at that time, a vote of two-thirds of Senators present and voting was required to succeed, which would have been the votes of 63 Senators in this case). A motion that consideration of the nomination be postponed until mid-January was defeated by a vote of 22-70. The Senate then agreed, by unanimous consent, to take a vote on the nomination at 5:00 p.m. that day. Rehnquist was confirmed by a vote of 68-26. (Subsequently, in 1986, he was confirmed as Chief Justice of the United States by a Senate vote of 65-33, after proceedings in which cloture was invoked).[29]

CHARACTERISTICS OF FLOOR ACTION

Senate floor proceedings on Supreme Court nominations might be distinguished in terms of a wide variety of different characteristics. The present study focuses chiefly on three that are readily identifiable and often referred to

- the kind of vote (or other action) by which the Senate disposed of the nominations;

- the amount of time the Senate spent considering them on the floor; and
- the forms of procedural action that occurred during their consideration.

Each of these represents a salient element of the procedural context in which a nomination is considered. Together, they may afford an indication of the amount of controversy, contention, or opposition that surrounds a nomination. For example, if the Senate approves a nomination by a voice vote after a single day of consideration, during which no procedural actions occur, one might reasonably conclude that it involved little opposition or controversy. As the following discussion indicates, however, none of these three characteristics, in itself, can simply be equated with the level of controversy.

Forms of Disposition

Varieties of Disposition

An obvious initial distinction among the 159 nominations concerns the ways the Senate disposed of them. In the broadest terms, the Senate confirmed 123 and failed to confirm the remaining 36. This breakdown, however, conflates the 11 nominations that the Senate affirmatively rejected with the 25 on which no final vote occurred. Further, the 25 without a final vote include 12 that never received floor consideration at all and 13 that were called up, but on which the Senate never finished action. The meaning and implications of each form of disposition may differ.

Nominations Confirmed

The 123 nominations confirmed make up 92% of the 134 on which the Senate reached a final vote. Well over half the 123 confirmations (73, or 59% of the 123 confirmed) took place by voice vote,[30] and the remaining 50 (41% of confirmations) by roll call. In earlier periods of American history, both voice and roll call votes occurred, but, as noted in the preceding section, in recent decades roll calls have become universal. The closest vote by which a nomination was confirmed was that of Matthews (1881-2), by 24-23; other close votes to confirm include those for Thomas (1991), by 52-48; Lamar (1888), by 32-28; and Clifford (1857), by 26-23.

Nominations Rejected

The 11 Supreme Court nominations the Senate has rejected make up the remaining 8% of those on which the Senate reached a final vote. All 11 of these rejections occurred on roll calls; the Senate has never rejected a nominee by voice vote. As with confirmations, these 11 rejections occurred at points scattered throughout American history. The earliest was Rutledge for Chief Justice in 1795; the most recent, the nomination of Robert Bork in 1987 to be an Associate Justice. Bork's was also the nomination rejected by the widest margin (42-58); the closest was that of Parker (1930), who was rejected by 39-41. The median margin of defeat, however, has been nine votes. Only in one instance (Spencer, 1844-2) has a President resubmitted a nomination the Senate had previously rejected, and then, not surprisingly, without success.

Table 1. Supreme Court Nominations That Received No Vote on Confirmation

Last Procedural Floor Action	Nomination	With-drawn?[a]	Later Action on Individual		Total
			Renom-inated?[a]	Con-firmed?[b]	
No Floor Action					12
None	Harriet Miers, 2005	yes			
	John Roberts, 2005	yes	yes	yes	
	Homer Thornberry, 1968	yes			
	John M. Harlan, 1954		yes	yes	
	Pierce Butler, 1922-1		yes	yes	
	William Hornblower, 1893-1		yes	rejected	
	Stanley Matthews, 1881-1		yes	yes	
	Caleb Cushing, 1874	yes			
	Henry Stanbery, 1866				
	William Micou, 1853				
	John C. Spencer, 1844-2	yes			
	William Paterson, 1793-1	yes	yes	yes	
Floor Action Without Vote on Confirmation					13
Tabled	Edward A. Bradford, 1852				
	Edward King, 1845	yes			
	Reuben H. Walworth, 1845	yes			
	Reuben H. Walworth, 1844-1	yes	yes	no	
	Edward King, 1844		yes	no	
Postponed[c]	George E. Badger, 1853				
	Roger B. Taney, 1835-1		yes	yes	
	John J. Crittenden, 1828				
Motion to consider defeated	Jeremiah S. Black, 1861				
Motion to consider met objection	Reuben H. Walworth, 1844-2		yes	no	
Cloture failed on motion to consider	Abe Fortas, 1968	yes			
Recommitted	George H. Williams, 1874	yes			
No procedures	John M. Read, 1845[d]				
Totals		11	10	6	25

Source: *Senate Executive Journal*. For 21st century nominations, congressional Legislative Information System (LIS) and *Congressional Record.*

a. Blanks indicate that the action in question did not occur. For details on the reasons for withdrawal, see accompanying text.

b. "No" indicates that no final vote occurred on the subsequent nomination. Blanks appear when there was no subsequent nomination.

c. For details on the means by which these postponements occurred, see section on "Procedural Complexity."

d. Nomination was taken up near the end of the session, and the Senate adjourned *sine die* before completing consideration.

Nominations without Final Vote

The Senate conducted no final vote on 25 nominations. **Table 1** lists these 25 nominations and notes some pertinent contextual features of each. They make up 16% of the total number of high court nominations submitted, an indication of the extent to which the Senate has not always considered itself obligated to proceed to a final up-or-down vote on every Supreme Court nomination presented to it.

These 25 nominations fall into two groups discussed separately in the following two subsections: (1) 13 on which the Senate initiated floor action, but never completed it; and (2) 12 that never reached the floor at all. For purposes of this chapter, all formal proceedings in the full Senate in relation to a nomination, once it was available for floor consideration, were counted as floor action. For example, a nomination was treated as receiving floor action even if the Senate never actually proceeded to its consideration, but did decline to grant unanimous consent to do so.[31] Overall, by this standard, the Senate has taken some floor action on 92% of all nominations submitted, and proceeded to a final vote on 84%.

No Floor Action

The 12 occasions on which the Senate has failed to bring a nomination to the floor have also been scattered throughout history. The circumstances of their occurrence have varied, as well. Five of the 12 were submitted quite late in a session, so that the Senate may simply have lacked time to act. Six others were withdrawn before floor consideration could commence, including instances from Paterson in 1793 (first nomination) to Miers in 2005. The last of the 12 (Stanbery, 1866) became moot because Congress reduced the size of the Court, thereby abolishing the vacancy.

This distribution of conditions for the lack of floor action suggests that the Senate has exhibited little tendency to leave Supreme Court nominations without a final vote simply out of reluctance to act, or to use inaction as an indirect means of denying confirmation. Four of the five nominations late in a session, and two of the six withdrawn, were later resubmitted (usually at the following session), and the Senate proceeded to a final vote on each of the resubmitted nominations. The other four withdrawn nominations were never resubmitted. Overall, therefore, only two of these 12 nominations continued to be available to the Senate and yet never received floor action. These included one of the late-session nominations and the one that became moot.

These observations show that the simple absence of floor consideration cannot be taken to imply that the Senate found the nomination less than acceptable. Of the five nominations in this group that were later resubmitted, the Senate confirmed four, rejecting only one. In addition, at least some of the withdrawals evidently occurred for reasons unrelated to Senate sentiment about the nomination. Paterson (1793-1), for example, who was among those later resubmitted and confirmed, was initially withdrawn only because he was constitutionally ineligible to sit on the Court at that point, as he had previously been elected to a Senate term that had not yet expired, and during which the salary of the Justices had been increased. The nomination of Roberts (2005-1) was withdrawn because the President decided to nominate him instead for the post of Chief Justice, which became available subsequent to his original submission of the Roberts' nomination.[32]

Among nominations not resubmitted, Thornberry's (1968) was withdrawn simply because the vacancy he was to fill was eliminated by the failure of a concurrent nomination of a sitting Justice to be Chief Justice. The late nomination of Micou (1853) presents a more ambiguous case, but the immediate reason it was not resubmitted was that the lame duck President who originally submitted it had left office.

On other nominations in this group, circumstances suggest that the Senate's inaction did reflect the presence of opposition. Most clearly, the congressional action to abolish Stanbery's vacancy (1866) appears to reveal emphatic objection to his nomination.[33] Also, after Hornblower's initial nomination received no action late in a session (1893-1), the Senate rejected his renomination outright (1893-2). In the case of Spencer, as discussed earlier, the Senate had already rejected the nomination once before President Tyler later resubmitted and withdrew it on the same day (1844).[34] There also appears reason to conclude that the withdrawals of both Cushing (1874) and Miers (2005) represent responses to expressed opposition.[35]

Floor Action without Final Vote

The 13 nominations that received floor action, but no final vote, reflect a different distribution of circumstances. Consideration of one of the 13 (Read, 1845) appears simply to have begun too late in a session to be completed, but the Senate appears to have laid aside each of the other 12 as a consequence of unfavorable action on some procedural motion. The specific actions taken in these cases, noted in **Table 1** and described in more detail in the section on "Procedural Complexity," were seldom ones that conclusively precluded further consideration. Instead, the Senate seems simply to have taken these actions as demonstrating a lack of sufficient support for confirmation. The President, correspondingly, subsequently withdrew six of these nominations.

The frequency of these proceedings may indicate the extent to which the Senate, in the presence of opposition to a Supreme Court nomination, has been willing to give it consideration and yet decline to proceed to an "up-or-down" vote. In recent times, the Senate has not often resorted to this form of proceeding. Nine of the 13 instances occurred in the decade from 1844 to 1853, and only two took place after the Civil War. The earliest instance occurred in 1828, when the Senate set aside the Crittenden nomination until after a reorganization of the Judiciary (by which point the nominating President would have left office).[36] The most recent case was the Fortas nomination for Chief Justice, which President Johnson withdrew in 1968 after supporters mustered only 45 votes for cloture on the motion to proceed to consider the nomination.[37]

Dispositions and the Extent of Opposition

The left-hand group of columns in **Table 2** summarizes the preceding discussion of how the Senate has disposed of Supreme Court nominations, showing that the Senate has confirmed more than three-quarters of all nominations submitted to it, and more than nine of every ten on which it voted. Indeed, as the middle group of columns shows, the Senate has confirmed almost half of all Supreme Court nominations ever submitted to it without even requiring a roll call vote. Roll calls, on the other hand, have by no means been uncommon, occurring on three of every seven final votes, including every one since 1967.

Neither the type nor the outcome of a vote, in itself, can be taken as affording a clear indication of the extent of the opposition a nomination may have generated. In particular, although a voice vote may reasonably be viewed as *failing* to indicate the *presence* of opposition, it could be rash to presume that it *demonstrates* an *absence* of opposition.[38]

Conversely, although a roll call vote may reflect the presence of extensive opposition, it may also occur when no such level of opposition is present. In the years since 1968, for example, eight of the 18 roll calls have registered fewer than four "no" votes. More broadly, as **Table 2** shows, half of all roll call votes on Supreme Court nominations throughout history have involved fewer than 10 votes in opposition.

Taking the appearance of at least 10 "nay" votes as a rough threshold for the presence of significant opposition permits a more meaningful judgment of the significance of these data on the disposition of nominations.[39] By this standard, 25 of the 50 roll calls by which nominations were confirmed revealed "significant" opposition. Combining these 25 nominations with the 11 that were rejected, it may be said that just 36 of the Senate's 134 votes on confirmation indicated the presence of "significant" opposition.

By incorporating nominations that received no final vote into this approach, a unified account may be given of what different outcomes on these nominations mean. The earlier discussion of nominations that received floor action but no final vote suggested that this outcome typically reflected the presence of opposition. The discussion of nominations that received no floor action, on the other hand, concluded that this outcome has come about, on different occasions, both when significant opposition was present and not. Accordingly, this disposition cannot, in itself, be taken as an indicator of either circumstance.

The results of these considerations are summarized in the right-hand columns of **Table 2**. The 13 nominations on which floor action failed to result in a final vote are counted as cases of "significant" opposition, but the 12 that never reached the floor are treated as permitting no definite conclusion about opposition. This classification yields a total of 49 nominations with dispositions that imply "significant" opposition.[40] From this perspective, accordingly, it can be held that just about two-thirds of the 147 Supreme Court nominations reaching the Senate floor have met no more than scattered opposition.

Length of Floor Action

Days of Floor Action

Another salient characteristic in terms of which Supreme Court nominations vary is the length of consideration they receive on the floor. As with forms of disposition, of course, length of consideration can be established only for those nominations on which consideration occurs. Accordingly, the data discussed in this section again reflect only the 147 nominations that reached the floor.

Table 2. Dispositions of Supreme Court Nominations, Types of Vote, and Extent of Opposition Indicated

Form of Disposition	Outcome			Type of Vote			Extent of Opposition Indicated by Form of Disposition (see text)		
	Confirmed	Rejected	No Final Action	Voice[a]	Roll Call	None	Scattered or None	"Significant"	Indeterminate
Confirmed, voice vote[a]	73			73			73		
Confirmed, roll call vote, fewer than 10 opposed	25				25		25		
Confirmed, roll call vote, 10 or more opposed	25				25			25	
Rejected (all by roll call vote)		11			11			11	
Floor action without final vote			13			13		13	
No floor action			12			12			12
Total	**123**	**11**	**25**	**73**	**61**	**25**	**98**	**49**	**12**
Percent of 159 total nominations	*77*	*7*	*16*	*46*	*38*	*16*	*62*	*31*	*8*
Percent of 134 nominations reaching a vote	*92*	*8*		*54*	*46*				
Percent of 147 nominations receiving floor action							*67*	*33*	

Source: *Senate Executive Journal*; **Table A-1**.

a. Includes unanimous consent.

Table 3. Length of Floor Action on Supreme Court Nominations

Days	Number of Nominations	Nominations	Disposition (if not confirmed)	For Chief Justice?
1	100	[individuals not listed]		
2	21	[individuals not listed]		
3	11	[individuals not listed]		
4	5	John G. Roberts, 2005		
		Charles Evans Hughes, 1930		yes
		Harlan F. Stone, 1925		yes
		Joseph P. Bradley, 1870		
		Alexander Wolcott, 1811	rejected	
5	4	Samuel A. Alito, 2005		
		Clarence Thomas, 1991		
		William H. Rehnquist, 1986		yes
		William H. Rehnquist, 1971		
6	2	Abe Fortas, 1968	unfinished	yes
		George E. Badger, 1853	unfinished	
7	1	Clement Haynsworth Jr., 1970	rejected	
8	1	John J. Parker, 1930	rejected	
9	1	John J. Crittenden, 1828	unfinished	
10-13	0			
14	1	G. Harrold Carswell,1970	rejected	
Total	147			

Source: *Senate Executive Journal*; **Table A-1**.

The length of consideration of Supreme Court nominations is identified in **Table 3** in terms of the number of calendar days on which Senate floor action took place on the nomination.[41] In general, each day was counted on which any formal procedural action in relation to a nomination occurred, even if the nomination itself was not formally under consideration on that day. For example, a day was counted on which a motion to proceed to consider a nomination was offered or debated, even if the motion was defeated, or was not adopted until the following day. Otherwise, for example, all Senate floor action on the Fortas nomination for Chief Justice (1968), which occurred in its entirety pending a motion to proceed to consider the nomination, would not be counted. Similarly, in relation to the 1828 Crittenden nomination, days on which the Senate debated the resolution to postpone action are counted as days of floor action on the nomination. On the other hand, days were not counted on which Senators made individual speeches in relation to a nomination, but the Senate did not formally have it under consideration on the floor, as happened extensively, for example, on the Rehnquist nomination for Associate Justice (1971).

The data presented, accordingly, are more precisely described as presenting the length of "floor action" than of formal "consideration" or of "debate." In compiling these data, however, a few actions were treated as exceptions to the standard just identified. Especially during the first half of the 19th century, for example, the Senate commonly referred newly received nominations to committee through action taken on the floor. In more recent times, the Senate has sometimes reached a unanimous consent agreement setting terms for consideration of a nomination in advance of any actual consideration. When either such action was the only one taken in relation to a nomination on a given day, the day was not counted as a day of consideration. A contrary practice would tend to overstate the length of consideration of these nominations relative to others to which the Senate actually devoted similar time, but on which similar actions occurred not on a preceding day, but on the same day as other steps.

Extended Consideration and Opposition

Table 3 shows that, historically, the Senate has found a single day sufficient for floor action on more than two-thirds of all the nominations submitted (although this form of action has ceased to be the norm in the years since 1967). For nominations receiving longer consideration, numbers decline quickly as length of consideration rises, so that 10% of those reaching the floor remained there for more than three days.

The more extended consideration given to this relative handful of nominations may rest on a variety of causes. Assessment of their nature is likely to begin from the well understood circumstance that opponents of a matter in the Senate may engage in extended debate as a means of delaying or blocking final action.[42] Accordingly, it might be natural to take the length of floor action as an indicator of the intensity of opposition to a nomination, and specifically of the determination with which opponents attempted to delay its confirmation. Such a supposition might be supported by the observation that none of the six nominations receiving more than five days' consideration was confirmed.

Other considerations, however, also may be pertinent. It may be significant, for example, that four of the 15 nominations considered for more than three days were for Chief Justice; it may plausibly be supposed that the Senate has generally tended to find these nominations as necessitating more sustained consideration. More broadly, the Senate may well have been likely to devote more time to nominations that were considered particularly important, for example, to the balance or future course of the Court.

In addition, the data in **Table 3** also suggest a trend toward longer consideration in more recent times. Although extended consideration was not unheard of even in very early years (e.g., Wolcott, 1811, and Crittenden, 1828), seven of the 10 nominations receiving more than four days' consideration occurred in 1968 or later, beginning with the Fortas nomination for Chief Justice. This trend may be associated either with generally observable developments in the way the Senate handles its business or with increases in controversy specifically over nominations to the Court.

These considerations suggest that the occurrence of extended consideration on Supreme Court nominations cannot, in itself, be taken as a reliable indicator of strong opposition. Not only may extended consideration occur for other reasons, but it is also not necessarily the case that even determined opponents have always expressed their position by attempting to protract proceedings. On the other hand, lengthy consideration may reasonably be viewed as a sign of the *possibility* that opposition may have been present. Correspondingly, although the completion of consideration on a single day cannot be taken to demonstrate an absence of opposition, it may appropriately be viewed, more cautiously, as *failing* to afford evidence that significant opposition *was* present.

Procedural Complexity

Optional Procedural Actions

Senate floor proceedings on Supreme Court nominations, like those on other matters, are distinguishable not only in terms of the means of disposition and the length of time consumed, but also by the procedural actions that may occur in the course of consideration. As with these other characteristics of floor action, procedural actions can be identified only for the 147 nominations that reached the floor. **Table 4** lists various forms of procedural action that have occurred in the course of Senate floor consideration on these nominations and how often each has appeared. It shows that no single procedure was used on more than about one in seven of the Supreme Court nominations reaching the floor, but also that a half-dozen different procedures were used at least half that often. No single procedure either stands out as especially characteristic of proceedings on these nominations or clearly identifies any distinctive subgroup among them.

Instead, floor proceedings on Supreme Court nominations are more readily categorized, in this respect, simply in terms of whether or not any procedural actions at all occurred beyond those required in the course of consideration itself. Throughout history, floor action on Supreme Court nominations has most often remained procedurally simple in this sense. Proceedings on 78 of the 147 nominations were procedurally simple in the sense of involving no optional procedural actions. The remaining 69 nominations (47% of the total) may be identified, in this minimal sense, as "procedurally complex."

Procedurally complex nominations might be further distinguished in several ways, such as by the number of procedural actions that occurred in the course of floor action or the extent to which procedural actions were applied to other procedural actions (e.g., a motion to table a motion to postpone). A more readily applicable criterion for this purpose, however, is whether any of the procedural actions taken resulted in a roll call vote. Again as **Table 4** shows, procedural roll calls occurred on 26 of the 69 nominations on which any optional procedures were used (18% of the total 147 nominations on which floor action occurred). This further distinction affords a rough indicator of the intensity with which procedural action was pursued.

For some kinds of optional procedure used in relation to Supreme Court nominations, the principal effect would have been to expedite rather than delay consideration. These included chiefly (1) actions, taken either by motion or unanimous consent, to proceed to consider a nomination on the same day reported; and (2) consent agreements assuring a final vote (either by limiting debate or setting a time certain) that were reached before consideration began or on its first day. In order to examine the potential use of optional procedures as means of pursuing opposition to Supreme Court nominations, it is appropriate to exclude these forms of action from consideration. The second column of **Table 4** presents a count of optional procedures that could potentially have been used for purposes of delay or opposition.

Using this criterion, 89 of the total 147 nominations reaching the floor (61%) may be said to have been subject to no optional procedures that could have had the effect of delaying or terminating consideration. This percentage is comparable to the 62% of nominations that faced no significant opposition and the 68% that received action on only a single day. As with those other characteristics of consideration, it would not be appropriate to take the absence of procedural complexity as demonstrating the absence of opposition. It could reasonably be said, nevertheless, that when nominations involve no procedural complexity, no positive inference may be drawn from the procedural features of consideration that opposition or contention was present. Conversely, the occurrence of procedural complexity, or even of procedural roll calls, cannot be regarded as sufficient in itself to *demonstrate* the presence of opposition or contention, but may reasonably be taken as cause to think that such opposition *may* have been present.

Table 4. Procedural Actions Occurring During Floor Action on Supreme Court Nominations

Procedural Action	Number of Nominations on Which the Procedural Action—			
	Occurred	Potentially Involved Delay	Received a Roll Call Vote	Had Effect of Terminating Consideration
Motion to postpone	19	19	8	3
Motion to recommit (or commit)	14	14	8	1
Intervention in calling up	23[a]	13[b]	n.a.[c]	n.a.[c]
Motion to proceed to consider	13[d]	13[d]	3	2
Motion to lay on the table	13	13	4	5
Live quorum call	11	11	n.a.[c]	n.a.[c]
Motion to adjourn or recess	7[e]	7	6	0
Consent agreement for final vote	18[f]	7[g]	n.a.[c]	n.a.[c]
Motion for cloture	4	4	4	1
Motion to reconsider	3	3	1	0
Total number of nominations	**69[h]**	**59[h]**	**26[h]**	**12**

Source: *Senate Executive Journal*. For 21st century nominations, congressional Legislative Information System (LIS) and *Congressional Record*.

a. Includes only the following: (1) objections to a request, made either by motion or by unanimous consent, to proceed to consider a nomination on the same day reported; (2) passing a nomination over on calendar call; and (3) unanimous consent arrangements (including those made by special order) providing for consideration at a future time.

b. Includes only the following: (1) objections to a request, made either by motion to unanimous consent, to proceed to consider a nomination on the same day reported; (2) passing a nomination over on calendar call; and (3) unanimous consent arrangements *before 1967* (including those made by special order) providing for consideration at a future time.

c. Not applicable (see accompanying text).

d. Includes special orders for consideration that were established by vote; excludes motions that could have been defeated by objection, which are included under (a)(1) and (b)(1) as "Interventions in calling up."

e. Includes only those motions to adjourn or recess that were offered in executive session, and so could have delayed or protracted consideration more than would normally have occurred.

f. Includes only consent agreements that assured the occurrence of a final vote, either by limiting total debate time, setting a time certain for a final vote, or otherwise.

g. Includes only consent agreements that assured the occurrence of a final vote and were not reached until after the first day of consideration.

h. For the first three data columns, the total displayed is less than the sum of the cell entries, because some nominations involved more than one procedural action.

The occurrence of optional procedural actions is also related to the occasions, previously detailed in **Table 1,** on which nominations reached the floor but failed to reach a final vote on confirmation. In 12 of the 13 cases of incomplete consideration listed in **Table 1**, some optional procedural action was the last one that occurred, and had the effect of terminating consideration. In order to indicate some potential effects of optional procedural actions, the last column of **Table 4** reproduces this information in summary form.

These 12 instances show that the effect of a procedural action in any individual case depends only in part on the prescribed effect of the action. It is also affected, in some cases, by the procedural context in which the action is undertaken, and in particular on whether it is integral to or divergent from the routine practice of the time. Procedural context changes from case to case, normal practice also has changed over the course of Senate history, and in some cases, the prescribed effect of procedural actions has changed as well. Accordingly, the potential significance of optional procedural actions may be clarified by reference to some of the points initially developed in the section on "Historical Trends." For this purpose, it is useful to look separately at actions that affect how the Senate has taken up nominations and those that can occur in the course of consideration. In both cases, however, the periods during which distinctive patterns of optional procedural action characteristically appear differ from those discussed in earlier sections, which were defined by changes in the normal terms of consideration. Each of the following sections, accordingly, is couched in terms of its own appropriate periodization.

Calling Up Nominations

The Senate has always taken up nominations under procedures that govern action in executive session, which are in some respects separate from those regulating legislative action. It has usually done so by going into executive session to consider the nomination, but occasionally by granting unanimous consent to consider the nomination "as in" executive session, without actually leaving legislative session for the purpose. As described earlier, in the section on "Historical Trends in Floor Consideration," it appears that the normal practice of the Senate for most of its history (from 1789 until roughly 1967) was to take up each nomination automatically when it was reached in the course of considering executive business. In order to be eligible for consideration under this procedure, a nomination apparently had to have become available for floor action at least one day previously. Initially, nominations became available when received from the President; after 1835, when nominations to the Supreme Court began routinely to be referred to committee, they normally became available for consideration when reported. After about 1922, it appears, this proceeding was formalized as a Call of the Calendar of nominations.

Sometimes, however, by unanimous consent, the Senate has taken up a nomination on the same day reported or submitted. As previously noted, in fact, this proceeding was used for nearly half of all nominations reaching the floor (18 of 41) from 1868 to 1922.

No departure from these routine forms of proceeding occurred before 1835, when the nominations of Taney and Barbour, though eligible for the normal procedures, were called up instead by a roll call vote on a motion to proceed to consider. Complications of a similar kind were faced by Badger in 1853, when the Senate was unable to reach a vote on a motion to proceed, and by Black in 1861, when the Senate defeated a motion to proceed on a roll call vote. During roughly this same period, however (1844-1874), motions to proceed to consider were also offered on seven other nominations that were eligible for normal consideration, but the Senate adopted these motions in short order and by voice vote.

In the cases of both Badger and Black, the Senate also attempted to bring the nomination to the floor through a special order providing that it proceed to consideration on a specified later day. The Senate ultimately adopted a special order of this kind for Badger by voice vote, but never accepted one for Black. On five Supreme Court nominations thereafter, through 1930, the Senate used unanimous consent to establish special orders of this kind. These special orders represent forerunners of the contemporary practice of reaching agreements in advance, by unanimous consent, to take a matter up. In these earlier times, however, special orders seem to have been used for these nominations only in unusual circumstances, to overcome difficulties in bringing a matter to the floor, and their effect was to put off its consideration until after the point at which it would normally have come up.

Another form of action that indicated an attempt to delay consideration appeared on four scattered occasions before 1967 when an attempt to call a nomination up on the same day it was reported or submitted was prevented by objection. A more definite, though still only temporary, form of delay was imposed on five nominations during this period (all after 1880), each of which was passed over for consideration at least once, upon demand of a Senator, when reached in its normal order.

From 1968 on, the Call of the Calendar of nominations fell into disuse for the consideration of Supreme Court nominations, and a different set of practices for initiating floor action on these nominations has become standard. All but one of the 20 nominations that have reached the floor since that time did so pursuant to a request for unanimous consent that the Senate proceed to consider it. For eleven nominations, this consent agreement provided for immediate consideration; for the remaining eight, it provided, like the earlier special orders, for consideration to begin at some future date. In addition, some of these consent agreements provided for the Senate not only to take up the nomination, but to go into executive session for the purpose, and some also limited debate or set a time certain for a final vote. Whether or not they included these additional provisions, however, these agreements represent a routine proceeding for taking up the nomination and fail to suggest any potential difficulties in bringing it to the floor. The only nomination in this recent period to experience difficulty at the point of calling up has been that of Fortas in 1968, on which a motion to proceed to consider was found necessary and could not be brought to a vote.

Proceedings in the Course of Floor Action

Senate rules do not establish separate procedures for the consideration of nominations and of legislation to the same extent that they do for calling up business of the two kinds. The most evident differences in forms of proceeding between the two kinds of matter may be that nominations, of course, cannot be amended. Otherwise, most of the same procedural mechanisms used for legislative business are also available on nominations.

1789-1835

The only optional procedures used during consideration of Supreme Court nominations in these years were motions to postpone temporarily, to commit with instructions, and to lay on the table. The use of any of these motions was rare, occurring on only five of the 31 nominations reaching the floor before 1835. Motions to postpone temporarily, however, were used as early as 1795, motions to commit with instructions by 1811, and motions to table by 1826.

During this period, a motion to postpone or table was sometimes offered at the point when the Senate was just proceeding to consider a nomination, so that the motions might in these instances have been treated as part of the proceedings for calling up nominations. In order to present a consolidated view of the use of each motion, however, the present discussion views all of them as having been offered in the course of consideration.

Occasionally, as well, action with effect similar to one of these motions also was proposed by resolution. For example, the Senate several times entertained a resolution that it postpone or table a nomination until enactment of legislation reorganizing the circuit courts (which could have the effect of eliminating the nominee's vacancy), or one that directed a committee to investigate a nominee further, but did not formally recommit the nomination. **Table 4** includes these proceedings in the count of corresponding motions.

In most instances during this period, when motions to postpone, commit, or table were offered, the Senate adopted them by voice vote. At that time, adoption of a motion to table evidently did not have the effect of a final negative disposition, as it does today, but only of putting off action for the time being. The normal effect of adopting any of these motions, accordingly, was only to delay further action by taking the nomination off the floor temporarily. The only exception to this pattern occurred in 1828, when adoption (by roll call) of the resolution postponing the Crittenden nomination until after a circuit court reorganization effectively terminated consideration of the nomination.

1835-1845

During the decade between 1835 and 1845, by contrast with earlier years, only five of the 16 Supreme Court nominations that reached the floor were considered without the intervention of optional procedures. The procedures used continued to include only motions to postpone, commit, and table, but the consequences of their use became more varied. Some of these motions continued to be adopted by voice vote, but others were either adopted or rejected on roll call votes. Adoption by voice vote may most likely suggest that supporters of the nomination may have been using the motion either to gain time or for routine purposes of agenda management; rejection by roll call suggests that the motions may have been offered by opponents seeking to bring about delays in consideration. Either of these results, however, normally permitted consideration to continue.

Especially when one of these motions was adopted by roll call, on the other hand, it often had the effect of terminating consideration before an up-or-down vote could occur. In 1835, the Senate tabled a resolution to postpone the Taney nomination until a circuit court reorganization, then adopted a motion to postpone it indefinitely. In 1844, the Senate, by roll call votes, tabled President Tyler's nominations of Walworth and King, and in the following year it did the same to their renominations, but by voice vote. The motion for indefinite postponement has the explicit purpose of terminating consideration, but, under the practice of the time, a similar consequence followed from adopting the motions to table only because the Senate never subsequently chose to resume consideration of the nomination. It appears highly likely that in taking these actions, the Senate understood that leaving consideration unfinished was their proponents' intent and would be the practical effect.

1845-1890

In the decades after 1845, political circumstances varied widely, but the overall incidence of procedural complexity on Supreme Court nominations declined, although not to early levels. A solid majority of the nominations reaching the floor between 1845 and 1890 (20 of 31) experienced no optional procedural action at all after being called up. (This figure, however, includes the five nominations confirmed during the Civil War, when any substantial opposition to the administration was absent from the Senate.)

During this period, the motions to postpone, to commit, and to table continued to be used on Supreme Court nominations, except that, because initial committee referral had become routine, the motion to recommit largely replaced the motion to commit. These three motions continued to be used in ways similar to the previous period, and continued to have a similar range of consequences. In 1870, however, a resolution was offered to lay two Supreme Court nominations on the table until Congress completed a circuit court reorganization, and this proved to be the last occasion on which an attempt was made in the Senate to table such a nomination. The Senate, accordingly, has never attempted to use this motion on Supreme Court nominations during the era when it would have the effect of a final negative disposition.

Beginning in 1853, however, the Senate also started to use motions to adjourn with the effect or apparent intent of putting off consideration of a Supreme Court nomination.[43] On the Badger nomination in 1853, such a motion was adopted by a roll call vote. Thereafter, the motion to adjourn was offered on six other nominations through 1889. On one occasion it was adopted by voice vote, but otherwise a roll call always rejected it.

For a brief period beginning in 1870, motions to reconsider a vote to confirm also appeared. The first such motion (on Strong in 1870) was withdrawn after three days' debate and the failure of a motion to postpone it. The second (on Harlan in 1877) never reached a vote. The last (on Woods in 1880) was tabled by roll call after a quorum failed on an initial roll call on the motion itself. After this third unsuccessful attempt, the Senate abandoned use of this motion in this context as well.

Neither the motion to adjourn nor the motion to reconsider was ever used with the effect of terminating consideration. The motions to postpone, to recommit, and to table, on the other hand, which had continued to appear since earlier times, were still occasionally used with this effect. The Bradford nomination was tabled in 1852 and received no further action, and the Badger nomination in the following year was postponed until a date after Congress was to adjourn. In 1873, the Williams nomination became the only one on which a recommittal ever terminated consideration.

On only one subsequent occasion (Fortas, 1968; see below) has the Senate ever again resorted to optional procedural actions to terminate action on a Supreme Court nomination short of an up-or-down vote. With this one exception, accordingly, such terminations came about only in the half century from 1828 through 1873. This period included not only the nine nominations on which floor action was terminated before a vote through optional procedures during consideration, but also the two on which this effect followed from Senate action on a motion to proceed to consider.[44] As already suggested in the case of the tabled Tyler nominations, it appears likely that in these instances, even when the procedures used did not, in themselves, definitively terminate consideration, the Senate understood in using them that this would be their practical effect.

1890-1967

After 1890, the frequency of optional procedural action during consideration declined further; from then through 1967, such action appeared on just 14 of the 50 nominations that reached the floor. Additional shifts also occurred in the forms of procedural action used. These shifts amounted principally to a substantial decline in the use of motions that required a vote of the Senate, and an increasing resort instead to live quorum calls, which can be demanded by a single Senator, and unanimous consent agreements, which require the absence of objection by any single Senator. Although the votable motions could potentially be used in ways that would have the effect of terminating consideration, such a result was not likely from either of these procedures that newly came into use on Supreme Court nominations during this period.

Early in this period, the Senate continued to adopt motions to recommit and to postpone by voice vote, and to reject them by roll call. After 1930, however, these motions became more unusual, and the motion to adjourn ceased to be used at all in this context. A motion to recommit or postpone has been offered on just four nominations since 1930, most recently in 1971 (on Rehnquist for Associate Justice), and all have been rejected on roll calls. Only routine motions to adjourn or recess have been offered during consideration of any Supreme Court nomination since 1890, except for one occasion (on the nomination of Hughes for Chief Justice in 1930) on which a roll call rejected a motion to recess. As noted earlier, the motion to reconsider had already become disused in this context, perhaps because the Senate now routinely tables this motion immediately after every successful action.

Beginning with the Stone nomination for Associate Justice in 1925, live quorum calls came to be used with some regularity during consideration (although a single such call had already occurred once previously, on the Woods nomination of 1880). At least 10 such calls each were demanded on the Hughes and Parker nominations in 1930. This procedure can be used to incur a certain amount of delay even if it succeeds in producing a quorum, although only once (in the consideration of Parker) did such a call ever result in the actual failure of a quorum. After 1930, live quorum calls occurred on seven more nominations, most recently in 1971, but no more than three times on any single nomination.

The unanimous consent agreements that are to be taken into account in this connection include only those that assured the ability of the Senate to reach a final vote on a nomination, usually by setting either a time certain for the vote or an overall limit on the time for debate.[45] Such an agreement was first reached for Brewer (1889), but appeared on just three other nominations between then and 1967. Three of these four agreements were reached either in advance of consideration or on its first day, and accordingly appear likely to represent consensual arrangements to facilitate consideration. The fourth agreement, by contrast (on Parker in 1930), was not reached until the seventh day of consideration, and so appears more likely to represent a response to attempts to delay or extend consideration.

1968-Present

From 1968 onward, however, consent agreements became the standard means of regulating consideration of Supreme Court nominations, as they increasingly did for other major matters. Such agreements appeared on 16 of the 20 nominations that have reached the floor during this period, and six of the 16 were established only after the first day of consideration. Many of these agreements, on the other hand, may have represented collegial arrangements rather than attempts to overcome any difficulties in consideration, especially inasmuch as, on 11 of the 16 nominations in question, the consent agreement was the only optional procedural action taken. Overall, indeed, consideration of 15 of the 20 nominations reaching the floor since 1968 involved no optional procedural actions other than the consent agreement.

On the remaining five of these 20 recent nominations, the only optional procedures used were to postpone (once), to recommit (once), and for cloture. The motion for cloture, which allows a super-majority to limit the time for consideration of a matter, started to be used on Supreme Court nominations at about the same time as consent agreements became routine. As explained in the section on "Historical Trends in Floor Consideration," this motion did not become available for use on nominations until 1949. It was not used on any nomination, however, until 1968, when the Senate rejected cloture on a motion to proceed to consider the Fortas nomination for Chief Justice (and thereafter abandoned action on the nomination). This action represents the only time since 1873 when the Senate has terminated floor action on a Supreme Court nomination short of an up-or-down vote. Subsequently, cloture was moved also on the two Rehnquist nominations, as noted in the case study presented earlier. On a 1971 nomination for Associate Justice the motion failed, but a consent agreement was subsequently reached that permitted the Senate to reach a vote on confirmation. On a 1986 nomination for Chief Justice, the Senate invoked cloture, the first time it had done so on a Supreme Court nomination. Cloture was invoked also on the fourth Supreme Court nomination on which it was moved, that of Alito in 2006.

Procedural Complexity and Opposition

As was the case for forms of disposition and length of consideration, the significance of procedural complexity is more difficult to ascertain than is its occurrence. The preceding discussion shows that, on some occasions, optional procedures may have been used routinely, with the apparent purpose of managing the flow of business, and with a potential effect only of expediting action. On other occasions, optional procedures may have been used as means of delaying consideration or even placing obstacles in the way of a final disposition. In cases when the occurrence of optional procedural action resulted in consideration being terminated before a final vote, for example, it might reasonably be conjectured that the procedural action in question could have been undertaken with the intent of bringing about this result. It is equally reasonable to suppose that similar actions, undertaken on other nominations, may at least sometimes have reflected similar intentions, even if the results did not successfully fulfill those intentions.

No definitive conclusions, of course, might be drawn about the purpose of optional procedural actions in any specific case in the absence of information about the intentions of Senators undertaking them. Even to offer inferences about specific occasions on which such intentions were present would require examination of the political and historical circumstances surrounding each nomination, a task beyond both the scope and the purpose of this chapter. The preceding discussion, nevertheless, permits some assessment about which optional procedures may have afforded the possibility of delaying consideration or forestalling a final vote, and, accordingly, which of them might, in principle, have been used in some instances for such a purpose.

As with the level of opposition manifested in the final vote and the length of floor action, it is plausible to consider the occurrence of procedural actions, or procedural roll calls, as an indication that contention or controversy *may* have been present, but it is insufficient to demonstrate that substantial contentiousness actually *was* present. At most, it may be appropriate to consider that the *absence* of optional procedural actions that could have been used for delay presents an *absence* of indication of controversy.

Relation among Characteristics of Proceedings

That none of the three indicators examined in this part of the report may be taken as a definitive demonstration of the presence or absence of controversy is substantiated by the observation that these three criteria do not always identify the same nominations as possibly controversial. On the other hand, substantial overlap does exist among the nominations picked out by each indicator. This circumstance suggests that a more reliable and comprehensive measure of the level of controversy on each nomination might be derived from a simultaneous consideration of all three indicators together. Such an analysis, however, is beyond the scope of this chapter.

APPENDIX. SELECTED CHARACTERISTICS OF SENATE ACTION ON SUPREME COURT NOMINATIONS

Selected Characteristics of Floor Proceedings

Table A-1 provides information on the extent of opposition to, length of consideration of, and procedural actions taken on, each Supreme Court nomination submitted by the President from 1789 through 2005. This table identifies each nomination by the name of the nominee, and nominations for Chief Justice are distinguished by *italics*. Each nomination is also identified by the year in which it was submitted (action on some nominations extended into the following year).

Nominations that received no floor consideration, or that were withdrawn by the President, are identified in the "Notes" column, and for those that received no floor consideration, the columns for characteristics of floor proceedings are blank.

The column on "final vote" gives the tally of each roll call vote on confirmation. Nominations confirmed by a voice vote are identified by the entry of "voice" in this column. If no vote on confirmation occurred, the column is left blank.

For nominations confirmed by voice vote, by unanimous consent, or with fewer than 10 "nay" votes, the "Extent of Opposition" column is left blank. Other entries in this column identify those nominations that

- received no final vote, by an entry of "unfinished;"
- were rejected, by an entry of "rejected;" and
- were confirmed with more than more than 10 "nay" votes, by an entry of "opposition."

The column on "Optional Procedural Actions" is blank only for those nominations on which no floor action occurred. For nominations on which floor action occurred, the extent of optional procedural actions is identified by entries of

- "n" if no such actions occurred;
- "op" if such actions occurred, but with no procedural roll calls; and
- "opr" if procedural actions with roll calls occurred.

Table A-1. Selected Characteristics of Floor Proceedings on Supreme Court Nominations

Year	Nominee	Final Vote	Extent of Opposition	Floor Days	Optional Procedural Action[a]	Notes
1789	*John Jay*	Voice		1	n	
1789	John Rutledge	Voice		1	n	
1789	William Cushing	Voice		1	n	
1789	Robert H. Harrison	Voice		1	n	Declined to serve
1789	James Wilson	Voice		1	n	
1789	John Blair	Voice		1	n	
1790	James Iredell	Voice		1	n	
1791	Thomas Johnson	Voice		1	n	
1793-1	William Paterson					No floor action; withdrawn
1793-2	William Paterson	Voice		1	n	
1795	*John Rutledge*	10-14	Rejected	2	op	
1796	*William Cushing*	Voice		1	n	Declined to serve
1796	Samuel Chase	Voice		1	n	
1796	*Oliver Ellsworth*	21-1		1	n	
1798	Bushrod Washington	Voice		1	n	
1799	Alfred Moore	Voice		3	op	
1800	*John Jay*	Voice		1	n	Declined to serve
1801	*John Marshall*	Voice		1	n	
1804	William Johnson	Voice		1	n	
1806	H. Brockholst Livingston	Voice		1	n	
1807	Thomas Todd	Voice		1	n	
1811	Levi Lincoln	Voice		1	n	Declined to serve
1811	Alexander Wolcott	9-24	Rejected	4	op	
1811	John Quincy Adams	Voice		1	n	Declined to serve
1811	Joseph Story	Voice		1	n	
1811	Gabriel Duvall	Voice		1	n	
1823	Smith Thompson	Voice		1	n	
1826	Robert Trimble	27-5		2	opr	

Table A-1. (Continued)

Year	Nominee	Final Vote	Extent of Opposition	Floor Days	Optional Procedural Action[a]	Notes
1828	John J. Crittenden		Unfinished	9	opr	
1829	John McLean	Voice		1	n	
1830	Henry Baldwin	41-2		1	n	
1835	James M. Wayne	Voice		1	n	
1835-1	Roger B. Taney		Unfinished	3	opr	
1835-2	*Roger B. Taney*	29-15	Opposition	3	opr	
1835	Philip P. Barbour	30-11	Opposition	1	opr	
1837	William Smith	23-18	Opposition	2	op	Declined to serve
1837	John Catron	28-15	Opposition	2	op	
1837	John McKinley	Voice		1	n	
1841	Peter V. Daniel	22-5		1	opr	
1844-1	John C. Spencer	21-26	Rejected	1	n	
1844-1	Reuben H. Walworth		Unfinished	1	opr	Withdrawn
1844	Edward King		Unfinished	1	opr	
1844-2	John C. Spencer					No floor action; withdrawn
1844-2	Reuben H. Walworth		Unfinished	1	op	
1845	Reuben H. Walworth		Unfinished	1	op	Withdrawn
1845	Edward King		Unfinished	1	op	Withdrawn
1845	Samuel Nelson	Voice		1	op	
1845	John M. Read		Unfinished	1	op	
1845	George W. Woodward	20-29	Rejected	2	opr	
1845	Levi Woodbury	Voice		1	n	
1846	Robert C. Grier	Voice		1	n	
1851	Benjamin R. Curtis	Voice		1	n	
1852	Edward A. Bradford		Unfinished	1	op	
1853	George E. Badger		Unfinished	6	opr	
1853	William C. Micou					No floor action
1853	John A. Campbell	Voice		1	n	
1857	Nathan Clifford	26-23	Opposition	2	op	
1861	Jeremiah S. Black		Unfinished	3	opr	
1862	Noah H. Swayne	38-1		1	n	
1862	Samuel F. Miller	Voice		1	n	
1862	David Davis	Voice		1	n	
1863	Stephen J. Field	Voice		1	n	
1864	*Salmon P. Chase*	Voice		1	n	
1866	Henry Stanbery					No floor action
1869	Ebenezer R. Hoar	24-33	Rejected	2	opr	
1869	Edwin M. Stanton	46-11	Opposition	1	n	Did not serve
1870	William Strong	Voice		3	opr	
1870	Joseph P. Bradley	46-9		4	opr	

Table A-1. (Continued)

Year	Nominee	Final Vote	Extent of Opposition	Floor Days	Optional Procedural Action[a]	Notes
1872	Ward Hunt	Voice		1	n	
1874	*George H. Williams*		Unfinished	2	op	Withdrawn
1874	*Caleb Cushing*					No floor action; withdrawn
1874	*Morrison R. Waite*	63-0		1	op	
1877	John M. Harlan	Voice		1	op	
1880	William B. Woods	39-8		2	opr	
1881-1	Stanley Matthews					No floor action
1881-2	Stanley Matthews	24-23	Opposition	3	op	
1881	Horace Gray	51-5		1	n	
1882	Roscoe Conkling	39-12	Opposition	1	n	Declined to serve
1882	Samuel Blatchford	Voice		1	n	
1888	Lucius Q.C. Lamar	32-28	Opposition	1	n	
1888	*Melville W. Fuller*	41-20	Opposition	1	n	
1889	David J. Brewer	53-11	Opposition	2	opr	
1890	Henry B. Brown	Voice		1	n	
1892	George Shiras, Jr.	Voice		1	n	
1893	Howell E. Jackson	Voice		2	op	
1893-1	William B. Hornblower					No floor action
1893-2	William B. Hornblower	24-30	Rejected	2	op	
1894	Wheller H. Peckham	32-41	Rejected	3	op	
1894	Edward D. White	Voice		1	n	
1895	Rufus W. Peckham	Voice		1	n	
1898	Joseph McKenna	Voice		2	op	
1902	Oliver W. Holmes	Voice		1	n	
1903	William R. Day	Voice		1	n	
1906	William H. Moody	Voice		1	n	
1909	Horace Lurton	Voice		1	n	
1910	Charles E. Hughes	Voice		1	n	
1910	*Edward D. White*	UC		1	n	
1910	Willis Van Devanter	Voice		1	n	
1910	Joseph R. Lamar	Voice		1	n	
1912	Mahlon Pitney	50-26	Opposition	3	n	
1914	James C. McReynolds	44-6		2	n	
1916	Louis D. Brandeis	47-22	Opposition	1	op	
1916	John H. Clarke	UC		1	n	
1921	*William H. Taft*	60-4		1	n	
1922	George Sutherland	Voice		1	n	
1922-1	Pierce Butler					No floor action
1922-2	Pierce Butler	61-8		1	opr	
1923	Edward T. Sanford	UC		1	n	

Table A-1. (Continued)

Year	Nominee	Final Vote	Extent of Opposition	Floor Days	Optional Procedural Action[a]	Notes
1925	Harlan F. Stone	71-6		4	op	
1930	*Charles E. Hughes*	52-26	Opposition	4	opr	
1930	John J. Parker	39-41	Rejected	8	op	
1930	Owen J. Roberts	UC		1	n	
1932	Benjamin N. Cardozo	UC		1	n	
1937	Hugo L. Black	63-16	Opposition	1	opr	
1938	Stanley F. Reed	UC		1	n	
1939	Felix Frankfurter	Voice		1	n	
1939	William O. Douglas	62-4		2	op	
1940	Frank Murphy	UC		1	n	
1941	*Harlan F. Stone*	UC		1	n	
1941	James F. Byrnes	UC		1	n	
1941	Robert H. Jackson	Voice		1	op	
1943	Wiley B. Rutledge	Voice		1	n	
1945	Harold H. Burton	UC		1	n	
1946	*Fred M. Vinson*	Voice		1	n	
1949	Tom C. Clark	73-8		2	n	
1949	Sherman Minton	48-16	Opposition	1	opr	
1954	*Earl Warren*	Voice		1	n	see note[b]
1954	John M. Harlan					No floor action
1955	John M. Harlan	71-11	Opposition	2	op	
1957	William J. Brennan, Jr.	Voice		2	op	
1957	Charles E. Whittaker	Voice		1	n	
1959	Potter Stewart	70-17	Opposition	1	op	
1962	Byron R. White	Voice		1	n	
1962	Arthur J. Goldberg	Voice		1	n	see note[c]
1965	Abe Fortas	Voice		1	n	
1967	Thurgood Marshall	69-11	Opposition	2	n	
1968	*Abe Fortas*		Unfinished	6	opr	Withdrawn
1968	Homer Thornberry					No floor action; withdrawn
1969	*Warren E. Burger*	74-3		1	n	
1970	Clement Haynsworth, Jr.	45-55	Rejected	6	op	
1970	G. Harrold Carswell	45-51	Rejected	14	opr	
1970	Harry A. Blackmun	94-0		2	n	
1971	Lewis F. Powell, Jr.	89-1		3	n	
1971	William H. Rehnquist	68-26	Opposition	5	opr	
1975	John Paul Stevens	98-0		1	n	
1981	Sandra Day O'Connor	99-0		1	n	
1986	*William H. Rehnquist*	65-33	Opposition	5	opr	
1986	Antonin Scalia	98-0		1	n	
1987	Robert H. Bork	42-58	Rejected	3	op	
1988	Anthony M. Kennedy	97-0		1	n	

Table A-1. (Continued)

Year	Nominee	Final Vote	Extent of Opposition	Floor Days	Optional Procedural Action[a]	Notes
1990	David H. Souter	90-9		2	n	
1991	Clarence Thomas	52-48	Opposition	6	op	
1993	Ruth Bader Ginsburg	96-3		3	n	
1994	Stephen G. Breyer	87-9		1	n	
2005-1	John G. Roberts					No floor action; withdrawn
2005-2	*John G. Roberts*	78-22	Opposition	4	n	
2005	Harriet Miers					No floor action; withdrawn
2005	Samuel A. Alito	58-42	Opposition	5	opr	
2009	Sonia Sotomayor	68-31	Opposition	3	n	

Source: *Senate Executive Journal.* For 21st century nominations, Legislative Information System (LIS) and *Congressional Record.*

Notes:

a. Includes only procedural actions having the potential for delaying consideration. For details, see **Table 4** and accompanying text.

b. Recorded as unanimous.

c. One Senator asked to be recorded in opposition.

Selected Characteristics of Committee Action

Table A-2 provides information about the course of committee action on Supreme Court nominations which, like that in **Table A-1**, may shed light on the extent and intensity of opposition thereto. Also like **Table A-1**, this table identifies nominees by name and by year of submission (which in some cases is not the year in which action was concluded), distinguishing nominations for Chief Justice by *italics*.

Table A-2 addresses only committee action that occurred before initial floor consideration. If a nomination was not referred to committee before initial floor consideration, the columns on "Days from receipt to committee report (or other final action)," and on ""Form of reporting (or other final committee action)" are left blank. Similarly, the column on "Days of open committee hearings" is left blank for cases in which no open committee hearings are known to have been held.

Finally, the column on "floor disposition" is left blank for nominations that were confirmed. For nominations not confirmed, a summary indication of floor disposition appears in this column, but greater detail appears in **Table A-1**, above.

The table provides the "Form of reporting (or other final committee action)" for each nomination that was referred to committee. In cases in which the committee action took any form other than the normal form of favorable action, the entry in this column is given in **bold face**. "Reported" was the normal form of favorable committee action from 1835 to 1865; "reported favorably" thereafter.

Table A-2. Selected Characteristics of Committee Action on Supreme Court Nominations

Year	Nominee	Days from receipt to committee report (or other final action)	Days of open committee hearings	Form of reporting (or other final committee action)	Floor Disposition
1789	*John Jay*				
1789	John Rutledge				
1789	William Cushing				
1789	Robert H. Harrison				
1789	James Wilson				
1789	John Blair				
1790	James Iredell				
1791	Thomas Johnson				
1793-1	William Paterson				no floor action; withdrawn
1793-2	William Paterson				
1795	*John Rutledge*				rejected
1796	*William Cushing*				
1796	Samuel Chase				
1796	*Oliver Ellsworth*				
1798	Bushrod Washington				
1799	Alfred Moore				
1800	*John Jay*				
1801	*John Marshall*				
1804	William Johnson				
1806	H. Brockholst Livingston				
1807	Thomas Todd				
1811	Levi Lincoln				
1811	Alexander Wolcott	see note[a]			rejected
1811	John Quincy Adams				
1811	Joseph Story				
1811	Gabriel Duvall				
1823	Smith Thompson				
1826	Robert Trimble				
1828	John J. Crittenden	39		**Recommended not to act**	unfinished
1829	John McLean				
1830	Henry Baldwin				
1835	James M. Wayne	2		reported	
1835-1	Roger B. Taney				unfinished
1835-2	*Roger B. Taney*	8		reported	
1835	Philip P. Barbour	8		reported	
1837	William Smith	5		reported	

Table A-2. (Continued)

Year	Nominee	Days from receipt to committee report (or other final action)	Days of open committee hearings	Form of reporting (or other final committee action)	Floor Disposition
1837	John Catron	5		reported	
1837	John McKinley	6		reported	
1841	Peter V. Daniel				
1844-1	John C. Spencer	21		reported	rejected
1844-1	Reuben H. Walworth	93		reported	unfinished; withdrawn
1844	Edward King	9		reported	unfinished
1844-2	John C. Spencer				no floor action; withdrawn
1844-2	Reuben H. Walworth				unfinished
1845	Reuben H. Walworth	42		reported	unfinished; withdrawn
1845	Edward King	42		reported	unfinished; withdrawn
1845	Samuel Nelson	2		reported	
1845	John M. Read	6		reported	unfinished
1845	George W. Woodward	28		reported	rejected
1845	Levi Woodbury	11		reported	
1846	Robert C. Grier	1		reported	
1851	Benjamin R. Curtis	11		reported	
1852	Edward A. Bradford	9		reported	unfinished
1853	George E. Badger				unfinished
1853	William C. Micou	1		**discharged**	no floor action
1853	John A. Campbell	1		reported	
1857	Nathan Clifford	28		reported	
1861	Jeremiah S. Black				unfinished
1862	Noah H. Swayne	2		reported	
1862	Samuel F. Miller				
1862	David Davis	2		reported	
1863	Stephen J. Field	2		reported	
1864	*Salmon P. Chase*				
1866	Henry Stanbery	see note[b]		**no action**	no floor action
1869	Ebenezer R. Hoar	7		**adversely**	
1869	Edwin M. Stanton				
1870	William Strong	6		favorably	
1870	Joseph P. Bradley	6		favorably	
1872	Ward Hunt	5		favorably	
1874	*George H. Williams*	9	see note[c]	favorably	unfinished; withdrawn
1874	*Caleb Cushing*	0		favorably	no floor action; withdrawn

Table A-2. (Continued)

Year	Nominee	Days from receipt to committee report (or other final action)	Days of open committee hearings	Form of reporting (or other final committee action)	Floor Disposition
1874	*Morrison R. Waite*	1		favorably	
1877	John M. Harlan	40		favorably	
1880	William B. Woods	5		favorably	
1881-1	Stanley Matthews	19[d]		**no action**	no floor action
1881-2	Stanley Matthews	53		**adversely**	
1881	Horace Gray	1		favorably	
1882	Roscoe Conkling	6		favorably	
1882	Samuel Blatchford	9		favorably	
1888	Lucius Q.C. Lamar	29		**adversely**	
1888	*Melville W. Fuller*	61		**without recommen-dation**	
1889	David J. Brewer	12		favorably	
1890	Henry B. Brown	6		favorably	
1892	George Shiras, Jr.	6		**without recommen-dation**	
1893	Howell E. Jackson	11		favorably	
1893-1	William B. Hornblower	see note[b]		**no action**	no floor action
1893-2	William B. Hornblower	33		**adversely**	rejected
1894	Wheller H. Peckham	21		**without Recommen-dation**	rejected
1894	Edward D. White				
1895	Rufus W. Peckham	6		favorably	
1898	Joseph McKenna	28		favorably	
1902	Oliver W. Holmes	2		favorably	
1903	William R. Day	4		favorably	
1906	William H. Moody	7		favorably	
1909	Horace Lurton	3		favorably	
1910	Charles E. Hughes	7		favorably	
1910	*Edward D. White*				
1910	Willis Van Devanter	3		favorably	
1910	Joseph R. Lamar	3		favorably	
1912	Mahlon Pitney	14		favorably	
1914	James C. McReynolds	5		favorably	
1916	Louis D. Brandeis	117	19	favorably	
1916	John H. Clarke	10		favorably	
1921	*William H. Taft*				

Table A-2. (Continued)

Year	Nominee	Days from receipt to committee report (or other final action)	Days of open committee hearings	Form of reporting (or other final committee action)	Floor Disposition
1922	George Sutherland				
1922-1	Pierce Butler	5		favorably	no floor action
1922-2	Pierce Butler	13		favorably	
1923	Edward T. Sanford	5		favorably	
1925	Harlan F. Stone	28	see note[e]	favorably	
1930	*Charles E. Hughes*	7		favorably	
1930	John J. Parker	27	1	**adversely**	rejected
1930	Owen J. Roberts	10		favorably	
1932	Benjamin N. Cardozo	8		favorably	
1937	Hugo L. Black	4		favorably	
1938	Stanley F. Reed	9	1	favorably	
1939	Felix Frankfurter	11	4	favorably	
1939	William O. Douglas	7	1	favorably	
1940	Frank Murphy	11		favorably	
1941	*Harlan F. Stone*	11	1	favorably	
1941	James F. Byrnes				
1941	Robert H. Jackson	18	1	favorably	
1943	Wiley B. Rutledge	21	1	favorably	
1945	Harold H. Burton	1		favorably	
1946	*Fred M. Vinson*	13	1	favorably	
1949	Tom C. Clark	10	3	favorably	
1949	Sherman Minton	18	1	favorably	
1954	*Earl Warren*	44	2	favorably	
1954	John M. Harlan	see note[b]		no action	no floor action
1955	John M. Harlan	59	2	favorably	
1957	William J. Brennan, Jr.	49	2	favorably	
1957	Charles E. Whittaker	16	1	favorably	
1959	Potter Stewart	93	2	favorably	
1962	Byron R. White	8	1	favorably	
1962	Arthur J. Goldberg	25	2	favorably	
1965	Abe Fortas	13	1	favorably	
1967	Thurgood Marshall	51	5	favorably	
1968	*Abe Fortas*	83	11	favorably	unfinished; withdrawn
1968	Homer Thornberry	see note[b]	11	**no action**	no floor action; withdrawn
1969	*Warren E.Burger*	11	1	favorably	
1970	Clement Haynsworth, Jr.	36	8	favorably	rejected
1970	G. Harrold Carswell	28	5	favorably	rejected

Table A-2. (Continued)

Year	Nominee	Days from receipt to committee report (or other final action)	Days of open committee hearings	Form of reporting (or other final committee action)	Floor Disposition
1970	Harry A. Blackmun	21	1	favorably	
1971	Lewis F. Powell, Jr.	32	5	favorably	
1971	William H. Rehnquist	32	5	favorably	
1975	John Paul Stevens	10	3	favorably	
1981	Sandra Day O'Connor	27	3	favorably	
1986	*William H. Rehnquist*	55	4	favorably	
1986	Antonin Scalia	51	2	favorably	
1987	Robert H. Bork	91	12	unfavorably	rejected
1988	Anthony M. Kennedy	58	3	favorably	
1990	David H. Souter	64	5	favorably	
1991	Clarence Thomas	81	8[f]	**without recommen-dation**	
1993	Ruth Bader Ginsburg	37	4	favorably	
1994	Stephen G. Breyer	63	4		
2005-1	John G. Roberts	see note[b]		**no action**	no floor action; withdrawn
2005-2	*John G. Roberts*	16	4	favorably	
2005	Harriet Miers	see note[b]		no action	no floor action; withdrawn
2005	Samuel A. Alito	75	5	favorably	
2009	Sonia Sotomayor	57	4	favorably	

Source: CRS Report RL33225, *Supreme Court Nominations, 1789 -2009: Actions by the Senate, the Judiciary Committee, and the President*, by Denis Steven Rutkus and Maureen Bearden. Also, for 21st century nominations, Legislative Information System (LIS) and *Congressional Record.*

Notes:

a. The Senate referred the Wolcott nomination to a special committee only subsequent to the start of floor consideration.

b. The nomination was referred, but the committee took no final action.

c. The committee held two days of closed hearings on the Williams nomination after it was recommitted subsequent to the start of floor consideration.

d. The committee took no action to report the first Matthews nomination, but at the end of the period stated voted to postpone it.

e. The committee held one day of hearings on the Stone nomination after it was recommitted subsequent to the start of floor consideration.

f. The committee held three additional days of hearings on the Thomas nomination subsequent to the start of floor consideration, although the nomination was not formally recommitted.

End Notes

[1] Michael J. Gerhardt, *The Federal Appointment Process: A Constitutional and Historical Analysis* (Durham, NC: Duke University Press, 2000), p. 162; out-of-print CRS Report 89-253, *Cabinet and Other High Level Nominations that Failed to be Confirmed*, 1789-1989, by Rogelio Garcia. For more information, Members of Congress and their staff should contact Betsy Palmer.

[2] CRS Report RL31171, *Supreme Court Nominations Not Confirmed, 1789-2009*, by Henry B. Hogue; out-of-print CRS Report 89-253, *Cabinet and Other High Level Nominations that Failed to be Confirmed*, 1789-1989.

[3] On May 10, 2010, the Senate received the nomination of Solicitor General Elena Kagan to be an Associate Justice of the Supreme Court. The data presented in this chapter do not include this nomination.

[4] A list of all 159 nominations appears as **Table A-1** in the Appendix to this chapter, giving for each the full name, year, disposition, and information on the form of consideration. Discussion in the text identifies nominations by surname and year, facilitating reference to fuller information in the **Appendix**. In cases in which an individual was nominated twice in the same year, the suffixes "-1" and "-2" are used after the date to distinguish the first from the second nomination.

[5] The 159 nominations involved only 140 different individuals, because on 11 occasions, a President resubmitted the name of an individual previously nominated but not confirmed, and on another eight occasions, a President nominated either a sitting or a former Justice to be Chief Justice. Of the 140 individuals nominated, the Senate confirmed 117, leaving 23 on whom the Senate never took favorable action. Of the 117 confirmed, five never served because they declined the office, and one died before assuming it, so that 111 people (all but three of them men) have served as Justices of the Supreme Court. See CRS Report RL33225, *Supreme Court Nominations, 1789 - 2009: Actions by the Senate, the Judiciary Committee, and the President,* by Denis Steven Rutkus and Maureen Bearden.

[6] See CRS Report RL31989, *Supreme Court Appointment Process: Roles of the President, Judiciary Committee, and Senate*, by Denis Steven Rutkus, and CRS Report RL32821, *The Chief Justice of the United States: Responsibilities of the Office and Process for Appointment*, by Denis Steven Rutkus and Lorraine H. Tong.

[7] **Table A-2** in the **Appendix**, however, provides some general information on committee consideration of Supreme Court nominees.

[8] CRS Report RL33118, *Speed of Presidential and Senate Actions on Supreme Court Nominations*, 1900-2010, by R. Sam Garrett and Denis Steven Rutkus.

[9] The Senate decided to open its deliberations to the public on treaties and nominations in 1929. See section below, "The Calendar Call Becomes Formalized, 1922-1967."

[10] U.S. Congress, Senate, *History of the Committee on Rules and Administration*, Senate Doc. 96-27, 96th Cong., 1st sess., prepared by Floyd M. Riddick, Parliamentarian Emeritus, with the assistance of Louise M. McPherson (Washington: GPO, 1980), p. 10. The Senate has adopted general revisions of its rules just seven times since 1789, and this book sets forth each of these revisions. The Senate routinely makes changes to its rules in a piecemeal fashion, and sometimes the general revisions include changes that had actually been made earlier in time. To date, however, this book is the best source for changes in Senate rules over time.

[11] *Journal of the Executive Proceedings of the Senate*, September 26, 1789, p. 29, available at http://memory.loc.gov/ cgi-bin/query/r?ammem/hlaw:@field(DOCID+@lit(ej00135)), accessed on May 12, 2010. (Hereafter cited as *Senate Executive Journal*).

[12] J. Myron Jacobstein and Roy M. Mersky, *The Rejected: Sketches of the 26 Men Nominated for the Supreme Court but Not Confirmed by the Senate* (Milpitas, CA: Toucan Valley Publications, 1993), pp. 19-23.

[13] *Senate Executive Journal*, January 26, 1829, p. 626.

[14] Ibid, p. 638.

[15] David G. Savage, ed., *Guide to the U.S. Supreme Court*, 4th ed. (Washington: CQ Press, 2004), pp. 945-946.

[16] Jacobstein and Mersky, *The Rejected*, pp. 33-41.

[17] *Senate Executive Journal*, June 17, 1844, p. 353.

[18] Ibid, p. 354.

[19] Riddick, *History of the Committee on Rules and Administration*, p. 26.

[20] Savage, *Guide to the U.S. Supreme Court*, pp. 958-959.

[21] Jacobstein and Mersky, *The Rejected*, pp. 53-59.

[22] Moorfield Storey and Edward W. Emerson, *Ebenezer Rockwood Hoar: A Memoir* (Boston: Houghton Mifflin Company, 1911), p. 182.

[23] Ibid., pp.189-190, 191.

[24] Joseph P. Harris, *The Advice and Consent of the Senate* (New York: Greenwood Press, 1968), pp. 249-255.

[25] "Senators Approve the Nomination of William O. Douglas," *New York Times*, Mar. 25, 1939, p. 3; Associated Press, "Committee Approval Is Given to Douglas for Supreme Court," *Chicago Daily Tribune*, March 28, 1939, p. 3.

[26] "Associate Justice of the Supreme Court of the United States," remarks in Senate, *Congressional Record*, vol. 84, April 3 and 4, 1939, pp. 3705-3713, 3773-3788. For more on Frazier's concerns, see "Frazier Attacks Choice of Douglas," *New York Times*, April 4, 1939, p. 15.

[27] Floyd M. Riddick and Alan S. Frumin, *Riddick's Senate Procedure*, 101st Cong., 2nd sess., S. Doc. 101-28 (Washington: GPO, 1992), p. 941.

[28] Glen Elasser, "Rehnquist Assailed as Segregationist," Chicago Tribune, November 10, 1971, p. 5; Spencer Rich, "Rehnquist Civil Liberties Stance Eyed," *Washington Post*, October 26, 1971, p. A1.

[29] "Court Nominees: Powell and Rehnquist Confirmed," *Congressional Quarterly Almanac* (Washington: Congressional Quarterly Press, 1971), pp. 851-859.

[30] For this purpose, confirmation by unanimous consent is included with voice votes. At least 10 nominations have been confirmed by unanimous consent, especially between 1923 and 1945.

[31] The use of this inclusive criterion of floor action accounts for certain small differences between the figures presented here and in CRS Report RL31171, *Supreme Court Nominations Not Confirmed, 1789-2009*, by Henry B. Hogue.

[32] Jacobstein and Mersky, *The Rejected*, p. 59.

[33] Ibid., pp. 70-72. In the following session, nevertheless, Stanbery was nominated and confirmed as Attorney General.

[34] Ibid., pp. 37-38.

[35] Ibid, pp. 87-93; Robin Toner, David D. Kirkpatrick and Anne E. Kornblut, "Steady Erosion in Support Undercut Nomination," *New York Times*, October 28, 2005, p. 16.

[36] Jacobstein and Mersky, *The Rejected*, pp. 21-23.

[37] Under the rule then in effect, two-thirds of Senators present and voting were needed to invoke cloture. On the vote in question, the required number would have been 59.

[38] A salient example is provided by the confirmation of Goldberg in 1962, when one Senator explicitly asked to be recorded in opposition even though the Senate was acting by voice vote.

[39] In early days, when the Senate was much smaller, fewer than 10 negative votes might still have represented a significant level of opposition. In practice, however, the rough standard proposed may reasonably be applied to all periods, because until 1870, all nominations opposed by fewer than 14 Senators were opposed by fewer than five.

[40] Alternatively, the 12 nominations without floor action might be incorporated into the classification on the basis of the individual circumstances identified in their earlier discussion. The observations offered there suggest that five of the 12 might be taken as representing responses to opposition. The addition of these five would result in counting 54 nominations with "significant" opposition out of a total of 159, or 34%, a result but slightly different from that displayed for only those nominations that reached the floor.

[41] A more detailed measure, such as the number of hours consumed, would have been impracticable to compile, especially for the years before 1929, when the Senate typically did all executive business in closed session. Number of days, however, could be readily and definitively ascertained from the *Executive Journal.*

[42] These possibilities are discussed in more detail in CRS Report RL30360, *Filibusters and Cloture in the Senate*, by Richard S. Beth, Valerie Heitshusen, and Betsy Palmer.

[43] Routine adjournments and recesses by voice vote or unanimous consent, most of which occurred outside executive session in any case, were not taken into account for this purpose.

[44] It also included the single case in which consideration lapsed without a vote in the absence of any procedural action (Read, 1845; see **Table 1**).

[45] Consent agreements providing that the Senate proceed to consider a nomination at a subsequent point were addressed in the previous section, on "Calling Up Nominations." Agreements that involved both features are counted in both groups and considered separately under both heads.

In: Supreme Court Appointments and Nominations
Editor: Edward P. Bennett
ISBN: 978-1-61209-249-2

Chapter 4

Supreme Court Nominations, 1789-2010: Actions by the Senate, the Judiciary Committee, and the President

Denis Steven Rutkus and Maureen Bearden

Summary

The process of appointing Supreme Court Justices has undergone changes over two centuries, but its most basic feature, the sharing of power between the President and Senate, has remained unchanged. To receive a lifetime appointment to the Court, a candidate must first be nominated by the President and then confirmed by the Senate. A key role also has come to be played midway in the process by the Senate Judiciary Committee.

Table 1 of this chapter lists and describes actions taken by the Senate, the Senate Judiciary Committee, and the President on all Supreme Court nominations, from 1789 to the present. The table provides the name of each person nominated to the Court and the name of the President making the nomination. It also tracks the dates of formal actions taken, and time elapsing between these actions, by the Senate or Senate Judiciary Committee on each nomination, starting with the date that the Senate received the nomination from the President.

Of the 43 Presidents in the history of the United States, 40 made nominations to the Supreme Court. They made a total of 160 nominations, of which 124 (more than three-quarters) received Senate confirmation. Also, on 12 occasions in the nation's history, Presidents have made temporary recess appointments to the Court, without submitting nominations to the Senate. Of the 36 unsuccessful Supreme Court nominations, 11 were rejected in Senate roll-call votes, 11 were withdrawn by the President, and 14 lapsed at the end of a session of Congress. Six individuals whose initial nominations were not confirmed were later re-nominated and confirmed to positions on the Court.

A total of 117 of the 160 nominations were referred to a Senate committee, with 116 of them to the Judiciary Committee (including almost all nominations since 1868). Prior to 1916, the Judiciary Committee considered these nominations behind closed doors. Since

1946, however, almost all nominees have received public confirmation hearings. Most recent hearings have lasted four or more days.

In recent decades, from the late 1960s to the present, the Judiciary Committee has tended to take more time before starting hearings and casting final votes on Supreme Court nominations than it did previously. The median time taken for the full Senate to take final action on Supreme Court nominations also has increased in recent decades, dwarfing the median time taken on earlier nominations.

INTRODUCTION

The procedure for appointing a Justice to the Supreme Court of the United States is provided for by the Constitution in only a few words. The "Appointments Clause" (Article II, Section 2, clause 2) states that the President "shall nominate, and by and with the Advice and Consent of the Senate, shall appoint ... Judges of the supreme Court." The process of appointing Justices has undergone changes over two centuries, but its most basic feature—the sharing of power between the President and Senate—has remained unchanged. To receive a lifetime appointment to the Court, a candidate must first be nominated by the President and then confirmed by the Senate. An important role also has come to be played midway in the process (after the President selects, but before the Senate considers) by the Senate Judiciary Committee.

On rare occasions, Presidents also have made Supreme Court appointments without the Senate's consent, when the Senate was in recess. Such "recess appointments," however, were temporary, with their terms expiring at the end of the Senate's next session. The last recess appointments to the Court were made in the 1950s.

The need for a Supreme Court nomination arises when a vacancy occurs or is scheduled to occur on the Court. The most recent Court vacancy was created when Associate Justice John Paul Stevens retired on June 28, 2010. Justice Stevens had given President Barack Obama advance notice, on April 9, of his intention to step down. In response, President Obama on May 10 nominated Elena Kagan, Solicitor General of the United States, to replace Justice Stevens. It was the 160th time a President of the United States has nominated someone to be a Supreme Court Justice. On July 20, following four days of confirmation hearings, the Senate Judiciary Committee, by a vote of 13-6, favorably reported the Kagan nomination to the Senate. Following three days of floor debate, the Senate, on August 5, confirmed Ms.Kagan to the Court by a vote of 63-37.

In the past, most, but not all, Supreme Court nominations have received Senate confirmation. From the first appointments in 1789, the Senate has confirmed 124 out of 160 Court nominations. Of the 36 unsuccessful nominations, 11 were rejected in Senate roll-call votes, while most of the rest, in the face of committee or Senate opposition to the nominee or the President, were withdrawn by the President, or were postponed, tabled, or never voted on by the Senate. The 36 unconfirmed nominations, however, included those of six individuals who were later re-nominated and confirmed.

DESCRIPTION OF REPORT'S CONTENTS

This chapter lists and describes actions taken by the Senate, the Senate Judiciary Committee, and the President on all Supreme Court nominations, from 1789 to the present. The listing appears in a Supreme Court nominations table, **Table 1**, later in this chapter. Preceding the table is summary text, which highlights certain nominations statistics derived from the table. The text also provides historical background information on the Supreme Court appointment process and uses nominations statistics from the table to shed light on ways in which the appointment process has evolved over time. Many of the statistical findings discussed, for example, provide historical perspective on the emergence, and then increased involvement, of the Senate Judiciary Committee in the appointment process.

Specifically, the table lists, for each Supreme Court nomination, the following:

- name of the person nominated (the nominee);
- name of the President who made the nomination;
- date the nomination was made by the President and received in the Senate;[1]
- date(s) of any committee hearings held on the nomination that were open to the public;
- type and date of final committee action; and
- type and date of final action by the Senate or, in rarer instances, by the President (when the final action taken on a nomination was its withdrawal by the President).

Table 1 also shows the speed with which action was taken on each nomination, specifically presenting the number of days that elapsed from the date the nomination was formally received in the Senate until the following:

- the first day of public confirmation hearings (if any);
- the date of final committee action (if any); and
- the date of final Senate action or presidential withdrawal of the nomination.

The table also lists all recess appointments to the Supreme Court, as well as the later nomination of each recess appointee.

Table 1, it should be emphasized, tracks the dates of *formal* actions taken by the President, the Senate, and the Senate Judiciary Committee on each Supreme Court nomination. The table, for example, records the dates that nominations were actually made and transmitted by the President to the Senate. The table, however, does not track the dates on which Presidents learned of prospective Court vacancies or announced their intention to nominate someone to be a Justice. A discussion focusing more closely on such informal steps in the Supreme Court appointment process can be found in CRS Report RL33118, *Speed of Presidential and Senate Actions on Supreme Court Nominations, 1900-2010*, by R. Sam Garrett and Denis Steven Rutkus.

Actions by the full Senate tracked systematically in **Table 1** are those on which the Senate took *final* action (ordinarily in the form of confirmation, and less often in the form of rejecting, tabling, or postponing action on a nomination). For certain Supreme Court nominations, **Table 1** also provides dates of procedural actions taken on the Senate floor, prior to or after final Senate action, in order to put the final action in fuller context. The table, however, does not account for all Senate procedural actions on, or for all dates of Senate floor consideration of, Supreme Court nominations. For more comprehensive information on procedural actions taken by the full Senate on past Supreme Court nominations, see CRS Report RL33247, *Supreme Court Nominations: Senate Floor Procedure and Practice, 1789-2010*, by Richard S. Beth and Betsy Palmer.

In listing all persons ever nominated to the Supreme Court, **Table 1** includes the names of those who were not confirmed as well as those who were confirmed but did not assume their appointive office.[2] A list solely of the 111 individuals who assumed office and served on the Court (with judicial oath dates and service termination dates for each Justice) is available on the Court's website.[3]

FINDINGS FROM THE NOMINATIONS TABLE

Number of Nominations and Nominees

Table 1 lists all 160 Supreme Court nominations since 1789. Each of the 160 nominations entailed a President signing a nomination message, which was then transmitted to, and received by, the Senate. A lesser number of separate individuals, 141, were actually nominated to the Court, with some of them nominated more than once.[4]

Of the 160 total nominations to the Court, 22 were to the position of Chief Justice and the other 138 to a position as Associate Justice. The 22 Chief Justice nominations involved 20 persons nominated once, and one person nominated twice.[5] The 138 Associate Justice nominations involved 121 persons nominated once, 7 persons nominated twice, and 1 person nominated three times.

Presidents Who Made the Nominations

Of the 43 Presidents in the history of the United States, 40 have made nominations to the Supreme Court.[6] These 40 are listed in the second column of **Table 1**. All but one of the 40 Presidents succeeded in having at least one Supreme Court nomination receive Senate confirmation. The one exception was President Andrew Johnson, whose only Court nomination, of Henry Stanbery in 1866, was thwarted when the Senate enacted legislation eliminating the Associate Justice position to which Stanbery had been nominated.[7]

As **Table 1** shows, the number of nominations made to the Supreme Court has varied greatly from President to President. For any given President, the number of nominations will be affected by various factors, including the length of time the President was in office, the number of vacancies occurring on the Court during that presidency, and whether more than one nomination was required to fill a Court vacancy due to a previous nomination's failure to be confirmed. Examination of the nominations to the Court for each President reveals that one less than half of the Presidents (21 of 43) made four or more nominations, and one more than half (22 of 43) made three or fewer. One less than half of the Presidents (21 of 43) saw three or more of their Court nominations confirmed, and one more than half (22 of 43) saw two or fewer confirmed.

The President with the most Supreme Court nominations and confirmations was George Washington with 14 nominations, 12 of which were confirmed.[8] The two Presidents with the second-largest number of Court nominations were John Tyler and Franklin D. Roosevelt, with nine each. Only one of Tyler's nine nominations, however, received Senate confirmation, while all nine of FDR's were confirmed. The President with the largest number of Supreme Court confirmations in one term (apart from the first eight of George Washington's nominations—all in his first term, and all confirmed) was William Howard Taft, who, during his four years in office, made six Court nominations, all of which were confirmed. Six Presidents made only one Supreme Court nomination each, with the nominations of five of these Presidents receiving confirmation.[9] And, as noted above, three of the nation's 43 Presidents were unable to make a single nomination to the Court, because no vacancies occurred on the Court during their presidencies.

Date That Nominations Were Received in Senate

The Supreme Court appointment process officially begins when the President signs a message to the Senate nominating someone for appointment to the Court. Usually on the date of the signing, the message is delivered to the Senate and recorded in the *Senate Executive Journal* as having been received that day.[10] However, in 30 instances (all but two prior to the 20th century), Supreme Court messages were recorded in the *Senate Executive Journal* as received in the Senate on a day after they were signed by the President—usually the next day. In **Table 1**, in the "Date received in Senate" column, a second date is provided in parentheses (as the "Nom. date"), whenever a President made a nomination on a day prior to its receipt by the Senate.

Referral of Nominations to Senate Judiciary Committee

Although referral of Supreme Court nominations to the Senate Judiciary Committee is now standard practice, such referrals were not always the case. **Table 1** shows that 117 of 160 Supreme Court nominations have been referred to a Senate committee, 116 of them to the Judiciary Committee.

The first standing legislative committees of the Senate, including the Judiciary Committee, were created in 1816. Only once previously was a Supreme Court nomination referred to committee, when, in 1811, the Senate referred the nomination of Alexander Wolcott to a select committee of three Members. For roughly half a century after the Judiciary Committee's creation, nominations, rather than being automatically referred to the committee, were referred by motion only. From 1816 to 1868, more than two-thirds of the nominations (26 out of 38 nominations), were referred to the committee. During this period, the confirmation success rate was roughly the same for nominations referred, 15 of 26, as it was for those not referred, seven out of 12.

In 1868, Senate rules were changed to provide that all nominations be referred to appropriate standing committees, unless otherwise ordered by the Senate.[11] Subsequently, from 1868 to the present day, 90 of 96 Supreme Court nominations have been referred to the Judiciary Committee. The seven nominations not referred to committee were of persons who, at the time of their nomination, were a former President, a Senator, a former Senator, an Attorney General and former U.S. Representative, a former Secretary of War, or a sitting Associate Justice,[12] and all were easily confirmed. The last Supreme Court nomination not referred to the Judiciary Committee was that of Senator James F. Byrnes in 1941. The Senate by unanimous consent considered and confirmed the Byrnes nomination, without referral to committee, on the day it received the nomination from the President.

Nominations That Received Public Confirmation Hearings

Table 1, in the "Public hearing date(s)" column, lists dates on which the full Judiciary Committee, or a Judiciary subcommittee, held public confirmation hearings on Supreme Court nominations. Included in this listing are public sessions of the committee at which either Supreme Court nominees testified on their own behalf and/or outside witnesses testified for or against the nominees.

Advent of Public Hearings

Before 1916, the Judiciary Committee considered Supreme Court nominations behind closed doors. Thus, until that year, there are no entries in the "Public hearing date(s)" column. Rather, committee sessions on Court nominations typically were limited to committee members discussing and voting on a nominee in executive session, without hearing testimony from outside witnesses.[13] In 1916, for the first time, the committee held open confirmation hearings on a Supreme Court nomination—that of Louis D. Brandeis to be an Associate Justice—at which outside witnesses (but not the nominee) testified. More days of public hearings (19) were held on the Brandeis nomination than on any Supreme Court nomination since. The Brandeis hearings, however, did not set immediately into place a new policy of open confirmation hearings for Supreme Court nominations, since each of the next six nominations (during the years 1916 to 1923) was either considered directly by the Senate, without referral to the Judiciary Committee, or was acted on by the committee without the holding of confirmation hearings.

From 1925 to 1946, public confirmation hearings for Supreme Court nominations became the more common, if not invariable, practice of the Judiciary Committee. In 1925, Harlan F. Stone became the first Supreme Court nominee to appear in person and testify at his confirmation hearings.[14] During the next two decades, the Stone nomination was one of 11 Court nominations that received public confirmation hearings before either the full Judiciary Committee or a Judiciary subcommittee,[15] while five other nominations did not receive public hearings. One of the five nominees not receiving a public confirmation hearing was Senator James F. Byrnes, whose nomination in 1941, as noted earlier, was considered directly by the Senate without referral to the Judiciary Committee.[16]

Not indicated in the "Public hearing date(s)"column is the precise length (in minutes or hours) of each public hearing session. The hearing sessions for a few Supreme Court nominations during the 1925 to 1946 period lasted for hours, extending over several days;[17] others, however, were brief and perfunctory in nature, held only long enough to accommodate the small number of witnesses who wished to testify against a nominee.[18]

From Tom C. Clark's appointment in 1949 through the nomination of Elena Kagan in 2010, all but three of 36 Supreme Court nominations have received public confirmation hearings before the Senate Judiciary Committee or a Judiciary subcommittee.[19] The first of the three exceptions involved the 1954 nomination of John M. Harlan II, made less than a month before the final adjournment of a Congress. At the beginning of the next Congress, however, Harlan was renominated, and hearings were held on that nomination.[20] The second and third exceptions involved the Associate Justice nominations of John G. Roberts Jr. and Harriet E. Miers in 2005, both of which were withdrawn by the President before the scheduled start of confirmation hearings.

Length of Hearings in Days

The number of days given to public confirmation hearings has varied greatly from one Supreme Court nomination to another, particularly in recent decades. Following the 19 days of hearings held on the Brandeis nomination in 1916, Court nominations through the Associate Justice nomination of Abe Fortas in 1965 typically received either one or two days of hearings. However, from 1967 through August 2010, 17 of the 23 Court nominations which advanced through the hearings stage received four or more days of open confirmation hearings. Four of the 17 nominations received 11 or more days of hearings,[21] while another received eight days of hearings.[22] By contrast, only three of the 23 nominations received two or fewer days of hearings.[23]

Nominations Reported Out of Committee to Full Senate

Supreme Court nominations referred to the Judiciary Committee have almost always been reported to the Senate. If a majority of its members oppose confirmation, the Judiciary Committee technically may decide not to report a Supreme Court nomination. (This tactic would prevent the full Senate from considering the nominee, unless the Senate were able to undertake successfully the discharge of the committee.) **Table 1**, however, shows that instances of the committee not reporting have been rare. Of the 116 Supreme Court nominations referred to the Judiciary Committee, 108 were reported to the Senate.[24] The committee has reported these nominations in the following four ways.

Reporting

For most of the first five decades in which the Judiciary Committee considered Supreme Court nominations (1828 to 1863), its usual practice was simply to report these nominations to the Senate, without any official indication of the committee members' opinions regarding them. Twenty-three nominations were reported to the Senate in this way, and 15 of them were confirmed.

Reporting with a Favorable Recommendation

In 1870, the Judiciary Committee initiated the practice of reporting to the Senate an explicit recommendation in favor of confirmation whenever a majority of members supported a Supreme Court nominee. Over the course of almost a century and a half, the committee has favorably reported 74 Supreme Court nominations, with 68 receiving Senate confirmation.[25]

Reporting without Recommendation

On four occasions—three times in the late 19th century and once in the late 20th century—the Judiciary Committee has voted to report a Supreme Court nomination while explicitly stating it was not making a recommendation to the Senate. On each occasion, the committee reported a nomination without urging the Senate either to confirm or to reject.[26] The Senate confirmed three of the nominations that were reported in this way, while rejecting the fourth.[27]

Reporting with an Unfavorable Recommendation

On seven occasions—five times in the 19th century and twice in the 20th century—the Judiciary Committee voted to report a Supreme Court nomination with a recommendation to the Senate that it reject the nomination. Only two of the seven nominations received Senate confirmation (and each only by a close roll call vote);[28] the Senate rejected four of the others[29] and postponed taking action on the fifth.[30]

Nominations Not Reported Out of Committee

Of the 116 Supreme Court nominations referred to the Judiciary Committee since its establishment, eight were not reported by the committee to the Senate. Although five of the nominees were never confirmed to the Court,[31] the other three ultimately were, after being renominated.[32]

Final Action by the Senate or the President

From the first Supreme Court appointments in 1789 to the present day, Presidents have made 160 nominations to the Court. **Table 1** shows, in the "Final action by Senate or President" column, that the Senate confirmed 124 of these nominations, or roughly three-fourths.[33] Of the 36 nominations that were not confirmed, 11 were rejected by the Senate (all in roll-call votes),[34] 11 were withdrawn by the President,[35] and 14 lapsed at the end of a session of Congress without a Senate vote cast on whether to confirm.[36] The 36 nominations not confirmed by the Senate represented 31 individuals, some of whom were nominated more than once.[37] Six individuals whose initial nominations were not confirmed were later re-nominated and confirmed for positions on the Court.[38]

While the invariable practice of the Senate in recent decades has been to vote on Supreme Court nominations by roll call, this historically was usually not the case. **Table 2**, at the end of this chapter, shows that of the 135 Senate votes on whether to confirm (resulting in 124 confirmations and 11 rejections), 62 decisions were reached by roll-call votes, and the other 73 by voice vote or unanimous consent.

Initially, for some 40 years, the Senate rarely used roll-call votes to decide Supreme Court nominations. Starting in the 1830s, however, and continuing through the 1880s, the Senate used roll-call votes on Supreme Court nominations somewhat more often than unrecorded votes. The trend reversed between 1890 and 1965, when fewer than one-third of Senate decisions on confirming Court nominations were by roll-call vote. Since 1967, though, every Senate vote on whether to confirm a Supreme Court nomination has been by roll call. **Table 2** shows these trends within the four historical periods just noted, by breaking down the number of Senate decisions on confirmation within each period according to whether made by voice vote or unanimous consent (UC) on the one hand, or by roll-call vote, on the other. As already mentioned, all 11 Senate rejections of Supreme Court nominations were accomplished by roll-call votes.

Historically, recorded vote margins on Supreme Court nominations have varied considerably. Some roll-call votes, either confirming or rejecting a nomination, have been close.[39] Most votes, however, have been overwhelmingly in favor of confirmation.[40] On other occasions, as occurred with the three most recent nominations to the Court, a solid majority of the Senate has voted in favor of confirmation, but with a minority of more than 30% of the Senate's Members voting against confirmation.[41]

Days from Date of Senate Receipt of Nomination to First Hearing

For Supreme Court nominations, the amount of time elapsing between Senate receipt and start of confirmation hearings has varied greatly. **Table 1** shows that, for all 45 Court nominations receiving public confirmation hearings (starting with the Brandeis nomination in 1916), the shortest time that elapsed between Senate receipt and start of hearings was four days, for the nominations of both Benjamin N. Cardozo in 1932 and William O. Douglas in 1939; the second shortest time interval of this sort was five days, for the nominations of both Stanley F. Reed in 1938 and Felix Frankfurter in 1939. The longest time elapsing between Senate receipt and first day of confirmation hearings was 82 days, for the nomination of Potter Stewart in 1959; the next-longest time interval of this sort was 70 days, for nominee Robert H. Bork in 1987.

In recent decades, from the late 1960s to the present, the Judiciary Committee has tended to take more time in starting hearings on Supreme Court nominations than it did previously. **Table 1** reveals that prior to 1967, a median of 10 days elapsed between Senate receipt of Supreme Court nominations and the first day of confirmation hearings. From the Supreme Court nomination of Thurgood Marshall in 1967 through the nomination of Elena Kagan to be Associate Justice in 2010,[42] a median of 26 days elapsed between Senate receipt and first day of confirmation hearings.[43]

Starting in the 1990s, the inclination of the Judiciary Committee has been to allow at least four weeks to pass between Senate receipt of Supreme Court nominations and the start of confirmation hearings. This block of time is intended to be used by the committee members and staff for thorough study and review of background information about nominees and issues relevant to their nominations, in preparation for the hearings. In the case of seven of the eight most recent Court nominations to receive confirmation hearings (starting with the David H. Souter nomination in 1990), the shortest elapsed time between Senate receipt and first day of hearings was 28 days.[44] While the elapsed time for the eighth nomination, of John G. Roberts Jr. to be Chief Justice in 2005, was only six days, another, longer time interval is more meaningful. **Table 1** shows that Roberts's earlier nomination to be Associate Justice—later withdrawn, in order to have Roberts be re-nominated for Chief Justice—was received by the Senate 45 days prior to the start of hearings on his Chief Justice nomination.

Days from Senate Receipt to Final Committee Vote

The time elapsing between Senate receipt of Supreme Court nominations from the President and final committee votes has also varied greatly. **Table 1** shows that, for the 110 Court nominations that received final committee votes,[45] the nomination receiving the most prompt committee vote was of Caleb Cushing in 1874, which was reported by the Judiciary Committee on the same day that the Senate received it from the President.[46] The committee votes on 14 other nominations to the court occurred three days or less after the dates of Senate receipt.[47] At the other extreme was the 1916 nomination of Louis D. Brandeis, on which the Judiciary Committee voted 117 days after Senate receipt and referral to the committee. Five other nominations as well, one in the 19th century and four in the 20th, received committee votes more than 80 days after Senate receipt from the President.[48]

In recent decades, the Judiciary Committee has taken much more time in casting a final vote on Supreme Court nominations than it did previously. **Table 1** shows that prior to 1967, a median of nine days elapsed between Senate receipt of Supreme Court nominations and the committee's final vote on reporting them to the full Senate.[49] From the Supreme Court nomination of Thurgood Marshall in 1967 through the nomination of Elena Kagan in 2010, a median of 51 days elapsed between Senate receipt and final committee vote.[50]

Somewhat earlier, during the presidency of Dwight D. Eisenhower (1953 to 1961), two of five Supreme Court nominations were pending, prior to Judiciary Committee vote, in excess of the 1967-to-2010 median of 51 days for that time interval (while two other nominations were pending 44 and 49 days respectively before receiving committee action);[51] however, the corresponding time intervals for the next three Court nominations (two by President John F. Kennedy and one by President Lyndon B. Johnson) were all well below the 51-day median.[52]

Table 1. Nominations to the Supreme Court of the United States, 1789-August 5, 2010

Nominee	President	Date received in Senate[a]	Senate committee actions			Final action by Senate or President		Days from date received in Senate to:		
			Public hearing date(s)	Final vote date[b]	Final vote	Date	Final action[c]	First public hearing date	Committee final vote date	Final action by Senate or President
John Jay of New York (Chief Justice, hereafter C. J.)	Washington	09/24/1789	Nomination predated creation of Judiciary Committee in 12/10/1816. No record of other committee referral.			09/26/1789	Confirmed	—	—	2
John Rutledge of South Carolina	Washington	09/24/1789				09/26/1789	Confirmed	—	—	2
William Cushing of Massachusetts	Washington	09/24/1789				09/26/1789	Confirmed	—	—	2
Robert Harrison of Maryland	Washington	09/24/1789				09/26/1789	Confirmed (Nominee declined)	—	—	2
James Wilson of Pennsylvania	Washington	09/24/1789				09/26/1789	Confirmed	—	—	2
John Blair Jr. of Virginia	Washington	09/24/1789				09/26/1789	Confirmed	—	—	2
James Iredell of North Carolina	Washington	02/09/1790 (Nom. Date 02/08/1790)				02/10/1790	Confirmed	—	—	1
Thomas Johnson of Maryland	Washington	*Recess Appointment, 08/05/1791*								
		11/01/1791 (Nom. Date 10/31/1791)				11/07/1791	Confirmed	—	—	6

Table 1. (Continued)

Nominee	President	Date received in Senate[a]	Senate committee actions			Final action by Senate or President		Days from date received in Senate to:		
			Public hearing date(s)	Final vote date[b]	Final vote	Date	Final action[c]	First public hearing date	Committee final vote date	Final action by Senate or President
William Paterson of New Jersey	Washington	02/27/1793	Nomination predated creation of Judiciary Committee in 12/10/1816. No record of other committee referral.			02/28/1793	Withdrawn	—	—	1
William Paterson of New Jersey	Washington	03/04/1793				03/04/1793	Confirmed	—	—	0
John Rutledge of South Carolina (C. J.)	Washington	*Recess Appointment, 07/01/1795*								
		12/10/1795	Nomination predated creation of Judiciary Committee in 12/10/1816. No record of other committee referral.			12/15/1795	Rejected (10-14)	—	—	5
William Cushing of Massachusetts (C. J.)	Washington	01/26/1796				01/27/1796	Confirmed (Nominee declined)	—	—	1
Samuel Chase of Maryland	Washington	01/26/1796				01/27/1796	Confirmed	—	—	1
Oliver Ellsworth of Connecticut (C. J.)	Washington	03/03/1796				03/04/1796	Confirmed (21-1)	—	—	1
Bushrod Washington of Virginia	J. Adams	*Recess Appointment, 09/29/1798*								
		12/19/1798	Nomination predated creation of Judiciary Committee in 12/10/1816. No record of other committee referral.			12/20/1798	Confirmed	—	—	1
Alfred Moore of North Carolina	J. Adams	12/04/1799				12/10/1799	Confirmed	—	—	6

Table 1. (Continued)

Nominee	President	Date received in Senate[a]	Senate committee actions			Final action by Senate or President		Days from date received in Senate to:		
			Public hearing date(s)	Final vote date[b]	Final vote	Date	Final action[c]	First public hearing date	Committee final vote date	Final action by Senate or President
John Jay of New York (C. J.)	J. Adams	12/18/1800				12/19/1800	Confirmed (Nominee declined)	—	—	1
John Marshall of Virginia (C. J.)	J. Adams	01/20/1801				01/27/1801	Confirmed	—	—	7
William Johnson of South Carolina	Jefferson	03/22/1804				03/24/1804	Confirmed	—	—	2
H. Brockholst Livingston of New York	Jefferson	*Recess Appointment, 11/10/1806*								
		12/15/1806	Nomination predated creation of Judiciary Committee in 12/10/1816. No record of other committee referral.			12/17/1806	Confirmed	—	—	2
Thomas Todd of Kentucky	Jefferson	02/28/1807				03/02/1807	Confirmed	—	—	2
Levi Lincoln of Massachusetts	Madison	01/02/1811				01/03/1811	Confirmed (Nominee declined)	—	—	1
Alexander Wolcott of Connecticut	Madison	02/04/1811	No record of hearing	Select Committee, 02/13/1811	Reported	02/13/1811	Rejected (9-24)	—	9	9
John Quincy Adams of Massachusetts	Madison	02/21/1811	Nomination predated creation of Judiciary Committee in 12/10/1816. No record of other committee referral.			02/22/1811	Confirmed (Nominee declined)	—	—	1
Joseph Story of Massachusetts	Madison	11/15/1811				11/18/1811	Confirmed	—	—	3
Gabriel Duvall of Maryland	Madison	11/15/1811				11/18/1811	Confirmed	—	—	3

Table 1. (Continued)

Nominee	President	Date received in Senate[a]	Senate committee actions			Final action by Senate or President		Days from date received in Senate to:		
			Public hearing date(s)	Final vote date[b]	Final vote	Date	Final action[c]	First public hearing date	Committee final vote date	Final action by Senate or President
Smith Thompson of New York	Monroe	*Recess Appointment, 09/01/1823*								
		12/08/1823 (Nom. date 12/5/1823)	Nomination was not referred to Judiciary Committee.			12/09/1823	Confirmed	—	—	1
Robert Trimble of Kentucky	J. Q. Adams	04/12/1826 (Nom. date 04/11/1826)	Motion to refer to Judiciary Committee rejected by Senate, 05/09/1826 (7-25)			05/09/1826	Confirmed (27-5)	—	—	27
John Crittenden of Kentucky	J. Q. Adams	12/18/1828 (Nom. date 12/17/1828)	No record of hearing	01/26/1829	Reported with recom-mendation not to act	02/12/1829	Postponed (23-17)	—	39	56
John McLean of Ohio	Jackson	03/06/1829	Nomination was not referred to Judiciary Committee.			03/07/1829	Confirmed	—	—	1
Henry Baldwin of Pennsylvania	Jackson	01/05/1830	Nomination was not referred to Judiciary Committee.			01/05/1830	Confirmed (41-2)	—	—	0
James M. Wayne of Georgia	Jackson	01/07/1835 (Nom. date 01/06/1835)	No record of hearing	01/09/1835	Reported	01/09/1835	Confirmed	—	2	2
Roger B. Taney of Maryland	Jackson	01/15/1835	Nomination was not referred to Judiciary Committee.			03/03/1835	Postponed (24-21)	—	—	47
Roger B. Taney of Maryland (C. J.)	Jackson	12/28/1835	No record of hearing	01/05/1836	Reported	Motion to proceed, 03/14/1836 (25-19)		—	8	78
						03/15/1836	Confirmed (29-15)			

Table 1. (Continued)

Nominee	President	Date received in Senate[a]	Senate committee actions			Final action by Senate or President		Days from date received in Senate to:		
			Public hearing date(s)	Final vote date[b]	Final vote	Date	Final action[c]	First public hearing date	Committee final vote date	Final action by Senate or President
Philip P. Barbour of Virginia	Jackson	12/28/1835	No record of hearing	01/05/1836	Reported	Motion to proceed, 03/15/1836 (25-20)		—	8	78
						03/15/1836	Confirmed (30-11)			
William Smith of Alabama	Jackson	03/03/1837	No record of hearing	03/08/1837	Reported	03/08/1837	Confirmed (23-18) (Nominee declined)	—	5	5
John Catron of Tennessee	Jackson	03/03/1837	No record of hearing	03/08/1837	Reported	03/08/1837	Confirmed (28-15)	—	5	5
John McKinley of Alabama	Van Buren	*Recess Appointment, 04/22/1837*								
		09/19/1837 (Nom. date 09/18/1837)	No record of hearing	09/25/1837	Reported	09/25/1837	Confirmed	—	6	6
Peter V. Daniel of Virginia	Van Buren	02/27/1841 (Nom. date 02/25/1841)	Nomination was not referred to Judiciary Committee.			03/02/1841	Confirmed (22-5)	—	—	3
John C. Spencer of New York	Tyler	01/09/1844 (Nom. date 01/08/1844	No record of hearing	01/30/1844	Reported	01/31/1844	Rejected (21-26)	—	21	22
Reuben H. Walworth of New York	Tyler	03/13/1844	No record of hearing	06/14/1844	Reported	Tabled, 06/15/1844 (27-20)		—	93	96
						06/17/1844	Withdrawn			
Edward King of Pennsylvania	Tyler	06/05/1844	No record of hearing	06/14/1844	Reported	06/15/1844	Tabled (29-18)	—	9	10

Table 1. (Continued)

Nominee	President	Date received in Senate[a]	Senate committee actions			Final action by Senate or President		Days from date received in Senate to:		
			Public hearing date(s)	Final vote date[b]	Final vote	Date	Final action[c]	First public hearing date	Committee final vote date	Final action by Senate or President
John C. Spencer of New York	Tyler	06/17/1844	Nomination was not referred to Judiciary Committee.			06/17/1844	Withdrawn	—	—	0
Reuben H. Walworth of New York	Tyler	06/17/1844	Nomination was not referred to Judiciary Committee.			Motion to proceed objected to, 06/17/1844. Senate adjourned on same day, with no record of further action.		—	—	—
Reuben H. Walworth of New York	Tyler	12/10/1844 (Nom. date 12/04/1844)	No record of hearing	01/21/1845	Reported	Tabled, 01/21/1845		—	42	58
						02/06/1845	Withdrawn			
Edward King of Pennsylvania	Tyler	12/10/1844 (Nom. date 12/04/1844)	No record of hearing	01/21/1845	Reported	Tabled, 01/21/1845		—	42	60
						02/08/1845	Withdrawn			
Samuel Nelson of New York	Tyler	02/06/1845 (Nom. date 02/04/1845)	No record of hearing	02/08/1845	Reported	02/14/1845	Confirmed	—	2	8
John M. Read of Pennsylvania	Tyler	02/08/1845	No record of hearing	02/14/1845	Reported	No record of action		—	6	—
George W. Woodward of Pennsylvania	Polk	12/23/1845	No record of hearing	01/20/1846	Reported	Motion to postpone rejected, 01/22/1846 (21-28)		—	28	30
						01/22/1846	Rejected			
Levi Woodbury of New Hampshire	Polk	*Recess Appointment, 09/20/1845*								
		12/23/1845	No record of hearing	01/03/1846	Reported	01/03/1846	Confirmed	—	11	11

Table 1. (Continued)

Nominee	President	Date received in Senate[a]	Senate committee actions			Final action by Senate or President		Days from date received in Senate to:		
			Public hearing date(s)	Final vote date[b]	Final vote	Date	Final action[c]	First public hearing date	Committee final vote date	Final action by Senate or President
Robert C. Grier of Pennsylvania	Polk	08/03/1846	No record of hearing	08/04/1846	Reported	08/04/1846	Confirmed	—	1	1
Benjamin R. Curtis of Massachusetts	Fillmore	*Recess Appointment, 09/22/1851*								
		12/12/1851 (Nom. date 12/11/1851)	No record of hearing	12/23/1851	Reported	12/23/1851	Confirmed	—	11	11
Edward A. Bradford of Louisiana	Fillmore	08/21/1852 (Nom. Date 08/16/1852)	No record of hearing	08/30/1852	Reported	08/31/1852	Tabled	—	9	10
George E. Badger of North Carolina	Fillmore	01/10/1853 (Nom. Date 01/03/1853)	Nomination was not referred to Judiciary Committee.			02/11/1853	Postponed (26-25)	—	—	32
William C. Micou of Louisiana	Fillmore	02/24/1853 (Nom. Date 02/14/1853)	No record of hearing	Referred to Judiciary Committee on 02/24/1853. Senate ordered committee discharged of nomination on same day; no record of Senate consideration after discharge.				—	—	—
John A. Campbell of Alabama	Pierce	03/21/1853	No record of hearing	03/22/1853	Reported	03/22/1853	Confirmed	—	1	1
Nathan Clifford of Maine	Buchanan	12/09/1857	No record of hearing	01/06/1858	Reported	01/12/1858	Confirmed (26-23)	—	28	34
Jeremiah S. Black of Pennsylvania	Buchanan	02/06/1861 (Nom. Date 02/05/1861)	Nomination was not referred to Judiciary Committee.			02/21/1861	Motion to proceed rejected (25-26)	—	—	15

Table 1. (Continued)

Nominee	President	Date received in Senate[a]	Senate committee actions			Final action by Senate or President		Days from date received in Senate to:		
			Public hearing date(s)	Final vote date[b]	Final vote	Date	Final action[c]	First public hearing date	Committee final vote date	Final action by Senate or President
Noah H. Swayne of Ohio	Lincoln	01/22/1862 (Nom. Date 01/21/1862)	No record of hearing	01/24/1862	Reported	01/24/1862	Confirmed (38-1)	—	2	2
Samuel F. Miller of Iowa	Lincoln	07/16/1862	Nomination was not referred to Judiciary Committee.			07/16/1862	Confirmed	—	—	0
David Davis of Illinois	Lincoln	*Recess Appointment, 10/17/1862*								
		12/03/1862 (Nom. date 12/01/1862)	No record of hearing	12/05/1862	Reported	12/08/1862	Confirmed	—	2	5
Stephen J. Field of California	Lincoln	03/07/1863 (Nom. date 03/06/1863	No record of hearing	03/09/1863	Reported	03/10/1863	Confirmed	—	2	3
Salmon P. Chase of Ohio (C. J.)	Lincoln	12/06/1864	Nomination was not referred to Judiciary Committee.			12/06/1864	Confirmed	—	—	0
Henry Stanbery of Ohio	A. Johnson	04/16/1866	No record of hearing	Referred to Judiciary Committee on 04/16/1866. No record of committee vote, and no record of Senate action after referral.				—	—	—
Ebenezer R. Hoar of Massachusetts	Grant	12/15/1869 (Nom. date 12/14/1869)	No record of hearing	12/22/1869	Reported adversely	02/03/1870	Rejected (24-33)	—	7	50
Edwin M. Stanton of Pennsylvania	Grant	12/20/1869	Nomination was not referred to Judiciary Committee			12/20/1869	Confirmed (46-11) (Nominee died before assuming office)	—	—	0

Table 1. (Continued)

Nominee	President	Date received in Senate[a]	Senate committee actions			Final action by Senate or President		Days from date received in Senate to:		
			Public hearing date(s)	Final vote date[b]	Final vote	Date	Final action[c]	First public hearing date	Committee final vote date	Final action by Senate or President
William Strong of Pennsylvania	Grant	02/08/1870 (Nom. date 02/07/1870)	No record of hearing	02/14/1870	Reported favorably	02/18/1870	Confirmed	—	6	10
Joseph P. Bradley of New Jersey	Grant	02/08/1870 (Nom. date 02/07/1870)	No record of hearing	02/14/1870	Reported favorably	Postponed, 03/02/1870 (31-26)		—	6	41
						Motion to postpone rejected, 03/02/1870 (23-28)				
						03/21/1870	Confirmed (46-9)			
Ward Hunt of New York	Grant	12/06/1872 (Nom. date 12/03/1872)	No record of hearing	12/11/1872	Reported favorably	12/11/1872	Confirmed	—	5	5
George H. Williams of Oregon (C. J.)	Grant	12/02/1873 (Nom. date 12/01/1873)	No record of hearing	12/11/1873	Reported favorably	Recommitted, 12/15/1873		—	9	37
			Closed hearings[d] 12/16/1873 12/17/1873	—	—	01/08/1874	Withdrawn			
Caleb Cushing of Massachusetts (C. J.)	Grant	01/09/1874	No record of hearing	01/09/1874	Reported favorably	01/14/1874	Withdrawn	—	0	5
Morrison R. Waite of Ohio (C. J.)	Grant	01/19/1874	No record of hearing	01/20/1874	Reported favorably	01/21/1874	Confirmed (63-0)	—	1	2

Table 1. (Continued)

Nominee	President	Date received in Senate[a]	Senate committee actions			Final action by Senate or President		Days from date received in Senate to:		
			Public hearing date(s)	Final vote date[b]	Final vote	Date	Final action[c]	First public hearing date	Committee final vote date	Final action by Senate or President
John Marshall Harlan of Kentucky	Hayes	10/17/1877	No record of hearing	11/26/1877	Reported favorably	11/29/1877	Confirmed	—	40	43
William B. Woods of Georgia	Hayes	12/15/1880	No record of hearing	12/20/1880	Reported favorably	12/21/1880	Confirmed (39-8)	—	5	6
						Tabled motion to reconsider, 12/22/1880 (36-3)				
Stanley Matthews of Ohio	Hayes	01/26/1881	No record of hearing	Considered , 02/07/1881		No record of action		—	19	—
				02/14/1881	Postponed					
Stanley Matthews of Ohio	Garfield	03/18/1881 (Nom. date 03/14/1881)	No record of hearing	05/09/1881	Reported adversely (6-1)	05/12/1881	Confirmed (24-23)	—	53	55
Horace Gray of Massachusetts	Arthur	12/19/1881	No record of hearing	12/20/1881	Reported favorably	12/20/1881	Confirmed (51-5)	—	1	1
Roscoe Conkling of New York	Arthur	02/24/1882	No record of hearing	03/02/1882	Reported favorably	03/02/1882	Confirmed (39-12) (Nominee declined)	—	6	6
Samuel Blatchford of New York	Arthur	03/13/1882	No record of hearing	03/22/1882	Reported favorably	03/22/1882	Confirmed	—	9	9
Lucius Q. C. Lamar of Mississippi	Cleveland	12/12/1887 (Nom. Date 12/06/1887)	No record of hearing	01/10/1888	Reported adversely (5-4)	01/16/1888	Confirmed (32-28)	—	29	35

Table 1. (Continued)

Nominee	President	Date received in Senate[a]	Senate committee actions			Final action by Senate or President		Days from date received in Senate to:		
			Public hearing date(s)	Final vote date[b]	Final vote	Date	Final action[c]	First public hearing date	Committee final vote date	Final action by Senate or President
Melville W. Fuller of Illinois (C. J.)	Cleveland	05/02/1888 (Nom. date 04/30/1888)	No record of hearing	07/02/1888	Reported without recommendation	07/20/1888	Confirmed (41-20)	—	61	79
David J. Brewer of Kansas	Harrison	12/04/1889	No record of hearing	12/16/1889	Reported favorably	Motion to postpone rejected, 12/18/1889 (15-54)		—	12	14
						Motion to postpone rejected, 12/18/1889 (25-45)				
						12/18/1889	Confirmed (53-11)			
Henry B. Brown of Michigan	Harrison	12/23/1890	No record of hearing	12/29/1890	Reported favorably	12/29/1890	Confirmed	—	6	6
George Shiras Jr. of Pennsylvania	Harrison	07/19/1892	No record of hearing	07/25/1892	Reported without recommendation	07/26/1892	Confirmed	—	6	7
Howell E. Jackson of Tennessee	Harrison	02/02/1893	No record of hearing	02/13/1893	Reported favorably	02/18/1893	Confirmed	—	11	16
William B. Hornblower of New York	Cleveland	09/19/1893	No record of hearing	Considered, 09/25/1893 and 10/25 & 30/1893		No record of action		—	—	—

Table 1. (Continued)

<table>
<tr><th rowspan="2">Nominee</th><th rowspan="2">President</th><th rowspan="2">Date received in Senate[a]</th><th colspan="3">Senate committee actions</th><th colspan="2">Final action by Senate or President</th><th colspan="3">Days from date received in Senate to:</th></tr>
<tr><th>Public hearing date(s)</th><th>Final vote date[b]</th><th>Final vote</th><th>Date</th><th>Final action[c]</th><th>First public hearing date</th><th>Committee final vote date</th><th>Final action by Senate or President</th></tr>
<tr><td rowspan="2">William B. Hornblower of New York</td><td rowspan="2">Cleveland</td><td rowspan="2">12/06/1893</td><td rowspan="2">No record of hearing</td><td colspan="2">Considered, 12/11, 14 & 18/1893</td><td rowspan="2">01/15/1894</td><td rowspan="2">Rejected (24-30)</td><td rowspan="2">—</td><td rowspan="2">33</td><td rowspan="2">40</td></tr>
<tr><td>01/08/1894</td><td>Reported adversely</td></tr>
<tr><td rowspan="2">Wheeler H. Peckham of New York</td><td rowspan="2">Cleveland</td><td rowspan="2">01/22/1894</td><td rowspan="2">No record of hearing</td><td colspan="2">On question of reporting favorably, committee vote divided, 02/12/1894 (5-5)</td><td rowspan="2">02/16/1894</td><td rowspan="2">Rejected (32-41)</td><td rowspan="2">—</td><td rowspan="2">21</td><td rowspan="2">25</td></tr>
<tr><td>02/12/1894</td><td>Reported without recommen-dation</td></tr>
<tr><td>Edward D. White of Louisiana</td><td>Cleveland</td><td>02/19/1894</td><td colspan="3">Nomination was not referred to Judiciary Committee</td><td>02/19/1894</td><td>Confirmed</td><td>—</td><td>—</td><td>0</td></tr>
<tr><td>Rufus W. Peckham of New York</td><td>Cleveland</td><td>12/03/1895</td><td>No record of hearing</td><td>12/09/1895</td><td>Reported favorably</td><td>12/09/1895</td><td>Confirmed</td><td>—</td><td>6</td><td>6</td></tr>
<tr><td>Joseph McKenna of California</td><td>McKinley</td><td>12/16/1897</td><td>No record of hearing</td><td>01/13/1898</td><td>Reported favorably</td><td>01/21/1898</td><td>Confirmed</td><td>—</td><td>28</td><td>36</td></tr>
<tr><td>Oliver Wendell Holmes of Massachusetts</td><td>T. Roosevelt</td><td>12/02/1902</td><td>No record of hearing</td><td>12/04/1902</td><td>Reported favorably</td><td>12/04/1902</td><td>Confirmed</td><td>—</td><td>2</td><td>2</td></tr>
<tr><td>William R. Day of Ohio</td><td>T. Roosevelt</td><td>02/19/1903</td><td>No record of hearing</td><td>02/23/1903</td><td>Reported favorably</td><td>02/23/1903</td><td>Confirmed</td><td>—</td><td>4</td><td>4</td></tr>
</table>

Table 1. (Continued)

Nominee	President	Date received in Senate[a]	Senate committee actions			Final action by Senate or President		Days from date received in Senate to:		
			Public hearing date(s)	Final vote date[b]	Final vote	Date	Final action[c]	First public hearing date	Committee final vote date	Final action by Senate or President
William H. Moody of Massachusetts	T. Roosevelt	12/03/1906	No record of hearing	12/10/1906	Reported favorably	12/12/1906	Confirmed	—	7	9
Horace H. Lurton of Tennessee	Taft	12/13/1909	No record of hearing	12/16/1909	Reported favorably	12/20/1909	Confirmed	—	3	7
Charles Evans Hughes of New York	Taft	04/25/1910	No record of hearing	05/02/1910	Reported favorably	05/02/1910	Confirmed	—	7	7
Edward D. White of Louisiana (C. J.)	Taft	12/12/1910	Nomination was not referred to Judiciary Committee.			12/12/1910	Confirmed	—	—	0
Willis Van Devanter of Wyoming	Taft	12/12/1910	No record of hearing	12/15/1910	Reported favorably	12/15/1910	Confirmed	—	3	3
Joseph R. Lamar of Georgia	Taft	12/12/1910	No record of hearing	12/15/1910	Reported favorably	12/15/1910	Confirmed	—	3	3
Mahlon Pitney of New Jersey	Taft	02/19/1912	No record of hearing	03/04/1912	Reported favorably	03/13/1912	Confirmed (50-26)	—	14	23
James C. McReynolds of Tennessee	Wilson	08/19/1914	No record of hearing	08/24/1914	Reported favorably	08/29/1914	Confirmed (44-6)	—	5	10
Louis D. Brandeis of Massachusetts	Wilson	01/28/1916	02/09/1916 02/10/1916 02/15/1916	05/24/1916	Reported favorably (10-8)	06/01/1916	Confirmed (47-22)	12	117	125

Table 1. (Continued)

Nominee	President	Date received in Senate[a]	Senate committee actions			Final action by Senate or President		Days from date received in Senate to:		
			Public hearing date(s)	Final vote date[b]	Final vote	Date	Final action[c]	First public hearing date	Committee final vote date	Final action by Senate or President
			02/16/1916 02/17/1916 02/18/1916 02/24/1916 02/25/1916 02/26/1916 02/29/1916 03/01/1916 03/02/1916 03/03/1916 03/04/1916 03/06/1916 03/07/1916 03/08/1916 03/14/1916 03/15/1916							
John H. Clarke of Ohio	Wilson	07/14/1916	No record of hearing	07/24/1916	Reported favorably	07/24/1916	Confirmed	—	10	10
William Howard Taft of Connecticut (C. J.)	Harding	06/30/1921	Nomination was not referred to Judiciary Committee.			06/30/1921	Confirmed (60-4)[e]	—	—	0
George Sutherland of Utah	Harding	09/05/1922	Nomination was not referred to Judiciary Committee.			09/05/1922	Confirmed	—	—	0
Pierce Butler of Minnesota	Harding	11/23/1922 (Nom. Date 11/22/1922)	No record of hearing	11/28/1922	Reported favorably	Placed on Executive Calendar, 11/28/1922, with no record of further action		—	5	—

Table 1. (Continued)

Nominee	President	Date received in Senate[a]	Senate committee actions			Final action by Senate or President		Days from date received in Senate to:		
			Public hearing date(s)	Final vote date[b]	Final vote	Date	Final action[c]	First public hearing date	Committee final vote date	Final action by Senate or President
Pierce Butler of Minnesota	Harding	12/05/1922	Closed hearings 12/09/1922 12/13/1922	12/18/1922	Reported favorably	Motion to recommit defeated, 12/21/1922 (7-63)		—	13	16
						12/21/1922	Confirmed (61-8)			
Edward T. Sanford of Tennessee	Harding	01/24/1923	No record of hearing	01/29/1923	Reported favorably	01/29/1923	Confirmed	—	5	5
Harlan F. Stone of New York	Coolidge	01/05/1925	Closed hearing 01/12/ 1925[f]	Reported favorably 01/21/1925		Recommitted 01/26/1925		—	28	31
			01/28/1925 (after 01/26/1925 recomt'l)[f]	02/02/1925	Reported favorably	02/05/1925	Confirmed (71-6)	23		
Charles Evans Hughes of New York (C. J.)	Hoover	02/03/1930	No hearing held	02/10/1930	Reported favorably (10-2)	Motion to recommit rejected, 02/13/1930 (31-49)		—	7	10
						02/13/1930	Confirmed (52-26)			
John J. Parker of North Carolina	Hoover	03/21/1930	04/05/1930	04/21/1930	Reported adversely (10-6)	05/07/1930	Rejected (39-41)	15	31	47
Owen J. Roberts of Pennsylvania	Hoover	05/09/1930	No hearing held	05/19/1930	Reported favorably	05/20/1930	Confirmed	—	10	11

Table 1. (Continued)

Nominee	President	Date received in Senate[a]	Senate committee actions			Final action by Senate or President		Days from date received in Senate to:		
			Public hearing date(s)	Final vote date[b]	Final vote	Date	Final action[c]	First public hearing date	Committee final vote date	Final action by Senate or President
Benjamin N. Cardozo of New York	Hoover	02/15/1932	02/19/1932	02/23/1932	Reported favorably	02/24/1932	Confirmed	4	8	9
Hugo L. Black of Alabama	F. Roosevelt	08/12/1937	No hearing held	08/16/1937	Reported favorably (13-4)	Motion to recommit rejected, 08/17/1937 (15-66)		—	4	5
						08/17/1937	Confirmed (63-16)			
Stanley F. Reed of Kentucky	F. Roosevelt	01/15/1938	01/20/1938	01/24/1938	Reported favorably	01/25/1938	Confirmed	5	9	10
Felix Frankfurter of Massachusetts	F. Roosevelt	01/05/1939	01/10/1939 01/11/1939 01/12/1939	01/16/1939	Reported favorably	01/17/1939	Confirmed	5	11	12
William O. Douglas of Connecticut	F. Roosevelt	03/20/1939	03/24/1939	03/27/1939	Reported favorably	04/04/1939	Confirmed (62-4)	4	7	15
Frank Murphy of Michigan	F. Roosevelt	01/04/1940	01/11/1940	01/15/1940	Reported favorably	01/16/1940	Confirmed	8	11	12
Harlan F. Stone of New York (C. J.)	F. Roosevelt	06/12/1941	06/21/1941	06/23/1941	Reported favorably	06/27/1941	Confirmed	9	11	15
James F. Byrnes of South Carolina	F. Roosevelt	06/12/1941	Nomination was not referred to Judiciary Committee.			06/12/1941	Confirmed	—	—	0

Table 1. (Continued)

Nominee	President	Date received in Senate[a]	Senate committee actions			Final action by Senate or President		Days from date received in Senate to:		
			Public hearing date(s)	Final vote date[b]	Final vote	Date	Final action[c]	First public hearing date	Committee final vote date	Final action by Senate or President
Robert H. Jackson of New York	F. Roosevelt	06/12/1941	06/21/1941 06/231941 06/27/1941 06/30/1941	06/30/1941	Reported favorably	07/07/1941	Confirmed	9	18	25
Wiley B. Rutledge of Iowa	F. Roosevelt	01/11/1943	01/22/1943	02/01/1943	Reported favorably	02/08/1943	Confirmed	11	21	28
Harold H. Burton of Ohio	Truman	09/18/1945	No hearing held	09/19/1945	Reported favorably	09/19/1945	Confirmed	—	1	1
Fred M. Vinson of Kentucky (C. J.)	Truman	06/06/1946	06/14/1946	06/19/1946	Reported favorably	06/20/1946	Confirmed	8	13	14
Tom C. Clark of Texas	Truman	08/02/1949	08/09/1949 08/10/1949 08/11/1949	08/12/1949	Reported favorably (9-2)	08/18/1949	Confirmed (73-8)	7	10	16
Sherman Minton of Indiana	Truman	09/15/1949	09/27/1949	10/03/1949	Reported favorably (9-2)	Motion to recommit rejected, 10/04/1949 (21-45)		12	18	19
						10/04/1949	Confirmed (48-16)			
Earl Warren of California (C. J.)	Eisenhower	*Recess Appointment, 10/02/1953*								
		01/11/1954	02/02/1954 02/19/1954	02/24/1954	Reported favorably (12-3)	03/01/1954	Confirmed	22	44	49
John M. Harlan II of New York	Eisenhower	11/09/1954	No hearing held	Referred to Judiciary Committee on 11/09/1954. No record of committee vote or Senate action.				—	—	—

Table 1. (Continued)

Nominee	President	Date received in Senate[a]	Senate committee actions			Final action by Senate or President		Days from date received in Senate to:		
			Public hearing date(s)	Final vote date[b]	Final vote	Date	Final action[c]	First public hearing date	Committee final vote date	Final action by Senate or President
John M. Harlan II of New York	Eisenhower	01/10/1955	02/25/ 1955[g]	03/10/1955	Reported favorably (10-4)	03/16/1955	Confirmed (71-11)	45	59	65
William J. Brennan Jr. of New Jersey	Eisenhower	*Recess Appointment, 10/15/1956*								
		01/14/1957	02/26/1957 02/27/1957	03/04/1957	Reported favorably	03/19/1957	Confirmed	43	49	64
Charles E. Whittaker of Missouri	Eisenhower	03/02/1957	03/18/1957	03/18/1957	Reported favorably	03/19/1957	Confirmed	16	16	17
Potter Stewart of Ohio	Eisenhower	*Recess Appointment, 10/14/1958*								
		01/17/1959	04/09/1959 04/14/1959	04/20/1959	Reported favorably (12-3)	05/05/1959	Confirmed (70-17)	82	93	108
Byron R. White of Colorado	Kennedy	04/03/1962	04/11/1962	04/11/1962	Reported favorably	04/11/1962	Confirmed	8	8	8
Arthur J. Goldberg of Illinois	Kennedy	08/31/1962	09/11/1962 09/13/1962	09/25/1962	Reported favorably	09/25/1962	Confirmed	11	25	25
Abe Fortas of Tennessee	L. Johnson	07/28/1965	08/05/1965	08/10/1965	Reported favorably	08/11/1965	Confirmed	8	13	14
Thurgood Marshall of New York	L. Johnson	06/13/1967	07/13/1967 07/14/1967 07/18/1967 07/19/1967 07/24/1967	08/03/1967	Reported favorably (11-5)	08/30/1967	Confirmed (69-11)	30	51	78

Table 1. (Continued)

<table>
<tr><th rowspan="2">Nominee</th><th rowspan="2">President</th><th rowspan="2">Date received in Senate[a]</th><th colspan="3">Senate committee actions</th><th colspan="2">Final action by Senate or President</th><th colspan="3">Days from date received in Senate to:</th></tr>
<tr><th>Public hearing date(s)</th><th>Final vote date[b]</th><th>Final vote</th><th>Date</th><th>Final action[c]</th><th>First public hearing date</th><th>Committee final vote date</th><th>Final action by Senate or President</th></tr>
<tr><td rowspan="2">Abe Fortas of Tennessee (C. J.)</td><td rowspan="2">L. Johnson</td><td rowspan="2">06/26/1968</td><td rowspan="2">07/11/1968
07/12/1968
07/16/1968
07/17/1968
07/18/1968
07/19/1968
07/20/1968
07/22/1968
07/23/1968
09/13/1968
09/16/1968</td><td rowspan="2">09/17/1968</td><td rowspan="2">Reported favorably (11-6)</td><td colspan="2">Cloture motion rejected, 10/01/1968 (45-43)[h]</td><td rowspan="2">15</td><td rowspan="2">83</td><td rowspan="2">100</td></tr>
<tr><td>10/04/1968</td><td>Withdrawn</td></tr>
<tr><td>Homer Thornberry of Texas</td><td>L. Johnson</td><td>06/26/1968</td><td>07/11/1968
07/12/1968
07/16/1968
07/17/1968
07/18/1968
07/19/1968
07/20/1968
07/22/1968
07/23/1968
09/13/1968
09/16/1968</td><td colspan="2">Referred to Judiciary Committee, 06/26/1968. No committee vote taken.</td><td>10/04/1968</td><td>Withdrawn</td><td>15</td><td>—</td><td>100</td></tr>
<tr><td>Warren E. Burger of Virginia (C. J.)</td><td>Nixon</td><td>05/23/1969</td><td>06/03/1969</td><td>06/03/1969</td><td>Reported favorably</td><td>06/09/1969</td><td>Confirmed (74-3)</td><td>11</td><td>11</td><td>17</td></tr>
</table>

Table 1. (Continued)

Nominee	President	Date received in Senate[a]	Senate committee actions			Final action by Senate or President		Days from date received in Senate to:		
			Public hearing date(s)	Final vote date[b]	Final vote	Date	Final action[c]	First public hearing date	Committee final vote date	Final action by Senate or President
Clement F. Haynsworth Jr. of South Carolina	Nixon	08/21/1969	09/16/1969 09/17/1969 09/18/1969 09/19/1969 09/23/1969 09/24/1969 09/25/1969 09/26/1969	10/09/1969	Reported favorably (10-7)	11/21/1969	Rejected (45-55)	26	49	92
George Harrold Carswell of Florida	Nixon	01/19/1970	01/27/1970 01/28/1970 01/29/1970 02/02/1970 02/03/1970	02/16/1970	Reported favorably (13-4)	04/08/1970	Rejected (45-51)	8	28	79
Harry A. Blackmun of Minnesota	Nixon	04/15/1970	04/29/1970	05/06/1970	Reported favorably (17-0)	05/12/1970	Confirmed (94-0)	14	21	27
Lewis F. Powell Jr. of Virginia	Nixon	10/22/1971	11/03/1971 11/04/1971 11/08/1971 11/09/1971 11/10/1971	11/23/1971	Reported favorably (16-0)	12/06/1971	Confirmed (89-1)	12	32	45
William H. Rehnquist of Arizona	Nixon	10/22/1971	11/03/1971 11/04/1971 11/08/1971 11/09/1971 11/10/1971	11/23/1971	Reported favorably (12-4)	Cloture motion rejected, 12/10/1971 (52-42)[i]		12	32	49
						Motion to postpone until 01/18/1972 rejected, 12/10/1971 (22-70)				

Table 1. (Continued)

Nominee	President	Date received in Senate[a]	Senate committee actions			Final action by Senate or President		Days from date received in Senate to:		
			Public hearing date(s)	Final vote date[b]	Final vote	Date	Final action[c]	First public hearing date	Committee final vote date	Final action by Senate or President
						12/10/1971	Confirmed (68-26)			
John Paul Stevens of Illinois	Ford	12/01/1975 (Nom. Date 11/28/1975)	12/08/1975 12/09/1975 12/10/1975	12/11/1975	Reported favorably (13-0)	12/17/1975	Confirmed (98-0)	7	10	16
Sandra Day O'Connor of Arizona	Reagan	08/19/1981	09/09/1981 09/10/1981 09/11/1981	09/15/1981	Reported favorably (17-1)	09/21/1981	Confirmed (99-0)	21	27	33
William H. Rehnquist of Arizona (C. J.)	Reagan	06/20/1986	07/29/1986 07/30/1986 07/31/1986 08/01/1986	08/14/1986	Reported favorably (13-5)	Cloture invoked, 09/17/1986 (68-31)[j] 09/17/1986	 Confirmed (65-33)	39	55	89
Antonin Scalia of Virginia	Reagan	06/24/1986	08/05/1986 08/06/1986	08/14/1986	Reported favorably (18-0)	09/17/1986	Confirmed (98-0)	42	51	85
Robert H. Bork of District of	Reagan	07/07/1987	09/15/1987 09/16/1987 09/19/1987 09/21/1987 09/22/1987 09/23/1987 09/25/1987 09/28/1987 09/29/1987 09/30/1987	Motion to report favorably rejected, 10/06/1987 (5-9) 10/06/1987	 Reported Unfavorably (9-5)	10/23/1987	Rejected (42-58)	70	91	108

Table 1. (Continued)

Nominee	President	Date received in Senate[a]	Senate committee actions			Final action by Senate or President		Days from date received in Senate to:		
			Public hearing date(s)	Final vote date[b]	Final vote	Date	Final action[c]	First public hearing date	Committee final vote date	Final action by Senate or President
On 10/29/1987, following the Senate's rejection of the nomination of Robert H. Bork, President Ronald Reagan announced his intention to nominate Douglas H. Ginsburg of the District of Columbia to be Associate Justice. Ginsburg, however, withdrew his name from consideration on 11/07/1987, before an official nomination had been made.										
Anthony M. Kennedy of California	Reagan	11/30/1987	12/14/1987 12/15/1987 12/16/1987	01/27/1988	Reported favorably (14-0)	02/03/1988	Confirmed (97-0)	14	58	65
David H. Souter of New Hampshire	G. H. W. Bush	07/25/1990	09/13/1990 09/14/1990 09/17/1990 09/18/1990 09/19/1990	09/27/1990	Reported favorably (13-1)	10/02/1990	Confirmed (90-9)	50	64	69
Clarence Thomas of Virginia	G. H. W. Bush	07/08/1991	09/10/1991 09/11/1991 09/12/1991 09/13/1991 09/16/1991 09/17/1991	Motion to report favorably failed, 09/27/1991 (7-7)[k]		UC agreement reached, 10/08/1991, to reschedule vote on confirmation from 10/08/1991 to 10/15/991, to allow for additional hearings		64	81	99
			09/19/1991 09/20/1991 10/11/1991 10/12/1991 10/13/1991	09/27/1991	Reported without recommen-dation (13-1)	10/15/1991	Confirmed (52-48)			
Ruth Bader Ginsburg of New York	Clinton	06/22/1993	07/20/1993 07/21/1993 07/22/1993 07/23/1993	07/29/1993	Reported favorably (18-0)	08/03/1993	Confirmed (96-3)	28	37	42

Table 1. (Continued)

Nominee	President	Date received in Senate[a]	Senate committee actions			Final action by Senate or President		Days from date received in Senate to:		
			Public hearing date(s)	Final vote date[b]	Final vote	Date	Final action[c]	First public hearing date	Committee final vote date	Final action by Senate or President
Stephen G. Breyer of Massachusetts	Clinton	05/17/1994	07/12/1994 07/13/1994 07/14/1994 07/15/1994	07/19/1994	Reported favorably (18-0)	07/29/1994	Confirmed (87-9)	56	63	73
John G. Roberts Jr. of Maryland	G. W. Bush	07/29/2005	Referred to Judiciary Committee, 07/29/2005. No hearing held and no committee vote taken.			09/06/2005	Withdrawn	—	—	39
John G. Roberts Jr. of Maryland (C. J.)	G. W. Bush	09/06/2005	09/12/2005 09/13/2005 09/14/2005 09/15/2005	09/22/2005	Reported favorably (13-5)	09/29/2005	Confirmed (78-22)	6	16	23
Harriet E. Miers of Texas	G. W. Bush	10/07/2005	Referred to Judiciary Committee, 10/07/2005. No hearing held and no committee vote taken.			10/28/2005	Withdrawn	—	—	21
Samuel A. Alito Jr. of New Jersey	G. W. Bush	11/10/2005	01/09/2006 01/10/2006 01/11/2006 01/13/2006	01/24/2006	Reported favorably (10-8)	Cloture invoked, 01/30/2006 (72-25)		60	75	82
						01/31/2006	Confirmed (58-42)			
Sonia Sotomayor of New York	Obama	06/01/2009	07/13/2009 07/14/2009 07/15/2009 07/16/2009	07/28/2009	Reported favorably (13-6)	08/06/2009	Confirmed (68-31)	42	57	66
Elena Kagan of Massachusetts	Obama	05/10/2010	06/28/2010 06/29/2010 06/30/2010 07/01/2010	07/20/2010	Reported favorably (13-6)	08/05/2010	Confirmed (63-37)	49	71	87

Table 1. (Continued)

Nominee	President	Date received in Senate[a]	Senate committee actions			Final action by Senate or President		Days from date received in Senate to:		
			Public hearing date(s)	Final vote date[b]	Final vote	Date	Final action[c]	First public hearing date	Committee final vote date	Final action by Senate or President
			Median number of days from date received in Senate, 1789-2010					14	11	10
			Median number of days from date received in Senate, 1789-1966					10	9	7
			Median number of days from date received in Senate, 1967-2010					26	51	69

Sources: U.S. Congress, Senate, *Journal of the Executive Proceedings of the Senate of the United States of America* (hereafter, *Senate Executive Journal*), various editions from the 1st Congress through the 110th Congress; Senate Committee on the Judiciary, *Legislative and Executive Calendar*, various editions from the 77th Congress through the 103rd Congress; various newspaper accounts accessed on-line through ProQuest Historical Newspapers (the primary source for recorded vote tallies in committee prior to the 1980s); CRS Report RL31171, *Supreme Court Nominations Not Confirmed, 1789-August 2010*, by Henry B. Hogue; and "Nominations" database in the Legislative Information System, available at http://www.congress.gov/nomis/.

Acknowledgments: Extensive preliminary research for this table was performed by Mitchel A. Sollenberger, former CRS Analyst. Calculations in this table, of median number of days for time intervals at different time periods, were performed by Susan Navarro Smelcer, CRS Aanalyst on the Federal Judiciary.

a. Usually the date on which the President formally makes a nomination, by signing a nomination message, is the same as the date on which the nomination is received, and these two dates are the same for any given nomination when only one date is shown in the "Date received in Senate" column. However, for the occasional nomination made by a President on a date prior to the nomination's receipt by the Senate, the earlier presidential nomination date ("Nom. date") is distinguished, in parentheses, from the date when the nomination was received by the Senate.

b. For nominations prior to 1873 that were referred to committee, the "Final vote date" is the date recorded in the *Senate Executive Journal* on which the committee's chairman or other member reported the nomination to the Senate. For nominations from 1873 to 2005, the "Final vote date" is the date on which the Judiciary Committee voted to report a nomination or, in one instance (on Feb. 14 1881, involving the first Stanley Matthews nomination), voted to postpone taking taking action.

c. "Final action," for purposes of this table, covers the following mutually exclusive outcomes: confirmation by the Senate ("Confirmed"), withdrawal of a nomination by the President ("Withdrawn") and Senate rejection by a vote disapproving a nomination ("Rejected"). In other instances, when none of the preceding three outcomes occurred, the last procedural action taken by the Senate on a nomination is indicated. On certain nominations, as indicated in the table, the last procedural outcome entailed tabling a nomination ("Tabled"), postponing consideration ("Postponed"), or rejecting a motion to proceed to consideration ("Motion to proceed rejected"). Final Senate actions taken by roll-call votes are shown in parentheses. Final Senate actions without roll-call votes shown in parentheses were reached by voice vote or unanimous consent. For roll-call votes shown above, the number of Yea votes always comes before the number of Nay votes. Thus, under "Confirmed" or "Rejected," the first number in the vote tally is the number of Senators who voted in favor of confirmation, and the second the number voting against confirmation.

d. On Dec. 16 and 17, 1873, the Judiciary Committee held closed-door sessions to examine documents and hear testimony from witnesses relevant to a controversy that arose over the Williams nomination only after the committee had reported the nomination to the Senate. The controversy prompted the Senate to recommit the nomination to the Judiciary Committee and to authorize the committee "to send for persons and papers." *Senate Executive Journal*, vol. 19, p. 211. After holding the two closed-door sessions, the committee did not re-report the nomination to the Senate. Amid press reports of significant opposition to the nomination in both the Judiciary Committee and the Senate as a whole, the nomination, at Williams's request, was withdrawn by President Ulysses S. Grant on Jan. 8, 1874. The Dec. 16 and 17 sessions can be regarded as an early, perhaps the earliest, example of a Judiciary Committee closed-door hearing. However, the above table, which focuses in part on the times that elapsed between dates nominations were received in the Senate and dates of *public* confirmation hearings, does not count the time that elapsed from the date the Williams nominations was received in the Senate until the Dec. 16 and 17, 1873, sessions, because they were closed to the public.

e. The 60-4 roll call vote to confirm Taft, conducted by the Senate in closed-door executive session, was not recorded in the *Senate Executive Journal*. Newspaper accounts, however, reported that a roll call vote on the nomination was demanded in the executive session, and that the vote was 60-4 to confirm, with an agreement reached afterwards not to make the roll call public. See Robert J. Bender, "Ex-President Taft New Chief Justice of United States," *Atlanta Constitution*, July 1, 1921, p. 1; Charles S. Groves, "Taft Is Confirmed, as Chief Justice," *Boston Daily Globe*, July 1, 1921, p. 1; and "Proceedings of Congress and Committees in Brief," *Washington Post*, July 1, 1921, p. 6.

f. The Jan. 12, 1925, hearing, held in closed session, heard the testimony of former Sen. Willard Saulsbury of Delaware. "Nomination of Stone Is Held Up Once More," *New York Times,* Jan. 13, 1925, p. 4. At the Jan. 28, 1925, hearing, which was held in open session, the nominee was questioned by the Judiciary Committee for four hours. This was the first confirmation hearing for a Supreme Court nomination at which the nominee appeared in person to testify. See Albert W. Fox, "Stone Tells Senate Committee He Assumes Full Responsibility for Pressing New Wheeler Case," *Washington Post*, Jan. 29, 1925, p. 1.

g. The Judiciary Committee held two days of confirmation hearings on the Harlan nomination, on Feb. 24 and 25, 1955. The Feb. 24 session, held in *closed* session, heard the testimony of nine witnesses (seven in favor of confirmation, and two opposed). Luther A. Huston, "Harlan Hearing Held by Senators," *New York Times,* Feb. 25, 1955, p. 8. The committee also began the Feb. 25 hearing in closed session, to hear the testimony of additional witnesses. However, for Judge Harlan, who was the last scheduled witness, the committee "voted to open the hearing to newspaper reporters for his testimony." Luther A. Huston, "Harlan Disavows 'One World' Aims in Senate Inquiry," *New York Times,* Feb. 26, 1955, p. 1.

h. The 45 votes in favor of the motion to close debate fell far short of the super-majority required under Senate rules—then two-thirds of Senators present and voting. The cloture motion, if approved, would have closed a lengthy debate (which had consumed more than 25 hours over a four-day period) on a motion to proceed to consider the Fortas nomination.

i. The 52 votes in favor of the motion to close debate fell short of the super-majority required under Senate rules—then two-thirds of Senators present and voting. Although the cloture motion failed, the Senate later that day (Dec. 10, 1971) agreed, without a procedural vote, to close debate and then voted to confirm Rehnquist 68-26.

j. The 68 votes in favor of the motion to close debate, by invoking cloture, exceeded the majority required under Senate rules—then, and currently, three-fifths of the Senate's full membership.

k. Motions to gain approval in Senate committees require a majority vote in favor and thus fail if there is a tie vote.

Days from Senate Receipt to Final Senate or Presidential Action

The Supreme Court confirmation process now typically extends over a much longer period of time than it once did. **Table 1** shows that from the appointment of the first Justices in 1789, continuing into the early 20th century, most Senate confirmations of Supreme Court nominees occurred within a week of the nominations being made by the President. In recent decades, by contrast, it has become the norm for the Court appointment process—from Senate receipt of nominations from the President to Senate confirmation or other final action (such as Senate rejection, or withdrawal by the President)—to take more than two months.

The last column of **Table 1** shows the number of days that elapsed from the dates Supreme Court nominations were received in the Senate until the dates of final Senate or presidential action. The number of elapsed days is shown for 152 of the 160 nominations listed in the table, with no elapsed time shown for eight nominations on which there was no record of any kind of official or effective final action by the Senate or by the President.[53] At the bottom of the table, the median number of elapsed days from initial Senate receipt until final action by the Senate or the President is shown for three historical periods—1789-2010, 1789-1966, and 1967-2010.

In recent decades, the median elapsed time for Supreme Court nominations to receive final action has increased dramatically, dwarfing the median time taken on earlier nominations. **Table 1** shows that from 1967 (starting with the nomination of Thurgood Marshall) through August 5, 2010 (the date on which the Senate confirmed the nomination of Elena Kagan) a median of 69 days elapsed from when a Supreme Court nomination was received in the Senate until the date it received final action, compared with a median of seven days for the same interval for the prior years of 1789 to 1966.[54] Most of the Supreme Court nominations receiving final action within a relatively brief period of time—for example, within three days of initial receipt in the Senate—occurred before the 20th century,[55] while most of the nominations receiving final action after a relatively long period of time—for example, 75 days or more after receipt in the Senate—occurred in the 20th century (and nearly all of these since 1967).[56]

The presence of Senate committee involvement has clearly tended to increase the overall length of the Supreme Court confirmation process. Of the 26 Court nominations made prior to the establishment of the Judiciary Committee in 1816, only one, of Alexander Wolcott in 1811, received final action more than seven days after initial Senate receipt (being rejected by the Senate nine days after receipt). It also was the only Court nomination prior to 1816 which was referred to, and considered by, a select committee. Subsequently, until the Civil War, six nominations received final action more than 50 days after initial Senate receipt. All six were first considered and reported by the Judiciary Committee. During the same period, other Court nominations were considered and acted on by the Senate more quickly—some with, and some without, first being referred to committee.

Subsequent historical developments involving the Senate Judiciary Committee further served to increase the median length of the Supreme Court confirmation process. One such development was the Senate's adoption of a rule in 1868 that nominations be referred to appropriate standing committees, resulting in the referral of nearly all Supreme Court nominations thereafter to the Judiciary Committee. Another was the increasing practice of the Judiciary Committee in the 20th century of holding public confirmation hearings on Supreme Court nominations (ultimately to become standard practice). A third, more recent, historical trend has involved the pace and thoroughness of the Judiciary Committee in preparing for and conducting confirmation hearings. Since the late 1960s, close and thorough examination of the background, qualifications, and views of Supreme Court nominees has become the norm for the Judiciary Committee, an approach that typically extends the confirmation process by at least several weeks, as a result of preparation for and holding of confirmation hearings.

Recess Appointments to the Supreme Court

On 12 occasions in the nation's history, Presidents have made temporary recess appointments to the Supreme Court without submitting nominations to the Senate. **Table 1** identifies all of these 12 appointments, showing how each was related to a later nomination of the appointee for the same position. The table shows that nine of the 12 recess appointments were made before the end of the Civil War,[57] with the last three made almost a century later, in the 1950s, during the presidency of Dwight D. Eisenhower.[58]

Each of the 12 recess appointments occurred when a President exercised his power under the Constitution to make recess appointments when the Senate was not in session.[59] Historically, when recesses between sessions of the Senate were much longer than they are today, recess appointments served the purpose of averting long vacancies on the Court when the Senate was unavailable to confirm a President's appointees. The terms of these recess appointments, however, were limited by the constitutional requirement that they expire at the end of the next session of Congress (unlike the lifetime appointments Court appointees receive when nominated and then confirmed by the Senate).[60]

Despite the temporary nature of these appointments, every person appointed during a recess of the Senate except for one—John Rutledge, to be Chief Justice, in 1795—ultimately received a lifetime appointment to the Court after being nominated by the President and confirmed by the Senate. As **Table 1** shows, all 12 of the recess appointees were subsequently nominated to the same position, and 11 (all except for Rutledge) were confirmed.

Table 2. Senate Votes on Whether to Confirm Supreme Court Nominations: Number Made by Voice Vote/Unanimous Consent (UC) or by Roll-Call Vote

Years	By voice vote or UC (all to confirm)	By roll-call vote (votes to reject in parentheses)	Totals
1789-1829	24	4 (2)	28
1830-1889	15	21 (3)	36
1890-1965	34	16 (3)	50
1966-2010	0	21 (3)	21
Totals	73	62 (11)	135 (11)

Sources: U.S. Congress, Senate, *Journal of the Executive Proceedings of the Senate of the United States of America,* various editions from the 1st Congress through the 110th Congress; also, "Nominations" database in the Legislative Information System, available at http://www .congress.gov/nomis/.

CONCLUDING OBSERVATIONS

The preceding discussion suggests that Senate treatment of Supreme Court nominations has gone through various phases during the more than 200 years of the Republic. Initially, such nominations were handled without Senate committee involvement. Later, from 1816 to 1868, most nominations to the Supreme Court were referred to the Judiciary Committee, but only by motion. Since 1868, as the result of a change in its rules, the Senate has referred nearly all Court nominations to the Judiciary Committee. During the rest of the 19th century and early 20th century, the committee considered nominations without public hearings. Subsequently, public hearings gradually became the more common, if not invariable, committee practice, although many of the earlier hearings were perfunctory and held simply to accommodate a small number of witnesses wishing to testify against the nominees. Gradually, however, in the latter half of the 20th century, public hearings on Supreme Court nominations lasting four or more days, with nominees present to answer extensive questioning from committee members, would become the usual practice; it would remain the Judiciary Committee's practice in considering the first two Supreme Court nominations in the 21st century.

Also, the overall length of time taken by the Supreme Court confirmation process has, in general, increased significantly over the course of more than 200 years. From the appointment of the first Justices in 1789, continuing well into the 20th century, most Supreme Court nominations received final action (usually, but not always, in the form of Senate confirmation) within a week of being submitted by the President to the Senate. In recent decades, by contrast, it has become the norm for the confirmation process to take from two to three months.

Other trends and historical phases may be discerned from **Tables 1** and **2**. Still other trends, of course, may be revealed by future nominations that Presidents make and by the actions taken on them by the Senate and its Judiciary Committee.

End Notes

1 Usually the date on which the President formally makes a nomination, by signing a nomination message, is the same as the date on which the nomination is received in the Senate. In **Table 1**, these two dates are the same for any given nomination when only one date is shown in the "Date received in Senate" column. However, for the occasional nomination made by a President on a date prior to the nomination's receipt by the Senate, the earlier presidential nomination date is distinguished, in parentheses, from the date when the nomination was received by the Senate.

2 **Table 1** identifies eight Supreme Court nominees who subsequent to Senate confirmation did not assume the office to which they had been appointed: Seven declined the office, and one died before assuming it. It should be noted, however, that one of the seven who declined the office, William Cushing—confirmed to be Chief Justice in 1796—was at the time serving on the Court as an Associate Justice, and continued to serve in that capacity until 1810. Another of the seven, John Jay—confirmed to be Chief Justice in 1800—had served earlier on the Court, as the Court's first Chief Justice, from 1789 to 1795.

3 The list, available at http://www.supremecourt.gov/about/members_text.aspx, presents first the names of 17 persons who have served as Chief Justice, followed by the 100 persons who have served as Associate Justices. The listing of 117 names in all (17 + 100) includes those of five Chief Justices who earlier had served as Associate Justices, hence reducing to 112 the total number of persons who have served as members of the Court.

4 Specifically, eight persons were nominated twice to the same Court position (seven to be Associate Justice, one to be Chief Justice); one person was nominated three times to be Associate Justice; and nine persons were

nominated first to be Associate Justice and later to be Chief Justice. The sum of 19 (the number of Court nominations that were not a person's first nomination to the Court) and 140 (the number of persons nominated to the Court at least once) is 159 (total Supreme Court nominations).

[5] The nation's first Chief Justice, John Jay, was nominated to that position twice. Jay was first nominated, and confirmed, in September 1789. He resigned as Chief Justice in 1795 to serve as governor of New York. In December 1800, Jay was nominated and confirmed a second time as Chief Justice, but declined the appointment. For analysis of the process by which a Chief Justice is appointed, accompanied by a list of all Chief Justice nominations from 1789 to the present (including the nomination, confirmation, judicial oath, and end-of-service dates of Chief Justice nominees, as well as their ages at time of appointment and upon termination of service), see CRS Report RL32821, *The Chief Justice of the United States: Responsibilities of the Office and Process for Appointment*, by Denis Steven Rutkus and Lorraine H. Tong.

[6] The three Presidents not to have made any Supreme Court nominations were William Henry Harrison, Zachary Taylor, and Jimmy Carter, with no Court vacancies having occurred while they were in office. See "Table 3. Supreme Court Nominations, by President, 1789 to 2008," in CRS Report RL31171, *Supreme Court Nominations Not Confirmed, 1789-August 2010*, by Henry B. Hogue, which lists the number of vacancies on the Court that existed during each presidency, from George Washington to George W. Bush. While it is unremarkable that no vacancies occurred during the short-lived presidencies of Harrison (Mar. 4 to Apr. 4, 1841) and Taylor (Mar. 5, 1849 to July 9, 1850), Jimmy Carter's presidency (Jan. 20, 1977 to Jan. 20, 1981) is remarkable as the only one lasting a full term during which no Supreme Court vacancies occurred.

[7] See Myron Jacobstein and Roy M. Mersky, *The Rejected* (Milpitas, CA: Toucan Valley Publications, 1993), pp. 69-74. (Hereafter cited as Jacobstein and Mersky, *The Rejected*.)

[8] President Washington, early in his first term of office, was presented with the opportunity to make six Supreme Court nominations, as the Judiciary Act of 1789 (1 Stat. 73 (1789)) set the number of Justice positions on the newly established Court at six. On September 24, 1789, the President nominated six persons to the Court, and two days later the Senate voted for their confirmation. However, one of the confirmed nominees, Robert Harrison of Maryland, declined the appointment, resulting in President Washington, in 1790, making a seventh nomination, of James Iredell of North Carolina, whose confirmation by the Senate put the six-member Court at full strength. Subsequently during the Washington presidency, four vacancies occurred on the Court, which resulted in the President making seven more nominations. Four of these seven nominations were confirmed by the Senate, with the nominees accepting their appointments to the Court. The other three nominations involved the first of two nominations of William Paterson of New Jersey in 1793 (who, after his first nomination was withdrawn, was re-nominated by President Washington and confirmed), John Rutledge of South Carolina (whose nomination in 1795 to be Chief Justice was rejected by the Senate), and William Cushing of Massachusetts (whose nomination in 1796 to be Chief Justice was confirmed by the Senate, but who declined the appointment).

[9] The five Presidents whose single Supreme Court nominations received Senate confirmation were Franklin Pierce, James A. Garfield, William McKinley, Calvin Coolidge and Gerald R. Ford. As mentioned above, the one President whose single Supreme Court nomination did not receive confirmation was Andrew Johnson.

[10] A President may announce the selection of a nominee well before transmitting a nomination message to the Senate. For instance, President George W. Bush announced his selection of Samuel A. Alito Jr. to be a Supreme Court nominee on Oct. 31, 2005, but formally signed and transmitted the nomination of Alito to the Senate on Nov. 10, 2005. For a complete list, from 1900 to 2009, of the dates on which Presidents announced their Supreme Court nominees (as distinguished from when they signed and transmitted nomination documents to the Senate), see CRS Report RL33118, *Speed of Presidential and Senate Actions on Supreme Court Nominations, 1900-2010*, by R. Sam Garrett and Denis Steven Rutkus.

[11] See U.S. Congress, Senate Committee on the Judiciary, *History of the Committee on the Judiciary, United States Senate, 1816-1981*. Sen. Doc. No. 97-18, 97th Cong., 1st sess. (Washington: GPO, 1982), p. iv; also, U.S. Senate, *History of the Committee on Rules and Administration—United States Senate,* prepared by Floyd M. Riddick, Parliamentarian Emeritus of the Senate, 96th Cong., 1st sess., S. Doc. No. 96-27 (Washington: GPO, 1980). Riddick provides, on pp. 21-28, the full text of the general revision of the Senate rules, adopted in 1868, including, on p. 26, the following rule: "When nominations shall be made by the President of the United States to the Senate, they shall, unless otherwise ordered by the Senate, be referred to appropriate committees.... "

[12] The nominations from 1868 to the present not referred to the Judiciary Committee were those of: Edwin M. Stanton in 1869 (at time of nomination, former Secretary of War); Edward D. White in 1894 (Senator); Edward D. White again, in 1910, this time to be Chief Justice (Associate Justice at time of nomination, and former Senator); William Howard Taft in 1921 (former President); George Sutherland in 1922 (former Senator); and James F. Byrnes in 1941 (Senator).

[13] At least once in the 19th century, however, in 1873, the Judiciary Committee did hear witnesses testify concerning a Supreme Court nomination—that of George H. Williams to be Chief Justice—but these two days of hearings, on Dec. 16 and 17, 1873, were held in closed session. The closed-door sessions were held to examine documents and hear testimony from witnesses relevant to a controversy that arose over the Williams nomination only after the committee had reported the nomination to the Senate. The controversy prompted the

Senate to recommit the nomination to the Judiciary Committee and to authorize the committee "to send for persons and papers." U.S. Congress, Senate, *Journal of the Executive Proceedings of the Senate of the United States of America*, vol. 19 (Washington: GPO, 1901), p. 189. After holding the two closed-door sessions on Dec. 16 and 17, the committee did not re-report the nomination to the Senate. Amid press reports of significant opposition to the nomination both in the Judiciary Committee and the Senate as a whole, the nomination, at Williams's request, was withdrawn by President Ulysses S. Grant on Jan. 8, 1874. See Jacobstein and Mersky, *The Rejected*, pp. 82-87.

[14] For a discussion of the advent of Supreme Court nominee appearances before the Senate Judiciary Committee, starting with Harlan F. Stone in 1925 (and carrying through the nominations of Abe Fortas and Homer Thornberry in 1968), see, James A. Thorpe, "The Appearance of Supreme Court Nominees Before the Senate Judiciary Committee," *Journal of Public Law,* vol. 18, 1969, pp. 371-402.

[15] A scholar examining the procedures followed by the committee in its consideration of 15 Supreme Court nominations referred to it between 1923 and 1946 found that, with two exceptions—the nominations of Charles Evans Hughes in 1930 and Harold H. Burton to be Associate Justices in 1945—all of the nominations were first "processed by a subcommittee prior to consideration by the full committee membership." David Gregg Farrelly, "Operational Aspects of the Senate Judiciary Committee," (Ph.D. diss., Princeton University: 1949), pp. 184-185. (Hereafter cited as Farrelly, "Operational Aspects.")

[16] The four other nominations not receiving public confirmation hearings even though referred to the Judiciary Committee were of former New York governor and former Supreme Court Associate Justice Charles Evans Hughes in 1930, former federal prosecutor Owen J. Roberts in 1930, Senator Hugo L. Black in 1937, and Senator Harold H. Burton in 1945.

Farrelly, in "Operational Aspects," also lists the Supreme Court nomination of former Michigan governor Frank Murphy in 1940 as one not receiving a confirmation hearing. Farrelly notes, at pp. 191-192, that the Senate Judiciary subcommittee which first processed the nomination "voted against public hearings." That vote notwithstanding, the nominee voluntarily appeared before the subcommittee on Jan. 11, 1940, in a public session at which four Senators "all questioned Mr. Murphy about his views of the Constitution and the duties of a Supreme Court Justice." "Senate Body Backs Murphy for Court," *New York Times*, Jan. 12, 1940, p. 1. Based on this and other similar newspaper accounts of the subcommittee session, Jan. 11, 1940 is listed below, in Table 1, as a public hearing date for the Murphy nomination.

[17] See, in **Table 1**, the multiple hearing days for the nominations of Felix Frankfurter in 1939 and Robert H. Jackson in 1941.

[18] For example, a Judiciary subcommittee hearing on the 1932 nomination of Benjamin N. Cardozo lasted only five minutes, during which one witness testified in opposition. Likewise, when the Judiciary Committee extended open invitations for witnesses to testify in opposition at the confirmation hearings for Stanley F. Reed in 1938, William O. Douglas in 1939, Harlan F. Stone (for Chief Justice) in 1941, Wiley B. Rutledge in 1943, and Fred M.Vinson (for Chief Justice) in 1946, no witnesses appeared to protest against Douglas or Stone, and "only one or two persons filed protests in each case against Reed, Vinson and Rutledge." Farrelly, "Operational Aspects," pp. 194-195.

[19] The last Supreme Court nomination on which a Senate Judiciary subcommittee held hearings was the 1954 nomination of Earl Warren to be Chief Justice. The subcommittee held public hearings on the nomination on Feb. 2 and 19, 1954, after which the full committee, on Feb. 24, 1954, voted to report the nomination favorably. All subsequent hearings on Supreme Court nominations were held by the full Judiciary Committee.

[20] The Judiciary Committee held two days of confirmation hearings on the second Harlan nomination, on Feb. 24 and 25, 1955. The Feb. 24 session, held in *closed* session, heard the testimony of nine witnesses (seven in favor of confirmation, and two opposed). Luther A. Huston, "Harlan Hearing Held by Senators," *New York Times,* Feb. 25, 1955, p. 8. The committee also began the Feb. 25 hearing in closed session, to hear the testimony of additional witnesses. However, for Judge Harlan, who was the last scheduled witness, the committee "voted to open the hearing to newspaper reporters for his testimony." Luther A. Huston, "Harlan Disavows 'One World' Aims in Senate Inquiry," *New York Times,* Feb. 26, 1955, p. 1.

[21] These were the nominations of Robert H. Bork in 1987 (12 hearing days), Clarence Thomas in 1991 (11 days), and Abe Fortas and Homer Thornberry in 1968 (11 days for their joint hearings).

[22] In 1969, eight days of confirmation hearings were held on the nomination of Clement F. Haynsworth.

[23] One day of hearings each was held on the nominations of Warren E. Burger (to be Chief Justice) in 1969 and Harry A. Blackmun in 1970, while two days of hearings were held on the nomination of Antonin Scalia in 1986.

[24] As noted earlier, only once prior to the establishment of the Judiciary Committee in 1816 was a Supreme Court nomination referred to committee, and that nomination was reported to the Senate as well. See, in Table 1the nomination in 1811 of Alexander Wolcott, which was considered by a select committee and then reported to the Senate, where it was rejected by a 9-24 vote.

[25] The six favorably reported nominations which failed to receive Senate confirmation involved these nominees: George H. Williams, for Chief Justice, in 1873 (nomination withdrawn); Caleb Cushing, in 1874 (nomination withdrawn); Pierce Butler in 1922 (no action taken by Senate); Abe Fortas, for Chief Justice, in 1968

(nomination withdrawn); Clement F. Haynsworth Jr. in 1969 (rejected by Senate); and G. Harrold Carswell in 1970 (rejected by Senate). Butler, it should be noted, was re-nominated and confirmed.

[26] A report that states it is not accompanied by a recommendation can be a way to alert the Senate that a substantial number of committee members have some reservations about the nominee which, however, do not rise, at that point, to the level of opposition; it might also be a way to bridge or downplay differences between committee members who favor confirmation and other members who oppose it. The latter, for example, was said to be the purpose for the Judiciary Committee in 1888 reporting the Chief Justice nomination of Melville W. Fuller without recommendation; the action was described in a news account as a "compromise between the Democratic minority who desired a report to the Senate in favor of confirmation, and the Republican majority, who desired to defeat the nomination .... " "Mr. Fuller's Nomination," *Washington Post,* July 3, 1888, p. 1.

[27] The three nominees confirmed by the Senate after the Judiciary Committee explicitly reported their nominations without recommendation were: Melville W. Fuller, for Chief Justice, in 1888; George Shiras Jr. in 1892; and Clarence Thomas in 1991. A fourth nomination reported without recommendation, Wheeler H. Peckham, in 1894, was rejected by the Senate.

[28] See, in **Table 1**, the second nomination of Stanley Matthews in 1881 (confirmed 24-23) and the nomination of Lucius Q. C. Lamar in 1888 (confirmed 32-28).

[29] The nominations reported unfavorably and then rejected by the Senate involved these nominees: Ebenezer R. Hoar in 1869 (rejected 24-33); William B. Hornblower in 1894 (rejected 24-30); John J. Parker in 1930 (rejected 39-41); and Robert H. Bork in 1987 (rejected 42-58).

[30] The Senate in 1829 postponed taking action on the nomination of John Crittenden after receiving an adverse report on the nomination from the Judiciary Committee.

[31] The final outcome for these five nominees, however, was determined not by the failure of their nominations to be reported out of committee, but by action, or lack of action, taken outside the committee—by the Senate, Congress as a whole, or the President. In 1853, the nomination of William C. Micou was referred to the Judiciary Committee and on the same day ordered discharged by the Senate, where no action was taken. In 1866, the nomination of Henry Stanbery was referred to the Judiciary Committee, but shortly afterwards, while the nomination was pending in the Senate, the Associate Justice position to which Stanbery had been nominated was eliminated by statute. In 1893, the nomination of William B. Hornblower was referred to the Judiciary Committee, but not reported; later that year, in a new session of Congress, Hornblower was re-nominated, reported unfavorably by the Judiciary Committee (in early 1894), and rejected by the Senate, 24-30. In 1968, the Judiciary Committee declined to report the nomination of Homer Thornberry to succeed Associate Justice Abe Fortas until the final outcome of the nomination of Fortas to be Chief Justice was determined. The Thornberry and Fortas nominations were both withdrawn by the President after a motion to close debate on the Fortas nomination failed to pass in the Senate. (The failure of Fortas's Chief Justice nomination eliminated the prospective Associate Justice vacancy that Thornberry had been nominated to fill.) In 2005, the nomination of Harriet E. Miers was withdrawn by the President before the Judiciary Committee held hearings on the nomination.

[32] In February 1881, just before the final adjournment of the 46th Congress, the Judiciary Committee voted to postpone taking action on the Supreme Court nomination of Stanley Matthews; shortly afterwards, however, in a special session of the 47th Congress, Matthews was re-nominated, and, although his second nomination was reported unfavorably by the Judiciary Committee, it was confirmed by the Senate, 24-23. In Nov. 1954, late in the 83rd Congress, the nomination of John M. Harlan II was referred to the Judiciary Committee, where no action was taken; in 1955, Harlan was re-nominated, considered and reported favorably by the Judiciary Committee, and confirmed by the Senate. In Sept. 2005, before the scheduled start of confirmation hearings, the nomination of John G. Roberts Jr. to be Associate Justice was withdrawn and, on the same day of the withdrawal, Roberts was re-nominated for Chief Justice; the second Roberts nomination was reported favorably by the Judiciary Committee and confirmed by the Senate.

[33] The exact confirmation percentage is 77.5%, reached by dividing 124 confirmations by 160 nominations.

[34] The earliest Senate rejection of a Supreme Court nomination occurred in 1795, when President George Washington's nomination of John Rutledge to be Chief Justice failed on a 10-14 vote. The latest instance was the Senate's rejection of Robert H. Bork in 1987, by a 42-58 vote. Between Rutledge and Bork, the following nominations were also rejected: Alexander Wolcott in 1811, John C. Spencer in 1844, George W. Woodward in 1846, Ebenezer R. Hoar in 1870, William B. Hornblower in 1894, Wheeler H. Peckham in 1894, John J. Parker in 1930, Clement F. Haynsworth Jr. in 1969, and G. Harrold Carswell in 1970.

[35] The following Supreme Court nominations were withdrawn, in the years indicated, with the Presidents who withdrew them shown in parentheses: The first nomination of William Paterson, in 1793 (George Washington); the first nomination of Reuben H. Walworth, in 1844 (John Tyler); the second nomination of John C. Spencer, in 1844 (John Tyler); the third nomination of Reuben H. Walworth, in 1845 (John Tyler); the second nomination of Edward King, in 1845 (John Tyler); George H. Williams and Caleb Cushing, both in 1874 (Ulysses S. Grant); Abe Fortas and Homer Thornberry, both in 1968 (Lyndon B. Johnson); John G. Roberts Jr. and Harrier E. Miers, both in 2005 (George W. Bush). Less than a week after his first nomination was withdrawn, Paterson was re-nominated by President Washington and confirmed by the Senate on the same

day. On the same day that President Bush withdrew the Roberts nomination to be Associate Justice, he re-nominated Roberts to be Chief Justice, and the latter nomination was confirmed.

36 The 14 nominations that lapsed at the end of a session of Congress, without a Senate confirmation or rejection vote or a withdrawal by the President having occurred, can be broken into the following groups according to Senate actions, or lack of Senate actions, taken: On three nominations (John Crittenden in 1829, the first nomination of Roger Taney in 1835, and George E. Badger in 1853), the Senate voted to postpone taking action; the Senate tabled two nominations (the first nomination of Edward King in 1844 and Edward A. Bradford in 1852); on one nomination, the Senate rejected a motion to proceed (Jeremiah S. Black in 1861, by a 25-26 vote); and on eight nominations, there was no record of any vote taken (the second nomination of Reuben H. Walworth in 1844, John M. Read in 1845, William C. Micou in 1853, Henry Stanbery in 1866, the first nomination of Stanley Matthews in 1881, the first nomination of William B. Hornblower in 1893, the first nomination of Pierce Butler in 1922, and the first nomination of John M. Harlan II in 1954). However, four of the 14 persons whose nominations lapsed in one session of Congress were renominated in the next congressional session and confirmed (Taney in 1835, Matthews in 1881, Butler in 1922, and Harlan in 1955).

37 For a list consisting solely of the 36 unconfirmed Supreme Court nominations (including dates that they were received in the Senate and received confirmation hearings, committee votes, and Senate debate), see Table 4 in CRS Report RL31171, *Supreme Court Nominations Not Confirmed, 1789-August 2010*, by Henry B. Hogue.

38 The six individuals who were not confirmed only to be later re-nominated and confirmed were, in the following years of confirmation shown in parentheses, William Paterson (1793), Roger B. Taneuy (1836), Stanley Matthews (1881), Pierce Butler (1922), John M. Harlan II (1955), and John G. Roberts Jr. (2005).

39 The closest roll calls ever cast on Supreme Court nominations were the 24-23 vote in 1881 confirming Stanley Matthews, the 25-26 vote in 1861 rejecting a motion to proceed to consider the nomination of Jeremiah S. Black, and the 26-25 Senate vote in 1853 to postpone consideration of the nomination of George E. Badger. Since the 1960s, the closest roll calls on Supreme Court nominations were the 52-48 vote in 1991 confirming Clarence Thomas, the 45-51 vote in 1970 rejecting G. Harrold Carswell, the 45-55 vote in 1969 rejecting Clement Haynsworth Jr., the 58-42 vote in 2006 confirming Samuel A. Alito Jr., the 42-58 vote in 1987 rejecting Robert H. Bork, the 63-37 vote in 2010 confirming Elena Kagan, and the 65-33 vote confirming William H. Rehnquist to be Chief Justice in 1986. Also noteworthy was the 45-43 vote in 1968 rejecting a motion to close debate on the nomination of Abe Fortas to be Chief Justice; however, the roll call was not as close as the numbers by themselves suggested, since passage of the motion required a two-thirds vote of the Members present and voting.

40 The most lopsided of these votes were the unanimous roll calls confirming Morrison R. Waite to be Chief Justice in 1874 (63-0), Harry A. Blackmun in 1970 (94-0), John Paul Stevens in 1975 (98-0), Sandra Day O'Connor in 1981 (99-0), Antonin Scalia in 1986 (98-0), and Anthony M. Kennedy in 1988 (97-0); and the near-unanimous votes confirming Noah H. Swayne in 1862 (38-1),Warren E. Burger in 1969 to be Chief Justice (74-3), Lewis F. Powell Jr. in 1971 (89-1), and Ruth Bader Ginsburg in 1993 (96-3).

41 In the case of the three most recent Supreme Court nominees, the Senate in 2006 confirmed Samuel A. Alito Jr. by a 58-42 vote, in 2009 confirmed Sonia Sotomayor by a 68-31 vote, and in 2010 confirmed Elena Kagan by a 63-37 vote. In the much more distant past, the Senate confimed two of President Andrew Jackson's nominees to the Court (Roger B. Taney to be Chief Justice in 1836 and John Catron in 1837) by comfortable vote margins, although on both occasions more than one-third of the votes cast were against confirmation, with the Senate confirming Taney 29-15 and Catron 28-15.

42 In calculating the median elapsed time for the contemporary period, the Marshall nomination in 1967 was selected as the starting point for the following reason. The Marshall nomination, it could be argued, marked the start of an era in which the confirmation hearings of most, if not all, Supreme Court nominees were highly charged events, covered closely by the news media, with nominees interrogated rigorously and extensively (and for more than a day) about their judicial philosophy as well as their views on constitutional issues and the proper role of the Supreme Court in the U.S. government. For the Marshall nomination, the elapsed time between Senate receipt and start of confirmation hearings was 30 days.

43 See bottom rows of **Table 1** for median number of days that elapsed from the date Supreme Court nominations were received in the Senate to first hearing dates, for three different time spans.

44 For the seven nominations, the elapsed time between Senate receipt of nomination and the first day of confirmation hearings was 50 days for David Souter in 1990, 64 days for Clarence Thomas in 1991, 28 days for Ruth Bader Ginsburg in 1993, 56 days for Stephen G. Breyer in 1994, 60 days for Samuel A. Alito Jr. in 2005-2006, 42 days for Sonia Sotomayor in 2009, and 49 days for Elena Kagan in 2010.

45 As already mentioned, the first such nomination, of Alexander Wolcott in 1811, was reported by a select committee; all subsequently reported nominations were reported by the Senate Judiciary Committee.

46 Ironically, five days after the committee's favorable, and extremely prompt, recommendation of Cushing, President Ulysses S. Grant withdrew the nomination.

47 Five nominations were voted on by the Judiciary Committee one day after their receipt by the Senate: Robert C. Grier in 1846; John A. Campbell in 1853; Morrison R. Waite, to be Chief Justice, in 1874; Horace Gray in 1881; and Harold H. Burton in 1945. Six nominations were voted on by the committee two days after Senate

receipt: James M. Wayne in 1835; Samuel Nelson in 1845; Noah H. Swayne in 1862; David Davis in 1862; Stephen J. Field in 1963; and Oliver Wendell Holmes in 1902. Three nominations were voted on by the committee three days after Senate receipt: Horace H. Lurton in 1909; Willis Van Devanter in 1910; and Joseph R. Lamar in 1910.

48 The first of Reuben H. Walworth's three nominations to the Court in 1844 was voted on by the Judiciary Committee 93 days after Senate receipt and committee referral. During the 20th century, the Judiciary Committee, in addition to its 1916 vote on the Brandeis nomination, voted on the following nominations more than 80 days after Senate receipt: Potter Stewart in 1959 (93 days); Robert H. Bork in 1987 (91 days), Abe Fortas, to be Chief Justice, in 1968 (83 days); and Clarence Thomas in 1991 (81 days).

49 All of the 15 aforementioned nominations on which the Judiciary Committee voted three days or less after Senate receipt were made prior to 1946, and 14 of the 15 were made prior to 1911.

50 See bottom rows of **Table 1** for median number of days that elapsed from the date Supreme Court nominations were received in the Senate to final Senate vote dates, for three different time spans.

51 The four Eisenhower nominations for which 44 or more days elapsed from the date received in the Senate to the date voted on by the Senate Judiciary Committee were those of: Earl Warren to be Chief Justice in 1954, 44 days; John M. Harlan II in 1955, 59 days; William J. Brennan Jr. in 1957, 49 days; and Potter Stewart in 1959, 93 days. Three of the nominees—Warren, Brennan, and Stewart—were already on the Court as recess appointees, a circumstance that served perhaps to make action on their nominations seem less urgent to the committee than if their seats on the Court had been vacant. Harlan, however, was not a recess appointee at the time of his nomination. See "The Harlan Nomination," *New York Times*, Feb. 25, 1955, p. 20, discussing, according to the editorial, the "inexcusable delay" on the part of the committee in acting on the nomination and the objections to the nomination voiced by a few of the committee's members. (Ultimately, the committee voted 10-4 to report the nomination favorably.) Receiving much more expeditious committee action was President Eisenhower's fifth Supreme Court nomination, of Charles E. Whittaker in 1957, which was approved by the Judiciary Committee 16 days after Senate receipt.

52 The days that elapsed from the date received in the Senate to the date voted on by the Senate Judiciary Committee were eight days and 25 days for the 1962 nominations of Byron R. White and Arthur J. Goldberg and 13 days for the 1965 nomination of Abe Fortas to be Associate Justice.

53 Besides nominations that received official final Senate action in the form of confirmation or rejection (124 and 11 respectively), or that were withdrawn by the President (11), six others are treated in the table as also receiving final action, albeit not of a definitive official sort—with three having been postponed by the Senate, two tabled, and one (the nomination of Jeremiah S. Black in 1861) not considered after a motion to proceed was defeated by a 25-26 vote. While the six nominations remained pending in the Senate after the noted actions, the effect of the actions, it can be argued, was decisive in eliminating any prospect of confirmation, and thus constituted a final Senate action for time measurement purposes. Accordingly, for these six nominations, the number of days elapsed is measured from date of Senate receipt to the dates of effective final action just noted.

54 At first glance, the nomination of John G. Roberts Jr. for Chief Justice in 2005 appears to be a deviation from the 1967 to 2009 median interval from date received to final action of 68 days, as the nomination was confirmed only 23 days after its initial receipt in the Senate. However, it can be argued that a more meaningful context is to see the Roberts Chief Justice nomination (received in the Senate on Sept. 6, 2005) in relation to the earlier July 29, 2005, nomination of Judge Roberts to be Associate Justice. After the death of Chief Justice William H. Rehnquist on Sept. 3, 2005, the Roberts Associate Justice nomination was withdrawn, and he was re-nominated to be Chief Justice. Hearings on the Roberts Associate Justice nomination, set to begin on Sept. 6, were cancelled, and rescheduled hearings, on the Chief Justice nomination, began on Sept. 12. The overall time that elapsed from the Associate Justice nomination of Judge Roberts on July 29 until Senate confirmation of his Chief Justice nomination on Sept. 29 was 62 days.

55 **Table 1** shows that 43 nominations received final Senate or presidential action three days or less after date of receipt in the Senate. Thirty-six of the 43 were pre-20th century nominations.

56 **Table 1** shows that 17 nominations received final Senate or presidential action more than 75 days after date of receipt in the Senate. Thirteen of the 17 were 20th or 21st century nominations, with 11 made since 1967.

57 See in **Table 1** the recess appointments of Thomas Johnson in 1791, John Rutledge (to be Chief Justice) in 1795, Bushrod Washington in 1798, H. Brockholst Livingston in 1806, Smith Thompson in 1823, John McKinley in 1837, Levi Woodbury in 1845, Benjamin R. Curtis in 1851, and David Davis in 1862.

58 See in **Table 1** the recess appointments of Earl Warren (to be Chief Justice) in 1953, William J. Brennan Jr. in 1956, and Potter Stewart in 1958.

59 Specifically, Article II, Section 2, clause 3 of the U.S. Constitution empowers the President "to fill up all Vacancies that may happen during the Recess of the Senate, by granting Commissions which shall expire at the End of their next Session."

60 For background on the history of recess appointments to the Supreme Court, and the policy and constitutional issues associated with those appointments, see CRS Report RL31112, *Recess Appointments of Federal Judges,* by Louis Fisher (out of print, available from author); and Henry B. Hogue, "The Law: Recess Appointments to Article III Courts," *Political Science Quarterly,* vol. 34, September 2004, p. 656.

In: Supreme Court Appointments and Nominations
Editor: Edward P. Bennett
ISBN: 978-1-61209-249-2

Chapter 5

SUPREME COURT NOMINATIONS NOT CONFIRMED, 1789-AUGUST 2010

Henry B. Hogue

SUMMARY

From 1789 through August 2010, Presidents submitted 160 nominations to Supreme Court positions. Of these, 36 were not confirmed by the Senate. The 36 nominations represent 31 individuals whose names were sent forward to the Senate by Presidents (some individuals were nominated more than once). Of the 31 individuals who were not confirmed the first time they were nominated, however, six were later nominated again and confirmed. The Supreme Court nominations discussed here were not confirmed for a variety of reasons, including Senate opposition to the nominating President, nominee's views, or incumbent Court; senatorial courtesy; perceived political unreliability of the nominee; perceived lack of ability; interest group opposition; and fear of altering the balance of the Court. The Senate Committee on the Judiciary has played an important role in the confirmation process, particularly since 1868.

All but the most recent of these nominations have been the subject of extensive legal, historical, and political science writing, a selected list of which is included in this chapter.

The announcement by Associate Justice Sandra Day O'Connor of her intention to retire and the death of Chief Justice William H. Rehnquist in the summer of 2005 created the need for two new Supreme Court appointments. The process for making these appointments led to three nominations to the Associate Justice position. The first two of these nominations were subsequently withdrawn by President George W. Bush, while the third—of Samuel A. Alito, Jr.—was confirmed by the Senate. The two withdrawn nominations—of John G. Roberts, Jr., and Harriet E. Miers—are the latest of 36 nominations to Supreme Court posts that have failed to be confirmed. These two nominations exemplify the range of this class of Supreme Court nominations. The Roberts nomination to Associate Justice was withdrawn as a formality so that the President could nominate him to be Chief Justice. Therefore, although the *first nomination* was not confirmed, the *nominee* was confirmed for another position. The

Miers nomination, on the other hand, was withdrawn without the expectation that she would subsequently be nominated for another position on the Court. Consequently, neither this particular nomination nor the nominee was confirmed.

Over the course of the nation's history, approximately one-quarter of the presidential nominations to the Supreme Court of the United States have failed to place a new Associate or Chief Justice on the bench. Of the 160 nominations to the Court between 1789 and August 2010, 116 individuals were confirmed and served, 7 individuals were confirmed and declined to serve, 1 confirmed nominee died before he could take his seat, and 36 nominations were not confirmed. This chapter discusses this last group of Supreme Court nominations. These 36 nominations that did not lead to confirmation represent 31 individuals whose names were sent forward to the Senate by Presidents (some of those 31 individuals were nominated more than once). The Supreme Court nominations discussed here were not confirmed for a variety of reasons, including Senate opposition to the nominating President, the nominee's views, or the incumbent Court; senatorial courtesy; perceived political unreliability of the nominee; perceived lack of ability; interest group opposition; and fear of altering the balance of the Court. The Senate Committee on the Judiciary has played an important role in the confirmation process, particularly since 1868.

Summary discussions of the Senate confirmation process and the unsuccessful nominations follow. The reasons some nominations have failed confirmation and the role of the Senate Judiciary Committee are also discussed. Finally, the report includes a detailed table that identifies each nomination and provides, for each, the facts that can be documented about the dates of relevant activity and votes in the Judiciary Committee and the full Senate (see **Table 4**). A list of additional relevant literature is also provided.

THE CONFIRMATION PROCESS

The Constitution of the United States provides for the appointment of a Justice to the Supreme Court in Article II, Section 2. This section states that the President "shall nominate, and by and with the Advice and Consent of the Senate, shall appoint ... Judges of the [S]upreme Court." The practices involved in following this constitutional mandate have varied over the years, but they have always involved the sharing of the appointment power between the President and the Senate.[1]

Nominations that failed to be confirmed by the Senate have been disposed of in a variety of ways, including withdrawal by the President, inaction in the committee, inaction in the Senate, postponement, tabling, rejection on the Senate floor, and filibuster on the Senate floor. **Table 1** provides a summary of the unsuccessful nominations by final disposition.

SUMMARY OF UNSUCCESSFUL NOMINATIONS

The 36 Supreme Court nominations not confirmed by the Senate represent 31 individuals. Six of these 31 were later re-nominated and confirmed for positions on the Court. Of the other 25 nominees, four were nominated and failed confirmation more than once. **Table 2** provides summary information concerning unsuccessful nominations.

The first of the six nominees who were not confirmed only to be later re-nominated and confirmed was William Paterson, nominated by President George Washington. Washington withdrew the nomination on the day following its submission. He noted that Paterson "was a member of the Senate when the law creating that office was passed, and that the time for which he was elected [had] not yet expired."[2] For this reason, President Washington felt that the nomination was in violation of the Constitution.[3] President Washington re-nominated Paterson at the beginning of the following Congress a few days later, and Paterson was immediately confirmed.[4] In this case, the failure of the first nomination was due to what might be considered formalities, rather than opposition to the nomination itself.

The last of these six nominations, that of John G. Roberts, Jr., to be an Associate Justice, might be similarly categorized. On July 29, 2005, President George W. Bush nominated Roberts to replace retiring Associate Justice Sandra Day O'Connor.[5] Subsequently, on September 3, Chief Justice William H. Rehnquist died. On September 6, President Bush withdrew Roberts's nomination to be Associate Justice and nominated him to be Chief Justice. The Senate confirmed this nomination on September 29, 2005.[6]

All of the other unsuccessful nominations faced opposition in the Senate.

Table 1. Supreme Court Nominations Not Confirmed, 1789-August 2010, by Final Disposition

Disposition	Number of Nominations
Rejected by a vote of the full Senate	11
Withdrawn by the President without Senate action	2
Referred to committee, withdrawn by the President without further Senate action	2
Postponed or tabled by the Senate, but not withdrawn by the President	5
Postponed or tabled by the Senate and withdrawn by the President	3
No record of referral, motion to consider unsuccessful	2
Referred to committee, but never reported or discharged from committee	4
Referred to committee, hearings held, withdrawn by the President without further Senate action	1
Discharged from committee, no record of action by the full Senate	1
Reported from committee, placed on the Executive Calendar, no record of action by the full Senate	1
Reported from committee, considered by the Senate, recommitted, and withdrawn by the President	1
Reported from committee, motion to consider unsuccessful	1
Reported from committee, withdrawn by the President	1
Withdrawn by the President after defeat of cloture motion	1
Total Supreme Court nominations not confirmed	**36**

Table 2. Summary of Supreme Court Nominations Not Confirmed, 1789-August 2010

Total Supreme Court nominations	160
Total Supreme Court nominations not confirmed	36
Nominees who failed to be confirmed at least once	31
Unconfirmed nominees who never served in the position to which they were nominated	24
Unconfirmed nominees later re-nominated and confirmed	6
Unconfirmed nominee who served as a recess appointee in a position to which he was nominated	1
Nominees subject to two or three failed nominations (for a total of nine nominations)	4
Unconfirmed nomination to elevate sitting Associate Justice to Chief Justice	1
Unconfirmed nomination of former Associate Justice to Chief Justice	1

Source: Total Supreme Court nominations calculated using data from Elder Witt, *Guide to the U.S. Supreme Court*, 2nd ed. (Washington: Congressional Quarterly, 1990), pp. 995-998; and Lee Epstein, Jeffrey A. Segal, Harold J. Spaeth, and Thomas G. Walker, *The Supreme Court Compendium: Data, Decisions, and Developments* (Washington: Congressional Quarterly, 1994), pp. 284-290. Other totals summarize information from **Table 4** of this chapter.

The other four nominees who were later re-nominated and confirmed were Roger B. Taney, nominated twice by President Andrew Jackson; Stanley Matthews, nominated first by President Rutherford B. Hayes and later by President James A. Garfield; Pierce Butler, nominated twice by President Warren G. Harding; and John Marshall Harlan II, nominated twice by President Dwight D. Eisenhower. Taney's first nomination, to Associate Justice, was postponed indefinitely by the Senate. During the next Congress, he was nominated and confirmed as Chief Justice, and he went on to author the *Dred Scott* decision. Matthews's first nomination was never reported out of committee, but in the following Congress, under a new President, he was re-nominated and confirmed by a one-vote margin.[7] Butler was first nominated to the high court during the third session of the 67th Congress. Confirmation was blocked during that session, but Butler was renominated and confirmed during the fourth session. Harlan was initially nominated to be an Associate Justice late in the 83rd Congress, and this nomination remained in committee at the time of adjournment. His second nomination, at the beginning of the following Congress, was confirmed a few months later.

Four individuals were the subjects of more than one unsuccessful nomination. The first three, John C. Spencer, Reuben H. Walworth, and Edward King, were nominees of President John Tyler. President Tyler had the opportunity to fill two vacancies on the high court. He made nine nominations of five men in the space of the last 15 months of his presidency. Eight of these nominations were not confirmed, giving President Tyler the highest tally of unconfirmed Supreme Court nominations. President Tyler nominated Spencer for the first vacancy. After the Senate rejected Spencer, Walworth was put forward for the position, and the Senate tabled this nomination. On June 17, 1844, the last day of the congressional session,[8] President Tyler withdrew the tabled Walworth nomination and re-nominated Spencer. Unable to gain unanimous consent for the Spencer nomination to be acted upon, Tyler then withdrew Spencer's name on the same day and re-nominated Walworth.[9] By this time, the nomination (June 5, 1844) of King for the second vacancy had also been tabled. Tyler went on to re-nominate Walworth and King at the beginning of the following congressional session. After these two nominations were once again tabled, they were both withdrawn. The nomination of John M. Read, which followed, was reported out of committee but never acted upon by the full Senate. Samuel Nelson was President Tyler's fifth nominee, and he was confirmed.

The fourth individual subject to multiple unconfirmed nominations was William B. Hornblower, who was nominated in successive sessions of Congress by President Grover Cleveland. His first nomination was never reported out of committee; the second nomination was reported out and rejected.

One of the unsuccessful nominees had previously been Associate Justice, had left the Court, and this time was being nominated for Chief Justice. Another was a sitting Associate Justice nominated for elevation to the Chief Justice position. The first of these was also the first nomination in which the Senate voted not to confirm. John Rutledge had previously served as one of the first Associate Justices from 1789 to 1791. In addition, he served as Chief Justice in 1795 under a recess appointment by President Washington. When the President nominated him later that year to succeed John Jay as permanent Chief Justice, however, the Senate asserted its constitutional power and voted against confirmation. The second such nominee, Justice Abe Fortas, was a sitting Associate Justice at the time of his nomination by President Lyndon B. Johnson to be Chief Justice in 1968. The nomination was favorably reported out of committee but filibustered on the floor of the Senate until the President withdrew the nomination.[10]

One unsuccessful nomination coincided with a legislative initiative to decrease the size of the Court. On April 16, 1866, President Andrew Johnson nominated Henry Stanbery to replace John Catron, who had died the previous May. By the time Stanbery was nominated, however, the House of Representatives had passed a bill decreasing the number of justices in the Supreme Court.[11] The act, as signed into law on July 23, 1866, called for a decrease in the number of Associate Justices from nine to six through the process of attrition.[12] At the time the bill was initiated and also at the time its final version was signed, only one position on the Court, that to which Stanbery was nominated, was vacant. Eight Associate Justice positions remained on the bench until the death of James M. Wayne in July 1867. Seven Associate Justice positions remained until a law was passed in April 1869 to increase the number to eight.[13]

Several scholars have suggested that, by reducing the number of Associate Justice positions,[14] the Republican Congress was trying to thwart the ability of Democratic President Johnson to shape the Supreme Court, although the record of House and Senate debate is silent as to each chamber's intention in this regard.[15] The law increasing the Associate Justice positions to eight was passed within two months of the beginning of the Administration of President Ulysses S. Grant.

FACTORS BEHIND UNSUCCESSFUL NOMINATIONS

There have often been multiple reasons behind the failure of the Senate to confirm a nomination. The official Senate records, particularly those prior to the 20th century, have usually been silent on the issues involved. Scholars have used other records in an effort to shed more light on the factors underlying unsuccessful Supreme Court nominations. This scholarship consists of analysis and interpretation of these records, and it provides a general understanding of the reasons that more than one in five nominations has failed to be confirmed by the Senate.

One widely cited scholar in the area of the Supreme Court appointments process and history, Henry J. Abraham, has developed categories of unsuccessful nominations:

> Among the more prominent reasons have been: (1) opposition to the nominating president, not necessarily the nominee; (2) the nominee's involvement with one or more contentious issues of public policy or, simply, opposition to the nominee's perceived jurisprudential or sociopolitical philosophy (i.e., politics); (3) opposition to the record of the incumbent Court, which, rightly or wrongly, the nominee presumably supported; (4) senatorial courtesy (closely linked to the consultative nominating process); (5) a nominee's perceived political unreliability on the part of the party in power; (6) the evident lack of qualification or limited ability of the nominee; (7) concerted, sustained opposition by interest or pressure groups; and (8) fear that the nominee would dramatically alter the Court's jurisprudential lineup.[16]

The sections below discuss the nominations with respect to these categories based on the preponderance of scholarly evidence. Many of the nominations fall into multiple categories. Two nominations that were not confirmed by the Senate—the first nomination of William Paterson and the nomination of John G. Roberts to be Associate Justice—do not appear to fall into any of the following categories. As discussed above, in both cases the nomination was withdrawn as a formality and the nominee was then renominated and confirmed.

Opposition to the President

Opposition to the nominating President played a role in at least 16 of the 36 nominations that were not confirmed. Many of the 16 were put forward by a President in the last year of his presidency—seven occurred after a successor President had been elected, but before the transfer of power to the new administration. Each of these "lame duck" nominations transpired under 19th century Presidents when the post-election period lasted from early November until early March. Four one-term Presidents made nominations of this kind. President John Quincy Adams nominated John J. Crittenden in December 1828, after losing the election to Andrew Jackson.[17] President Tyler's third nomination of Walworth, second nomination of King, and only nomination of Read all came after Tyler had lost to James Polk.[18] President Millard Fillmore nominated George E. Badger and William C. Micou after Franklin Pierce had been elected to replace him.[19] Finally, President James Buchanan forwarded the name of Jeremiah S. Black to the Senate less than a month before Abraham Lincoln's inauguration.[20] Other nominations where opposition to the President was a major factor include the remaining unsuccessful Tyler nominations, Fillmore's nomination of Edward A. Bradford, and Andrew Johnson's nomination of Henry Stanbery.[21]

President Lyndon B. Johnson's two unsuccessful nominations (Fortas and Thornberry) occurred during the last seven months of his presidency, when, having announced he was not seeking re-election, he was considered by some to be a lame duck even before the election of his successor. Nineteen Senators issued a statement indicating that, on this basis, they would oppose any nomination by President Johnson.[22] The committee report accompanying the nomination of Abe Fortas to be Chief Justice, however, suggests that the opposition to Justice Fortas was based, to a considerable extent, on concern about money received by Fortas for delivering university lectures while an Associate Justice, Fortas's close relationship and advisory role with President Johnson while an Associate Justice, and his judicial philosophy.[23]

President Rutherford B. Hayes nominated Stanley Matthews in late January 1881, about six weeks before the transfer of power to the Garfield administration. In this case, however, the opposition seems to have centered on the nominee and his views, as discussed below, rather than on the nominating President.

Opposition to the Nominee's Views

President Washington's nomination of John Rutledge to Chief Justice, in 1795, was the first unsuccessful nomination to fail based on the nominee's political views. Shortly after his nomination, Rutledge made a strong speech denouncing the controversial and newly ratified Jay Treaty between the United States and Great Britain. The Senate, which was dominated by Federalists and had ratified the treaty, rejected the Rutledge nomination. Of the 14 who voted for rejection, 13 were Federalists, putting them in the position of rejecting a nomination by a President from their own party.[24]

Alexander Wolcott's nomination to the Court 15 years later, by President James Madison, was the next to be rejected by the Senate. Wolcott's strong enforcement of the controversial embargo and non-intercourse acts while a U.S. collector of customs cost him support in the press and the Senate. His qualifications for the position were also questioned.[25]

Andrew Jackson's first nomination of Roger B. Taney in 1835 was the third nomination for which the lack of success is often attributed to the nominee's views. In this case, there was also opposition to the nominating President's policies. Prior to the nomination, President Jackson had given a recess appointment to Taney to be Secretary of the Treasury. In that capacity, Taney had, under Jackson's direction, removed the government's deposits from the United States Bank. Jackson's Whig opponents in the Senate were incensed by this move, and this led first to the rejection of Taney as permanent Secretary of the Treasury and then to the failure of his first nomination to the Court.[26]

President James Polk's nomination of George W. Woodward in 1845 was rejected when six Democrats, led by a Senator from the nominee's home state of Pennsylvania, joined with the Whigs to oppose it. Woodward's nativist views have been cited as the principal reason for the failure of his nomination.[27]

Ebenezer R. Hoar served as President Ulysses S. Grant's Attorney General prior to his nomination to be Associate Justice in 1869. In that capacity, Hoar had alienated Senators by recommending to Grant nominees for circuit judge without regard for the Senators' preferences. In addition, the majority of the Senate disliked "his active labors on behalf of a merit civil service system for the federal government ... and his opposition to Andrew Johnson's impeachment."[28] Despite praise for Hoar's nomination in the press, the Senate rejected it.

Stanley Matthews was nominated first by President Rutherford B. Hayes in 1881, in the last weeks of Hayes's presidency. The Senate opposed the nomination because of Matthews's close ties to railroad and financial interests, and the Judiciary Committee postponed the nomination. Although Matthews was subsequently re-nominated by President James Garfield and confirmed, concerns about him persisted, and the Senate vote, at 24-23, was the closest for any successful nominee.[29]

Pierce Butler's first nomination, by President Warren G. Harding in 1922, was reported favorably by the Judiciary Committee but blocked from consideration on the Senate floor, in part because of alleged pro-corporation bias and his previous advocacy for railroad interests in cases that were to be coming before the Court.[30] During the succeeding session, Butler was re-nominated and confirmed, with 61 Senators in favor and eight opposed.[31]

John J. Parker, nominated by President Herbert Hoover in 1930, was opposed by the National Association for the Advancement of Colored People (NAACP) and organized labor based on his previous statements and writings.[32] The NAACP testified in opposition to Parker's racial views at his confirmation hearing. Their testimony was based on a statement Parker had made in the course of an unsuccessful campaign for governor of North Carolina in 1920, in which he opposed the participation of African-Americans in politics.[33] In addition, Parker's record on labor issues, as chief judge of the U.S. Fourth Circuit Court of Appeals, was criticized by labor at the hearing. The American Federation of Labor (AFL), representing several labor groups, objected in particular to an opinion, authored by Parker, that affirmed a lower court opinion in support of "yellow dog" contracts, in which employees agreed not to join a union as a condition of employment.[34]

President Dwight D. Eisenhower first nominated John Marshall Harlan II to be an Associate Justice in late 1954, but that nomination was never reported from committee. Among the objections to his nomination was the perception by some Senators that Harlan was "'ultra-liberal,' hostile to the South, [and] dedicated to reforming the Constitution by 'judicial fiat.'"[35] Eisenhower re-nominated Harlan at the beginning of the next Congress, in early 1955, and he was then confirmed.

As noted previously, President Lyndon B. Johnson's nomination of Justice Abe Fortas in 1968 for elevation to Chief Justice failed for several reasons, including his judicial philosophy. Although the Committee on the Judiciary reported the nomination favorably, several committee members strongly dissented in the committee's printed report. One Senator wrote that Fortas's "judicial philosophy disqualifies him for this high office." Another criticized Fortas as part of the majority on the Supreme Court led by Chief Justice Earl Warren (the Warren Court) making an "extremist effort ... to set itself up as a super-legislature." A third Senator also found Fortas lacking on the "broader question of the nominee's judicial philosophy which includes his willingness to subject himself to the restraint inherent in the judicial process." Yet another Senator objected to "positions taken by Justice Fortas since he went on the Supreme Court as Associate Justice [which had] reflected a view to the Constitution insufficiently rooted to the Constitution as it is written."[36] Opposition to Fortas was also based on money he received for delivering university lectures while an Associate Justice and his close relationship and advisory role with President Johnson while an Associate Justice.

President Richard M. Nixon's nomination of Clement F. Haynsworth, Jr. in 1969 also failed partly on the basis of his perceived views. Like the Fortas nomination, the Haynsworth nomination was reported favorably by the Committee on the Judiciary. In this case, the dissenting views in the committee's written report focused on perceived ethical lapses on the part of Judge Haynsworth. In addition, a joint statement by five Senators referred to "doubts about his record on the appellate bench," and one Senator opposed the nomination on the basis of the judge's record on civil rights issues.[37] Furthermore, Haynsworth drew criticism from labor and minority groups on the basis of his record. One historian has suggested that because of the recent rejection of Fortas on the basis of ethical questions, the ethical questions concerning Haynsworth played the largest role in his rejection.[38]

President Nixon's nomination of G. Harrold Carswell in 1970 was also opposed partly on the basis of his perceived views. The Committee on the Judiciary reported the nomination favorably with several dissenting views. One statement, issued jointly by four Senators, opposed the nomination in part because his "decisions and his courtroom demeanor [had] been openly hostile to the black, the poor, and the unpopular."[39] A more persistent theme in the dissent, however, was a perceived lack of competence and qualification for the position.[40]

Robert H. Bork, nominated by President Reagan in 1987, was also rejected on the basis of his views. Much has been written about this nomination, and it remains controversial. The Committee on the Judiciary reported the nomination unfavorably after 12 days of hearings. Although the written report raised some concerns about the nominee's evaluation by the American Bar Association and academic and legal communities and his role in the firing of Special Prosecutor Archibald Cox during the Nixon administration, the bulk of the report detailed concerns about and opposition to his publicly stated positions and judicial philosophy.[41]

Opposition to the Incumbent Court

The rejection by the Senate of a Supreme Court nominee on the basis of opposition to the incumbent Court is closely related to opposition on the basis of the nominee's views. In this case, the views and record of the incumbent Court majority are opposed, whereas the nominee is presumed to support the Court's views. In the case of Abe Fortas's nomination for Chief Justice, for example, the opposition of many Senators to the Warren Court has been cited as an influential factor. Fortas had been an Associate Justice for almost three years at the time of his nomination, and some opposition hinged on his positions while on the Court, as discussed above. In addition, however, his elevation was opposed because of his affiliation with the Warren Court and its wider reputation. This opposition to the Warren Court in the context of the Fortas nomination is reflected in the individual views of a Senator in the committee report.[42] In addition, during the confirmation hearings, another Senator pointedly brought up a Warren Court opinion with which he disagreed, *Mallory v. United States*,[43] although, as he acknowledged, the case had preceded Fortas's appointment as Associate Justice by eight years.[44]

Senatorial Courtesy

At least seven Supreme Court nominations have failed to be confirmed partly on the basis of deference to the objections of the nominees' home-state Senators. New York's Senators objected to the nominations of Reuben H. Walworth by President Tyler.[45] President Polk's nomination of George W. Woodward of Pennsylvania was rejected, in part, due to the objection of one of the Senators from that state.[46] The last failed Supreme Court nominations that were attributed, in part, to senatorial courtesy came before the Senate in 1893-1894, when opposition by New York's Senators was instrumental in the failure of the nominations of William Hornblower and Wheeler H. Peckham, both also of New York.[47] No unsuccessful Supreme Court nomination since that time has been attributed to senatorial courtesy.[48]

Allegations of Political Unreliability

One unsuccessful nominee was opposed in the Senate in part because of the perception that he was a "political chameleon."[49] One of President Grant's nominees for Chief Justice, Caleb Cushing, "had been, in turn, a regular Whig, a Tyler Whig, a Democrat, a[n Andrew] Johnson Constitutional Conservative, and finally a Republican."[50] The failure of his nomination has also been attributed to his advanced age (74) and a letter of introduction of a friend Cushing wrote to Confederate President Jefferson Davis in 1861.[51]

Perceived Lack of Qualification or Ability

As noted previously, President Madison's nomination of Alexander Wolcott[52] and President Nixon's nomination of G. Harrold Carswell[53] were opposed in part because of their perceived lack of qualification and ability. President Grant's nomination of George H. Williams faced similar opposition.[54] Williams also suffered from allegations of ethical misconduct.[55]

Interest Group Opposition

Interest groups were involved in confirmation fights as far back as 1881, when the Grange mounted a campaign in opposition to the Matthews nomination.[56] Interest groups testified in opposition to (and, in some cases, support of) many of the Supreme Court nominations that were not confirmed in the 20th century, including Parker, Fortas, Thornberry, Haynsworth, Carswell, and Bork. The number of organized interest groups testifying at the confirmation hearings grew from two for the Parker nomination to more than 20 for the Bork nomination.[57] Interest groups have been active in unsuccessful Supreme Court confirmation processes in a number of other ways, as well, including conducting research on nominees' positions, lobbying Senators, providing information to the media, conducting television ad campaigns, sending mailings, and organizing constituent letters and calls.[58] Observers of the Supreme Court confirmation process have suggested that interest group opposition has not only grown, but has also been effective in preventing confirmations. The impact of interest group opposition relative to other factors is a matter of continuing study.[59]

Fear of Altering the Court

In addition to the above-mentioned reasons for not confirming a nomination, the Senate may fear altering the jurisprudential philosophy of the Court. In this case, opposition would be not only to the perceived views of the nominee, but also to the impact the nominee could have on the Court's ideological balance. The best-documented case where this factor appears to have been influential was President Reagan's nomination of Robert H. Bork. Bork was nominated to replace Associate Justice Lewis F. Powell, Jr., who had been the swing voter on an often evenly divided bench. If confirmed, Bork was expected to tip the Court to the conservative side, and some of the opposition to his nomination came from those who opposed this change.[60]

Application of the Factors to the Miers Nomination

Scholars have only begun to assess the unsuccessful nomination of Harriet E. Miers to be Associate Justice. Analysis of the factors contributing to the nomination's failure is therefore preliminary. Both Miers and President Bush cited the Senate requests for White House documents as the chief reason for the withdrawal of her nomination.[61] Journalistic accounts of the Miers nomination, however, have suggested that a combination of factors led to the withdrawal.[62] Many of the factors identified by Abraham seem to apply in the Miers case. Opposition to the nominee's perceived views, for one, appears to have played a role. For example, a position Miers took in a 1993 speech reportedly contributed to opposition to her nomination by at least one conservative interest group, and it raised concerns for some conservative Senators.[63] In addition, some conservative observers expressed concern that Miers, a self-identified conservative, would be ideologically unreliable. Addressing concerns about Miers's views and ideological reliability was made more difficult for her supporters by the relatively sparse available record of her views on controversial constitutional issues. As a close legal advisor to President Bush, much of her most relevant writing in these areas would likely be found in White House documents, and these documents were not made publicly available because of their confidential nature.[64]

Three other factors identified by Abraham—perceived lack of qualifications, interest group opposition, and fear of altering the Court—also seemed to contribute to the nomination's failure. Some observers raised questions about Miers's qualifications for the position, and these concerns appear to have intensified as she met individually with Senators. Furthermore, her response to the questionnaire of the Senate Committee on the Judiciary was seen as inadequate by the chair and ranking member of that committee.[65] Miers also faced interest group opposition, but this case was unusual because the opposition came predominantly from conservative groups that had previously been allied with the President who submitted the nomination.[66] Finally, in a variation on Abraham's "fear of altering the Court" factor, it seemed that some conservatives feared that Miers, if confirmed, would *not* alter the Court, as they had long hoped an appointee of a Republican President would do.[67]

In addition to the factors identified by Abraham, another factor that may have played a part in the failure of this nomination was the close proximity of the nominee to the President. Miers's position in the Bush Administration, as Counsel to the President, raised questions for some about whether she would be able to rule fairly on presidential power issues that might come before the Court.[68] In addition, many documents related to her work for the President, which might have shed light on her views and qualifications, were not made available by the White House, despite bipartisan requests.

The Committee on the Judiciary and Unsuccessful Nominations

Since 1816, the Senate has had a standing Committee on the Judiciary. Prior to that development, one of the three unsuccessful nominations was referred to a select committee. Between 1816 and 1868, 11 of the 16 unsuccessful nominations were referred to the Judiciary Committee. Since 1868, almost all Supreme Court nominations, including all that were ultimately not confirmed, have been automatically referred to the Judiciary Committee.[69]

Of the unsuccessful nominations that have been referred to the Judiciary Committee, seven were never reported or discharged. The first four, Henry Stanbery, Stanley Matthews, William Hornblower, and John Marshall Harlan II, are discussed above. The fifth was Homer Thornberry, nominated by President Lyndon B. Johnson to replace Justice Abe Fortas as Associate Justice when he was nominated for elevation to Chief Justice. When Fortas's nomination was withdrawn by the President, the open position for Thornberry was effectively eliminated, and his nomination was also withdrawn. At that time, the Thornberry nomination had not been reported by the Judiciary Committee. The sixth of these nominations was that of John G. Roberts to be Associate Justice. Before the Judiciary Committee acted on this nomination, Chief Justice William H. Rehnquist died, creating a vacancy. Roberts's nomination to be Associate Justice was withdrawn, shortly before hearings on the nomination were to begin, so that he could be nominated to be Chief Justice. The last of this group of seven nominations is that of Harriet E. Miers. Although the Judiciary Committee had scheduled hearings on her nomination to be Associate Justice, her nomination was withdrawn in the face of opposition before any formal committee action.

Although their first nominations were never reported, second nominations of Matthews, Hornblower, and Harlan in subsequent sessions of Congress were reported to the full Senate, and Roberts's nomination to be Chief Justice during the same session of Congress was also reported to the full Senate. Only in the cases of Stanbery, Thornberry, and Miers did nominations that had been referred to committee fail to be reported out of committee on any occasion. The first two of these nominations were to fill Associate Justice vacancies that ceased to exist while the nominations were pending,[70] and the last, as just mentioned, was withdrawn prior to any formal committee action.

Additional Information on Nominations

This chapter provides two additional tables of information concerning Supreme Court nominations through August 2010. **Table 3** shows, by President, the number of vacancies, number of nominations, and disposition of nominations. **Table 4** provides detailed information on the course and fate of each of the 36 unsuccessful Supreme Court nominations.[71] A variety of sources were used to develop this table, as identified in the table notes. Although most of these sources are widely available, some, particularly older committee records, are located at the National Archives and Records Administration. Among the official sources, the *Journal of the Executive Proceedings of the Senate of the United States of America* and committee records, where available, provided the most information. Where the *Journal* showed no evidence of a debate or vote on the floor of the Senate, the indices of other official sources were also checked for evidence of any other Senate activity related to the nomination. These sources included the *Congressional Globe*, *Congressional Record, Annals of Congress*, and *Senate Journal.* Where the table indicates that there was no debate or further Senate action, there is no known official record that provides additional information. A list of related literature follows **Table 4**.

Table 3. Supreme Court Nominations, by President, 1789-August 2010

President (party)	Actual or Prospective Vacancies During Presidency[a]	Nominations	Confirmed and Served	Not Confirmed	Confirmed and Declined or Died Prior to Service
Washington (Federalist)	10	14	10	2	2
J. Adams (Fed.)	3	4	3	0	1
Jefferson (Democratic-Republican)	3	3	3	0	0
Madison (Dem.-Rep.)	2	5	2	1	2
Monroe (Dem.-Rep.)	1	1	1	0	0
J. Q. Adams (Dem.-Rep.)	2	2	1	1	0
Jackson (Democratic)	7	8	6	1	1
Van Buren (Dem.)	2	2	2	0	0
W. H. Harrison (Whig)	0	0	0	0	0
Tyler (Whig)	2	9	1	8	0
Polk (Dem.)	2	3	2	1	0
Taylor (Whig)	0	0	0	0	0
Fillmore (Whig)	2	4	1	3	0
Pierce (Dem.)	1	1	1	0	0
Buchanan (Dem.)	2	2	1	1	0
Lincoln (Republican)	5	5	5	0	0
A. Johnson (Dem.)	2[b]	1	0	1	0
Grant (Rep.)	4	8	4	3	1
Hayes (Rep.)	3	3	2	1	0
Garfield (Rep.)	1	1	1	0	0
Arthur (Rep.)	2	3	2	0	1

Table 3. (Continued)

President (party)	Actual or Prospective Vacancies During Presidency[a]	Nominations	Confirmed and Served	Not Confirmed	Confirmed and Declined or Died Prior to Service
Cleveland (1) (Dem.)	2	2	2	0	0
B. Harrison (Rep.)	4	4	4	0	0
Cleveland (2) (Dem.)	2	5	2	3	0
McKinley (Rep.)	1	1	1	0	0
T. Roosevelt(Rep.)	3	3	3	0	0
Taft (Rep.)	6	6	6	0	0
Wilson (Dem.)	3	3	3	0	0
Harding (Rep.)	4	5	4	1	0
Coolidge (Rep.)	1	1	1	0	0
Hoover (Rep.)	3	4	3	1	0
F. D. Roosevelt (Dem.)	9	9	9	0	0
Truman (Dem.)	4	4	4	0	0
Eisenhower (Rep.)	5	6	5	1	0
Kennedy (Dem.)	2	2	2	0	0
L. B. Johnson (Dem.)	4[c]	4	2	2	0
Nixon (Rep.)	4	6	4	2	0
Ford (Rep.)	1	1	1	0	0
Carter (Dem.)	0	0	0	0	0
Reagan (Rep.)	4	5	4	1	0
G. H. W. Bush (Rep.)	2	2	2	0	0
Clinton (Dem.)	2	2	2	0	0
G. W. Bush (Rep.)	2	4	2	2	0
Obama (Dem.) [through August 2010]	2	2	2	0	0
Totals	**126**	**160**	**116**	**36**	**8**

a. Includes unfilled vacancies remaining from previous administration; some vacancies are counted for more than one administration. The term "prospective vacancy" refers to those cases in which a Justice has announced his or her intention to leave office, but remains in the position pending the appointment of a replacement.

b. Both positions were abolished, one until the Grant administration, the other permanently.

c. One of these vacancies was the expected Associate Justice vacancy created when Johnson nominated Abe Fortas for elevation to Chief Justice. When the Fortas nomination was not successful, this expected vacancy ceased to exist.

Table 4. Supreme Court Nominations Not Confirmed, 1789-August 2010

Nominee	President	Date Received in Senate[a]	Confirmation Hearing Date(s)[b]	Committee Votes, Reports, and Recommendations	Date(s) of Senate Debate	Final Disposition (Vote)
William Paterson[c]	Washington	Feb. 27, 1793	Nomination predates standing Judiciary Committee; no record of other committee referral		No record of debate	Withdrawn, message received Feb. 28, 1793
John Rutledge (for Chief Justice)[d]	Washington	Dec. 10, 1795	Nomination predates standing Judiciary Committee; no record of other committee referral		Dec. 11, 15, 1795	Rejected (10-14), Dec. 15, 1795
Alexander Wolcott[e]	Madison	Feb. 4, 1811	Nomination predates standing Judiciary Committee; referred to select committee on Feb. 7, 1811. The committee reported on Feb. 13, 1811; no record of committee hearings, vote or recommendation		Feb. 5, 6, 7, 13, 1811	Rejected (9-24), Feb. 13, 1811
John J. Crittenden[f]	J. Q. Adams	Dec. 18, 1828 (referred)	No record of hearings	Reported on Jan. 26, 1829 with the recommendation that the Senate not act on the nomination during that session	Jan. 29, 30, 1829; Feb. 2, 3, 4, 5, 9, 12, 1829	Postponed[g] (23-17), Feb. 12, 1829
Roger B. Taney[h]	Jackson	Jan. 15, 1835	No record of referral to the Judiciary Committee		Jan. 20, 1835; Feb. 2, 1835; Mar. 3, 1835	Postponed indefinitely (24-21), Mar. 3, 1835
John C. Spencer[i]	Tyler[j]	Jan. 9, 1844 (referred)	No record of hearings	Reported on Jan. 30, 1844; no record of committee vote or recommendation	Jan. 31, 1844	Rejected (21-26), Jan. 31, 1844
Reuben H. Walworth[k]	Tyler	Mar. 13, 1844 (referred)	No record of hearings	Reported on June 14, 1844; no record of committee vote or recommendation	June 15, 1844	Tabled (27-20), June 15, 1844; withdrawn, message received June 17, 1844
Edward King[l]	Tyler	June 5, 1844 (referred)	No record of hearings	Reported on June 14, 1844; no record of committee vote or recommendation	June 15, 1844	Tabled (29-18), June 15, 1844
John C. Spencer[m]	Tyler	June 17, 1844 (withdrawn	No record of referral to the Judiciary Committee		No record of debate on the nomination	Withdrawn, message received June 17, 1844

Table 4. (Continued)

Nominee	President	Date Received in Senate[a]	Confirmation Hearing Date(s)[b]	Committee Votes, Reports, and Recommendations	Date(s) of Senate Debate	Final Disposition (Vote)
		on the same day)				
Reuben H. Walworth[n]	Tyler	June 17, 1844	No record of referral to the Judiciary Committee		Motion to consider the nomination was objected to, June 17, 1844	No record of further action
Reuben H. Walworth[o]	Tyler	Dec. 10, 1844 (referred)	No record of hearings	Reported on Jan. 21, 1845; no record of committee vote or recommendation	No record of debate	Tabled, Jan. 21, 1845 (no record of vote); withdrawn, message received Feb. 6, 1845
Edward King[p]	Tyler	Dec. 10, 1844 (referred)	No record of hearings	Reported on Jan. 21, 1845; no record of committee vote or recommendation	No record of debate on the nomination	Tabled, Jan. 21, 1845 (no record of vote); withdrawn, message received Feb. 8, 1845
John M. Read[q]	Tyler	Feb. 8, 1845 (referred)	No record of hearings	Reported on Feb. 14, 1845; no record of committee vote or recommendation	Unsuccessful motion to consider nomination, Feb. 26, 1845	No further record of action
George W. Woodward[r]	Polk	Dec. 23, 1845 (referred)	No record of hearings	Reported on Jan. 20, 1846; no record of committee vote or recommendation	Jan. 21, 22, 1846; motion to postpone rejected (21-28), Jan. 22, 1846	Nomination rejected (20- 29), Jan. 22, 1846
Edward A. Bradford[s]	Fillmore	Aug. 21, 1852 (referred)	No record of hearings	Reported on Aug. 30, 1852; no record of committee vote or recommendation	Aug. 31, 1852	Tabled Aug. 31, 1852 (no record of vote)
George E. Badger[t]	Fillmore	Jan. 10, 1853	No record of referral to the Judiciary Committee		Jan. 14, 20, 24, 1853; Feb. 7, 11, 1853	Postponed (26-25), Feb. 11, 1853

Table 4. (Continued)

Nominee	President	Date Received in Senate[a]	Confirmation Hearing Date(s)[b]	Committee Votes, Reports, and Recommendations	Date(s) of Senate Debate	Final Disposition (Vote)
William C. Micou[u]	Fillmore	Feb. 24, 1853 (referred and discharged on the same day)	No record of hearings	No record of committee vote; ordered discharged on Feb. 24, 1853, the same day as referred	No record of debate	No record of action after discharge
Jeremiah S. Black[v]	Buchanan	Feb. 6, 1861	No record of referral to the Judiciary Committee		Motions to consider the nomination unsuccessful, Feb. 6, 12, 21, 1861	No record of further action
Henry Stanbery[w]	A. Johnson	Apr. 16, 1866 (referred)	No record of hearings	No record of committee action[x]	No record of debate	No record of action after referral[y]
Ebenezer R. Hoar[z]	Grant	Dec. 15, 1869 (referred)	No record of hearings	Reported adversely on Dec. 22, 1869; no record of committee vote	Dec. 22, 1869, Feb. 3, 1870	Rejected (24-33), Feb. 3, 1870
George H. Williams (for Chief Justice)[aa]	Grant	Dec. 2, 1873 (referred Dec. 4, 1873)	Hearings held Dec. 16, 17, 1873 after recommittal	Reported favorably on Dec. 11, 1873; no record of committee vote Hearings held after recommittal; nomination withdrawn by the President; committee returned nomination to the Senate[bb]	Debated Dec. 11, 15, 1873; nomination recommitted to the Judiciary Committee, Dec. 15, 1873	Withdrawn, message received Jan. 8, 1874
Caleb Cushing (for Chief Justice)[cc]	Grant	Jan. 9, 1874 (referred)	No record of hearings	Reported favorably on Jan. 9, 1874[dd]	No record of debate	Withdrawn, message received Jan. 14, 1874
Stanley Matthews[ee]	Hayes	Jan. 26, 1881 (referred)	No record of hearings	Addressed on Feb. 7, 1881; addressed and postponed Feb. 14, 1881[ff]	No record of debate	No record of action after committee postponement[gg]
William B. Hornblower[hh]	Cleveland	Sept. 19, 1893 (referred)	No record of hearings	Addressed on Sept. 25, 1893; October 25, 30, 1893	No record of debate	No record of further action

Table 4. (Continued)

Nominee	President	Date Received in Senate[a]	Confirmation Hearing Date(s)[b]	Committee Votes, Reports, and Recommendations	Date(s) of Senate Debate	Final Disposition (Vote)
William B. Hornblower	Cleveland	Dec. 6, 1893 (referred)	No record of hearings	Addressed on Dec. 11, 14, 18, 1893; Reported adversely, Jan. 8, 1894[ii]	Jan. 15, 1894	Rejected (24-30), Jan. 15, 1894
Wheeler H. Peckham[jj]	Cleveland	Jan. 22, 1894 (referred)	No record of hearings	Addressed Jan. 29, 1894; Feb. 5, 6, 12, 1894; committee reportedly equally divided;[kk] reported without recommendation, Feb. 12, 1894	Feb. 15, 16, 1894	Rejected (32-41), Feb. 16, 1894
Pierce Butler[ll]	Harding	Nov. 23, 1922 (referred)	No record of hearings	Reported Nov. 28, 1922	No record of debate	Placed on the Executive Calendar on Nov. 28, 1922; No record of further action[mm]
John J. Parker[nn]	Hoover	Mar. 21, 1930 (referred)	April 5, 1930[oo]	Reported adversely, Apr. 21, 1930[pp]	Apr. 28, 29, 30, 1930; May 1, 2, 5, 6, 7, 1930	Rejected (39-41), May 7, 1930
John Marshall Harlan II[qq]	Eisenhower	Nov. 9, 1954 (referred)	No record of hearings	No record of committee vote or report	No record of debate	No record of further action[rr]
Abe Fortas (for Chief Justice)[ss]	L. B. Johnson	June 26, 1968 (referred)	July 11, 12, 16, 17, 18, 19, 20, 22, 23, 1968; Sept. 13, 16, 1968[tt]	Committee voted to approve on Sept. 17, 1968[uu]; reported favorably on Sept. 20, 1968	Sept. 24, 25, 26, 27, 30, 1968; Oct. 1, 1968	Cloture motion defeated (45-43), Oct. 1, 1968; Withdrawn, message received Oct. 4, 1968
Homer Thornberry[vv]	L. B. Johnson	June 26, 1968 (referred)	July 11, 12, 16, 17, 18, 19, 20, 22, 23, 1968; Sept. 13, 16, 1968[ww]	No record of committee vote or report	No record of debate	Withdrawn, message received Oct. 4, 1968[xx]
Clement F. Haynsworth, Jr.[yy]	Nixon	Aug. 21, 1969 (referred)	Sept. 16, 17, 18, 19, 23, 24, 25, 26, 1969[zz]	Committee voted 10-7 in favor of confirmation on Oct. 9, 1969[aaa]; reported favorably on Nov. 12, 1969	Nov. 13, 14, 17, 18, 19, 20, 21, 1969	Rejected (45-55), Nov. 21, 1969

Table 4. (Continued)

Nominee	President	Date Received in Senate[a]	Confirmation Hearing Date(s)[b]	Committee Votes, Reports, and Recommendations	Date(s) of Senate Debate	Final Disposition (Vote)
G. Harrold Carswell[bbb]	Nixon	Jan. 19, 1970 (referred)	Jan. 27, 28, 29, 1970; Feb. 2, 3, 1970[ccc]	Committee voted 13-4 in favor of recommending for confirmation on Feb. 16, 1970[ddd]; reported on Feb. 27, 1970	Mar. 13, 16, 17, 18, 19, 20, 23, 24, 25, 26, 31, 1970; Apr. 3, 6, 7, 8, 1970	Rejected (45-51), Apr. 8, 1970
Robert H. Bork[eee]	Reagan	July 7, 1987 (referred)	Sept. 15, 16, 17, 18, 19, 21, 22, 23, 25, 28, 29, 30, 1987[fff]	5-9 against on Oct. 6, 1987; reported on Oct. 13, 1987[ggg]	Oct. 21, 22, 23, 1987	Rejected (42-58), Oct. 23, 1987
John G. Roberts, Jr.[hhh]	G.W. Bush	July 29, 2005 (referred)	No hearings	No committee action	No Senate debate	Withdrawn, message received Sept. 6, 2005
Harriet E. Miers[hhh]	G.W. Bush	Oct. 7, 2005 (referred)	No hearings	No committee action	No Senate debate	Withdrawn, message received Oct. 28, 2005

a. The date of the President's nomination and the date the nomination is received in the Senate are often, but not always, the same. As used in this column, "referred" indicates that the nomination was referred to the Senate Committee on the Judiciary on that date.

b. The committee's deliberations were held in closed session until the early 20th century. CRS Report RL31989, *Supreme Court Appointment Process: Roles of the President, Judiciary Committee, and Senate*, by Denis Steven Rutkus.

c. Nomination information from U.S. Congress, Senate, *Journal of the Executive Proceedings of the Senate of the United States of America*, vol. 1, pp. 134-135. (Hereafter cited as nominee, *Executive Journal*.) Paterson was later nominated again and confirmed.

d. Rutledge, *Executive Journal*, vol. 1, pp. 194-196. Rutledge served as an Associate Justice from February 15, 1790, through March 5, 1791. Although Rutledge was never confirmed as Chief Justice, he served in the position from August 12, 1795, through December 15, 1795, under a recess appointment by President Washington. ("Members of the Supreme Court of the United States," at http://www.supremecourtus.gov/about/about.html.)

e. Wolcott, *Executive Journal*, vol. 2, pp. 165-67.

f. Crittenden, *Executive Journal*, vol. 3, pp. 622-623, 636-639, 643-644.

g. Although the Senate did not take up a motion to "postpone indefinitely," as it did on other similar occasions, it passed a resolution which had the effect of postponing.

(See Crittenden, *Executive Journal*, vol. 3, p. 644.)

h. Taney, *Executive Journal*, vol. 4, pp. 459, 463, 465, 484. Taney was later nominated to be Chief Justice and confirmed.

i. Spencer was the subject of two nominations not confirmed. Information concerning the first nomination can be found at *Executive Journal*, vol. 6, pp. 207-208, 227, 229.

j. In 1844 and 1845, President John Tyler forwarded nine nominations involving only five men. Eight of the nine were not confirmed. Of those nominees who were not confirmed, Walworth was nominated three times, Spencer and King were nominated twice, and Read was nominated once. Samuel Nelson was nominated once and confirmed.

k. Walworth was the subject of three nominations not confirmed. Information concerning the first nomination can be found at *Executive Journal*, vol. 6, pp. 243-244, 332, 344-345, 353.

l. King was the subject of two nominations not confirmed. Information concerning the first nomination can be found at *Executive Journal,* vol. 6, pp. 306, 332, 345.

m. Spencer, *Executive Journal*, vol. 6, pp. 353-354.

n. Walworth, *Executive Journal*, vol. 6, p. 354.

o. Walworth, *Executive Journal,* vol. 6, pp. 355, 357, 387, 391.

p. King, *Executive Journal,* vol. 6, pp. 355, 357, 387, 392.

q. Read, *Executive Journal*, vol. 6, pp. 392, 396.

r. Woodward, *Executive Journal*, vol. 7, pp. 10, 36-38.

s. Bradford, *Executive Journal,* vol. 8, pp. 440-441, 448, 452.

t. Badger, *Executive Journal*, vol. 9, pp. 10, 18-20, 26-28, 34. President Millard Fillmore indicated that he regarded the postponement of the Badger nomination as "equivalent to a rejection" in his message nominating William C. Micou (p. 34).

u. Micou, *Executive Journal*, vol. 9, pp. 34-36.

v. Black, *Executive Journal*, vol. 11, pp. 260-261, 271, 278.

w. Stanbery, *Executive Journal*, vol. 15, part 1, pp. 720-721.

x. Senate Judiciary Committee minutes are available for the session during which this nomination was pending. Specific information regarding this nomination or any other nomination, however, was not recorded. See U.S. Congress, Senate Committee on the Judiciary, "Senate Judiciary Committee, 39th-40th Congress, 1st sess.: Minutes," RG 46.15, U.S. National Archives.

y. There is no record of action on this nomination. The Associate Justice position to which Stanbery was nominated was eliminated by statute after his nomination. He was nominated and confirmed for U.S. Attorney General in July 1866.

z. Hoar, *Executive Journal,* vol. 17, pp. 314, 316, 328-330.

aa. Williams, *Executive Journal,* vol. 19, pp. 119, 166, 183, 188-189, 210.

bb. The date of this action is not specified in committee records. See U.S. Congress, Senate Committee on the Judiciary, "Papers re Nominations (P-W)," drawer Sen: 43B-A5 12, RG 46.15, U.S. National Archives.

cc. Cushing, *Executive Journal*, vol. 19, pp. 212-213, 218.

dd. The official vote of the committee is not reported. According to one press account, the committee was unanimous ("The Chief Justiceship," *New York Tribune*, January 10, 1874, p. 1), while another reported a waiving of the formal referral of the nomination ("The Chief Justiceship," *New York Times*, January 10, 1874, p. 1).

ee. Matthews, *Executive Journal,* vol. 22, p. 469.

ff. According to committee minutes, "The nomination of Stanly [sic] Matthews was taken up and on motion the further consideration of same was postponed until next Monday [February 21, 1881]." The committee minutes contain no further report of action on the nomination during the remaining days of the 46th Congress. (U.S. Congress, Senate Committee on the Judiciary, *Senate Judiciary Committee 46th-48th Congress, 1st Session: Minutes,* pp. 53-54.)

gg. Matthews was later nominated by President James A. Garfield and confirmed.

hh. Hornblower was the subject of two nominations not confirmed. The first was at the end of the first session of the 53rd Congress, and the second was at the beginning of the second session of the same Congress. *Executive Journal,* vol. 29, part 2, pp. 138, 142, 243, 251, 339, 352-353.

ii. The official vote of the committee was not recorded. *The New York Times* reported the vote as 7-4 against ("Unfavorable to Mr. Hornblower," *New York Times*, January 9, 1894, p. 1), and the *New York Tribune* reported 5-3 against ("To Reject Mr. Hornblower," *New York Tribune*, January 9, 1894, p. 2).

jj. Peckham, *Executive Journal*, vol. 29, part 2, pp. 356, 408, 421-423.

kk. The official vote of the committee was not recorded. *The New York Times* reported the vote as 5-5 ("Peckham's Friends Hopeful," *New York Times*, February 13, 1894, p. 1).

ll. Butler, *Executive Journal*, vol. 60, pp. 29, 63.

mm. Butler was later re-nominated by President Harding and confirmed.

nn. Parker, *Executive Journal*, vol. 69, part 1, pp. 525, 643, 655, 673, 682, 691, 695-696, 699, 705, 710, 718-722.

oo. See U.S. Congress, Senate Committee on the Judiciary, *Confirmation of Hon. John J. Parker to Be an Associate Justice of the Supreme Court of the United States,* hearings, 71st Cong., 2nd sess. (Washington: GPO, 1930).

pp. The official committee vote was not reported in the *Executive Journal*. *The New York Times* reported a 10-6 vote against the nomination on April 21, 1930 ("Committee, 10 to 6, Rejects Parker," *New York Times*, April 22, 1930, pp. 1, 23). Another source provides a different vote count, 9-8, with the same outcome (Joseph P. Harris, *Advice and Consent of the Senate* [New York: Greenwood Press, 1968], p. 129).

qq. Harlan, *Executive Journal*, vol. 96, p. 834.

rr. Harlan was later re-nominated by President Eisenhower and confirmed.

ss. Fortas, *Executive Journal*, vol. 110, pp. 332, 516, 521, 527, 529, 554-556, 569-570, 592.

tt. U.S. Congress, Senate Committee on the Judiciary, *Nomination of Abe Fortas*, report to accompany the nomination of Abe Fortas, 90th Cong., 2nd sess., Exec. Rept. 8 (Washington: GPO, 1968). See also U.S. Congress, Senate Committee on the Judiciary, *Nominations of Abe Fortas and Homer Thornberry*, hearings, 90th Cong., 2nd sess. (Washington: GPO, 1968).

uu. The official committee vote was not reported in the *Executive Journal*. *The New York Times* reported an 11-6 vote in favor of the nomination on September 17, 1968 ("Fortas Approved by Senate Panel; Filibuster Looms," *New York Times*, September 18, 1968, pp. 1, 13).

vv. Thornberry, *Executive Journal*, vol. 110, pp. 332, 592.

ww. The Thornberry hearings were conducted in conjunction with the Fortas hearings. See U.S. Congress, Senate Committee on the Judiciary, *Nominations of Abe Fortas and Homer Thornberry*, hearings, 90th Cong., 2nd sess. (Washington: GPO, 1968).

xx. With the nomination of Abe Fortas to be Chief Justice withdrawn, an Associate Justice vacancy was no longer anticipated.

yy. Haynsworth, *Executive Journal*, vol. 111, pp. 590, 768-770, 772-773, 776.

zz. See U.S. Congress, Senate Committee on the Judiciary, *Nomination of Clement F. Haynsworth, Jr.*, hearings, 91st Cong., 1st sess. (Washington: GPO, 1969).

aaa. Vote tally from U.S. Congress, Senate Committee on the Judiciary, *Nomination of Clement F. Haynsworth, Jr.*, report to accompany the nomination of Clement F. Haynsworth, Jr., 91st Cong., 1st sess., Exec. Rept. 91-12 (Washington: GPO, 1969); date of vote from U.S. Congress, Senate Committee on the Judiciary, *Legislative and Executive Calendar*, 91st Cong., 1st and 2nd sess. (Washington: GPO, 1970), p. 434.

bbb. Carswell, *Executive Journal*, vol. 112, pp. 1, 79, 117, 121, 125, 127-130, 139-141, 144-148.

ccc. See U.S. Congress, Senate Committee on the Judiciary, *George Harrold Carswell*, hearings, 91st Cong., 2nd sess. (Washington: GPO, 1970).

ddd. Vote tally from U.S. Congress, Senate Committee on the Judiciary, *Nomination of George Harrold Carswell*, report to accompany the nomination of George Harrold Carswell, 91st Cong., 2nd sess., Exec. Rept. 91-14 (Washington: GPO, 1970); date of vote from U.S. Congress, Senate Committee on the Judiciary, *Legislative and Executive Calendar*, 91st Cong., 1st and 2nd sess. (Washington: GPO, 1970), p. 442.

eee. Bork, *Executive Journal*, vol. 129, pp. 493, 665, 669-771.

fff. See U.S. Congress, Senate Committee on the Judiciary, *Nomination of Robert H. Bork to Be Associate Justice of the Supreme Court of the United States*, hearings, 5 parts, 100th Cong., 1st sess. (Washington: GPO, 1987).

ggg. U.S. Congress, Senate Committee on the Judiciary, *Legislative and Executive Calendar*, S.Prt. 100-153, 100th Cong., 1st and 2nd sess. (Washington: GPO, 1989). See also U.S. Congress, Senate Committee on the Judiciary, *Nomination of Robert H. Bork to be an Associate Justice of the United States Supreme Court*, report to accompany the nomination of Robert H. Bork, 100th Cong., 1st sess., Exec. Rept. 100-7 (Washington: GPO, 1987).

hhh. Information concerning the nominations of John G. Roberts, Jr., and Harriet E. Miers was obtained from the Senate nominations database of the Legislative Information System, available to congressional staff at http://www.congress.gov/nomis/.

ADDITIONAL RESOURCES

Other Resources

Abraham, *Henry J. Justices, Presidents, and Senators: A History of the U.S. Supreme Court Appointments from Washington to Clinton*, 4th ed. (Lanham, MD: Rowman & Littlefield, 1999).

Ginsburg, Ruth Bader. "Confirming Supreme Court Justices: Thoughts on the Second Opinion Rendered by the Senate." *University of Illinois Law Review, vol. 1988, pp. 101-117.*

Greenburg, Jan Crawford. *Supreme Conflict: The Inside Story of the Struggle for Control of the United States Supreme Court* (New York: Penguin Press, 2007).

Harris, Joseph P. *The Advice and Consent of the Senate: A Study of the Confirmation of Appointments by the United States Senate* (New York: Greenwood Press, 1968).

Jacobstein, J. Myron, and Roy M. Mersky. *The Rejected: Sketches of the 26 Men Nominated for the Supreme Court but Not Confirmed by the Senate* (Milpitas, CA: Toucan Valley Publications, 1993). (Note: The authors do not include the Paterson nomination.)

Maltese, John Anthony. *The Selling of Supreme Court Nominees* (Baltimore, MD: The Johns Hopkins University Press, 1995).

Massaro, John. *Supremely Political: The Role of Ideology and Presidential Management in Unsuccessful Supreme Court Nominations* (Albany, NY: State University of New York Press, 1990).

Massey, Calvin R. "Getting There: A Brief History of the Politics of Supreme Court Appointments." *Hastings Constitutional Law Quarterly, vol. 19* (fall 1991), pp. 1-21.

Sulfridge, Wayne. "Ideology as a Factor in Senate Consideration of Supreme Court Nominations." *The Journal of Politics, vol. 42*, no. 2 (May 1980), pp. 560-567.

Thorpe, James A. "The Appearance of Supreme Court Nominees Before the Senate Judiciary Committee." In *The First Branch of American Government: The United States Congress and Its Relations to the Executive and Judiciary, 1789-1989, vol. 2*, Joel Sibley, ed. (Brooklyn, NY: Carlson, 1991), pp. 515-546.

Tulis, Jeffrey K. "The Appointment Power: Constitutional Abdication: The Senate, the President, and Appointments to the Supreme Court." *Case Western Reserve Law Review, vol. 47* (summer 1997), pp. 1331-1357.

Whittington, Keith E. "Presidents, Senates, and Failed Supreme Court Nominations." In *The Supreme Court Review*, 2006, Dennis J. Hutchinson, David A. Strauss, and Geoffrey R. Stone, eds. (Chicago: University of Chicago Press, 2007), pp. 401-438.

End Notes

[1] For a more detailed history of the Supreme Court nominations process, see CRS Report RL31989, *Supreme Court Appointment Process: Roles of the President, Judiciary Committee, and Senate*, by Denis Steven Rutkus; CRS Report RL33247, *Supreme Court Nominations: Senate Floor Procedure and Practice, 1789-2009*, by Richard S. Beth and Betsy Palmer; CRS Report RL33225, *Supreme Court Nominations, 1789-2010: Actions by the Senate, the Judiciary Committee, and the President*, by Denis Steven Rutkus and Maureen Bearden; and CRS

Report RL32821, *The Chief Justice of the United States: Responsibilities of the Office and Process for Appointment*, by Denis Steven Rutkus and Lorraine H. Tong.

[2] U.S. Congress, Senate, *Journal of the Executive Proceedings of the Senate of the United States of America*, vol. 1, p. 135. (Hereafter cited as *Executive Journal.*)

[3] Article I, Section 6 of the Constitution provides that, "No Senator or Representative shall, during the Time for which he was elected, be appointed to any civil Office ... , which shall have been created ... during such time.... " The office to which Washington was nominating Paterson, Associate Justice, was created by the Judiciary Act of 1789 on September 24, 1789, during which time Paterson was a Senator. Paterson began serving in the Senate on March 4, 1789 and resigned on November 13, 1790, having been elected Governor of New Jersey (U.S. Congress, House, *Biographical Directory of the American Congress*, H.Doc. 607, 81st Cong., 2nd sess. [Washington: GPO, 1950], p. 1655). His term, however, did not conclude until March 3, 1793 (U.S. Congress, Senate, *Senate Manual*, S.Doc. 106-1, 106th Cong., 1st sess. [Washington: GPO, 2000], p. 859), and so his appointment to Associate Justice prior to that date would have been unconstitutional. President Washington re-nominated, and a special session of the Senate of the new Congress confirmed, Paterson on March 4, 1793. Paterson's Senate position had covered four years, rather than six, due to the staggering of Senate terms at the outset of the First Congress, which was called for in the Constitution (Article I, Section 3) and was implemented in the Senate in May 1789.

[4] *Executive Journal*, vol. 1, p. 139.

[5] Senate nominations database of the Legislative Information System, available to congressional staff at http://www.congress.gov/nomis/.

[6] Ibid.

[7] *Executive Journal,* vol. 23, pp. 14, 75-76.

[8] 28th Congress, 1st sess.

[9] "Washington: Adjournment of Congress," *Daily National Intelligencer* (Washington), June 18, 1844, p. 3.

[10] For more on the Senate's consideration of the Fortas nomination, see CRS Report RL31948, *Evolution of the Senate's Role in the Nomination and Confirmation Process: A Brief History*, by Betsy Palmer.

[11] H.R. 334 (39th Congress), passed March 8, 1866.

[12] An Act to fix the Number of Judges of the Supreme Court of the United States, and to change certain Judicial Circuits, *Statutes at Large* 14, chap. 210, sec.1, p. 209 (1866).

[13] An Act to amend the Judicial System of the United States, *Statutes at Large* 15, chap. 22, sec. 1, p. 44 (1869).

[14] See Joseph P. Harris, *The Advice and Consent of the Senate* (New York: Greenwood Press, 1968), p. 304; Henry J. Abraham, *Justices and Presidents*, 3rd ed. (New York: Oxford University Press, 1992), pp. 124-125; and J. Myron Jacobstein and Roy M. Mersky, *The Rejected: Sketches of the 26 Men Nominated for the Supreme Court but Not Confirmed by the Senate* (Milpitas, CA: Toucan Valley Publications, 1993), pp. 67-74.

[15] See "Supreme Court of the United States," *The Congressional Globe*, vol. 72, March 8, 1866, p. 1259; "Supreme Court Judges," *The Congressional Globe,* vol. 74, July 10, 1866, p. 3697; "United States Supreme Court," *The Congressional Globe,* vol. 75, July 18, 1866, p. 3909.

[16] Abraham, *Justices and Presidents*, p. 39.

[17] Charles Warren, *The Supreme Court in United States History*, revised edition, vol. 1 (Boston: Little, Brown, and Company, 1926), pp. 701-704; William F. Swindler, "The Politics of 'Advice and Consent,'" *American Bar Association Journal*, v. 56, 1970, p. 537.

[18] Warren, *The Supreme Court in United States History*, vol. 2, pp. 115-120; Swindler, "The Politics of 'Advice and Consent,'" pp. 537-538. Notably, Tyler also put forth his one successful nomination out of nine, of Samuel Nelson, a month before the transfer of power.

[19] Warren, *The Supreme Court in United States History*, vol. 2, pp. 242-245; Swindler, "The Politics of 'Advice and Consent,'" pp. 538-539.

[20] Warren, *The Supreme Court in United States History*, vol. 2, pp. 363-365.

[21] Abraham, *Justices and Presidents*, pp. 39-41, 124-125. As previously discussed, Congress initiated legislation to reduce the number of Associate Justices around the time of Stanbery's nomination.

[22] Jacobstein and Mersky, *The Rejected*, pp.131-132.

[23] U.S. Congress, Senate Committee on the Judiciary, *Nomination of Abe Fortas*, report to accompany the nomination of Abe Fortas, 90th Cong., 2nd sess., Exec. Rept. 8 (Washington: GPO, 1968).

[24] See Warren, *The Supreme Court in United States History*, vol. 1, pp. 129-139; Harris, *The Advice and Consent of the Senate*, pp. 42-43; Ruth Bader Ginsburg, "Confirming Supreme Court Justices: Thoughts on the Second Opinion Rendered by the Senate," *University of Illinois Law Review*, Winter 1988, pp. 101-117, at 106; Swindler, "The Politics of 'Advice and Consent,'" pp. 534-535.

[25] Warren, *The Supreme Court in United States History*, vol. 1, pp. 410-413; Swindler, "The Politics of 'Advice and Consent,'" pp. 535-536; Abraham, *Justices and Presidents*, pp. 41, 88.

[26] Harris, *The Advice and Consent of the Senate*, pp. 59-64; Warren, *The Supreme Court in United States History*, vol. 1, pp. 798-802.

[27] Abraham, *Justices and Presidents*, pp. 41, 109; Warren, *The Supreme Court in United States History*, vol. 2, pp. 146-147; Harris, *The Advice and Consent of the Senate*, p. 69.

[28] Abraham, *Justices and Presidents*, p. 127. See also Warren, *The Supreme Court in United States History*, vol. 2, pp. 501-504, 507; Harris, *The Advice and Consent of the Senate*, pp. 74-75.

[29] Warren, *The Supreme Court in United States History*, vol. 2, pp. 622-623; Abraham, *Justices and Presidents*, pp. 135-137.

[30] Abraham, *Justices and Presidents*, pp. 190-192; "Senate Sends Back Butler Nomination," *New York Times*, December 5, 1922, p. 1; and "Shipstead Attacks Butler on 4 Points," *New York Times*, December 9, 1922, p. 5.

[31] *Executive Journal*, vol. 61, part 1, pp. 76, 104-105.

[32] For a description of the Parker nomination and a differing perspective on his record, see Harris, *The Advice and Consent of the Senate*, pp. 127-132. Abraham, *Justices and Presidents*, (pp. 42-43) also discusses the nomination and contests the claims offered by opponents.

[33] U. S. Congress, Committee on the Judiciary, Subcommittee, *Confirmation of Hon. J. Parker to be an Associate Justice of the Supreme Court of the United States*, hearings, 71st Cong., 2nd sess., April 5, 1930 (Washington: GPO, 1930), pp. 74-79.

[34] Ibid., pp. 23-60.

[35] Abraham, *Justices and Presidents*, p. 263.

[36] All quotes from U.S. Congress, Senate Committee on the Judiciary, *Nomination of Abe Fortas*, report to accompany the nomination of Abe Fortas, 90th Cong., 2nd sess., Exec. Rept. 8 (Washington: GPO, 1968), pp. 15-44. See also Abraham, *Justices and Presidents*, pp. 43-45.

[37] U.S. Congress, Senate Committee on the Judiciary, *Nomination of Clement F. Haynsworth, Jr.*, report to accompany the nomination of Clement F. Haynsworth, Jr., 91st Cong., 1st sess., Exec. Rept. 91-12 (Washington: GPO, 1969), pp. 24, 48.

[38] Abraham, *Justices and Presidents*, pp. 14-15.

[39] U.S. Congress, Senate Committee on the Judiciary, *Nomination of George Harrold Carswell*, report to accompany the nomination of George Harrold Carswell, 91st Cong., 2nd sess., Exec. Rept. 91-14 (Washington: GPO, 1970), p. 13.

[40] Abraham, *Justices and Presidents*, pp. 15-18.

[41] U.S. Congress, Senate Committee on the Judiciary, *Nomination of Robert H. Bork to be an Associate Justice of the United States Supreme Court*, 100th Cong., 1st sess., Exec. Rept. 100-7 (Washington: GPO, 1987).

[42] U.S. Congress, Senate Committee on the Judiciary, *Nomination of Abe Fortas*, report to accompany the nomination of Abe Fortas, 90th Cong., 2nd sess., Exec. Rept. 8 (Washington: GPO, 1968), pp. 20-30.

[43] 354 U.S. 449 (1957). For the Senator's remarks, see U.S. Congress, Senate Committee on the Judiciary, *Nominations of Abe Fortas and Homer Thornberry*, hearings, 90th Cong., 1st sess., July 11, 12, 16, 17, 18, 19, 20, 22, 23, 1968 (Washington: GPO, 1968), p. 191.

[44] Abraham, *Justices and Presidents*, p. 44.

[45] Abraham, *Justices and Presidents*, pp. 27-28.

[46] Swindler, "The Politics of 'Advice and Consent,'" p. 538; Abraham, *Justices and Presidents*, p. 41.

[47] Swindler, "The Politics of 'Advice and Consent,'" p. 541; Abraham, *Justices and Presidents*, pp. 27-28.

[48] For a discussion of senatorial courtesy, see Harris, *The Advice and Consent of the Senate*, pp. 215-237.

[49] Abraham, *Justices and Presidents*, p. 45. See also Harris, *The Advice and Consent of the Senate*, p. 76; Swindler, "The Politics of 'Advice and Consent,'" pp. 540-541.

[50] Abraham, *Justices and Presidents*, p. 45.

[51] Harris, *The Advice and Consent of the Senate*, p. 76; see also Jacobstein and Mersky, *The Rejected*, pp. 87-93 for a description of this nomination.

[52] Abraham, *Justices and Presidents*, p. 41; Jacobstein and Mersky, *The Rejected*, pp. 14-17; Swindler, "The Politics of 'Advice and Consent,'" p. 535.

[53] Abraham, *Justices and Presidents*, 16-17. See also U.S. Congress, Senate Committee on the Judiciary, *Nomination of George Harrold Carswell*, report to accompany the nomination of George Harrold Carswell, 91st Cong., 2nd sess., Exec. Rept. 91-14 (Washington: GPO, 1970), pp. 13-17, 32-33, 36-38.

[54] Abraham, *Justices and Presidents*, pp. 45-56; Harris, *The Advice and Consent of the Senate*, pp. 75-76.

[55] Jacobstein and Mersky, *The Rejected*, pp. 82-87.

[56] John A. Maltese, *The Selling of Supreme Court Nominees* (Baltimore: The Johns Hopkins University Press, 1995), chapter 3.

[57] Maltese, *The Selling of Supreme Court Nominees*, chapter 6.

[58] Christine DeGregorio and Jack E. Rossotti, "Campaigning for the Court: Interest Group Participation in the Bork and Thomas Confirmation Processes," in *Interest Group Politics*, 4th ed., Allan J. Cigler and Burdett A. Loomis, eds. (Washington: CQ Press, 1995), p. 215; and Gregory A. Caldeira, Marie Hojnacki, and John R. Wright, "The Lobbying Activities of Organized Interests in Federal Judicial Nominations" (paper presented at the 1996 Annual Meeting of the Midwest Political Science Association).

[59] See, for example, Jeffrey A. Segal, Charles M. Cameron, and Albert D. Cover, "A Spatial Model of Roll Call Voting: Senators, Constituents, Presidents, and Interest Groups in Supreme Court Confirmations," *American Journal of Political Science*, vol. 36 (February 1992), p. 96; and Gregory A. Caldeira and John R. Wright,

"Lobbying for Justice: Organized Interests, Supreme Court Nominations, and the United States Senate," *American Journal of Political Science*, vol. 42 (April 1998), p. 499.

[60] Abraham, *Justices and Presidents*, pp. 356-359; Jacobstein and Mersky, *The Rejected*, pp. 160-170.

[61] U.S. President (G. W. Bush), "Statement Announcing the Withdrawal of the Nomination of Harriet E. Miers To Be an Associate Justice of the United States Supreme Court," *Weekly Compilation of Presidential Documents*, vol. 41 (Oct. 27, 2005), p. 1608; Harriet E. Miers, "The Letter of Withdrawal," *Washington Post*, October 28, 2005, p. A7.

[62] For press accounts in the immediate aftermath of Miers's withdrawal, see, for example, Elisabeth Bumiller and Carl Hulse, "Court in Transition: The Overview," *New York Times*, October 28, 2005, p. A1; John Harwood, John D. McKinnon, Jeanne Cummings, and Jess Bravin, "Hot Seat: In Seeking New Court Nominee, Bush Has Little Margin of Error—As Miers Withdraws, Pleasing Right Will Spark Big Fight; Consensus Pick Has Risks—CIA Leak Probe Adds to Woes," *Wall Street Journal*, October 28, 2005, p. A1; and Peter Baker and Amy Goldstein, "Nomination Was Plagued By Missteps From the Start," *Washington Post*, October 28, 2005, p. A1. For a later, more detailed account, see Jan Crawford Greenburg, *Supreme Conflict: The Inside Story of the Struggle for Control of the United States Supreme Court* (New York: Penguin Press, 2007), pp. 248-284.

[63] Jo Becker, "In Speeches From the 1990s, Clues About Miers Views," *Washington Post*, October 26, 2005, p. A1; Charles Hurt and Ralph Z. Hallow, "Women's Group Calls for Miers Withdrawal," *Washington Times*, October 27, 2005, p. 1; David D. Kirkpatrick, "Nominee Is Pressed on Her Abortion Views," *New York Times*, October 27, 2005, p. A18.

[64] Charlie Savage, "Bush Says He Won't Air Memos from Miers," *Boston Globe*, October 25, 2005, p. A1.

[65] Elisabeth Bumiller and Carl Hulse, "Bush's Court Choice Ends Bid After Attack by Conservatives," *New York Times*, October 28, 2005, p. A1; Robin Toner, David D. Kirkpatrick, and Anne E. Kornblut, "Weeks Erosion in Support for the Nomination," *New York Times*," October 28, 2005, p. A16.

[66] Charles Hurt and Ralph Z. Hallow, "Women's Group Calls for Miers Withdrawal," *Washington Times*, October 27, 2005, p. 1.

[67] David D. Kirkpatrick, "Kansas Senator, Looking at Presidential Bid, Makes Faith the Bedrock of Campaign," *New York Times*, October 14, 2005, p. A18; Jonathan Weisman, "The Rift's Repercussions Could Last Rest of Term," *Washington Post*, October 28, 2005, p. A8.

[68] Amy Goldstein and Charles Babington, "Miers's Autonomy Will Be at Issue," *Washington Post*, October 27, 2005, p. A1.

[69] U.S. Congress, Senate Committee on the Judiciary, *History of the Committee on the Judiciary, United States Senate, 1816-1981*, Senate Document no. 97-18, 97th Cong., 1st sess. (Washington: GPO, 1982), p. iv.

[70] As previously discussed, on April 16, 1866, President Andrew Johnson nominated Henry Stanbery to replace John Catron, who had died the previous May. By the time Stanbery was nominated, however, the House of Representatives had passed a bill decreasing the number of justices in the Supreme Court. As discussed just above, the anticipated vacancy to which Thornberry was nominated ceased to exist when Fortas failed to be confirmed as Chief Justice.

[71] For information all Supreme Court nominations (i.e., those that were unsuccessful and those that were successful), see CRS Report RL33225, *Supreme Court Nominations, 1789 - 2010: Actions by the Senate, the Judiciary Committee, and the President*, by Denis Steven Rutkus and Maureen Bearden.

CHAPTER SOURCES

The following chapters have been previously published:

Chapter 1 – This is an edited, excerpted and augmented edition of a United States Congressional Research Service publication, Report Order Code RL31989, dated September 3, 2010.

Chapter 2 – This is an edited, excerpted and augmented edition of a United States Congressional Research Service publication, Report Order Code RL33118, dated August 6, 2010.

Chapter 3 – This is an edited, excerpted and augmented edition of a United States Congressional Research Service publication, Report Order Code RRL33247, dated May 17, 2010.

Chapter 4 – This is an edited, excerpted and augmented edition of a United States Congressional Research Service publication, Report Order Code RL33225, dated August 23, 2010.

Chapter 5 – This is an edited, excerpted and augmented edition of a United States Congressional Research Service publication, Report Order Code RL31171, dated August 20, 2010.

INDEX

D

E

F

S

T

U

V

W

Y